NOLO Products & Services

➪ Books & Software

Get in-depth information. Nolo publishes hundreds of great books and software programs for consumers and business owners. Order a copy—or download an ebook version instantly—at Nolo.com.

➪ Legal Encyclopedia

Free at Nolo.com. Here are more than 1,400 free articles and answers to common questions about everyday legal issues including wills, bankruptcy, small business formation, divorce, patents, employment and much more.

➪ Plain-English Legal Dictionary

Free at Nolo.com. Stumped by jargon? Look it up in America's most up-to-date source for definitions of legal terms.

➪ Online Legal Documents

Create documents at your computer. Go to Nolo.com to make a will or living trust, form an LLC or corporation or obtain a trademark or provisional patent. For simpler matters, download one of our hundreds of high-quality legal forms, including bills of sale, promissory notes, nondisclosure agreements and many more.

➪ Lawyer Directory

Find an attorney at Nolo.com. Nolo's consumer-friendly lawyer directory provides in-depth profiles of lawyers all over America. From fees and experience to legal philosophy, education and special expertise, you'll find all the information you need to pick the right lawyer. Every lawyer listed has pledged to work diligently and respectfully with clients.

➪ Free Legal Updates

Keep up to date. Check for free updates at Nolo.com. Under "Products," find this book and click "Legal Updates." You can also sign up for our free e-newsletters at Nolo.com/newsletters/index.html.

NOLO® The Trusted Name
(but don't take our word for it)

"In Nolo you can trust."
THE NEW YORK TIMES

"Nolo is always there in a jam as the nation's premier publisher of do-it-yourself legal books."
NEWSWEEK

"Nolo publications…guide people simply through the how, when, where and why of the law."
THE WASHINGTON POST

"[Nolo's]…material is developed by experienced attorneys who have a knack for making complicated material accessible."
LIBRARY JOURNAL

"When it comes to self-help legal stuff, nobody does a better job than Nolo…"
USA TODAY

"The most prominent U.S. publisher of self-help legal aids."
TIME MAGAZINE

"Nolo is a pioneer in both consumer and business self-help books and software."
LOS ANGELES TIMES

4th edition

Win Your Lawsuit

Sue in California Superior Court Without a Lawyer

by Judge Roderic Duncan

Fourth Edition	AUGUST 2010
Book Design	TERRI HEARSH
Cover Design	SUSAN PUTNEY
Proofreading	ROBERT WELLS
Index	JANET PERLMAN
Printing	DELTA PRINTING SOLUTIONS, INC.

Duncan, Roderic, 1932-

Win your lawsuit : sue in California Superior Court without a lawyer / by Roderic Duncan. -- 4th ed.

p. cm.

Includes index.

Summary: "Many lawsuits involve too much money for Small Claims Court, but the participants cannot afford an attorney. This book shows how to prepare and try a case in Califorina Superior Court. This edition has been completely updated and reflects current court procedures and all forms are explained in detail"-- Provided by publisher.

ISBN-13: 978-1-4133-1075-7 (pbk.)

ISBN-10: 1-4133-1075-3 (pbk.)

1. District courts--California--Popular works. 2. Civil procedure--California--Popular works. 3. Small claims courts--California--Popular works. 4. Pro se representation--California--Popular works. I. Title.

KFC968.D86 2010

347.794'05--dc22

2010009292

Copyright © 2003, 2005, 2007, and 2010 by Nolo.
All rights reserved. The NOLO trademark is registered in the U.S. Patent and Trademark Office.
Printed in the U.S.A.

No part of this publication may be reproduced, stored in a retrieval system, or transmitted in any form or by any means, electronic, mechanical, photocopying, recording, or otherwise without prior written permission. Reproduction prohibitions do not apply to the forms contained in this product when reproduced for personal use. For information on bulk purchases or corporate premium sales, please contact the Special Sales Department. Call 800-955-4775 or write to Nolo, 950 Parker Street, Berkeley, California 94710.

Please note

We believe accurate, plain-English legal information should help you solve many of your own legal problems. But this text is not a substitute for personalized advice from a knowledgeable lawyer. If you want the help of a trained professional—and we'll always point out situations in which we think that's a good idea—consult an attorney licensed to practice in your state.

Dedication

One of the most important things a person venturing into court without a lawyer can hope for is an understanding judge. So this book is dedicated to the many understanding California judges who will try to make your experience in their courtroom as easy as possible. The next most important thing I wish for you is a courtroom clerk sympathetic to the problems of a newcomer in this foreign land. In my 20 plus years as a judge, I've been fortunate to work with many such clerks. This book is dedicated to all of the user-friendly courtroom clerks in this state—in particular, to former Municipal Court clerks Barbara Bliefert, Jackie Eklund, Connie Harvey, Mike and Leslye Robey, Mark Montgomery, Suzy Johnston, Bernice Garcia, Mary Trafton-Oxendine, and Geny Fabella, and to my Superior Court regulars, Nancy Regas, Leo Tungohan, Miranda Edgerly, and Mary McGlothin. In retirement, I have been fortunate to work with three excellent and consumer-friendly clerks, Deborah Wanzo in Oakland, Angelique Andreozzi in San Francisco, and Jami Jacobson in Siskiyou County.

And to my wife, Carol B. Thompson, who always made coming home from a harrowing day on the bench something to look forward to.

Acknowledgments

The author gratefully acknowledges the assistance of:

Judge Robert Freedman and attorney Walter Stemmler (both of my alma mater, the Alameda County Superior Court) who carefully guided me through the ever-changing rules and procedures of the California courts. On the statewide scene, Patrick O'Donnell, staff attorney for the California Administrative Office of the Courts, likewise was invaluable in keeping me up to date on new and anticipated changes in the forms that are displayed throughout the book and in the appendix.

Bonnie Hough, Supervising Attorney for the Equal Access Program of the Administrative Office of the Courts. On top of all of her other accomplishments in making courts more accessible, Ms. Hough designed the "Welcome to the Superior Court" form reproduced in Chapter One after a suggestion I'm proud to have made to her.

Nolo Executive Publisher Jake Warner, who conceived the idea for this book and contributed many important suggestions as it went through the editing process; and Steve Elias, who helped form the concept and edited numerous drafts.

And, finally, Janet Portman, who edited this book and contributed immensely to making sure the book speaks understandably to those who have never before ventured into a system developed by lawyers for lawyers.

Table of Contents

Your Courtroom Companion 1

1 Is This Book for You? 3
Who Can Use This Book 4
Lawsuits Covered in This Book 5
Lawsuits This Book Does Not Cover 10
When You Have a Choice: Small Claims Court 12
The Pros and Cons of Representing Yourself 13
The Course of a Typical Limited Jurisdiction Case 17
Finding the Law, on Paper and Online 18
General Instructions for Filling Out Your Forms 19

2 Do You Have a Good Case? 21
Is Your Case Fresh Enough? 22
Evaluating the Evidence 23
Preserve Your Evidence Now 26
Can You Collect the Judgment If You Win? 29
How Much Should You Sue For? 30

3 Can't We Settle Somehow? 35
Why Would You Want to Settle Out of Court? 36
How Much Are You Willing to Settle For? 36
Should You Use a Third Person to Help You Settle? 37
Making a Settlement Offer 39
Taking Care of the Details 43
Should a Lawyer Review the Settlement Agreement? 45
If You're Worried About Getting Paid 48

4 Deciding Where and Whom to Sue 49
- Selecting the Plaintiff(s) 50
- Selecting the Defendant(s) 51
- Making Sure You Can Sue in California 63
- Selecting the Right Court 65

5 Preparing the Complaint 69
- Beginning Your Tort or Contract Complaint 70
- Tort Complaints: Personal Injury, Property Damage, and Wrongful Death 73
- Contract Complaints 92
- Complaints for Other Types of Lawsuits 108
- Preparing the Summons and Cover Sheet 110
- Preparing a Case Questionnaire 112
- Requesting a Waiver of the Filing Fee 113
- Preparing an Attachment 117

6 Filing the Papers 119
- Call the Clerk's Office 120
- Photocopy Your Documents 120
- Filing the Papers 121

7 Serving the Papers on the Defendants 125
- Completing the Summons 126
- Serve Your Papers by Mail 126
- Selecting a Process Server 128
- Serving the Summons and Complaint 128
- Completing the Proof of Service 130
- Serving Other Papers as the Case Proceeds 134

8 Lawsuits from the Defendant's Point of View 135
- Initial Steps 136
- Decide Whether to Represent Yourself 142
- Ask for More Time 143
- Prepare an Answer 144
- Prepare a Cross-Complaint 160
- File and Serve the Answer and Cross-Complaint 164
- What Happens Next? 164

9 If Defendant Doesn't Respond 167
Taking the Defendant's Default 168
Applying for a Judgment 174
Court Hearings on Your Default 180
Setting Aside a Default Judgment 181

10 Discovery 185
Types of Discovery 186
Discovery Rules and Limits 187
Doing Your Own Discovery 188
Responding to Discovery 193
Less-Used Methods of Discovery 198
Failing to Respond to a Discovery or Case Questionnaire Request 199
Discovering Doe Defendants 203

11 The Opposition Gets Nasty: Summary Judgment and Other Motions 205
Motion for Summary Judgment 206
Motion for Summary Adjudication of Issues 217
Motion for Judgment on the Pleadings 218
Other Motions: Demurrers, Motions to Quash, and Motions to Strike 218
Demand for Bill of Particulars 219

12 Moving Your Case to Arbitration and Trial 221
Meeting With Your Opponent 222
Completing the Case Management Statement 223
Arbitration or Mediation? 227
Preparing for the Arbitration Hearing 229
Attending the Arbitration Hearing 231
The Arbitration Decision 232

13 Preparing for a Trial or Arbitration 235
A Short Course in the Rules of Evidence 236
Live Witnesses or Written Declarations 239
Using Written Declarations 239
Having Witnesses Attend a Trial or Arbitration Hearing 246
Making a Chart of Your Evidence 252
Making a Trial Binder 253
Drafting Questions to Ask Your Witnesses 253
Attending a Settlement Conference 254

14 Trial Before a Judge 257
Sizing Up the Judge 258
Rules of Courtroom Etiquette... 261
The Trial Begins 262
Plaintiff's Case 262
Defendant's Case 266
Plaintiff's Rebuttal 266
Closing Arguments 267
Judgment 268

15 Trial Before a Jury 269
If Your Opponent Requests a Jury Trial 270
Jury Selection 270
Challenging Jurors 272
Preparing Jury Instructions 273
The Trial 274
Jury Deliberations 275

16 After the Trial 277
Requesting a New Trial 278
Appealing the Judgment 279

17 Finding a Good Lawyer 281
Your Choices 282
Checking Out the Lawyer 284

A Tear-Out Forms 285

Forms for Filing a Lawsuit

Complaint—Personal Injury, Property Damage, Wrongful Death

Cause of Action—Motor Vehicle

Cause of Action—Premises Liability

Cause of Action—General Negligence

Cause of Action—Intentional Tort

Exemplary Damages Attachment

Complaint—Contract

Cause of Action—Breach of Contract

Cause of Action—Breach of Warranty (Merchantability)

Cause of Action—Breach of Warranty (Fitness

Civil Case Cover Sheet

Civil Case Cover Sheet Addendum and Statement of Location

Case Questionnaire—For Limited Civil Cases

Request to Waive Court Fees

Summons

Notice and Acknowledgement of Receipt—Civil

Proof of Service by First-Class Mail—Civil

Proof of Service of Summons

Forms for Responding to a Lawsuit

Answer—Personal Injury, Property Damage, Wrongful Death

Answer—Contract

General Denial

Cross-Complaint—Personal Injury, Property Damage, Wrongful Death

Forms to End Your Lawsuit

Request for Dismissal

Request for Entry of Default

Judgment

Forms for Discovery/Evidence

Form Interrogatories—Limited Civil Cases (Economic Litigation)

Requests for Admission

Declaration

Request for Statement of Witnesses and Evidence

Civil Subpoena for Personal Appearance at Trial or Hearing

Civil Subpoena (Duces Tecum)

Other Forms

Blank Pleading Paper

Attachment to Judicial Council Form

Application and Order for Appointment of Guardian ad Litem—Civil

Amendment to Complaint (Fictitious/Incorrect Name)

Case Management Statement

Request for Trial De Novo After Judicial Arbitration

Index 431

Your Courtroom Companion

Whether you're filing a lawsuit or responding to one filed against you, going to court is rarely fun. On top of the stress of trying to collect money owed to you, recover from an injury, or get your insurance company to honor your policy, you've got to figure out the complexities of dealing with the legal system. The stress can be even worse if a process server has just handed you papers informing you that you are being sued. And if you're doing it without the help of a lawyer, it's up to you to understand important things like how to file and serve papers, when to settle, and what to say and how to act in the courtroom.

Thankfully, it's not as complicated as it may look from the outside. In fact, if you're going to court in California for a case involving $25,000 or less, you can do most things on your own. To be ready to act as your own lawyer, though, you need to be informed about the process and ready to follow the rules. That's what this book will show you. It covers all the ins and outs of a limited jurisdiction case—a case involving $25,000 or less—in California Superior Court. I'll explain:

- how to file a lawsuit and how to respond if you have been sued
- settlement procedures that may help you resolve the case early on, without the need for a trial
- how to gather evidence to support your case
- how to write motions to request the court's help, and how to argue them in the courtroom if you need to, and
- how to prepare for and conduct a trial.

Dealing with a lawsuit doesn't have to be confusing and overwhelming. If you're well informed, you can handle the process and paperwork, decide whether to settle, and even argue your case before a judge or jury. Read this book, and you'll be ready to go to court—and win your lawsuit.

CHAPTER 1

Is This Book for You?

Who Can Use This Book	4
Lawsuits Covered in This Book	5
Tort Cases	6
Breach of Contract Cases	7
Lawsuits This Book Does Not Cover	10
When You Have a Choice: Small Claims Court	12
Small Claims Court and Out of Staters	12
Disadvantages of Small Claims Court	12
The Pros and Cons of Representing Yourself	13
The Up Side of Self-Representation	13
The Down Side of Self-Representation	14
The Course of a Typical Limited Jurisdiction Case	17
Finding the Law, on Paper and Online	18
California Statutes	18
California and Local Court Rules	19
Cases	19
Getting Information About Your County on the Web	19
General Instructions for Filling Out Your Forms	19

This book shows you how to sue a person or a business for up to $25,000 in a California Superior Court, without using a lawyer. It also shows you how to defend yourself in some lawsuits where you are sued for less than $25,000. I'll take you step-by-step through the set of rules and printed forms that everyone needs to use, and I'll guide you when there are decisions to be made or strategy to plan.

Before we get down to the nuts and bolts of how to handle your case, I need to explain a bit of history, which will make the terms I use in this book understandable. Until 1998, California trial courts were divided into two tiers—Superior Court for cases involving more than $25,000, and Municipal Courts for cases involving less than that (like yours). California voters decided to allow counties to merge Municipal Courts into Superior Courts, and by 2001 all had done so. Cases that used to go to "Muni" court now go to Superior Court, where they're known as "limited jurisdiction" cases because they involve less than $25,000 (cases concerning more than that amount are known as "unlimited jurisdiction" cases).

For convenience sake, when I'm talking about a Superior Court that's handling a limited jurisdiction case, I refer to the Superior Court's "limited jurisdiction division," but there really isn't a formal division involving separate buildings or court personnel. Just keep in mind that the Superior Court judge frequently changes hats (or robes) to hear limited jurisdiction cases for a while, then unlimited jurisdiction cases. Fortunately, the rules and procedures in the limited division of the court are simpler than those used in an unlimited Superior Court case, where lawyers abound and frequently use all sorts of technical procedures to make suing or defending yourself far more complicated than it should be.

Your opponent may seek to change your case from limited to unlimited if he answers your complaint with a claim against you for more than $25,000. The rules on situations such as this are a little complicated. If this happens, the best thing to do is tell the judge you oppose a switch that will make it more difficult for you to represent yourself, and leave it to the judge to make a decision.

Each of California's 58 counties has at least one Superior Court courthouse that handles limited jurisdiction cases. In counties with small populations, such as Amador and Trinity, all of the court cases (limited and unlimited) are handled at one courthouse, located at the county seat. In more populous counties where there are many branches of the Superior Court, several branches (but not necessarily all) may handle limited jurisdiction cases.

This chapter introduces you to the process of handling your own case, by describing what this book can—and cannot—do for you. In particular, I explain:

- people who can use this book
- the types of legal disputes this book covers
- the types of cases this book will *not* cover, either because the law requires them to be brought in the unlimited division of the Superior Court or in another court altogether, or because they're the type of cases where you really should have a lawyer
- cases that *could* be handled in unlimited jurisdiction divisions but should instead be handled in Small Claims Court
- the pros and cons of representing yourself
- the course of a typical limited jurisdiction case
- how to find the law, on paper and online, and
- how to fill out the court forms you'll encounter as you wend your way through the lawsuit.

Who Can Use This Book

If you are a competent adult (you are if able to read and understand this book) or a legally emancipated minor, you have the right to bring your own lawsuit or defend yourself if a case is filed against you. Someone who represents him- or herself is usually referred to as "self-represented," although occasionally the old-fashioned Latin terms "in pro per" or "in pro se" are still used.

Specifically, you can sue or defend on behalf of:
- yourself as an individual
- a partnership of which you are a partner, or
- your business, if you are a sole proprietor.

You cannot, however, represent another person—others must represent themselves or hire an attorney to represent them. Thus, you cannot sue or defend on behalf of:
- a corporation (which the law considers to be a person), even if it's a small business in which you own all the stock; or an LLC
- family members (but adults can join you in suing on their own behalf)
- an incapacitated or incompetent person, even if you are the court-appointed conservator or guardian (you must have an attorney)
- a minor, even if you are the parent or guardian (you also must have an attorney)
- a person for whom you serve as the attorney-in-fact under a durable or regular power of attorney, or
- an unincorporated association (see "Selecting the Defendant(s)" in Chapter 4 for an explanation of this term). In certain situations, you may file suit on behalf of an unincorporated association—see Witkin, *Summary of California Law*, 10th Edition, Corporations §§ 37-47B.

Lawsuits Covered in This Book

Most of the cases this book deals with are what the law calls tort or contract cases. A tort case involves personal injury or property damage, the result of an intentional or negligent act by another person. For example, a lawsuit arising out of a traffic accident is a tort case. So is a lawsuit involving a slip and fall at a supermarket.

A contract case is normally one in which someone did not keep his or her side of a bargain. If you lend your brother-in-law $10,000 and he fails to repay it as promised, you have a contract

Can You Force the Defendant Into Court?

The first question any plaintiff must ask is whether their chosen court has the power to compel the defendant to show up. That power, known as having "personal jurisdiction" over the defendant, depends on whether the defendant has sufficient ties to California, by living here, doing business here, or even soliciting business here.

Most of the time, you won't have a "jurisdiction problem," because your defendant will be a California resident or will have done enough in California to enable a judge to say, "You must answer to the call of this court." But sometimes it's not so clear. Take a look at the expanded discussion of jurisdiction in Chapter 4 for more guidance.

Typical Court Costs

Even if you save money by not hiring a lawyer, you'll face expenses such as filing fees, a fee to serve court papers, and, in some cases, the cost of taking a deposition. In a typical case, these costs can add up to several hundred dollars. Some of the costs can be waived if you qualify as a low-income person.

The typical fees for a plaintiff seeking $20,000 in a lawsuit might include:

Filing fee	$250–$330	(see Chapter 6)
Process server's fee	75	(see Chapter 7)
Deposition cost	300	(see Chapter 10)
Photocopying	15	
Postage	10	
Miscellaneous	50	

If you win the case, the court will most likely order the other side to pay your costs (but usually not any attorney fees you may have incurred). If you lose the case, not only must you pay your own costs, you'll probably be ordered to pay your opponent's as well.

A defendant can expect to incur similar costs, except a process server's fee.

case. If the telephone you bought doesn't operate as the salesman said it would, you have a contract case.

Most tort and contract cases are fairly easy to handle in the limited jurisdiction division because the court gives both plaintiffs and defendants straightforward, check-the-box forms.

Tort Cases

When a plaintiff claims that a defendant intentionally or carelessly caused injury or damage, the plaintiff's case is called a tort case. Tort cases have three basic legal requirements (lawyers call them elements):
- the defendant acted either carelessly or intentionally
- the plaintiff was injured physically or emotionally, or the plaintiff's property was damaged, or both, and
- the defendant's act was the direct cause of the plaintiff's injury or the property damage.

Below are several examples of torts, each containing all of the three elements. If your situation also has all these elements, you probably have a tort case.

EXAMPLE 1: While driving his car, Fred carelessly runs a red light and hits Sue's car in an intersection. The side of Sue's car is smashed and her neck is injured.

EXAMPLE 2: Someone accidentally drops some fresh produce on the floor in a supermarket. It doesn't get cleaned up and 30 minutes later, Leroy is injured when he slips and falls on a piece of fruit still lying there.

EXAMPLE 3: Sandy and Leslie are arguing. Sandy grows increasingly angry and suddenly hits Leslie in the face, breaking Leslie's nose.

EXAMPLE 4: Mike walks down the street pushing a dolly carrying an expensive piece of computer equipment. A painter working on a building project above the sidewalk drops a bucket of paint that hits and ruins Mike's computer.

Some types of tort cases are more complex than others. This book focuses on the straightforward cases that sensibly can be brought by a plaintiff without a lawyer. You probably should not use this book for the following, more complex types of cases:

- **Professional malpractice.** These are lawsuits against lawyers, doctors, or other professionals for negligent performance of their duties. If you paid someone to remove your appendix or prepare your taxes and the person botched the job—causing you to suffer permanent injury or pay a big penalty to the IRS—you may have a professional malpractice claim. (On the other hand, if the person simply failed to do the work, you can sue for breach of contract, as explained in the next section.) Malpractice cases are very complex, usually require the help of a lawyer, and involve more than $25,000 in damages. If you're set on representing yourself in a malpractice case, Chapter 5 explains the basics of how to do it if your damages are less than $25,000.
- **Civil rights and civil liberties cases.** These are lawsuits involving a deprivation of rights under the federal or state Constitution, or discrimination on account of race, sex, religion, or the like. Cases involving sexual harassment on the job fall into this category.
- **Libel and slander.** These are lawsuits in which a plaintiff claims the defendant wrote or said something untrue and harmful about the plaintiff. Because the Constitution protects many types of expression, these cases are hard for plaintiffs to win. In addition, it's usually hard for the plaintiff to prove that the defendant's writings or statements caused an actual loss. Winning such cases (and successfully defending against them) usually

requires a lawyer who knows this area of the law.
- **Fraud.** Here, a plaintiff claims that a defendant misrepresented or concealed a fact, usually in connection with a contract, with the intention to deceive. Plaintiffs must prove they reasonably relied on the misrepresentation to their harm. Fraud cases are complex and usually require a lawyer's involvement.
- **Product liability.** In these cases, plaintiffs claim that a manufactured item had a defect that caused them physical injury. Plaintiffs who receive a defective item but aren't injured can sue for breach of contract or breach of warranty (see the next section). But if a product malfunctioned and physically injured the plaintiff, the matter usually requires a lawyer.
- **Exemplary or punitive damages.** Sometimes outrageous conduct by a defendant entitles the plaintiff to recover not only out-of-pocket losses but also an added amount meant to punish the defendant or serve as an example for others. These "punitive" damages are rarely awarded, and usually only in cases involving more than $25,000. Chapter 5 includes a discussion of punitive damages.
- **Cases in which your auto or homeowner's insurance company has already paid you some money for your damages.** If this describes your situation, talk to your company before suing. The company may have negotiated a settlement with the defendant that legally prevents you from suing.

Breach of Contract Cases

A contract is an agreement between individuals, businesses, or an individual and a business. Many transactions involve contracts, even if nothing is written down. A plaintiff might bring a breach of contract lawsuit after buying something that wasn't what it was represented to be, or after hiring someone who didn't do what he or she was supposed to do.

In general, your case will involve a breach of contract if one party failed to perform his or her end of a binding agreement, thereby causing the other party to suffer an economic loss. Binding agreements come in many forms. They include:
- buying or selling goods to be delivered now or in the future
- renting a product, such as an automobile or a rug shampooer
- doing work in exchange for goods or services
- hiring someone to perform services
- borrowing or lending money, or
- extending credit for goods or services.

The contract or agreement can be written, oral, or, in some cases, implied from the circumstances (but some contracts must be written and signed to be enforceable; see "Contracts That Must Be in Writing," below).

To win a contract case, it is up to you, as the plaintiff, to prove that:
- you and the defendant had a legally binding agreement
- you did everything you were required to do under the agreement
- the defendant failed to perform as was required under the agreement, and
- the defendant's failure to perform caused you actual economic loss.

Here are some examples of breached contracts:

EXAMPLE 1: Uncle Walter borrowed $10,000 from Audrey, orally promising to pay her back in two months. Four months later, Uncle Walter hasn't paid and won't return Audrey's phone calls.

EXAMPLE 2: Marc paid a plumber $20,000 to install a new bathroom in his storefront. He later discovered that the plumber hooked up the toilet to the sewer incorrectly. Now the plumber won't fix it unless Marc gives him another $3,000.

Contracts That Must Be in Writing

Under a law called the Statute of Frauds, a judge won't enforce certain kinds of contracts unless the agreement is written up as a contract, a note, or a memo. The writing must be signed by the person you are suing. If you try to enforce such an unwritten or unsigned agreement, the defendant can point out that the agreement doesn't comply with the Statute of Frauds, and your case is likely to be dismissed.

The following are the most important types of contracts that must be in writing:

- Contracts that cannot be fully performed within one year, such as an agreement to work for someone for five years
- Leases that extend for more than one year (the lease is enforceable for up to one year; after that, the rental changes to month to month)
- Contracts for the sale of goods for $500 or more, unless the buyer makes a partial payment or the goods are delivered at the time of the sale
- Contracts for the sale of real estate
- Contracts employing a real estate agent, and
- Contingency fee contracts with a lawyer, when a lawyer represents you in exchange for a percentage of what you recover and earns nothing if you don't win.

Normally it's useless to try to enforce one of these kinds of agreements if it's unwritten or unsigned. But there are several ways to get around the Statute of Frauds, so you may want to consult a lawyer if it appears you have a Statute of Frauds problem. You can also visit a law library to consult *Summary of California Law* (10th edition), by Bernard Witkin, at Vol. 1, Contracts §§ 342-418.

EXAMPLE 3: Sheila owns a clothing store. A supplier convinced her to carry a line of sweaters and agreed to take them back for full credit if they didn't sell. The sweaters didn't sell and now the supplier refuses to take them back.

EXAMPLE 4: Chris sold his boat through a classified ad for $19,000. Milt gave him $5,000 down and a written promise to pay the additional $14,000 within ten days. Two weeks later, Milt called Chris to say that he lost his job and can't pay the rest of the money for a while. Milt wants to return the boat, but Chris wants the money.

EXAMPLE 5: The day after Elaine bought a two-year-old used car from a used car dealer, the engine seized up. The dealer had claimed that the car was almost new and that the engine was in great shape. But Elaine's mechanic told her that the engine was shot and that replacement and repairs will cost more than $8,000. The dealer won't discuss it.

EXAMPLE 6: Francisco told a salesperson at a computer store that he needed a system to handle a sizable database and state-of-the-art software. The salesperson talked him out of a national brand that would do the job and instead recommended the house brand for $9,500. Francisco bought it and took it home, only to discover that it can't handle his database or his software. The store offers to sell Francisco memory enhancements and a larger hard disk, but won't take back the computer or return his money.

EXAMPLE 7: Ruth runs an import-export business. A year ago she signed a five-year commercial lease that included the landlord's promise to put in a loading dock within the first year. Ruth is still waiting for the dock.

EXAMPLE 8: Art paid a lawyer a "nonrefundable" $8,000 retainer to represent him in the purchase of a business. The lawyer talked to Art several times and wrote a few letters, but has otherwise done nothing in the past three months. Escrow is due to close next week and the lawyer's secretary says he is too busy to talk to Art.

> **Some Contracts You Might Miss**
>
> We enter all sorts of written contracts in our daily life. You may not always retain copies of them, but they legally bind you all the same. Here are some examples:
> - credit card agreements
> - automobile and truck leases
> - insurance policies
> - agreements you sign with contractors who work on your house, and
> - invoices a delivery person asks you to sign.

Two types of breach of contract cases could cause special problems if you tried to bring or defend them yourself in Superior Court. They are contracts with arbitration clauses and contracts that are illegal or require someone to engage in illegal behavior.

Arbitration Requirements

Some written contracts require that before you file a lawsuit, you must attempt to resolve any dispute using arbitration or mediation. These are alternative avenues for solving legal disagreements, involving a neutral third party who acts as either a mediator—helping the parties come to a compromise—or an arbitrator—deciding the outcome much as a judge would, but without some of the formalities and procedures of going to court. We'll explain these two processes in greater detail in Chapter 3.

Sometimes this is advantageous, because the case can be resolved more simply and quickly. But if the terms of the arbitration or mediation don't seem fair and you want to avoid it and go directly to court, you will need a lawyer's help. For a very helpful discussion of mediation, see *Mediate, Don't Litigate*, by Peter Lovenheim and Lisa Guerin (Nolo).

Illegal Contracts

Most contracts between consenting adults are legal and enforceable. Some, however, are not. You will probably need the help of a lawyer if your contract involves one of the following problems:

Illegal interest rate (usury). California has a complicated set of rules, called "usury law," that prohibit interest charges on loans or other credit transactions in excess of 10%. But the law contains several exceptions, making it difficult to be sure just what transactions are covered. For example, it doesn't apply to banks, loan companies, credit card companies, and many merchants, some of whom can charge as much as 30%.

Virtually all businesses are aware of the rate they are permitted to charge, so it is rare to find a business violating the usury law. In private transactions, however, any agreement to pay more than 10% interest for money or goods intended for personal, family, or household purposes is illegal. If you lent money to a friend or relative and charged interest over 10%, don't accept any payment for the interest; instead, offer to rewrite the contract at 10%. If you don't and you sue to collect, you'll be entitled to a judgment only for the principal (the amount you loaned). A borrower who paid you any interest can sue and ask for a penalty of triple the amount of the interest already paid.

Gambling. All gambling is illegal in California except horse racing, the casinos operated by some Indian tribes, card rooms permitted by some cities, and the state lottery. Lawsuits to collect debts based on gambling are usually unenforceable. If you want to sue on a contract involving illegal gambling or some other criminal activity, consult a lawyer.

Services by an unlicensed person. The law requires dozens of businesspeople, such as building contractors, architects, real estate agents, real estate brokers, attorneys, and beauticians to have licenses

Checking Up on Licenses

To learn whether certain work must be performed by a licensed individual, check with the State Department of Consumer Affairs. The department supervises 2.6 million licensees in California and provides information about them on its website, www.dca.ca.gov. You'll find an alphabetical index listing the occupations that are subject to license requirements, from accountants to vocational nurses.

Once you've determined that the work that's the subject of your lawsuit requires a license, you'll want to know whether the individual who did the work is in fact licensed. Contact the agency that does the licensing. Use the same website to access the listing of licensed individuals. Lawyers' licenses can be checked at the State Bar website, www.calbar.ca.org.

Phone numbers for some of the major agencies are listed below. If you can't find the agency you want, the Department of Consumer Affairs can probably assist you at 800-952-5210.

Accountants	916-263-3680
Architects	916-574-7220
Automobile Repair Shops	800-952-5210
Chiropractors	916-263-5355
Contractors	800-321-2752
Dentists	916-263-2300
Doctors (and many other health care professionals)	800-633-2322
Electronic and Appliance Repair	916-574-2069
Engineers	866-780-5370
Funeral Directors	916-574-7870
Lawyers (State Bar)	800-843-9053
Marriage & Family Therapists	916-574-7830
Nurses	916-322-3350
Optometrists	866-585-2666
Pharmacists	916-574-7900
Psychologists	916-263-2699
Real Estate Brokers, Salespeople	916-227-0864
Structural Pest Control (termites)	916-561-8708
Veterinarians	916-263-2610

to perform their services. If you've performed such a service but you don't have the required license, the person receiving the services doesn't have to pay. (The law provides a small exception for building contractors: If the total cost of labor and materials is less than $500, the contractor, licensed or not, has the right to be paid. But if the bill is higher and the buyer won't pay, the contractor won't win in court if he or she didn't have a contractor's license, no matter how well the job was done.)

Lawsuits This Book Does Not Cover

This book is designed primarily to help you bring or defend lawsuits that ask for money damages, rather than lawsuits that seek to compel someone to do (or not do) something. The court forms used in most money damages cases are straightforward and easy to explain. In cases not about money damages, the forms are far more complicated, and so are the legal theories involved.

If you are a plaintiff and plan to ask the court for something other than money damages, or if you are a defendant and the plaintiff has requested something other than money damages, you will need to consult a lawyer or do some extensive legal research on your own. More specifically, if your case falls within one of the following groups, this book is not for you:

- **Criminal cases.** All Superior Court cases are classified as either criminal or civil. Criminal cases can be brought only by the district attorney, not private individuals, and usually seek an order that the defendant be put in jail or required to pay a fine. If you want to learn more about a criminal case, *The Criminal Law Handbook: Know Your Rights, Survive the System*, by Paul Bergman and Sara J. Berman

(Nolo), is a good source of information (but it does not equip you to defend your own criminal case).

- **Lawsuits to dissolve a partnership, divide up jointly owned land, or declare someone as the rightful owner of property.** These cases involve complicated accounting issues or complex real estate laws that require expert knowledge.
- **Lawsuits to dissolve or annul a marriage, declare the paternity of a child, or decide who will have the power to handle the affairs of a child or incompetent person.** Less complicated cases can be handled without an attorney (such as an uncontested conservatorship or guardianship proceeding). But the court procedures are so different from the ones that are explained in this book that you should seek help from other sources, such as the office of the Family Law Facilitator at your county courthouse.

RESOURCE

If you want to do an uncontested guardianship, see *The Guardianship Book for California: How to Become a Child's Legal Guardian,* by David Brown and Emily Doskow (Nolo).

- **Lawsuits to probate an estate.** This process is quite complicated and is covered in *How to Probate an Estate in California,* by Julia Nissley (Nolo).
- **Lawsuits to rewrite or cancel a contract.** This is a complex area of the law that should be handled by a lawyer.
- **Lawsuits requesting an injunction or temporary restraining order to prevent someone from doing something.** Although a limited jurisdiction court can grant a temporary restraining order and a preliminary injunction, preparing the paperwork for these cases is tricky and requires expert assistance.
- **Lawsuits to evict a tenant or fight an eviction.** *The California Landlord's Law Book: Evictions,* by David Brown (Nolo), includes information for landlords on this subject; *California Tenants' Rights,* by Janet Portman and David Brown (Nolo), has information for tenants.
- **Lawsuits for back wages that an employer owes you.** If you have such a claim, check with a local office of the California Labor Commissioner, listed under the state government offices in your phone book. The office will assist you in preparing a complaint against the employer through its own internal procedure; if necessary, it may even provide a lawyer to sue on your behalf. You can find more information, including office locations, at www.dir.ca.gov/DLSE.
- **Lawsuits involving an issue covered by federal law, such as the patent laws or the bankruptcy laws.** Cases involving federal laws cannot be heard in state Superior Court. They must be brought in a federal court.
- **Cases brought against you by the government for back taxes.** Most of these cases are brought in federal court, and a lawyer specializing in tax law can probably explain defenses you would not have known about.

Finally, if you are a plaintiff with a claim for significantly more than $25,000 and you don't want to reduce the amount you're seeking (which would allow you to remain in limited jurisdiction), you must file your case in the court's unlimited jurisdiction division. The procedures are more complicated than those discussed in this book, and so are the forms. Either side can appeal if they lose. If you believe your claim entitles you to significantly more than $25,000, this book is not for you.

But think twice before heading for the big leagues if you're suing for slightly over $25,000—it might make sense to trim your demand to $25,000 and stay in the limited jurisdiction division. If you are suing someone who you think will have a lawyer, this could make a lot of sense, primarily because you'll experience less harassment. Unfortunately, some lawyers mistreat litigants who don't have a lawyer, filing unnecessary motions, bombarding them with excessive requests for information and documents to help them defend the case, and generally being as intimidating as they can. The rules in the limited division prevent a lot of that harassment. Additionally, the very helpful Case Questionnaire (discussed in Chapter 5) is available only in the limited division.

On the other hand, you can use the court forms in Chapter 5 of this book in both limited and unlimited cases and it is always possible that the lawyer representing your opponent will turn out to be more cooperative.

When You Have a Choice: Small Claims Court

In Small Claims Court, the most you can sue for is $7,500 if you are an individual, and $5,000 if you are suing on behalf of a business. In the limited jurisdiction division, on the other hand, you can sue for any amount from $1 to $25,000. As you can see, if you are a individual with a claim for less than $7,500 and it involves the type of case explained above, your case may qualify for either court.

When you can use either the limited jurisdiction of Superior Court or Small Claims Court, I recommend using Small Claims. One huge advantage of Small Claims Court is that lawyers can't appear in this court on behalf of clients—so if you're representing yourself, you won't face a lawyer for the other side. Also, Small Claims cases move quickly, the court clerks do most of the paperwork, there are no formal rules of evidence, there are no jury trials, and the judges or commissioners who hear the cases are accustomed to helping people who represent themselves.

Small Claims Court is so advantageous that you may want to use it even if your case involves more than $7,500—say $8,000 or $9,000. To do this, you must reduce the amount you are seeking to $7,500. If you believe you are entitled to significantly more than $7,500, however—say $15,000—it probably makes more sense to learn how to file a lawsuit in the limited jurisdiction division.

Small Claims Court and Out of Staters

Small Claims Courts are designed for California litigants. This means that even if your lawsuit fits within the Small Claims requirements—it's a claim for money damages and you're asking for no more than $7,500—you won't be able to sue in Small Claims unless you can serve the defendant with papers in California. For example, if the expensive fishing rod you purchased in Idaho while on vacation turns out to be a piece of junk, you won't be able to sue the sporting goods store in a California Small Claims Court. Instead, you'll have to turn to the limited jurisdiction division of Superior Court.

There are a few welcome exceptions to this rule. You may use Small Claims Court if:
- you intend to sue a corporation whose headquarters is out of state, as long as the corporation has offices here or has an agent designated for service with the Secretary of State. (If the corporation does business here but has no offices or agent here, you will have to sue in the limited division of Superior Court. (Code of Civil Procedure § 116.340(e).)
- your lawsuit involves California real estate and the defendant is the owner (for example, you can sue an out of state landlord), and
- you intend to sue the owner or operator of a motor vehicle involved in an accident in California.

Disadvantages of Small Claims Court

Most of the time, if your lawsuit can be brought in Small Claims Court, you'll want to do so, for the reasons explained above. But before you turn your sights in that direction, consider whether, in your case, you might be better off heading for the unlimited jurisdiction division of Superior Court. There are three issues to think about.

Losing Plaintiffs Can't Appeal

A Small Claims judgment against a plaintiff is final, so if you lose, you can't appeal. However, if you sue in the limited jurisdiction division of Superior Court and you lose, you can appeal if you believe the judge has made a legal mistake. (As explained in Chapter 16, an appeal can be quite expensive and complicated, but in the right case it can be an important protection.)

The Losing Defendant Can Get a Second Shot

A second disadvantage for Small Claims Court plaintiffs is that if the defendant loses, the defendant can ask that the case be tried all over again before another judge of the Superior Court. And this isn't just an appeal, which is limited to arguing that the judge below incorrectly applied the law. Instead, the defendant will get a chance to try the case all over, even with new evidence. Although most losing defendants don't go to this extreme, the right of appeal can mean that your first win will be essentially wiped away and any tactical advantage you enjoyed in the first trial will be lost.

By contrast, either a defendant or plaintiff can appeal after losing a limited jurisdiction case. This appeal won't involve arguing the facts again, and will be confined to arguing whether the judge made a legal mistake.

No Frequent Visitors

California's Small Claims Court has one more wrinkle: You can sue for over $2,500 only twice in one calendar year. There is no limit to the number of cases you can bring for $2,500 or less.

RESOURCE
For help in going to Small Claims Court, see *Everybody's Guide to Small Claims Court in California,* by Ralph Warner (Nolo).

The Pros and Cons of Representing Yourself

If you have a lawsuit that fits in the limited jurisdiction division of Superior Court and is within the scope of this book, you still have an important decision to make: Do you *want* to represent yourself? Should you instead hire an attorney? There are pros and cons for each option.

The Up Side of Self-Representation

The main advantage of representing yourself is that you can save a lot of money. Assuming you find an attorney you want to hire, that person will probably charge at least $150–$250 per hour for all tasks, no matter how mundane: meeting with you, talking to you on the phone, attempting to reach a settlement with the other side, studying your case in the library, driving to court, waiting for the case to be called by the judge, and finally arguing it for you.

This bill will add up fast—lawyers usually bill in six-minute increments. If you have a lawyer file suit for you, your bill will probably exceed $2,000 within a very short time, and the total is likely to run to many times that amount if you end up going to trial. Unless you have a contingency fee agreement with your lawyer, you will have to foot the bill whether you win or lose. Under the American legal system, the winning party's legal fees rarely get paid by the losing party (but there are exceptions; see "Contracts and Laws That Provide for Attorney's Fees," below).

> **EXAMPLE:** You've won a case against your brother-in-law for the $16,000 he borrowed from you. But the lawyer you hired charged $4,000 for her services. To make matters worse, she will expect to be paid pronto even though it will probably take years to collect your judgment from your sister's bum of a husband. Had you served as your own lawyer and won the case, the victory would have been $4,000 sweeter.

> **Contracts and Laws That Provide for Attorney's Fees**
>
> Some contracts include a clause saying that if the person who provided (or wrote) the contract sues the other party and wins, that person is entitled to have his or her legal fees paid by the loser. Such a clause is perfectly valid. But the law requires a clause like this to run both ways, and if you win, you're entitled to fees whether you're the plaintiff or the defendant (Civil Code § 1717; *Shandoan v. World Sav. & Loan Ass'n*, (1990) 219 Cal.App.3d 97). For example, suppose you sign a contract with a service provider, promising to pay for services rendered, which contains a clause stating that if the provider sues you for payment and wins, he is entitled to attorney's fees. If you sue *him* for failure to provide the services and win, you'll get attorney's fees as well.
>
> There are other situations in which plaintiffs (but not defendants) may be entitled to attorney fees. California legislators have decided that, in many kinds of cases, it's important to encourage plaintiffs to assert their rights. One way to do so is to provide that a losing defendant will pay the winning plaintiff's attorney fees. (This actually encourages lawyers to take the case, since it guarantees a source of payment that's independent of the settlement or judgment.) Such cases involve civil rights, tenants' rights, and consumer issues. You'll need to read the text of the law you're relying on (or have been sued under) to find out whether the Legislature has specifically directed how fees should be paid. The paying of attorney's fees in various cases is covered in the Code of Civil Procedure, beginning at Section 1021. For help in locating these statutes, see "Finding the Law, on Paper and Online," below.

Lawyers in accident cases (known as personal injury cases) normally have contingency agreements. If you win your case, the lawyer will receive 33% to 50% of any money you recover at the end of the case. If you have a legitimate $20,000 claim against someone whose negligent behavior caused your injury, you'll pay anywhere from $6,600 to $10,000 if you hire a lawyer to help you collect. If you bring the lawsuit yourself in Superior Court, that money is yours.

Many people who represent themselves also experience a feeling of pride and accomplishment after navigating successfully through this system designed by lawyers for lawyers. Winning in court is something akin to solving a crossword puzzle; those who venture into this system without a lawyer deserve to be proud of themselves.

The Down Side of Self-Representation

There are disadvantages to representing yourself. The negatives shouldn't be overemphasized, but you must understand and accept what you are up against.

Superior Court Is Geared Toward Lawyers

Superior Court was created by and for lawyers, although nonlawyers are representing themselves more frequently, especially in the limited jurisdiction division. Nevertheless, Superior Court judges are all former lawyers. Although many are helpful to self-represented people, others may patronize you or, worse, be openly hostile. Similarly, many clerks and other court personnel have been socialized to work with lawyers who know the ropes, and sometimes resent nonlawyer "pro pers." And the lawyer representing your opponent may even feel it his or her duty to take advantage of your lack of legal knowledge by filing all sorts of pretrial paperwork and using other obscuring tactics. But the news is not all bad. Many judges and court clerks are sympathetic to pro pers, and many people like you handle their own cases successfully every day.

> ### Dealing With Court Clerks
>
> As you go through the process described in this book, you will deal many times with persons known as Clerks of the Superior Court. Some of them work behind counters in large public rooms. Others sit at a desk just beneath the judge's bench in a courtroom.
>
> As in many government and private offices, clerks come with different attitudes toward dealing with the public. A few consider dealing with the public a bit of a pain. They seem to enjoy telling you that you are doing something the wrong way—and that they can't tell you the right way. But fortunately, more than 80% of the clerks I have observed enjoy working with anyone who treats them with courtesy and respect.
>
> The California Judicial Council recently got serious about reminding the court clerks of their role as helpers, not just gatekeepers. You may see the notice reproduced below when you go to the Clerk's office to file papers. It clarifies what the clerks can—and cannot—do for litigants. Even if your county does not display the sign, all counties in California are bound to abide by its teachings.
>
> Keep in mind that court clerks have a specific job to do. They are not allowed to give you legal advice, tell you what they think the judge will do in your case, or tell you what they think you should do. Even though it may sometimes be frustrating, it's designed to be fair—your opponent isn't getting any extra help, either. For more on dealing with court clerks, see Chapter 6.

Representing Yourself Will Take Time

If you are the plaintiff and the defendant contests your lawsuit—or if you are the defendant and plan to defend yourself—your case may take a substantial amount of your time. If the other side hires a lawyer, count on spending even more time on the case, because you may be bombarded with legal papers to decipher and respond to.

In most lawsuits, you'll have to prepare legal papers and learn court procedures. You also may need to gather evidence from your opponent before the trial, or respond to the other side's pretrial requests for evidence—a process called discovery. And before the trial begins, you'll find yourself waiting around courtrooms for your case to be heard. If the other side or the judge aren't ready, the hearing may even be postponed. When the day and hour finally arrives, the trial could take several days.

If the defendant *doesn't* contest the case, you can normally get a judgment in your favor—called a "default judgment"—without much delay. But the likelihood that your case will be contested is difficult to predict. If the defendant is a businessperson or is covered by insurance, he or she will probably fight. If the defendant clearly owes you money and has no legal defense, there is a decent chance you'll be unopposed.

You'll Need to Rely on Others for Impartial Advice

Have you heard the saying, "The lawyer who represents himself has a fool for a client?" The truth behind this adage is that a smart lawyer realizes that personal involvement with a case is likely to interfere with the ability to make sound decisions. It's much safer to have a wise sounding board—literally, good counsel. The self-represented litigant is likely to have the same problem—one I've unhappily observed almost every day in court. Whether you're a lawyer or not, most people have difficulty making sensible decisions about tactics and settlement possibilities when their emotions are running high.

Because representing yourself means that you will face this problem, I recommend that you set up a mechanism to cope with it. Find a mature, knowledgeable person (your "Sounding Board") whose advice you will seek and respect each time you must make an important decision in your case.

Your Sounding Board may be a friend, relative, or colleague who can help you separate emotion

WELCOME TO THE SUPERIOR COURT OF CALIFORNIA, COUNTY OF

WE ARE HAPPY TO HELP YOU IF WE CAN. HOWEVER, WE ARE ALLOWED TO HELP YOU ONLY IN CERTAIN WAYS, SINCE WE MUST BE FAIR TO EVERYONE.

This is a list of some things the court staff can and cannot do for you.

We can	explain and answer questions about how the court works.	**We cannot**	tell you whether or not you should bring your case to court.
We can	provide you with the number of the local lawyer referral service, legal services program, family law facilitator program, and other services where you can get legal information.	**We cannot**	tell you what words to use in your court papers. (However, we can check your papers for completeness. For example, we check for signatures, notarization, correct county name, correct case number, and presence of attachments.)
We can	give you general information about court rules, procedures, and practices.	**We cannot**	tell you what to say in court.
We can	provide court schedules and information on how to get a case scheduled.	**We cannot**	give you an opinion about what will happen if you bring your case to court.
We can	provide you information from your case file.	**We cannot**	talk to the judge for you.
We can	provide you with court forms and instructions that are available.	**We cannot**	let you talk to the judge outside of court.
We can	usually answer questions about court deadlines and how to compute them.	**We cannot**	change an order signed by a judge.

Since court staff may not know the answers to all questions about court rules, procedures, and practices, and because we don't want to give you wrong information, we have been instructed not to answer questions if we do not know the correct answers. For additional information, please contact a lawyer or your local law library, or check the California Courts Self-Help Center Web site at *www.courtinfo.ca.gov/selfhelp*.

Form Approved for Optional Use
Judicial Council of California
MC-800 [New January 1, 2002]

Court Clerks Office: signage

from fact and analyze your situation objectively. He or she should listen critically to your legal theories, as well as to the practical side of your case. You need someone who will treat your views with a little skepticism and ask tough questions. Your Sounding Board should not be someone who always agrees with you! Anything short of honest assessments from your Sounding Board will hurt you in the long run.

Especially if your case is complicated, I recommend that you find a lawyer who will sell you an hour or two of time to consult on your case from time to time for a reasonable fee. That way, if you have a question about a point of law or procedure, you'll be able to pick up the phone and get an answer. It used to be very difficult to find a lawyer who would help you with just a portion of your case—they wanted to handle every aspect or none of it. However, an increasing number of lawyers are now agreeing to "unbundle" their services and help you evaluate your case, prepare a difficult document, or coach you before you go to court. An unbundled lawyer can also be a good Sounding Board, although consulting a lawyer will obviously cost more than arranging for less formal feedback. There has been a lot written on unbundling, and if you are interested, I recommend an article in the magazine of the Wisconsin Bar Association at www.wisbar.org/wislawmag/1997/09.

The Course of a Typical Limited Jurisdiction Case

A limited jurisdiction lawsuit starts when the plaintiff—who can be either a person or a business—files a formal document called a Complaint with the clerk's office in the Superior Court. The Complaint identifies:
- who the plaintiff is
- who the defendant is (the person or business being sued)
- the date the Complaint was filed with the court
- why the pl... breach of co... problem), and
- what the plainti... the defendant.

Chapter 5 and the app... the-box Complaint forms t... of lawsuits discussed in this u... instructions for completion.

After filling out the Complai... .in and some other forms discussed later (Chapter 5) and filing them with the court, the plaintiff must have a friend or a professional process server deliver copies of these documents to the defendant. (There's also a way to serve the papers by mail, as explained in Chapter 7.) One of these documents, called a Summons, informs the defendant that he or she is being sued and what action to take to contest the suit.

If you are a defendant, note the date the papers were served on you. Within 30 days—31 won't do—you must file either a document challenging some legal defect in the Complaint or, in most cases, a form in response called an Answer. This document must be served on the plaintiff. As explained in Chapter 7, this can be accomplished by mail. Check-the-box Answer forms for defendants are in Chapter 8 and the appendix.

If the defendant files no response within 30 days, the plaintiff can move for a quick resolution of the lawsuit under the "default judgment" procedure. The court takes the defendant's failure to file on time as an indication that he or she has chosen not to participate in the case. Normally, the court can grant a default judgment when the plaintiff requests it (and follows the procedure described in Chapter 9), and does not have to follow the more complicated procedures described in the second half of this book.

If, however, the defendant files an Answer or other written response, the case progresses along a time-worn legal path. Often, the plaintiff and defendant conduct "discovery," the phase of a lawsuit in which each side seeks to find out the

the other is relying on (see Chapter ...). ... limited jurisdiction cases, discovery ... of asking the other side some written questions (called "interrogatories") or asking the other side to answer questions in person (called a "deposition").

Before a trial is scheduled, the court will probably require the parties to meet and attempt to settle the case (see Chapter 3). This is often a great opportunity to arrive at an acceptable compromise, avoiding the time and anxiety of a trial. If the settlement attempt fails, the case goes on to trial.

In the overwhelming majority of cases, a limited jurisdiction trial takes place before a judge alone. It is possible, however, for either the plaintiff or the defendant to force the case to be tried before a jury (see Chapter 15).

From the day the complaint in a limited jurisdiction case is filed and served on the defendant to the day the trial concludes, more than a year may pass. But more likely, if both sides meet court-imposed deadlines, the lawsuit will take less than a year. The actual time your case takes will depend on the following:

- the amount of discovery conducted (see Chapter 10)
- whether pretrial requests, called motions, are filed (see Chapter 11)
- the backlog of cases in your county, and
- whether a jury trial is requested, since a jury trial usually takes longer than a trial before a judge.

If a jury is involved, deliberations usually go fairly quickly, but the lawsuit is not over until three-quarters of the jurors agree and notify the judge of their conclusion. If the case is tried by a judge, he or she may announce a decision within minutes. But sometimes a judge will "take the matter under submission," sending the parties home and informing them of the decision by mail within a few days.

After the trial is over, the losing party may request a new trial by filing a motion with the trial judge. Or, if the loser believes the judge or jury made a serious error in applying the law, that person can appeal to the Appellate Division of the Superior Court. In practice, in most limited jurisdiction cases, however, the trial court's decision ends the lawsuit.

Finding the Law, on Paper and Online

If you've stayed with me so far, it means you're ready and willing to keep thinking about representing yourself. Succeeding chapters will help you evaluate your case and see it through filing and trial. As you go through the rest of the book, you'll find references to California law, both judge-made (cases) and that made by the Legislature (statutes). This section explains how to get your eyes and hands on the law. It also shows you how to get extra copies of the forms you'll need to file or defend your case.

California Statutes

Throughout this book, I refer to California codes such as the Vehicle Code, the Evidence Code, the Civil Code, and the Code of Civil Procedure. These codes collect all the laws, or statutes, in a particular legal subject area. The statutes were written by the Legislature and signed by the Governor. They're organized into 29 separate codes (some with multiple volumes) and are available at many general libraries, all law libraries, and on the Internet.

Most of the time, when I refer to a statute in one of the code books, I explain what it says and how you can use it. But sometimes you will need the exact wording of the law. If so, refer to Nolo's website as described below, or visit a law library and ask a librarian to help you locate it. When you find it, look up the particular statute in the appropriate bound volume. Then, look for the statute in the pamphlet tucked into the back of the book (the "pocket part"). The pocket part will contain any changes to the statute passed by the Legislature since the bound volume was published.

Some code books also contain cases that have relied upon or interpreted the statutes. These are called annotated code books. In some situations, you'll want to read the case summaries that appear under the statute you're interested in, because they tell you how courts have applied the law in specific situations.

Use Nolo.com to Find the Statute

To find a particular California statute, you can start at Nolo's website, www.nolo.com. Choose "Legal Research" at the top of the page, then the State Law link. Choose "California" and pick the California Code that contains your statute. Most of them will be in the Code of Civil Procedure.

California and Local Court Rules

In addition to the codes, various court rules will apply to your case. The rules determine how the courts conduct business. Statewide rules are published in a volume called the *California Rules of Court*, which you can find at any law library. Also, your local court will have a set of rules that govern just that court. You can find both the statewide and local county court rules on the Internet. For the state rules, go to www.courtinfo.ca.gov and click on "Rules." For local rules, follow the same procedure, and click on "Local Rules" on the left side of the page. Then scroll down the list of counties to select your county.

Cases

I refer occasionally to court cases or decisions— for example, *Armendariz v. Foundation Health Psychcare Services*, (2000) 24 Cal. 83—that have interpreted or applied a particular point of law. These written decisions are available at any law library. With the citation, the libraria you locate the decision.

Finding court cases on the Internet easy as finding statutes. A few recent C court decisions are available for free at www.courtinfo.ca.gov (click on "Opinions"). But most decisions can be read only by going to a law library or by using a commercial legal research service. Most of these services are designed for law firms with extensive needs (and clients who will pay), and they're expensive. Fortunately, there's one outfit that is designed for the solo user like yourself. At www.versuslaw.com, you can have unlimited access to their database of cases (and more) for a modest fee ($13.95 per month at the time of writing). Although it is not usually necessary, it can be a good investment if your case involves a complicated dispute over the meaning of a law.

Getting Information About Your County on the Web

Each of California's 58 Superior Courts has a website that you can reach via www.courtinfo.ca.gov. Click the "Courts" heading at the top of the page, and then "Superior Courts" and "Court Web Sites." Pick the county you are interested in and you will find tons of useful information.

General Instructions for Filling Out Your Forms

The rest of the chapters in this book will guide you as you think about whether to file suit (or defend against one), whether to settle or, in some cases, to hire an attorney after all. If you progress to the point of filing a lawsuit or defending against one on your own, you're going to need to fill out court forms, which tell the judge and your opponent what your case is all about and what it is that you're asking for (or refusing to give up). All of the forms you'll need are in the appendix and, as explained below, you can download additional copies from the Internet.

All official forms contain some identical elements, such as the requirement that you identify the case, its number, your name, and so on. Follow the instructions below when you begin to fill out any official form. Directions for the balance of the individual forms are in the chapters that discuss the forms in detail.

ATTORNEY OR PARTY WITHOUT ATTORNEY (Name and Address): Type your full name, as it appears on your driver's license. If you choose to handwrite your forms, you must use black or blue-black ink. (California Rule of Court 2.106.) While the court clerk cannot reject your papers just because they are handwritten, that hasn't always been the rule; clerks are used to receiving typed papers, and they may reject your papers anyway. Your safest bet is to type them.

Do not use nicknames. If you are suing (or being sued) on behalf of a business, write the business's name (see "Suing a Business" in Chapter 4 for information on how to describe a business). Then add your address and telephone number. After the words "ATTORNEY FOR," type "In Pro Per." This tells the court that you are representing yourself, without a lawyer.

Insert name of court and name of judicial district and branch court, if any: Fill in the name and address of the county and court at the top of the next box, and the name of the branch you are using, if any. Consult "Selecting the Right Courthouse" in Chapter 4 for information on the courts in your county that will hear limited jurisdiction cases.

PLAINTIFF/PETITIONER: Write the name of the plaintiff—the person bringing the lawsuit.

DEFENDANT/RESPONDENT: This is the person or business being sued—again, refer to Chapter 4 for proper format.

FOR COURT USE ONLY: Leave this box blank. The clerk will stamp the form in this space when you file it.

CASE NUMBER: Once you've filed a lawsuit, the clerk will assign it a number. Always enter this number in this space.

Downloading Court Forms

To obtain a Judicial Council form from the Internet, go to www.courtinfo.ca.gov and click "Forms" at the top of the page. Then choose to view "All forms listed by number." The form's number is in the upper right corner, as you'll see when you look at the forms in the appendix. Now click "See Forms," and scroll down the page to find that number, choose it, and print the form on your printer. You can also fill in the form online. Click the link in the "Fillable Form" column, which allows you to type your answers into the form on your computer. One word of caution—you must complete the form in one session and print it right away. You cannot save this completed form to your hard drive (and if you quit midway, your work will be lost).

If you need a form designed by Nolo, you'll have to photocopy the form as it appears in the appendix.

CHAPTER 2

Do You Have a Good Case?

Is Your Case Fresh Enough?	22
Evaluating the Evidence	23
Is the Evidence Convincing?	23
Is the Evidence Admissible?	24
Can You Prove Each Legally Required Fact?	26
The Defendant's Perspective	26
Preserve Your Evidence Now	26
Can You Collect the Judgment If You Win?	29
How Much Should You Sue For?	30
Tort Cases	30
Breach of Contract Cases	33

> **SKIP AHEAD**
> **If you are a defendant, some of this chapter isn't directly relevant.** However, it's still a good idea to read the whole chapter carefully. It will help you evaluate the strength of the plaintiff's case as well as the strength of your own defense. It will also give you an idea of some arguments the plaintiff might make and the amount the plaintiff might try to collect.

Before you file a lawsuit, ask yourself two questions: How good are my chances of winning? If I win, will I be able to collect? If your answers lead you to conclude your chances are good, then you need to ask a third question: How much should I sue for?

This chapter guides you through these questions. Specifically, it shows you how to:

- determine whether the deadline for filing your kind of lawsuit has passed
- evaluate the strength of your evidence
- preserve your evidence
- figure out whether you can collect if you win, and
- decide how much to sue for.

> **CAUTION**
> **Never sue just to "get even."** If you don't care about recovering money and only have a burning desire to get even with someone, I'd advise you not to file a civil lawsuit. Judges figure out your motives and treat these cases harshly, and everyone loses—the plaintiff and the defendant. But if court is the only place you can go to right a wrong, then file. Remember, however, the ancient Gypsy curse "May you be involved in a lawsuit in which you know you are right."

Is Your Case Fresh Enough?

For all sorts of reasons, lawmakers have decided that courts should decide recent cases, not old ones. The main reason is that evidence (especially people's memories) is more accessible and trustworthy when it's fresh. There's a practical side to things, too—many courts are very busy and would be overwhelmed if they entertained old cases. There's also an element of fairness involved—would-be defendants shouldn't have to spend years wondering whether a lawsuit is about to fall on them.

Laws called "statutes of limitations" govern the time period within which you're permitted to sue after the incident that led to the lawsuit occurred. If the statute of limitations period has passed, in most cases it's useless to sue. (But see "Don't automatically give up on old claims," below.) The statute of limitations period differs according to the type of case, as explained in "Statutes of Limitations," below.

> **SEE AN EXPERT**
> **For claims against the federal government, the time limits are different than for claims against state or local government.** If your claim is against a federal government agency, it's best to consult a lawyer.

In some situations, more than one statute of limitations may apply. For example, suppose you've been hurt in a car accident. You'd have two years from the date of the accident to sue for the injuries to your body, and three years to sue for the damage to your car. However, you should handle it all in one suit within two years.

The statute of limitations is shorter for an oral contract than for a written one. Most of your contracts, though, are probably at least partially written. The work order you sign at a garage, your cousin's IOU for a loan, a credit account with a department store, and many other transactions do not require signing a document labeled "Contract," but they all involve written agreements.

It's important to understand that the statute of limitations for a breach of contract starts to run on the day the contract was broken, not the day it was written. If the contract called for installment payments, the statute runs separately for each installment as it becomes due. For example, suppose your written contract with a customer calls for one payment on March 15, 2011, and a second payment on September 15, 2011. If the customer failed to pay on March 15, 2011, you can sue to collect on that payment until March 15, 2015. If the customer doesn't make the September 15, 2011, payment either, you can sue to collect on that payment until September 15, 2015. Of course, if you wait that long to sue, you won't be able to recover the payment that was due March 15, 2011, because more than four years will have passed.

Statutes of Limitations

The table below lists common statutes of limitations. For limitations periods for other, more unusual cases, see the Code of Civil Procedure, §§ 312-365.

Injury to your body resulting from an intentional or negligent act	2 years
Damage to property	3 years
Oral contracts	2 years from when the contract was broken
Written contracts	4 years from when the contract was broken
Hidden defects in a construction project (such as a home)	10 years after the completion of the project or within 3 years of discovery of the defect
Claims against state or local government entity or agency	You must file a special claim form with the government entity or agency within six months. If they reject your claim, you can file your case in court, subject to the statute of limitations for that type of case.

SEE AN EXPERT
Don't automatically give up on old claims. Determining if the statute of limitations has expired can get complicated. If you think that your claim may be too old, but you aren't sure, consult a lawyer. On rare occasions, a lawyer may be able to figure out a way around a statute of limitations time limit.

Evaluating the Evidence

Before deciding to file a lawsuit, you should realistically examine your chance of winning. The same is true if you've been sued and must decide whether to defend or settle out of court.

Lawsuits are won by people who have the facts and the law on their side, not by those who have the saddest stories. Sometimes nice people are surprised when they lose a case because they had assumed that courts always arrive at results that are just. Unfortunately, it isn't that simple.

If you are a potential plaintiff, to analyze your chances of winning you'll need to assess:
- whether your evidence will convince the court to award you damages
- whether your evidence is admissible in court, so that it can be considered by the judge or jury, and
- whether you can prove each fact required under the law for your type of suit.

If you are a defendant, you'll need to look at:
- whether the plaintiff's theory about what he or she needs to prove to win is correct
- whether your evidence is admissible in court so that it can be considered by the judge or jury, and
- whether your evidence is strong enough to convince the court that the facts are not as the plaintiff claims.

Is the Evidence Convincing?

Let's look at each of these important issues in more detail, first from the plaintiff's perspective.

A plaintiff's first step should be to consult his or her adviser—the Sounding Board or legal coach, discussed in Chapter 1. Carefully explain the facts of your case and the evidence you plan to use. Ask for an honest assessment. Then urge your Sounding Board or legal coach to play devil's advocate—that is, to challenge your conclusions and evidence and to state the other side's case as strongly as possible. Ask how your helper would decide the case if he or she were the judge. If your case doesn't look so hot to your wise adviser, it probably won't look any better in court.

Such a review would have been helpful to a couple that once appeared in my courtroom. They described how their Volkswagen engine had burst into flames while they were driving down the freeway with their young child in the back seat. They pulled over quickly and got out safely, but their car was a total loss. They sued the local Volkswagen dealer who had done repairs on the gas lines about two weeks earlier.

After hearing their testimony, I asked if they'd had a mechanic examine their ruined car to try to determine the cause of the fire. They hadn't thought it necessary, assuming anyone would conclude that the dealer had done the gas line repair incorrectly. I was sympathetic and even understood how they had come to that conclusion. Unfortunately, I also knew that they'd flubbed their task of proving to me that the fire had been caused by the dealer's negligence. Unproven probabilities or suppositions weren't enough for me to rule in their favor—they needed some hard evidence that the fire really was the dealer's fault. Or to put it another way, I could declare them the winner only if their evidence led to the conclusion that their theory was more likely to be correct than any other explanation. Because they lacked that sort of evidence, judgment was for the defendant.

I think a good advisor could have helped this couple see that in their outrage about the fire, they had jumped to an unproven conclusion that couldn't stand on its own in the harsh light of the courtroom. A good advisor would have asked:

"Why is it more likely that the fire resulted from the repair than from one of a hundred other causes?" And once this question was asked, I think it would have been obvious to the couple that they'd need to ask a mechanic to do a detailed examination of the burned car.

Is the Evidence Admissible?

Okay, you believe your evidence is convincing —that a court would be convinced that the defendant's actions led directly to the harm you suffered. Now you must figure out if it is admissible. That means that it is the type of evidence the court is legally authorized to hear and consider. Evidence includes any witnesses who can support your case, as well as photographs, documents, and the like.

The study of evidence is a yearlong course at most law schools and, as you will readily understand, I cannot cover it in depth here. But I can summarize the most important principles. This material is discussed in more detail in Chapter 13.

In assessing your evidence, follow these general rules:

Most witnesses must have personal knowledge. Unless a witness qualifies as an expert (see next paragraph), a witness must have been present at some significant event and have personal knowledge of what happened in the story of your case to be able to testify in court about those facts. Possible witnesses include you, your friends and your relatives, as well as complete strangers, as long as they have firsthand knowledge. For the most part, people who merely heard about the events from someone else can't testify.

Opinion evidence is allowed infrequently. Generally, only a person with specialized training in a scientific or technical field (called an "expert witness") can give an opinion in court. In fact, all sorts of experts give opinions in court, often in exchange for a fee. For example, an experienced mechanic would normally be considered as an expert witness who could give an opinion about whether a car repair was done properly. Similarly, an electrician could testify about a wiring installation. In some fields, college professors can give helpful testimony or know of other experts who may be able to help you.

RESOURCE
For a more thorough review of evidence rules, see *Represent Yourself in Court*, by Paul Bergman and Sara J. Berman (Nolo). Also, if you need the help of an expert witness, see *California Expert Witness Guide*, 2nd ed., published by the California Continuing Education of the Bar (CEB) and available at most law libraries. Chapter 13 has some excellent tips on locating a good expert.

When You Need an Expert

You won't need an expert witness in every case. But you should consider hiring one if your case involves:
- a car in need of repair
- plumbing, electrical, construction, or similar work around the home, or
- an accident in which skid marks or other markings may indicate negligent or reckless driving.

If you are claiming that a lawyer, doctor, accountant, or other professional you hired committed malpractice, it's absolutely essential to get an expert opinion on that subject.

There are a few areas in which a nonexpert can offer an opinion, if relevant. A nonexpert can offer testimony regarding:
- the identity of a person, including descriptive features such as voice or physical traits
- a person's appearance, state of intoxication, health, or age
- the witness's own intention, motive, or emotion
- the value of the witness's own property or services
- measurements such as speed, distance, or size, and
- the directions from which sounds came.

Written statements are usually not allowed. Most of the time, you can't use written statements by witnesses in court. This rule applies to most police reports and even to notarized affidavits and declarations made under penalty of perjury.

There is an exception, however: Routine business and public records may be brought into court by their "custodian" (the person responsible for maintaining the records). Here are some examples:
- a bank officer can present monthly bank statements as evidence
- a landlord or property manager can introduce rent receipts, and
- a creditor can introduce business records showing when bills were sent and payments received, as long as the person who supervises the record keeping is available to testify.

A knowledgeable witness must identify photos and other physical objects. For photographs, a witness needs to be able to testify in court that the photo accurately depicts how a particular scene looked at a particular time. However, you don't have to produce the photographer to testify as to the contents of the photo or to the process used. Other physical objects may be used as evidence as long as a witness can link them to the case using the witness's own personal knowledge.

Impartial witnesses are preferable. An impartial witness who didn't know any of the parties before the event is a more valuable witness than your friends and relatives. These witnesses are unbiased and have nothing to gain if you win your case. If, however, your only testimony is from your spouse and your sister, by all means use them—their testimony is a lot better than nothing.

You can't introduce evidence about a person's character. Evidence showing what a good person you are—and what a bad person the other side is—is generally not allowed.

Can You Prove Each Legally Required Fact?

The final test in assessing your chances of winning is harder to explain to people without formal legal training: For every type of lawsuit, a plaintiff must prove a list of required facts (called "elements") to win. The elements of lawsuits are what law students study for three years and legal authorities write about almost endlessly. Sometimes the requirements change as the Legislature enacts new laws and amends old ones, and courts interpret the laws.

For the relatively simple lawsuits I discuss in this book, I don't believe you need torture yourself over whether you can prove each required fact. Instead, read over the descriptions of tort and contract lawsuits in Chapter 1. If your facts seem to fit these molds, your major pieces of evidence are admissible, and your Sounding Board or legal coach agrees that you have a solid case, then proceed to prepare your suit. If your case is more complicated, check "Complaints for Other Types of Lawsuits" in Chapter 5, where I discuss the elements of some other claims.

The Defendant's Perspective

If you're a defendant, your part in the case formally begins when you receive a Summons and Complaint from the plaintiff. At this early stage, you can follow much the same path as a plaintiff in evaluating the strength of your own case.

First, determine whether the plaintiff has filed the lawsuit within the permitted period of time allowed by law. Check the statute of limitations that covers the type of case that the plaintiff has brought to find out. If the case is too old, your most cost-effective alternative is to raise the statute of limitations problem in your Answer, the document a defendant files in response to the plaintiff's Complaint. Preparing an Answer is discussed in Chapter 8. Another alternative is to file a complicated motion called a Demurrer, which could cause the case to go away after some legal wrangling and a court appearance. But preparing and filing a Demurrer generally requires the assistance of a lawyer.

After checking to see whether the plaintiff has filed in time, read over the Complaint to see whether the plaintiff seems to have covered the basic elements of the particular type of case, whether it's a tort case or a contract case. If it is another type of case, consult the resources discussed in "Complaints for Other Types of Lawsuits" in Chapter 5, and make the same decision.

Go over the facts of the case as you perceive them, noting where and how your account differs from the version in the plaintiff's Complaint. Lay out your evidence—your account of events, documents supporting your account, statements by potential witnesses—and try to determine whether it would be admissible in court, as explained above.

Then present your case to a trusted adviser—a Sounding Board or legal coach. You're looking for help in spotting any weaknesses in your case, along with suggestions about additional ways to prove your key points.

Preserve Your Evidence Now

If you've concluded that your evidence is convincing and admissible, it's time to preserve any evidence you might use. Bruises and skid marks disappear in time. Work orders and cash register receipts are often misplaced. Witnesses move and memories fade.

To preserve your evidence, set up some files in a safe place. Make one file for repair bills, another for medical reports, and as many more as you need for your different kinds of evidence. I can't emphasize too much how important this is. Many times I've seen witnesses in court say that they've lost an important document. If they ask for a few more days to search, I usually can't allow it. Evidence produced after the trial is over is useless.

Here are some of the things you should put in your files.

Photographs. Try to take pictures as close to the time of an event as possible, before the scene changes. Photos taken later may be used, but only if nothing else is available. Here are some pointers on particular situations:

- If the subject is difficult to photograph, such as a loose rug in a dark hallway, or a botched paint job on the underside of a roof overhang, hire a professional photographer.
- If the condition of a car is important and the car is being held in a garage, go and take a picture before it is repaired or moved.
- If the presence or absence of a sign is important, photograph the scene before it changes. To prove that the photograph was not taken before a particular date, place a copy of that day's newspaper in the picture.
- Use color film to photograph bruises or wounds. If they are changing rapidly, take a picture every day or two and record the date each was taken. Again, to prove that a photograph was not taken before a particular date, place a copy of that day's newspaper in the picture.

Medical evaluation. Seek a medical evaluation of any physical or emotional injury as soon as possible. Begin with your regular physician. If you're getting treatment from a chiropractor or another non-M.D., a medical doctor still should evaluate you. Most injury cases are settled with insurance companies, which are notoriously skeptical of chiropractors and other alternative healers. If you don't have an M.D., ask your chiropractor or other healer for a referral.

Physical objects. Keep all relevant physical objects. You don't want to have to testify that you threw an important piece of evidence into a garbage can. Also, try to keep damaged items in their damaged condition so that you can introduce them as evidence in court. Where this is impractical—for example, if you need to repair or replace your faulty wiring or car—get at least two written estimates before having the work done. Some insurance adjusters will tell you they need three estimates and that you must have the work done by the lowest bidder. This simply isn't true.

You can use the estimates in settlement negotiations and at any arbitration hearing, and you can have the people who gave the estimates testify at trial. If a particular part of the about-to-be repaired item shows the damage, have the mechanic (or other repairperson) save the part.

Witnesses. If you know of any witnesses to the event in question, find them and ask them what they saw. Police reports sometimes list witnesses' addresses and phone numbers. (If the witness doesn't have deep roots in the community, try to get the name, address, and phone number of someone who will be able to help you locate your witness for a future trial date.)

How to Interview a Witness

If a witness agrees to be interviewed and taped, begin the interview by stating the date, where the interview is taking place, and who is in the room. Then ask the witness if he or she understands that the interview is being recorded.

For the actual interview, start by asking the witness's location and what he or she saw. Then develop the story slowly, moving step by step. Ask questions that bring out the most basic facts. Try to imagine that the story is being told to someone who knows nothing about what happened.

When talking to witnesses, don't put words in their mouths or argue with them, even if you violently disagree with what they say.

Be sure to get explanations of imprecise words. If the witness says the defendant was acting "crazy," ask what "crazy" means.

If a witness seems helpful, explain how important his or her testimony is and ask if yo[u can] conduct an interview with a video or tape [recorder]. If the witness doesn't want to be on ta[pe,]

description of what the person said and ask him or her to sign it. If the witness refuses to sign, ("I don't want to get involved"), an unsigned statement can still be valuable under some circumstances, as long as a third person was present at the interview and will testify that it is a true statement of what the witness said.

Recorded statements of witnesses are not allowed in court under most circumstances, but they can be very effective in settlement negotiations. They are also useful as a reminder for a witness who plans to testify in court. And if the witness changes his or her testimony at trial, the video or tape recording can be played for the judge or jury to show the witness's lack of reliability (this is called "impeaching the witness").

Pain diary. If you've been physically or emotionally injured—no matter how minor or severe—keep a daily "pain diary." Every few days, describe briefly how you feel, whether you are having problems with sleep, mobility, or other consequences, and any drugs you are taking. This information is nearly impossible to remember accurately months later. Don't lay it on too thick, however. Your opponent will probably see your diary eventually and will try to get it in front of the judge if you are too melodramatic.

Police reports. Police reports of vehicle accidents are generally not admissible as evidence in court, but they can help you investigate and settle your case. Insurance adjusters often base their settlement offers on the opinions of investigating police officers. To obtain a police report, visit the applicable police department, sheriff's office, or California Highway Patrol office. Ask for a copy of the officer's report. You'll probably have to pay a few dollars for copying charges.

Accident reconstruction experts. These experts investigate accidents (usually vehicle crashes) by examining vehicles and accident sites and scientifically determining such factors as distance, time, and rate of speed. If you want to show that a police officer's opinion was wrong or if your accident was complicated, consider consulting an accident reconstruction expert. You can find them in the yellow pages for major cities. Some are quite good; others have little real expertise. To find a good one, ask for references (and check them out) and credentials. Make sure you know what the fee is in advance.

Reading a Police Report

Police reports come in many formats. Study the report carefully; you'll often find a box where the reporting officer gives his or her opinion as to who might have been at fault for the accident.

The officer's opinion may be indicated by reference to a section of the Vehicle Code, the set of laws governing traffic safety. For instance, if you're identified as "Dr...   er driver is "Driver 2," you
                            d "Driver 2" with the number
                            Vehicle Code section dealing
                            bably means that the officer
                            as making an unsafe turn at

                            about who was violating a
                            in a police report even

if the officer didn't issue a ticket. But even if there is no Vehicle Code section in the police report, the officer may still have an opinion about who caused the accident. The opinion probably won't be admissible in court, but it can be persuasive in settlement negotiations.

If the police officer doesn't agree with your version of what happened, it doesn't necessarily mean you don't have a case. Police officers make mistakes like everyone else. You just have to look elsewhere for your evidence.

If you don't understand the report, take it back to the police department and ask for help.

Can You Collect the Judgment If You Win?

When I was a judge, I often felt a little sad after telling some self-represented plaintiffs that I was ruling in their favor. Their faces would brighten, their eyes would dart around the courtroom nervously, and then they'd ask what seemed to be the next logical question: "When do I get paid?" It was almost as if they thought the courthouse had a window where winning plaintiffs could go and watch a clerk count out the money due. "The sad truth is," I'd say, "you've just finished the easy part of your case. Now you must start the hard part—collecting."

In fact, some judgments are aptly described as "not worth the paper they are printed on." This isn't the court's fault. The Legislature has passed many laws to protect people who have little money from losing what is left. These are called "exemptions," and exempt property includes basic household goods, furnishings, and clothing; 75% of wages; $2,300 of equity in a car; and between $75,000 and $175,000 of equity in a house, depending on the age and family status of the debtor.

If you win your case, the judge or jury will decide how much the defendant should pay you. Some defendants pay right away. Some never pay. The point is to ask yourself "Can I collect if I win?" before you file your case. Don't sue unless you can answer, "Yes." If the defendant won't pay voluntarily, you can use certain collection techniques to force payment.

Court judgments last for ten years in California and can be renewed indefinitely. This means that even if the defendant doesn't have any money or property now, you may be able to collect some time in the future.

Here are some ideas about collecting from certain defendants:

Large businesses. If the defendant is an airline, department store, or other established business, collecting should be no problem. Big corporations normally pay off judgments under $25,000 within a month or two. Although they can appeal any case they lose, they usually don't because the legal fees they'd incur don't justify appealing. Paying a judgment of under $25,000 won't break them.

Small businesses. If a small business has a regular store or office where it pays rent, issues paychecks to employees, or operates a cash register, collecting probably won't be a big problem. By contacting the appropriate county official, you can have a sheriff or marshal actually go to the business and take your money. However, if the business is run by one person who operates informally out of his home with no cash register or bank account, you may have problems collecting.

Individuals. People who receive public assistance, Social Security, or disability payments, or who have no recognizable assets or bank accounts, are difficult to collect from. On the other hand, the following defendants are usually not hard to collect from:

- people with applicable insurance policies—the insurance company pays on their behalf
- wage earners—the sheriff can collect about 25% of their paycheck, with some exceptions, and
- owners of real estate—you can place a lien and either foreclose or get paid when they sell the property.

If the defendant files for bankruptcy. If the defendant filed for Chapter 7 bankruptcy before your case arose, it normally won't affect your suit. (Chapter 7 bankruptcies erase most debts; Chapter 13 bankruptcies prioritize the debts and impose a plan for repayment on the debtor. Under the new bankruptcy laws that went into effect in 2005, some higher-income persons who could afford to pay back a portion of their debt over a five-year period aren't allowed to proceed under Chapter 7 and may be forced to file under Chapter 13.) However, if the defendant files for bankruptcy after losing your case, your judgment will often be wiped out along with other debts. In a few instances, you may still be entitled to collect your court judgment after the bankruptcy case is over. For instance, debts that arise from drunk driving can't be erased in bankruptcy. Also, court judgments that arise from willful or malicious injury to another person or the person's property may remain after bankruptcy. And sometimes liens on real property arising from court judgments remain after bankruptcy. Suing someone who declares bankruptcy is covered in Chapter 4.

How Much Should You Sue For?

Okay—you have a reasonable chance of winning and you think you can collect. Now the question is, "How much should you sue for?" You can sue in the limited jurisdiction division for anywhere from $1 to $25,000. Before you pick an exact amount, take a look at what types of money damages are routinely awarded in breach of contract and tort cases.

RESOURCE

If your case is under $7,500, you are almost always better off in Small Claims Court, discussed in Chapter 1. *Everybody's Guide to Small Claims Court in California*, by Ralph Warner (Nolo), can guide you through the process.

Tort Cases

If your lawsuit is based on a tort (intentional or careless behavior directly resulting in injury or damage to you or your property), you may be able to recover for the following kinds of damages:

Property damage. Legally, property falls into two categories: real property (land and buildings) and personal property (everything else). When I speak of property, I mean both real and personal. You can collect the cost of repairing an item of property, but if the repair exceeds the market value, you get only the market value. The market value is the property's worth just before it was damaged, not its replacement cost. For instance, if your car is totaled, use the car's value as reflected in the Edmunds guide (www.Edmunds.com) or the Kelley Blue Book (www.kbb.com), not what it is going to cost you to replace it.

Medical bills. You can sue both for costs you've already incurred and for those you expect to incur in the future for medical treatment for both physical and emotional injuries. These costs might include ambulance charges, emergency room service, hospital costs, X-rays, chiropractors, orthopedists, plastic surgeons, and therapists who have helped you recover from your trauma. See "If Your Insurance Is Paying for Your Medical Bills," below.

Lost wages and benefits. The amount you seek should include compensation for income you didn't or won't receive as a result of the injury or damage. Be sure to include estimated future lost wages if you'll have to take more time off.

If you were paid through an insurance or sick leave plan, request compensation for the regular wages you missed. Insurance and sick leave payments are benefits you earn; they should not be a windfall to the defendant. Similarly, if you were forced to use up vacation time to recuperate, ask for wages during that period. But if you have a dream employer who ignored your absence and paid your regular wages while you missed work, don't ask to be compensated for the time you missed. If you're self-employed, you may need an accountant to help you figure out what you would have earned had you been able to work.

Another type of damages that will apply in a few cases is your loss of "earning capacity" in the future. If your injury will prevent you from being promoted to a better job, or if you now cannot do the job you used to do and must take a lower-paying job, you can sue for the difference between what you could have reasonably expected to earn preaccident, minus your expected, lower earnings, postaccident. (If you have a significant injury and hence sizable loss of earning capacity damages, chances are you'll be suing for much more than

If Your Insurance Is Paying for Your Medical Bills

If you are covered by health insurance, your insurance company is probably paying for any ambulance, doctor, hospital, and physical therapy bills as they are incurred. And most likely, the defendant and the defendant's insurance company will not want to pay you for services that aren't costing you anything. Should you sue to collect medical expenses that you're already insured for?

Before you decide how to handle this issue, you'll have to take the trouble to read your health insurance policy (or, if you have insurance through your employer or some other group, the booklet that describes your coverage). Does the policy say anything about having to reimburse the insurance company if you recover those costs from someone else? If you can't find the policy or booklet or if you pale at the thought of reading fine print, you can call the broker who sold you the policy, or if you have a group policy, you can talk to the person who handles insurance for your employer or group. Explain what happened to you and that your health insurance company is paying your bills.

In some cases, you will find the insurance policy has no reimbursement clause and that there is no need to inform the company of your lawsuit. In that event, list your medical expenses as part of your damages. If, in the course of the lawsuit, the defendant asks whether your bills are covered by your own insurance, tell the truth, but point out that the defendant is not entitled to benefit from the fact that you provide pro[tection] for yourself.

It's more likely, however, that your insurance [policy] states that the insurer will get reimbursed—through what's called a lien claim—if you recover medical expenses through a lawsuit. In other words, the insurance company will come after you to reimburse them for the bills they've paid on your account. That's true for most private health insurers as well as for governmental insurance such as Medicare, Medi-Cal, and workers' compensation.

If your policy allows the company to seek reimbursement, you should still include your medical bills in the amount you are seeking in your lawsuit. Be aware that you probably will face a lien claim from the insurance company after you settle your case or win at trial. You might be able to negotiate with an adjuster from your insurance company, however. The insurance company may agree to accept less than the full amount of your medical expenses if your injuries were particularly painful or if you recovered less than you sued for. At any rate, contact your insurance company now so that there won't be surprises later.

If you don't have health insurance and your medical bills are being paid through your automobile insurance policy (something that doesn't occur often), your insurance company is normally entitled to repayment from any recovery you make.

$25,000 and will have a lawyer representing you in the unlimited division of Superior Court.)

Pain and suffering. Money awarded for pain and suffering compensates you for your stiff back, the pain you feel when you hobble down the stairs, and your general discomfort. It also includes compensation for fright, nervousness, anxiety, and apprehension caused by the incident. Be sure to include both past pain and suffering and any you are likely to experience in the future.

A typical approach to calculating pain and suffering is to begin by multiplying your medical bills by a factor of three to five. If your pain and suffering is extreme or out the ordinary, increase it from there.

> **EXAMPLE:** Nick's total medi[cal bills were] $4,000. To figure out his in[jury and pain and] suffering loss, he multiplie[d $4,000 by] three. He didn't have any

and suffering, so he asks for $12,000 for this portion of his damages.

This formula is used because pain and suffering is usually loosely related to the amount of an injured person's medical expenses. Insurance companies deny that they use any such formula, but at least it gives you a place to start your bargaining. After a quick trip to an emergency room and one follow-up appointment with a doctor, most people won't experience much pain and suffering. But if you required an operation and physical therapy, your pain and suffering would likely be much greater.

No Pain & Suffering for Drunk or Uninsured Drivers

In 1996 California voters adopted a new law that restricts the damages you can recover from a motor vehicle accident if you were uninsured at the time or if you are later convicted of having been driving under the influence of alcohol or drugs when the accident occurred. The law does not affect your right to recover for your medical bills or the damage to your property, but it does say that you cannot receive damages for pain, suffering, inconvenience, physical impairment, disfigurement, or other nonmonetary damages. It also says that insurance companies are not required to cover for these damages in this type of situation. (Civil Code § 3333.4.)

There are complicated details regarding some parts of this law—for instance, an uninsured driver is not prevented from a full recovery against a drunk driver—so if you were uninsured or under the influence at the time of an accident, you should consult a lawyer before filing a lawsuit. As explained above, pain and suffering are frequently the major part of any plaintiff's recovery in a motor vehicle case, and if this law applies to you, it may not be worthwhile for you to sue.

Other Ways to Estimate Pain and Suffering

Rarely will two experienced personal injury lawyers agree on an exact pain and suffering award in a contested court case. This is because the lawyers are trying to guess what the members of a jury will feel is fair to compensate someone for something that's difficult to evaluate monetarily.

Pain and suffering awards depend on the facts of a particular situation. For example, if your medical care was limited to a doctor sewing up a major wound, but you had a lot of pain and a permanent scar, multiplying your medical bills by three to five wouldn't come close to compensating you for your pain and suffering. At the same time, if your injury is minor (such as a sprained wrist), the fact that you visited a doctor ten times and ran up a big bill shouldn't mean you're entitled to a huge pain and suffering award. In these situations, insurance companies often offer a flat pain and suffering award, such as $1,000 per month while you were recovering.

Good personal injury lawyers often can get juries to make large pain and suffering awards, usually far in excess of what an inexperienced self-represented plaintiff can reasonably expect to recover. But, as explained in Chapter 1, the lawyer's fee is usually one-third to one-half the award. Nevertheless, if you have sustained a serious injury and suffered a high amount of pain, I'd recommend that you at least consult with a lawyer and get an estimate of what you can expect to recover after the lawyer's fee gets paid. For a more detailed discussion of this issue and about personal injury cases in general, see *How to Win Your Personal Injury Claim,* by Joseph Matthews (Nolo).

> **CAUTION**
>
> **Were you partially at fault?** If you were injured or your property was damaged because of the defendant's act, but your carelessness contributed to the injury or damage, your recovery may be reduced proportionately under a legal doctrine known as "comparative negligence." Comparative negligence means that a person who was partially at fault gets charged for his or her share of the blame. For example, suppose Linda and Jason collided in a car accident. The judge rules for Linda, and finds that her damages—auto repair, lost wages, medical bills, and pain and suffering—total $10,000. The judge also finds that Jason was 75% responsible for the accident (he made an unsafe lane change) and that Linda was 25% responsible (she was driving too fast). Linda's recovery would be reduced to $7,500.

Breach of Contract Cases

If you're suing because the defendant breached a contract, the amount of your damages will likely depend on the type of contract involved. Because damages in a contract case are related directly to the contract itself, and what the defendant's breaking the agreement cost you, the damages are usually easier to determine. On the flip side, they're also more limited—for example, you can't recover for pain and suffering for breach of a contract. Look at the breach of contract categories below and see which type most nearly matches yours.

Unpaid loans. If you lent someone money and he or she hasn't paid you back, you're entitled to the unpaid loan amount, plus any interest specified in the contract, not to exceed 10% per year. If you forgot to include interest in your contract, you can recover 10% per year from the time the loan was due, under Civil Code § 3289.

> **EXAMPLE 1:** Wayne lent John $10,000. John signed a promissory note that said nothing about interest. John failed to pay Wayne. Wayne sued for $10,000 plus 10% per year interest from the time the money was due.

> **EXAMPLE 2:** This time Wayne lent John $10,000 for two years at 8% interest. When John fails to pay Wayne back, Wayne sues for the $10,000 plus 8% interest from the time the money was loaned.

If the loan was to be paid in installments, you can sue on each installment as it becomes due or wait until all the installments are owed and sue then—assuming the statute of limitations hasn't run on the earlier installments. If, however, your loan agreement has an acceleration clause—a provision that if any payment is missed the full amount becomes due immediately—you can "accelerate" the loan and sue on the full amount as soon as the borrower misses a single payment.

> **EXAMPLE:** Missy loaned Nora $8,000 to be paid back at $200 per month. The agreement contains an acceleration clause—that is, if Nora misses any payment, the balance amount becomes due immediately. Nora makes one payment and then misses several. Missy accelerates the loan and sues for the full balance plus interest.

Failure to provide a service. If you had a contract with someone to provide you a service, you can recover any damages that could have been reasonably predicted. You're certainly entitled to recover any money you've paid out. You can also recover any extra money you paid to get the services done elsewhere. In exchange, you must take reasonable steps to minimize your damages—by choosing a reasonably priced substitute, for example, and by acting quickly.

> **EXAMPLE 1:** Mac's bathtub pipes spring several leaks and soak his house. Mac calls a plumber and tells him about the extensive damage the water is causing. The plumber promises to be over within ten minutes. Mac tells him that if he can't make it right away, he will call someone else. The plumber tells Mac not to worry, but then takes 70 minutes to get there.

Mac is entitled to any damage that occurred during the 60-minute period, but nothing else. If Mac let the leak go unrepaired for a week, his recovery would be limited to the damage incurred before he should have realized the plumber was not going to honor his commitment.

EXAMPLE 2: In August, Ann hired Ajax Roofing to repair her roof at a bargain rate of $4,000. Ajax promised to complete the work by October 1, when rain was expected. On September 25, Ajax calls to say it couldn't begin until the end of October. Ann hires Zeus Roofing at $5,000, to begin work on October 5. From October 1 until October 5 she puts a tarp over the holes in her roof. Her damages are the extra $1,000 she paid to Zeus and the cost of putting up the tarp.

Providing defective goods. If you receive defective goods, you can recover your costs to repair or replace the item, and any other damages reasonably foreseeable to the defendant, as long as you:
- didn't cause the damage by improper use, and
- follow reasonable terms of any warranty or agreement from the seller about returning the goods for credit or repair. When you buy goods, you often get a brochure telling you what to do if the goods are defective. The law regarding these matters is covered in Chapter 4. Unless there is a brochure that says otherwise, the seller must repair or replace the item within a reasonable time. Otherwise, you're entitled to your costs of repair or replacement.

CHAPTER 3

Can't We Settle Somehow?

Why Would You Want to Settle Out of Court? 36

How Much Are You Willing to Settle For? 36
    For Plaintiffs 36
    For Defendants 37

Should You Use a Third Person to Help You Settle? 37
    Mediation 37
    Arbitration 39

Making a Settlement Offer 39
    Offering to Settle Before a Lawsuit Is Filed 39
    Offering to Settle After a Lawsuit Is Filed 42

Taking Care of the Details 43
    Getting the Settlement Agreement in Writing 43
    Does the Release Cover Unforeseen Damages? 44
    Dismissing the Lawsuit 45

Should a Lawyer Review the Settlement Agreement? 45

If You're Worried About Getting Paid 48
    Turn the Settlement Into a Court Judgment 48
    Warn the Defendant That You *May* Turn the Settlement Into a Judgment 48
    When You Haven't Filed Your Lawsuit Yet 48

Before you sue or defend a case in court, stop and consider if there's another way to resolve the matter. As you've probably gathered by now, lawsuits are expensive, stressful, and time-consuming. If it's possible, it's almost always better to settle than to litigate, even if you have to compromise somewhat in the process.

If you are offered a fair settlement, grab it. If you're offered a settlement that's a little less fair but in the ballpark, at least consider it, or think about negotiating with the defendant. If you wait for the case to develop, you take the chance the other side will reduce or withdraw the offer.

Why Would You Want to Settle Out of Court?

As a judge, I have overseen more than a thousand trials, several hundred of which were before a jury. In at least half these cases, one side or the other was shocked by the result, and sometimes both sides were shocked—it was so different from what they had predicted. Many lawyers, for both plaintiffs and defendants, have sadly told me of times that they pushed a case to trial aggressively, only to achieve a far worse outcome than if they had accepted the other side's last settlement offer.

By settling your case, you have a say in the result. It may not be everything you hoped for. It may not even put you back to where you were before the events that led to the lawsuit. But it's predictable.

Also, by settling you'll save a lot of time, expense, and stress. And if you are the plaintiff, you're more likely to be paid. This is because plaintiffs have relatively fewer problems collecting in cases that are settled. The defendant, who agreed to an outcome rather than facing one imposed by a court, usually does not resist paying.

Of course, it's one thing to reach a settlement—it's another to get paid. If you and the defendant reach a settlement but the defendant reneges, what happens? You can:

- sue on your original case, just as if no settlement had been reached—as long as the statute of limitations hasn't run out
- sue to enforce the settlement agreement itself, if you feel the settlement is reasonable, or
- use one of the procedures described in "If You're Worried About Getting Paid," below.

How Much Are You Willing to Settle For?

Before you can settle your case, you must figure out how much you're willing to accept, or if you're the defendant, how much you're willing to pay.

For Plaintiffs

First, arrive at an initial amount by following the approach discussed in "How Much Should You Sue For?" in Chapter 2. This is the amount you would hope to recover if everything in your suit goes perfectly. In determining how much you'd settle for, scale this figure back in light of the following:

- the possibility you will lose the case
- your chances of collecting from the defendant if you win the case
- the value of your own time, and
- how much time you're likely to spend litigating and collecting the judgment if you win.

EXAMPLE: In a recent accident, Stacy was hurt and her car was damaged. She evaluates her case against Gary, the other driver, considering the factors set out in Chapter 2. She concludes that her injuries, pain and suffering, lost earnings, and property losses would reasonably allow her to recover $16,000.

Stacy believes the accident was all Gary's fault. However, a police report says that Stacy may have made an unsafe lane change. Thus, Stacy deducts 25% from the $16,000. She also realizes that although her claim for time lost from work is justified, it may be questioned because her doctor's notes on her work return date were vague and the doctor has retired and moved away. As a result, Stacy cuts her $3,800 lost wages figure in half. She deducts another $2,000 for the time and stress she will save if she settles now. The result is $8,100—her "bottom line" settlement amount.

In some circumstances, the terms of your settlement may involve things other than money. If the defendant runs a business or provides a service, you might consider bartering for goods or services—especially if you think the defendant might be difficult to collect from. For example, in the above scenario if Gary is a house painter, Stacy might consider taking $5,500 and having Gary repaint her house.

CAUTION

Don't pick a settlement amount prematurely. It may be too soon to agree on a settlement amount if you were injured only recently and the full extent of your injuries is unknown, or if your total medical costs or lost wages can't be estimated yet. You may need to take some time to gather this information. But it's also important not to delay indefinitely. If you're going to sue, you must do so within the time specified in the applicable statute of limitations.

For Defendants

Read the material above for plaintiffs, and review Chapter 2. That should help you estimate how much the plaintiff might reasonably be entitled to if successful in the lawsuit. Then scale back this figure as follows:

- Subtract an amount to cover the value of the time and trouble the plaintiff will save by settling without going to court.
- Consider whether, as a practical matter, you will be hard to collect from. Perhaps you can help the plaintiff realize that it will be difficult to collect any judgment you don't pay voluntarily. For example, do you have little available cash or property? Do you lack insurance that might have covered the plaintiff's claim?
- If you are able to make an all-cash offer, subtract some more. Cash in hand is worth far more than a promise to pay in installments.

TIP

Remember to consider the plaintiff's fault. When making a settlement offer, remember that a court will reduce a plaintiff's award if the plaintiff's own negligence contributed to the damage. Your settlement offer can reflect that reduction, too.

Should You Use a Third Person to Help You Settle?

Some of the best settlements involve a neutral third person who helps the parties resolve their dispute through what lawyers call alternative dispute resolution (ADR). ADR is usually informal, fast, and comparatively inexpensive. You are usually not constrained by formal procedures and rules of evidence. Under either of the two primary ADR options, mediation and arbitration, you just tell your story.

Mediation

Mediation is a voluntary, informal, private process in which the parties discuss their dispute with a person who is skilled at helping them reach an agreement. Typically, the mediator doesn't express an opinion on how the case should come out; he or she simply helps the parties find acceptable middle ground. If the parties don't come to a resolution, the mediator won't impose one.

Mediation can be done privately before a s is even filed, or in the court system after f some counties, judges will require litigants to try mediation before the case will be considered by the judge. Los Angeles County has a very successful mediation program, operating since 1993. The court can order any case into mediation where the amount in controversy is under $50,000. (Code of Civil Procedure § 1775.) As a practical matter, the court doesn't make such an order unless both parties agree. The court has experienced mediators and has had a very high rate of success in helping parties reach settlements before trial.

Everything that is said during the mediation remains confidential. And either party can call off the mediation at any time and take the dispute to court. Many skilled mediators have success rates as high as 70% to 90%.

Mediation is the type of ADR that is most commonly used to resolve small disputes. Its use has grown enormously in the past few years, as lawyers and litigants alike have found that successfully resolving legal battles through simple discussion is not just some do-gooders' pipe dream. Several experienced trial lawyers have told me recently that they want to refocus their entire practices toward mediation because, as one of them said, "I have just gotten tired of this angry, expensive litigation game."

Although most mediators allow the parties to be represented by an attorney in mediation sessions, many people represent themselves in cases involving less than $25,000.

RESOURCE

For a complete understanding of mediation, how it works, and how you might use it to resolve your particular issues, see *Mediate, Don't Litigate,* by Peter
rin (Nolo).

he best way to get the other
e direct approach. Show
local mediation providers
e that one or both of you
them to find out more about

their programs and the cost. Then set up a meeting at a mediator's office. Frequently, all that is needed is for an experienced mediator to explain how the process works. The low cost and simplicity of the process will usually sell itself.

If the direct approach fails, you can always try the indirect approach. Ask someone who provides mediation services to contact the other side about participating. Mediators are surprisingly good at this. Indeed, if they are in private practice, their bottom line may depend upon it. You should tell the other side in advance that you are contacting a mediation service and that it will be in touch.

Finding a Mediator

Finding a good mediator outside the court system at a reasonable price can take a little time. Some mediators charge several hundred dollars an hour. Others work as volunteers in community programs and receive no compensation. If you have Internet access, the best place to start your search is at the website for the Superior Court in your county. You can find your local Superior Court's website by going to www.courtinfo.ca.gov and by following the instructions in "Getting Information About Your County on the Web" in Chapter 1. The websites of the courts in many of the larger counties have excellent local information on mediation and arbitration.

California's Department of Consumer Affairs has an excellent Web page listing various low-fee dispute resolution groups throughout the state. You can reach the site through www.dca.ca.gov. Click on the heading "For Consumers," and scroll down to "Mediation Programs." If you prefer, the department can provide references in your area at 800-952-5210.

You may find additional listings in the yellow pages under the heading "Mediation." If a local bar association or some other nonprofit agency is listed there, give them a call and ask them to send you some information about who their mediators are and what they charge.

Arbitration

Arbitration is a more formal and traditional form of alternative dispute resolution. It may be voluntary or ordered by the court. Under the voluntary model, you and the other side agree to submit your dispute to a neutral arbitrator for a decision. Normally, you agree in advance either that the decision will be binding or that either party may reject it and take the case to court. The process may involve only the two parties and the arbitrator or, if you both agree, you can call witnesses. As with mediation, arbitration proceedings are often conducted without attorneys, although parties may bring them. (For more on court-ordered arbitration, see Chapter 12.)

After considering the evidence, the arbitrator makes a written decision. If both sides have agreed, the winner can take the arbitrator's decision to court if the loser fails to pay up. (See "If You're Worried About Getting Paid," below, for more on enforcing arbitration awards.)

To locate an arbitrator, use the sources suggested above in "Finding a Mediator." Many local programs offer up to four hours of service with no fee: one hour for an initial consultation, an hour for the mediator or arbitrator to prepare the case, and up to two hours for mediation or arbitration. Parties may qualify for additional services at below-market rates (or for free) by completing financial eligibility forms.

Making a Settlement Offer

I'm often asked, "When is the best time to make (or accept) a settlement offer?" The answer is simple: Before you sue (or are sued), after you sue (or are sued), during the litigation, just before trial, during the trial, or even when the judge is contemplating a final decision. (Judges frequently do not make their decisions as soon as a trial is over. Instead, they take the case "under submission" and announce their decision a few days or weeks later.) In short, the best time to settle is any time you and the other side agree.

When the Contract Demands Arbitration

Buried in the small type in many contracts is a "mandatory arbitration" clause—a clause requiring that any dispute about the contract terms must be arbitrated. In other words, the contract prohibits you from taking the other party to court for breaching (breaking) the contract. These clauses are found in many health insurance contracts, in building contractor and architect agreements, and in the agreements that many employees sign when they are hired.

These clauses may give you good reason for concern—especially if the arbitration requires you to pay a large fee, if the amount of damages you can receive is narrowly limited, or if the contract specifies a particular arbitrator who you think might not be impartial.

If you have a dispute over a contract that contains such a clause and you are concerned about being forced into arbitration, you might buy an hour of an attorney's time to explore the subject.

Also, be aware that courts have found *some* mandatory arbitration agreements to be so one-sided that they're unlawful and unenforceable. If you'd like to review some recent California court cases in which particular mandatory arbitration agreements were ruled invalid, start with the state Supreme Court case *Armendariz v. Foundation Health Psychcare Services, Inc.* (2000) 24 Cal.4th 83. The librarian at your local law library can help you find these cases.

Offering to Settle Before a Lawsuit Is Filed

Before you file a lawsuit, you can write a nice, straightforward business letter telling the potential defendant about your claim and suggesting a settlement. It is surprising how few people do this. Many people assume that the person or business causing them grief is stubborn, stupid, angry, intransigent, or crazy (or all five), and that sett

Settlement Negotiating Tips

Follow these suggestions to improve your chances of settling your dispute:

1. **Organize the documents that show your damages.** Use a photo-album-type notebook to display copies (never the originals) of your bills, photographs, medical reports, and other papers that support your claim. Send it to the potential defendant or the defendant's insurance company. This will show the other side that you are not an amateur.

2. **Understand the personal dynamics of what is happening.** Be polite and cooperative, but not excessively so. In some instances, one side won't settle—or won't offer to settle for very much—simply because the other side is insulting or rude. At the same time, your opponent isn't going to offer you a good settlement if he or she feels you are so nice you won't assert your rights.

3. **State your demand in your letter.** Start at an amount reasonably above your "bottom line" to give yourself room to go lower. It's seldom feasible to raise an initial demand once you've made it. But don't go so high that the other side concludes you're hopeless to deal with and refuses to negotiate. Use your Sounding Board or legal adviser to help you determine an opening amount that is reasonable. You will have plenty of chances to lower it, especially if the other side makes a decent counteroffer.

4. **Keep cool and don't get bulldozed by a tough negotiator.** If your offer is rejected, press the other side to make a counteroffer of a specific amount. Remember that most first offers are less than the other side ultimately settles for. Your next job is to counter the defendant's counteroffer.

5. **Don't split the difference.** Sometimes, after you demand a particular amount to settle, the other side will name a lower amount and then immediately propose that you accept a number halfway between the two figures. Don't agree to it. Treat this split-the-difference number as a new low and propose an amount between that figure and your original offer.

6. **Consult a negotiation guide.** An excellent book about the negotiating process is *Getting to Yes*, by Roger Fisher, William Ury, and Bruce Patton of the Harvard Negotiation Project (Penguin Books).

---

is out of the question. A lot of potential defendants recognize their mistakes and know that it's cheaper to pay for them sooner rather than later. Also, some people worry about having a court judgment on their credit record.

Many retailers and service agencies have people on staff whose only job is to head off lawsuits by settling. If the potential defendant has insurance, you may benefit from the fact that some insurance companies tell their adjusters to settle cases quickly if the plaintiff has no lawyer. They know that if the ly hires a lawyer, defense costs will

r before suing accomplishes three

her side know you're serious
ing

- you set out what you believe you are entitled to, and
- you open up a channel of communication.

Don't be concerned that your offer will be used against you later in court. By law, settlement offers and settlement demands, no matter what motivates them, cannot be disclosed in court. (Evidence Code § 1152.)

Below are two sample settlement demand letters. Remember that the amount you request should be at least a little higher than what you'd be willing to settle for. Also, if the defendant is represented by an insurance company and that insurance company has contacted you, write directly to the company and send a copy to the defendant.

In your letter, present your version of the facts, state your damages, and show a willingness to

Sample Settlement Letter (Breach of Contract)

947 Elm Street
San Rafael, California 94299

January 6, 20xx

Brad Caruso
ABC Plumbing Company
456 Market Street
San Anselmo, California 94301

Dear Mr. Caruso:

On December 6, 20xx, Sam Jones, who works for you, attempted to replace a leaking pipe at the address shown above. After working for several days, he told me he was finished and presented me with a bill for $2,156 for materials and labor. I paid the bill.

On December 14, 20xx, the pipe burst where Mr. Jones had repaired it. My basement flooded and many items of furniture were ruined. I contacted you on December 14, and from December 15-17 your employee, Ralph Sanchez, did more work on the pipe.

On December 20, 20xx, I hired XYZ Plumbing to inspect the work done by your employees and offer an opinion as to the cause of the burst pipe. XYZ concluded that Mr. Jones did not repair the pipe correctly, and that his negligence caused my damages, as follows:

Cost of first repair	$ 2,156
XYZ Plumbing's bill	225
Rug and furniture damage	7,500
Materials spent for cleanup	500
Time spent for cleanup	425
Total	$10,806

Please send me a check in that amount. If I do not hear from you within 10 days, I will assume you are not interested in resolving this matter and will promptly file a formal legal action.

Yours very truly,

Joan Wintucket

Joan Wintucket

Sample Settlement Letter (Tort)

8999 Jefferson Blvd.
Canoga Park, California 90528

May 1, 20xx

Robert Wong
333 Green Street
Gardena, California 90777

Dear Mr. Wong:

This letter concerns the automobile accident that occurred at the corner of 9th and Main Streets in Santa Monica on April 11, 20xx. I believe the accident was caused by your failing to stop at the stop sign on 9th Street. The police report and several eyewitnesses I have contacted confirm this.

As a result of the accident, I suffered a painful sprained spine and missed five days of work. Also, I had substantial pain and trouble sleeping for 13 days. Today I still have occasional twinges of pain between my shoulders. My doctor has indicated this will continue for at least six months.

My damages as a result of the accident were as follows:

Damage to my automobile (see enclosed estimates from two body shops)	$ 4,987
Mercy Hospital emergency room expenses (see enclosed bill)	879
Three visits to Albert Condon, M.D. (see enclosed bill)	100
Lost wages (see enclosed letter from payroll department)	750
Pain and suffering	5,200
Total	$11,926

Please send me a check in that amount or make arrangements to pay it to me within 10 days. If I do not hear from you within that time, I will assume you are not interested in resolving this matter and I will file a legal action.

Sincerely,

Beth Herzog

Beth Herzog

settle. Don't insult the other side or make remarks about his or her lousy motives, bad characteristics, or outrageous behavior—even if it's true. Few people will settle if they have to take a lot of insults as part of the package.

Also, don't make threats about what you will do if the defendant doesn't send you a check right away. It's okay to say you'll exercise your right to sue if the matter isn't settled within some stated period. But threatening to tell the DMV that the other driver was uninsured or to ask the police to make an arrest for a crime usually falls within the crime of extortion. (Penal Code §§ 518–527.) Penal Code § 518 defines "extortion" as obtaining something from another person by the wrongful use of fear. Under Penal Code § 523, sending a threatening letter with the intent to extort money is a crime. While few district attorneys would prosecute you for crossing the line, I've seen supposed settlement letters that clearly constituted criminal extortion.

Finally, be ready to follow up on your statement that you will file a lawsuit if the other person doesn't respond within a certain number of days. Otherwise, the other side will decide you aren't serious.

If the other side responds to your letter with an unacceptable counteroffer, consider suggesting mediation.

Offering to Settle After a Lawsuit Is Filed

If you've already filed your lawsuit—or if you're a defendant—you can still try to settle, whether or not you tried to before the case was filed. More than 90% of all cases settle before trial. If they don't settle right after the papers are filed, they do during a deposition, at a court settlement conference, or some other time. There usually will come a time when your opponent realizes his or her case has more problems than originally believed, and will want to talk settlement.

Many cases settle right after the legal papers are filed and served on the defendant. This is when the defendant must face the fact that the plaintiff is not just an angry loudmouth who makes empty threats. The defendant has solid evidence of the plaintiff's seriousness and must decide whether to settle or to fight in court.

> ### A Personal Experience: How Filing a Lawsuit Can Change Your Defendant's Attitude
>
> Just as an earlier edition of this book was being prepared, I had a personal experience that proved again that just filing the papers that initiate a lawsuit can produce some amazing results.
>
> I had a dispute with a large national corporation about a product sold to me. I had numerous unproductive conversations with different representatives of the company, some of whom were rude and dismissive. I wrote letters to them and a government agency that I thought might be interested in the matter. Nothing happened. Communications went from bad to worse.
>
> I finally took an hour or so and prepared a legal complaint like the one discussed in Chapter 5. I filed it with the court and had a summons and complaint filed and served on the company's representative. Within days, my problem was "escalated" (as the defendant described it) to a person who supervised many of the representatives I had talked to previously. And within hours, she offered a quick settlement agreeing that if I dismissed the suit, the company would pay me everything I had asked for in the lawsuit. Just filing the lawsuit changed everything.

If the defendant is represented by an insurance company, however, it's unlikely the case will settle right away. Instead, the case will be transferred from a claims adjuster to an insurance company lawyer, who won't be ready to settle until after investigating the case. The insurance company lawyer will probably conduct some "discovery," most likely by taking the plaintiff's deposition—a formal interview allowing the lawyer to ask the plaintiff questions about what happened, under oath. (Depositions are covered in Chapter 10.) If the lawyer thinks the plaintiff's case is weak, he or she may even file a motion for summary judgment. This motion essentially says, "Even if you assume everything the plaintiff says is true, the plaintiff still doesn't have a case." Unlike many other types of motions, which may just resolve issues that are part of a case prior to trial, a successful summary judgment motion ends the case for good. (See Chapter 11.) Some insurance companies pride themselves in never increasing an opening settlement offer once they've made it.

In any event, whether the other side has an insurance company or not, you should get the idea across that you are willing to talk settlement or engage in ADR at any time. Just because you were far apart during your previous settlement talks shouldn't mean you won't talk again. Judges who see hundreds of settlement conferences know that parties often posture during negotiations. Cases in which the parties are thousands of dollars apart one day mysteriously settle the next.

You can talk to the other side without communicating weakness. If you're very far apart, try saying something like: "We don't seem to be making much progress here. Is there anything to be gained by our talking settlement today?"

Taking Care of the Details

If you and the other side settle, first get it in writing. Then dismiss any lawsuit that had been filed.

Getting the Settlement Agreement in Writing

It's essential to have a record of the settlement, because even the most honest people remember events differently. I've seen dozens of cases in which the parties came to court, announced their case had settled, and then couldn't agree on what they thought they agreed to.

Any settlement agreement should contain the following elements:
- a brief description of the facts that led to the dispute
- a statement that the parties disagree about those facts or their implications
- a statement that all claims involved in the incident are being settled (called a "release"), and
- a statement of the terms of the settlement.

The following settlement agreement resolves the dispute between Joan Wintucket and her plumber, Brad Caruso, described above.

Sample Settlement Agreement (Breach of Contract)

Joan Wintucket and Brad Caruso, who does business under the name of ABC Plumbing, agree as follows:

1. On December 6, 20xx, ABC Plumbing ("ABC") did certain plumbing repair work on the home of Joan Wintucket ("Wintucket") at 947 Elm Street, San Rafael. Wintucket paid ABC $2,156 for doing that work.

2. On December 14, 20xx, a pipe that ABC worked on burst and caused damage to items in Wintucket's house. Between December 15-17, at no cost to Wintucket, ABC repaired that break.

3. Wintucket contends the damage that occurred on December 14 was caused by poor workmanship by ABC.

4. ABC contends all work done for Wintucket was performed in a competent manner and was not the cause of her damage, if any.

5. In order to settle all claims of Wintucket for damages as the result of the incidents referred to above, ABC agrees to pay her $5,000, payable within five days of when Wintucket signs this Agreement.

Joan Wintucket   6/6/xx
Joan Wintucket   Date

Brad Caruso   6/6/xx
Brad Caruso, ABC Plumbing   Date

Here's another settlement agreement. This one is between Robert Wong and Beth Herzog, who were in the car accident described earlier in this chapter.

Sample Settlement Agreement (Tort)

Robert Wong and Beth Herzog agree as follows:

1. On April 11, 20xx, Herzog was driving her car south on Main Street in Santa Monica, California;
2. At the same time, Wong was driving his car east on 9th Street in Santa Monica, California;
3. The two automobiles collided at the intersection of Main and 9th, causing damage to both cars and physical injuries to Herzog;
4. Wong contends that the accident was caused by Herzog's negligence;
5. Herzog contends that the accident was caused by Wong's negligence;
6. In order to settle and release the claims of each party against the other for:
   a. damage to their automobiles, and
   b. personal injury claims including medical bills, lost wages, and pain and suffering, already sustained and which may occur in the future;
7. Wong agrees to pay Herzog the sum of $9,250 within five days of when this Agreement is signed by both parties, as a full and complete compromise of all claims between them.

Beth Herzog   6/6/xx
Beth Herzog   Date

Robert Wong   6/6/xx
Robert Wong   Date

Sometimes cases settle in the hallway outside a courtroom or in the judge's office at a settlement conference (settlement conferences are covered in Chapter 13). If you can't get the settlement reduced to writing, ask the judge or the courtroom clerk if you can put the agreement "on the record." This usually involves the court reporter or the clerk taking down the terms of your settlement as part of the court's official records.

Does the Release Cover Unforeseen Damages?

The sample agreements above both contain what's called a "general release," saying all claims that arose in the dispute are now settled, or "released." This means that the plaintiff can't change his or her mind later and demand more money.

Like lots of issues in the law, however, there is one important wrinkle in the law of releases. Under Civil Code § 1542, the defendant may still be responsible for claims that were unknown or unsuspected when the release was signed. For this reason, the party who's making the payment often insists that the settlement include a clause releasing him or her from future unknown damages. In fact, almost all insurance companies, and almost all defendants represented by attorneys, will demand a "Section 1542 waiver" in a settlement agreement.

If you're the party getting paid and you aren't completely sure you won't have unforeseen damages in the future, what should you do? Well, if you're up against a lawyer or an insurance company, you may have no choice but to sign. Some lawyers insist: "Waive future damages, or don't settle." But it may be possible for you to use signing the release as a bargaining chip. You might agree to include it if the other party pays 10% to 20% more than what you'd accept otherwise.

Here's how such a future waiver clause might read if Herzog and Wong were to add it to their agreement:

Sample Settlement Agreement With Release

> 8. The releases recited in this Agreement shall cover all claims under California Civil Code § 1542 and Herzog and Wong hereby waive the provisions of § 1542, which read as follows:
>
> "A general release does not extend to claims which the creditor does not know or suspect to exist in his favor at the time of executing the release, which if known by him must have materially affected his settlement with the debtor."

Dismissing the Lawsuit

If you're the plaintiff and you've settled your case after the lawsuit was filed, you'll need to file a document dismissing the lawsuit as soon as the releases are signed and settlement funds are paid. California provides a simple form, called a Request for Dismissal, to accomplish this task.

FORM

The appendix contains a tear-out version of Form CIV-110, Request for Dismissal, and you can download one from the Judicial Council website at www.courtinfo.ca.gov. A filled-out sample is shown below.

Follow the instructions below for completing this form. General instructions for filling out the top portion are in Chapter 1.

Item 1a. This asks the plaintiff to check "With prejudice" or "Without prejudice." "Without prejudice" means the plaintiff can renew the lawsuit in the future—which is exactly what you don't want if you've reached a settlement. The plaintiff should not be allowed to resume the case. Check "With prejudice."

Item 1b. This portion of the form identifies what part of the lawsuit it is that you want the court to dismiss. If both sides have fully settled their claims against one another, check "Entire action …."

Item 2, Signature. The plaintiff must sign the signature line under Item 2, adding the date and the plaintiff's typed or printed name.

Item 3. This portion is for the defendant, but not all defendants will need to fill it out. If the defendant filed a cross-complaint (see Chapter 8), he or she must sign and date the second signature line, including a typed or printed full name. Items 4 through 7 will be filled out by the clerk.

The second page applies only if the winning party received a waiver of the court fees in the case (see Chapter 5).

Should a Lawyer Review the Settlement Agreement?

If your case is more complicated than the two examples above, consider having your settlement agreement reviewed by a lawyer, or even having the lawyer draw it up. If you have a lawyer coach who is already familiar with your case, he or she should be able to help you do this for a very modest fee. If neither party has a lawyer, you might want to hire one jointly and split the cost. If one party has a lawyer who drafts the agreement, the other may want to pay for an hour of a different lawyer's time to review it.

CAUTION

Be sure your lawyer will really help. The danger in hiring a lawyer to draft your settlement agreement is that some will feel a duty to construct a complex document filled with legalese. *The Prairie Home Companion* radio show used to have a segment entitled "Worst Case Scenario," in which Garrison Keillor described an innocent event and another actor described the worst possible (and most outlandish) things that could happen as a result. Many lawyers are like that. Asked to draft a simple document when a dispute has already been resolved, some lawyers will

	CIV-110
ATTORNEY OR PARTY WITHOUT ATTORNEY *(Name, State Bar number, and address):* Beth Herzog 914 Spruce Street San Jose, CA 92471 TELEPHONE NO.: 408-238-9954 FAX NO. *(Optional):* E-MAIL ADDRESS *(Optional):* ATTORNEY FOR *(Name):* In Pro Per	
SUPERIOR COURT OF CALIFORNIA, COUNTY OF Santa Clara STREET ADDRESS: 191 N. First Street MAILING ADDRESS: CITY AND ZIP CODE: San Jose, CA 95113-1090 BRANCH NAME: Downtown	
PLAINTIFF/PETITIONER: Beth Herzog DEFENDANT/RESPONDENT: Robert Wong	
REQUEST FOR DISMISSAL [✓] Personal Injury, Property Damage, or Wrongful Death 　　[✓] Motor Vehicle　[ ] Other [ ] Family Law　[ ] Eminent Domain [ ] Other *(specify):*	CASE NUMBER: 947 623

- A conformed copy will not be returned by the clerk unless a method of return is provided with the document. -

1. TO THE CLERK: Please **dismiss** this action as follows:
    a. (1) [✓] With prejudice　(2) [ ] Without prejudice
    b. (1) [ ] Complaint　(2) [ ] Petition
    　(3) [ ] Cross-complaint filed by *(name):*　　　　　　　　　　　　on *(date):*
    　(4) [ ] Cross-complaint filed by *(name):*　　　　　　　　　　　　on *(date):*
    　(5) [✓] Entire action of all parties and all causes of action
    　(6) [ ] Other *(specify):**

2. *(Complete in all cases except family law cases.)*
    [ ] Court fees and costs were waived for a party in this case. *(This information may be obtained from the clerk. If this box is checked, the declaration on the back of this form must be completed).*

Date:

Beth Herzog　　　　　　　　　　　　　　　▶ _____
(TYPE OR PRINT NAME OF [ ] ATTORNEY [✓] PARTY WITHOUT ATTORNEY)　　　(SIGNATURE)

*If dismissal requested is of specified parties only of specified causes of action only, or of specified cross-complaints only, so state and identify the parties, causes of action, or cross-complaints to be dismissed.

Attorney or party without attorney for:
[✓] Plaintiff/Petitioner　[ ] Defendant/Respondent
[ ] Cross-Complainant

3. **TO THE CLERK:** Consent to the above dismissal is hereby given.**
Date:

_____　　▶ _____
(TYPE OR PRINT NAME OF [ ] ATTORNEY [ ] PARTY WITHOUT ATTORNEY)　　　(SIGNATURE)

** If a cross-complaint – or Response (Family Law) seeking affirmative relief – is on file, the attorney for cross-complainant (respondent) must sign this consent if required by Code of Civil Procedure section 581 (i) or (j).

Attorney or party without attorney for:
[ ] Plaintiff/Petitioner　[ ] Defendant/Respondent
[ ] Cross-Complainant

(To be completed by clerk)
4. [ ] Dismissal entered as requested on *(date):*
5. [ ] Dismissal entered on *(date):*　　　　　　　as to only *(name):*
6. [ ] Dismissal **not entered** as requested for the following reasons *(specify):*

7. a. [ ] Attorney or party without attorney notified on *(date):*
   b. [ ] Attorney or party without attorney not notified. Filing party failed to provide
       [ ] a copy to be conformed　[ ] means to return conformed copy

Date: _____ Clerk, by _____, Deputy

Form Adopted for Mandatory Use
Judicial Council of California
CIV-110 [Rev. July 1, 2009]

REQUEST FOR DISMISSAL

Code of Civil Procedure, § 581 et seq.;
Gov. Code, § 68637(c); Cal. Rules of Court, rule 3.1390
www.courtinfo.ca.gov

		CIV-110
PLAINTIFF/PETITIONER: Beth Herzog DEFENDANT/RESPONDENT: Robert Wong	CASE NUMBER: 947 623	

Declaration Concerning Waived Court Fees

The court has a statutory lien for waived fees and costs on any recovery of $10,000 or more in value by settlement, compromise, arbitration award, mediation settlement, or other recovery. The court's lien must be paid before the court will dismiss the case.

1. The court waived fees and costs in this action for *(name)*:
2. The person in item 1 *(check one)*:
   a. ☐ is not recovering anything of value by this action.
   b. ☐ is recovering less than $10,000 in value by this action.
   c. ☐ is recovering $10,000 or more in value by this action. *(If item 2c is checked, item 3 must be completed.)*
3. ☐ All court fees and costs that were waived in this action have been paid to the court *(check one)*: ☐ Yes ☐ No

I declare under penalty of perjury under the laws of the State of California that the information above is true and correct.

Date: _____

_____ ▶ _____
(TYPE OR PRINT NAME OF ☐ ATTORNEY ☐ PARTY MAKING DECLARATION)   (SIGNATURE)

CIV-110 [Rev. July 1, 2009] **REQUEST FOR DISMISSAL**

include pages of unlikely issues. This can cost you a lot in legal fees, and it may jeopardize the settlement. So if you hire a lawyer to draft an agreement, spell out exactly what you want.

If You're Worried About Getting Paid

Most settlement agreements include a provision saying that the plaintiff will be paid the agreed amount when the release is signed or within a few days thereafter. If you're worried that the defendant won't follow through, there are several procedures to consider.

Turn the Settlement Into a Court Judgment

This procedure will be available to you only if a lawsuit has been filed and you and the defendant later signed a written settlement agreement. As soon as you realize you may have trouble getting the defendant to perform, file a motion in court— Chapter 10 explains the procedure for filing a motion—to have your settlement agreement turned into an official court judgment. Code of Civil Procedure § 664.6 authorizes this motion. Adapt either of the forms described in "File a Motion to Compel" in Chapter 10, and entitle your motion "Motion to Enter Judgment Per C.C.P. § 664.6." In the body of the form, state that you request the court to enter a judgment on the terms of the attached settlement agreement.

After your motion is granted, prepare the Judgment form. You will find a filled out sample of Form JUD-100 in the appendix. In paragraph 6, enter the details of your agreement. Give the form to the clerk for the judge's signature.

Warn the Defendant That You *May* Turn the Settlement Into a Judgment

Rather than immediately turning a settlement into a judgment, you may instead choose to have that happen if the defendant doesn't comply with the agreement. This procedure also applies only when a lawsuit has been filed and the parties have later reached a settlement. Use the same form referred to above and entitle it "Stipulation for Entry of Judgment." In the body of the form, state the following: "If the defendant does not perform all of the terms of the agreement attached hereto by the time provided for, it is hereby stipulated that judgment may be entered against him [or her] in the amounts provided for herein." Both of you should sign and date the form, and have the signatures notarized in case the defendant becomes difficult to find.

If the defendant doesn't perform, you'll need to file the motion explained in the previous section. In this situation, your motion should move through the court without difficulty.

When You Haven't Filed Your Lawsuit Yet

Sometimes the looming possibility of a lawsuit convinces a soon-to-be defendant to settle quickly, before the other side has filed the papers (the Complaint) that formally signal a lawsuit. If you haven't filed your papers yet and your opponent has indicated a willingness to settle, hopefully you will get paid and that will be that. However, if you see the defendant going sideways, get yourself down to the courthouse and file those papers now. Serving the defendant with a Summons and Complaint shows the other side that you are not to be fooled with.

CHAPTER 4

Deciding Where and Whom to Sue

Selecting the Plaintiff(s) 50

Selecting the Defendant(s) 51

    Defendants in Personal Injury and Property Damages Cases................................... 52

    Breach of Contract Cases 53

    Suing a Business 56

    Suing the Government... 58

    Suing Someone Who Has Died 59

    Suing Someone Who Has Filed for Bankruptcy 61

    Suing for Libel or Slander 61

    Suing a Minor 62

    Dealing With Unknown Defendants 63

Making Sure You Can Sue in California 63

Selecting the Right Court 65

    Selecting the Right County.. 65

    Selecting the Right Courthouse 65

    Special Rules for Los Angeles 67

    The Consequences of Picking the Wrong County or Branch 67

> **SKIP AHEAD**
>
> **If you're a defendant, you don't need to decide whom to sue or where to sue, so you can skip this chapter for now,** even if you plan to file your own lawsuit against the plaintiff or against a third party (this is called a cross-complaint). Cross-complaints are covered in Chapter 8. If necessary, you can come back here after reading that material.

Before you file your lawsuit, you must decide three things:

- who will be the plaintiff(s)
- who will be the defendant(s), and
- which Superior Court you will sue in.

Answering these questions can be simple and take only a minute or two of your time. For example, suppose you're an adult and were in a car accident with another adult who lives in the same city. The accident happened in that city while each of you was driving your own car. The decisions are clear: You are the plaintiff, the other driver is the defendant, and you sue in the Superior Court in the city in which both of you live.

But it's not always so easy. You may have other options if one driver was a minor; the other driver comes from another city, county, or state; either driver was driving an employer's vehicle at the time; or the accident happened somewhere besides the city or county where you live. This chapter will help you understand these issues and will guide you as you:

- Select plaintiff(s) and defendants
- Confirm that you can bring your case in a California court, and
- Choose the right county in which to bring your suit.

Plaintiff(s)

..., the plaintiff is the person ... . In most situations, this will ... else—remember, as a nonlawyer you can't represent other people. And most of the time, you'll simply list your name as the plaintiff.

But suppose your case concerns harm to your business. If you run your business as a sole proprietor (Henry's Taco Shop) or a partnership (for example, Lynn and Lydia's Restaurant), name yourself and your business as the plaintiffs. You can represent the business if it's a sole proprietorship. If your business is a partnership, you can represent it only if you're a general partner. If your business is a corporation or an LLC, you will need to hire a lawyer to handle the suit, since by law corporations and LLCs must be represented by lawyers.

> **Suing in the Name of Your Business**
>
> If you plan to name your business as the plaintiff, check to see whether you need to have filed a "fictitious business name" certificate with your county. Every sole proprietor, partnership, or association that does business in a name that doesn't include all the real names of the owners must file this certificate with the clerk of the county where the company has its principal place of business. Business and Professions Code §§ 17910 and 17911. (Certain nonprofit organizations are exempt from this law.) If you plan to sue in the name of such a business (remember, corporations and associations must be represented by a lawyer), be sure you've filed the certificate before you file the lawsuit. Ask the county clerk for the certificate form and instructions.

Two or more self-represented people can join together to file a lawsuit. They're known as coplaintiffs. A coplaintiff must be someone who was injured or damaged in the same incident, accident, or business transaction that harmed you. The most common coplaintiffs are spouses or living-together partners who were simultaneously hurt or financially damaged. The rules explained above regarding representation of a plaintiff apply equally to a coplaintiff—if your coplaintiff is a corporation, that plaintiff will need to hire an attorney (which might, in some circumstances, be helpful to you, too).

Some examples of appropriate coplaintiffs are:
- you and your passenger, if both were injured when your car was hit by another driver
- several tenants whose personal belongings are damaged when a fire spreads through an apartment house, and
- you and your spouse, if you pay a repairperson to fix a problem in your house and the work is defective.

Each coplaintiff can sue for up to $25,000 if the coplaintiffs suffered their damages individually. Thus, in the examples above, you and your passenger can each sue for up to $25,000. So can each of the tenants in the apartment building where the fire spread. But the spouses in the above example are limited to a total of $25,000, not $25,000 each, because they co-own the house and suffered the damage jointly.

Suing to Enforce a Contract

To sue to enforce a contract, you normally must be one of the parties who signed the contract. For example, if you and a tradesperson sign a contract describing work that will be done on your house, either you or the worker can sue to enforce its terms. It gets tricky when you stand to benefit from a contract, but you didn't actually sign it. For instance, suppose you are a real estate salesperson working for a real estate broker and you sell a house listed by your broker—but the seller doesn't pay your commission. Because the sales agreement was between the broker and the seller, you don't have the right to sue the seller. Any suit for your unpaid sales commission has to be brought by the broker.

In rare situations, someone in your position (known as a "third-party beneficiary" in legalese) can bring such a suit, but you'll probably need the assistance of a lawyer if you fit that description. If you're unsure, check it out with a lawyer before carrying on.

Once you've determined whether you'll be the only plaintiff or whether there will be coplaintiffs, make a record of the information. Chapter 5 explains where to put the plaintiff's name (or names) on your court papers.

CAUTION

Each coplaintiff must act for himself or herself. If more than one person is plaintiff in a lawsuit, all plaintiffs must sign the court papers and appear in court at the appropriate times. One plaintiff cannot speak for the others.

Selecting the Defendant(s)

The defendant is the person, business, or governmental entity you sue. In some cases, it's easy to pick out the principal "bad guy": That's the one who won't pay you, bashed your car, or sold you defective merchandise. Often, however, the defendant is more than one person or business.

CAUTION

Special rules apply if the government, a governmental agency, or a government employee is a defendant. We'll discuss those considerations below.

When selecting defendants, the basic rule is to name every person, business, or agency that is legally responsible for your injury or damage. (The discussion below explains what I mean by "legally responsible.") If you sue multiple defendants and win, under a legal principle called joint and several liability you can recover the full amount of your out-of-pocket damages from any responsible party, no matter how slight that party's contribution to your damages. California limits this principle to out-of-pocket losses, or economic damages, only. "Noneconomic damages," such as pain and suffering, must be collected according to percentage of fault. (Judges and juries typically assess responsibility for a loss by using percentages.)

In other words, suppose one defendant is judged 75% responsible for your out-of-pocket damages and a second is judged 25% responsible. The law gives you the right to collect the whole amount from the second defendant, even though the other defendant caused 75% of the damage. A defendant who pays more than his or her share can then sue other defendants to be reimbursed. But that's the paying defendant's problem, not yours.

EXAMPLE: Alice was hurt in a car accident. She sued the drivers of two other vehicles: one who swerved into her car and knocked it across several lanes and another who was speeding and smashed into her car after it had come to a stop. The jurors concluded the first driver was responsible for 70% of Alice's damages and the second driver was responsible for 30%. They awarded her $12,000 to compensate for her medical expenses, damage to the car, and lost salary. They awarded an additional $8,000 for the pain and suffering she endured. Alice has the right to collect the $12,000 in out-of-pocket damages from either defendant. But she can recover only 30% of her pain and suffering award from the second driver and must look to the first driver for the rest.

While it's advantageous to sue all defendants responsible for your damages, don't name people who bear no legal responsibility. First, it is morally not right to do so. You may be a sophisticated person who doesn't get particularly upset if sued every once in a while, but many people have never been sued and will be severely disturbed if they are. Don't put them through the process unnecessarily.

Second, a judge can impose a significant penalty on you if you sue someone against whom you have no real claim. After you carefully read the rest of this section, review your decision on whom you want to sue with your Sounding Board or legal adviser. Explain your theory of fault for each potential defendant and get your adviser's advice.

Business Owners' Liability for Debts

There are several ways to structure a business in California. The list below notes the liability of the owners for debts—such as court judgments—of the business.

- **Sole Proprietorship.** This is the simplest business entity. The owner is personally liable for business debts.
- **Associations.** These are businesses ("joint ventures") or charitable ventures whose members haven't formed a partnership, corporation, or LLC. It's common for unincorporated associations to run small labor unions, country or social clubs, neighborhood organizations, and the like. The members are personally liable for the association's debts.
- **General Partnership.** The partners are personally liable for business debts.
- **Limited Partnership.** General partners are personally liable for business debts, but limited partners have limited personal liability as long as they don't participate in management.
- **Regular Corporations and S Corporations.** Shareholders and owners have personal liability for business debts only in very limited situations.
- **Limited Liability Companies.** Owners have limited liability for business debts even if they participate in management.

Defendants in Personal Injury and Property Damages Cases

The general idea in personal injury and property damage (tort) cases is to sue everyone whose careless or intentional behavior contributed even a little bit to the injury or damage.

Vehicle Accidents

If your suit arises out of a vehicle accident, these are some of the parties you might name as defendants:
- the driver of the other car
- the parents of the driver of the other car, if the driver was a minor
- the owner of the other car—and if the owner is married, the owner's spouse, too
- the responsible mechanic, if a defective repair possibly contributed to the accident
- the employer of the person driving the other car, if the other driver was on the job when the accident happened
- the government agency responsible for upkeep of the road, if a road condition or lack of proper signs contributed to the accident
- the driver of the car you were riding in, if you were a passenger
- the parents of the driver of the car in which you were a passenger, if the driver was a minor, and
- anyone who entrusted a vehicle to someone who they knew or had reason to know was incompetent, reckless, or intoxicated (see "Suing an Entrustment Defendant," below).

Suing an Entrustment Defendant

The law may hold someone responsible for an accident if he or she lets an incompetent, reckless, or intoxicated person use his or her vehicle. Normally, a defendant in this situation—known as an entrustment defendant—is a parent, an employer, or someone who lent a car to someone else. In some situations, a car dealer, the giver of a gift car, or a co-owner might also be liable as an entrustment defendant. Proving a defendant is liable for having entrusted a car to someone else requires some legal expertise. If this is your situation and a lawyer is out of the question, you'll need to do some research. Look at *Summary of California Law* (10th edition), by Bernard Witkin, Vol. 6, Torts §§ 1221-1226 and 1256-1272.

Slip-and-Fall Accidents

Suppose you were injured when you fell on a piece of fruit, roll of toilet paper, or loaf of bread on the supermarket floor. You might name as defendants:
- the company that operates the store
- the store manager
- the employee whose duty it was to sweep it up, and
- the owner of the building (if there was a defect in the floor covering).

Use the same inclusive approach in other slip-and-fall cases. If you tripped over a cracked sidewalk in a residential neighborhood, possible defendants might include the homeowner whose house fronts the sidewalk and the city whose agency is responsible for repairing public property.

Other Accidents

In tort cases that fall into categories other than "vehicle" or "slip-and-fall," follow the same approach and sue anyone who is possibly responsible for your damages or injuries. For example, if you were hurt when a painter on a scaffold let a can of paint fall on you as you walked below, possible defendants might include the:
- painting contractor who employed the painter
- general contractor on the job
- owner of the building on which the work was being done
- painter
- scaffolding company (which should have but didn't provide protection for people on the sidewalk), and
- a governmental agency (if it issued a permit for the work without requiring adequate protection).

Breach of Contract Cases

In lawsuits for breach of contract, sue the pers business, or agency that failed to perform d required by the contract. If a person was behalf of her employer when breaching (see "Suing an Employer When the F at Fault"), you may sue both the employee and the employer.

Breach of Service Contracts

A service contract is one in which one person promises to perform a service for another person. Examples of such services are contracts to play music at your wedding reception, to paint your house, to design a brochure for your new business, or to repair your front porch. Here are some common breach of service contract cases and the defendants in those cases:

- If a supplier promises to deliver a load of lumber to you by August 1 and misses the deadline, causing you to incur major expenses on your construction project, you would sue the supplier.

- If a salesperson falsely represents what the service he or she sells would accomplish ("Quinn Carpet Cleaners will remove all these stains on your rugs without any damage"), you'd sue the person who made the false statement.

- If you had an agreement with a business that its employee would perform a service and the employee failed to do so properly, you may sue both the business and the employee, to the extent the employer's actions led to the breach. For example, suppose you hired an auto repair shop to tighten your brakes and they were loosened instead, causing you to have an accident. Possible defendants include the repair shop, the mechanic who worked on your car, and the shop manager or foreman who gave the orders.

Suing an Employer When the Employee Is at Fault

If someone is harmed by an employee's actions, the employer is usually responsible (along with the employee)—as long as the employee was acting "in the scope of employment" when the harmful act happened. This principle applies to both tort (accident) cases and breach of contract cases. So if a driver totals your car while making deliveries, the delivery company is liable. And if a contractor's workers fail to finish your new house on time or make a serious construction error, it's the contractor that's responsible for the breach of contract.

The key is to find out whether the act was in the scope of an employee's employment—that is, done to further the company's purposes. For example, if the delivery company driver sneaks off to the movies in the van (without the company's knowledge or consent) and totals your car on the way, that's outside the scope of employment and the company probably isn't responsible (unless they knew this was going on and did nothing to stop it).

A company also isn't responsible for a person's harmful act if it can show the person was not an employee but an "independent contractor"—someone who works under contract for several clients and retains control over how the work is done. Lawyers are sometimes able to convince a judge that a worker who might appear to be an independent contractor was really working as an employee, even if the hiring firm didn't treat the person as one. The result—you get to look to the employer as well as the worker for compensation—is beneficial to you. Consult an attorney if you suspect that someone who caused harm to you was misclassified as an independent contractor and was really performing the work of an employee.

In all employer/employee lawsuits, name as a defendant the employee as well as the employer. When you win, you'll probably be paid by the employer, who will usually be jointly responsible with the defendant for the amount you win. However, there are a few situations where the employee may be easier to collect from than a small or weak corporate employer. And once in a while, the fact that you have the employee as a defendant may also result in his or her being more interested in talking to you about the facts of the case than would be true otherwise. You will also be entitled to a reply to your Case Questionnaire (explained in Chapter 5) and other discovery from each individual defendant (discovery is covered in Chapter 10).

- If the business you hired used a subcontractor or some other additional business you didn't hire yourself, you can sue both businesses if the second seems partly at fault. For example, suppose you brought your car to a dealer for repairs and the dealer sent your car to an outside repair shop for some of the work. If the repairs were faulty, you can sue both the dealer and the repair shop.

Breach of Purchase Contracts

A purchase contract is one in which one party sells a product to another. If the product is defective, doesn't do what the seller promised it would do, or wasn't delivered as promised, you can sue for breach of a purchase contract. In all cases, you would sue the business that sold you the item. There may be other defendants as well, as the following examples illustrate.

- If the product was defective in any way, sue the manufacturer of the item. (Here, you'll need to understand something about the law of warranty, which we'll explain in the next section.)
- If the manufacturer is a defendant, you may also sue any distributor or "middleperson" that provided the product to the retailer.
- If the item was modified by someone other than the seller or manufacturer, sue that person or business.
- If the item was damaged during delivery, sue the delivery company and any business or person who hired the company.
- If a business's employee was responsible for the breach of a purchase contract, you may sue both the business and the individual to the extent he or she caused the breach. For example, if a company vice president orders salespeople not to deliver goods to you, you may sue the company and the vice president.

Breach of Warranty

A warranty is a guarantee that a product will work for a period of time and is fit for the purpose for which it was sold. Some warranties are express—an expression in words, either written or spoken, that the product will be suitable. Others are implied—no actual guarantee is given, but the law infers from the circumstances that the manufacturer or retailer is responsible if the product doesn't work.

Express written warranties are normally drafted by company lawyers deep in the workings of corporate headquarters. They mostly state what your rights *aren't* if you are unhappy with the product. A written warranty may be in a little folder that falls out of the box when you open your new coffee maker, or it may be a whole booklet of information that comes with your new car. A written warranty promises that the manufacturer or retailer will try to fix the product if you return it. This is not usually a problem. The problem arises when the manufacturer or retailer denies that there's a defect or tries several times, without success, to make the repair.

Implied warranties fall into two categories:

An *implied warranty of merchantability* means that a product is fit for the ordinary purposes for which it was designed, and conforms to any statements of fact made on the container or label.

An *implied warranty of fitness* is less common. It can arise after you tell a seller that the item will be put to a particular use ("We plan to install this water heater in the basement of a four-story building"). You must rely on the seller's skill and judgment to select and furnish suitable goods ("Which model would you suggest?"). If the item proves unsuitable for this purpose, the implied warranty of fitness has been breached.

Implied warranties of merchantability apply to anyone who manufactures, distributes, or sells any consumer goods used, bought, or leased primarily for personal, family, or household purposes, except these:

- clothing
- products intended for consumption (food and drink)
- products used for personal care, and
- products consumed in household tasks.

For example, a rug shampoo solution (a product consumed in household tasks) is not covered, but a rug shampoo machine is. Eye drops aren't covered, but eyeglasses are. Purchases from a corner video store are covered; something bought from your neighbor (assuming he isn't in that business) is not.

Sometimes a seller attempts to do away with the implied warranty of merchantability by stating that the product is sold "as is" or words to that effect. But these words won't let the seller avoid responsibility if you received a written warranty to the contrary.

How Long Does Your Implied Warranty Last?

Implied warranties don't last forever. Here are the rules:

- **New goods sold with an express warranty.** An implied warranty on the sale of new goods lasts just as long as any express warranty you were given, but no less than 60 days and no more than one year.
- **New goods sold without any express warranty.** If you received no written warranty, the implied warranty lasts one year on new products.
- **Used products sold with an express warranty.** On used products, the implied warranty lasts as long as the express warranty, but no less than 30 days and no more than 90.

The intricate provisions of the implied warranty law are contained in the Song-Beverly Consumer Warranty Act, Civil Code §§ 1790 and following.

If you plan to sue a retailer or manufacturer who refuses to stand behind a product, you need to notify that person or company before filing suit. Send a letter to the manufacturer or retailer describing the product and its failure. Also state when and where the item was purchased. Ask that the product be repaired or replaced. If the product came with a written warranty, follow the procedures described in those materials. A little assertiveness at the beginning will often solve the problem and eliminate your need to sue.

Send the letter by certified mail, return receipt requested, and keep a copy for yourself. I can't tell you how many intelligent people come to court and tell me they wrote a great letter to the defendant before they sued but forgot to keep a copy of it. It helps your credibility with the judge if you have copies of everything you send.

The Lemon Law

A special kind of warranty covers new cars that need continual repairs. If you've bought a new car that has a serious problem, or several problems, California's Lemon Law, Civil Code § 1793.22, requires that you give the manufacturer the opportunity to fix it before you can sue. (The Lemon Law is part of the Song-Beverly Consumer Warranty Act.)

Specifically, the manufacturer is liable under certain conditions if the car has serious problems within 18 months or 18,000 miles from delivery. If this is your situation, read the provisions of the law above (see how to find it in "Finding the Law, on Paper and Online" in Chapter 1) for the rules on how many times you must have had it in for service (or for how long it must have been inoperable) before you can sue under this law.

Suing a Business

In both tort cases and breach of contract cases, when one of the defendants is a business, you'll have to sue the business itself and sometimes the individuals who own the business. Before you can sue a business or business owner, you must know the legal form under which the business operates (corporation, partnership, etc.). And you may need to find the names of individual owners if that's not obvious.

Discovering the Names Behind the Businesses

In some cases, you will want to name individual owners as defendants but may not know their names. The way you'll discover the names depends on the type of business entity you're dealing with.

Sole proprietorships, partnerships, and associations. The first place to check is the Fictitious Names Index at the County Clerk's office. As previously explained, every sole proprietor, partnership, or association that does business in a name that doesn't include all the real names of the owners must file a "fictitious business name" certificate with the clerk of the county where the company has its principal place of business. The certificate includes the owners' real names and addresses. Use the Index, which contains the filings of all those who have complied with the fictitious business names law. Bear in mind, however, that not all business owners comply with this law.

If you come up empty-handed after you check the Fictitious Names Index, try the Business Tax Office of the city or county where the business is located or does substantial business. These taxing agencies aggressively collect taxes from local businesses and usually have up-to-date ownership records. The drawback is that some city offices are poorly run, their records may be hard to research, and the personnel are sometimes not prepared to handle requests by people representing themselves without a lawyer.

LLCs, limited partnerships, and corporations. Corporations, limited partnerships, and limited liability companies (LLCs) are not required to file a fictitious name certificate with the county clerk unless they are using some name other than their official title while doing business. Obtaining similar information about these organizations is covered in the next section.

Choosing Business Defendants

Who should be named as defendants in your case? If you're dealing with an individually owned business—that is, a sole proprietorship—the individual should be sued in the name of the business and as an individual. For example, if Jeff Taylor owns and operates a store under the name of Saville Row Tailors, your court papers should name both as defendants.

Partnerships. Partnerships should be sued in the name of the business. This could be the last names of the partners (Barney, Barney, and Hill) or a fictitious name (Party Time Catering). You may also want to sue some or all of the principal partners. That's because if you get a judgment against individual partners, you can try to collect from their assets without having to ask the court to declare them responsible for the business's debts. Also, naming the individuals will probably encourage settlement efforts, because the named individuals will suddenly realize they may be personally liable for the "business problem."

Limited partnerships. Limited partnerships are those in which certain partners, called limited partners, typically contribute money or resources but have little say in running the business, which is done by the general partners. Again, you will want to name the partnership as a defendant and possibly individual partners as well, either limited or general.

Unincorporated associations. Naming an unincorporated association as a defendant works the same way as naming a partnership. You will want to sue the organization under its name; you may also want to sue some of its members if they had an individual role in the cause for your suit.

Corporations. Corporations are usually sued only in the name of the business. You normally won't name any shareholders or officers. You'd sue a corporation's shareholders or officers only if the corporation is a shell that has few or no assets, or if it appears that officers of a corporation were acting outside the scope of corporate authority. The latter process is called "piercing the corporate veil," and is a complicated procedure requiring a lawyer who specializes in business litigation.

Nonprofits. Nonprofit corporations, like for-profit corporations, are normally sued only in their corporate name. In the unusual case when you want to sue an officer or director of a nonprofit corporation and the person receives no compensation for the work he or she does, you'll need to proceed cautiously—California law protects volunteer officers and directors from personal liability in certain situations (Corporations Code §§ 5047.5 and 5239). Code of Civil Procedure § 425.15 describes special papers that must be filed with the court before you can sue.

Both profit and nonprofit corporations should be sued in their correct corporate name as well as any other name they do business under. So if Creamy Dairies, Inc., operates Frosty Ice Cream Stores, sue the company in both names.

Get Corporate, LLC Information Online

You can get information about some California businesses—such as their address and the name of their agent for service of court documents—by going to the California Secretary of State's website at www.ss.ca.gov. Click "Business Entities" and then, in the upper left corner, "Business Search." You can enter the names of corporations, limited liability companies, and limited liability partnerships, all of which must register with the Secretary of State. The agent may be an easy person for you to serve once you have prepared and filed your court papers (see Chapters 5, 6, and 7).

General partnerships do not have to file with the Secretary of State (although some choose to do so). To discover their address and agent for service of court papers, you're better off looking in the County Clerk's fictitious name index.

SKIP AHEAD

Skip ahead unless you are suing minors, government agencies, people who have died or filed for bankruptcy, defendants in libel and slander cases, or if you don't know the identity of one or more of the defendants. The next few sections cover these topics.

But don't leave this chapter before reading the last section, "Selecting the Right Court."

Suing the Government

If you are suing the state, county, or city government, or any of their agencies, you must first file a special claim with that governmental body within a specific time frame. That's also the case if you're suing a government employee over something that occurred in the scope of employment. Lawsuits against the federal government or any of its agencies must be filed in federal court and are beyond the scope of this book.

Government Code §§ 910 and following provides that you have a year to file a claim with the government if your case involves damage to real estate or a breach of contract. In other kinds of cases, you must file within six months of when the incident occurred.

Suing a government employee doesn't always require filing a government claim. The "scope of employment" theory applies (see "Suing an Employer When the Employee Is at Fault," above). If the government employee was doing something logically unrelated to his or her job, such as hiking in the mountains on vacation, don't file the claim. Sue the individual and forget about the government. If you're uncertain—suppose the hiking government employee is a park ranger—file the government claim. If you don't, you may lose important rights.

It's not always easy to recognize that an agency responsible for your injury or damage is part of the government. Many government entities that are not technically part of city or county government operate hospitals, run bus lines, manage irrigation projects, and provide other services. Private companies often carry out the same types of activities, so you may need to do some research. Every government agency except cities and counties themselves must be on file in the Roster of Public Agencies maintained by county clerks and the

Secretary of State. If the agency hasn't filed its name, address, and names of its board members with the county clerk, you won't be penalized for failing to file a Government Code claim.

All government agencies should have a printed claim form available for your use. If your claim is against the State of California, you can request a form from the California Victims Compensation and Government Claims Board; you can also download the form from the Web at www.boc.ca.gov or call 800-955-0045. Claims against a county or special district are normally handled by the clerk of the governing board (such as a county Board of Supervisors). In a city, it's normally the city clerk or the city auditor. A copy of the Alameda County form is shown below.

After having you fill in your name and address, the claim form asks for the amount of your claim. The way you answer depends on whether you are seeking more or less than $10,000. If your claim is for under that amount, state the precise amount you are asking for and, if you can, break it down on the lines where itemization is called for. If your claim is for $10,000 or more, say it is "within the limited jurisdiction division of Superior Court," meaning it is between $10,000 and $25,000, and forget about the itemization. If it is for more than $25,000, leave this blank empty.

The form also asks for a description of the event that led you to make a claim. Be honest and be sure to include the important dates, locations, and the name of the government agency or employee you dealt with. Do *not* make any admissions about your own responsibility for the incident. If you end up in court, it's the other party's job to prove that you were wholly or partially at fault or did not carry out your end of a contract. You certainly do not want to say something on the form that could be used against you.

Once you've prepared the claim form, make several copies. (The form will say how many you need to file.) Make an extra copy for yourself and then file the claim at the office where you picked it up. There's a $25 filing fee, which you can ask to be waived. Ask the clerk to stamp the date and place where you filed it. As long as you're not filing just before the deadline, you can also send it by certified mail.

Next you must wait. The agency has 45 days from receipt to either deny your claim or take no action on it (which is the same as a denial). You can start working on your lawsuit papers while you are waiting.

CAUTION
You can still file a claim if you miss the deadline. If there was a six-month limit on your government claim and you've exceeded it, you can still file after the deadline if your late filing was due to excusable mistake, inadvertence, surprise, or excusable neglect; or if you were a minor or physically or mentally unable to file the claim during the entire six months. But if you missed the filing period, you are in a precarious place and probably need a lawyer's immediate help.

RESOURCE
If you need help filing a claim against the government, use *California Government Tort Liability Practice*, 4th ed., by Fisher et al. (California Continuing Education of the Bar), considered the bible in this area. You can find this book in most large law libraries. It covers all sorts of claims, not just torts, and is kept up-to-date by loose-leaf inserts. You'll find a less expensive and very good summary of this area of the law in an Action Guide published by California Continuing Education of the Bar, "Handling Claims Against Government Entities," available in most law libraries. Or, you can buy one online at www.ceb.com or by phoning CEB at 800-232-3444.

Suing Someone Who Has Died

To sue a person who has died, or if the defendant dies while your lawsuit is pending, you sue—or continue the lawsuit through—the defendant's estate. In most cases, an executor or administrator

CLAIM AGAINST THE COUNTY OF ALAMEDA

PLEASE TYPE OR PRINT

Please complete the form, retain one (1) copy for your records
and **return the original to:**
Clerk, Board of Supervisors Office,
Administration Building, 1221 Oak Street,
Room 536, Oakland, CA 94612. Phone: (510) 208-4949.

Please include all attachments which would support your
claim (estimates, bills, receipts, police report, etc.)

CBS CLAIM NO._____

FOR CLERK'S USE ONLY

**FOR FUTURE INFORMATION ON YOUR CLAIM
PLEASE CONTACT:
Acclamation Insurance Management Services**
P.O. Box 2147, Oakland, CA 94621
Phone No.: (510) 633-5650   Fax: (510) 633-5673

1. *Claimant's Name:*_____
   (Last, First, Middle Initial)
1.5 *Claimant's PFN (if applicable):*_____
2. *Address:*_____ - _____
   (number, street, city, state & zip code)   (phone number)
3. *Address to which notices are to be sent, if different from1 & 2:*
   Name: _____
   Address: _____ - _____
   (number, street, city, state & zip code)   (phone number)
*4. *Total Amount of Claim:* $_____   5. *Date of Accident/Loss:*_____
6. *Location of Accident/Loss:*_____
7. *How did Accident/Loss Occur?:*_____
   _____
8. *Describe Injury/Damage/Loss:*_____
   _____
9. *Name of Public Employee(s) Causing Injury/Damage/Loss, if known:*_____
   _____
10. *Itemization of Claim (List items totaling amount set forth in line #4). (Use separate sheet for additional items.)*

ITEM	AMOUNT	ITEM	AMOUNT
_____	$_____	/ _____	$_____
_____	$_____	/ _____	$_____
		*TOTAL AMOUNT OF CLAIM	$_____

11. *Signed by or on behalf of claimant:*_____ Date:_____

NOTICE: Section 72 of the Penal Code provides:

"Every person who, with intent to defraud, presents for allowance or for payment to any state board or officer, or to any county, city or district board or officer, authorized to allow or pay the same if genuine, any false or fraudulent claim, bill, account, voucher, or writing, is punishable either by imprisonment in the county jail for a period of not more than one year, by a fine of not exceeding one thousand ($1,000), or by both such imprisonment and fine; or by imprisonment in the state prison, or by a fine not exceeding ten thousand ($10,000), or by both such imprisonment and fine."

v:\claims\claim form updated 12_05.doc

is appointed to represent the deceased's estate. This is the person against whom you must file your claim.

The process of distributing a person's assets is called probate, and it takes place in the Probate Division of the Superior Court in the county in which the deceased lived. You should be able to find out whether probate has been filed and who the executor or administrator is by phoning the office of the county clerk in the Superior Court and giving the name of the deceased and the date of death. As part of the probate proceedings, the court will issue "letters" to the executor or administrator, usually within 30 days of death. Letters are legal papers showing that the executor or administrator has authority to represent the estate.

If you're filing a claim against the estate, usually you must do so within four months after the letters have been issued. You must use a Creditor's Claim form, which you can obtain from the court clerk or on the Internet, as described in Chapter 1. Specify form DE 172. Filing instructions are on the form. You don't need to file a Creditor's Claim against the estate if the deceased's insurance policy covers the incident you're suing over and the policy's monetary limit exceeds the damages you're seeking. But if you don't know whether the deceased had insurance, file a Creditor's Claim to protect yourself.

The executor or administrator has 30 days to accept or reject your claim and must notify you of his or her action. If your claim is approved, you don't have to file a lawsuit. If it's rejected, you have three months to sue the estate.

SEE AN EXPERT
If a defendant has very few assets or has taken steps to pass property outside of probate, there may be no probate proceeding after death, and therefore no executor or administrator. Anyone receiving the deceased's assets is liable for his or her debts, and it is possible to sue those people. You will probably need to hire an attorney.

The rules regarding suits against an estate are covered in Probate Code §§ 9000 et seq. They are somewhat complicated. If you appear to have missed a deadline, consult an attorney, preferably one who specializes in probate matters.

Suing Someone Who Has Filed for Bankruptcy

If you want to sue someone who has filed for bankruptcy, you may have to rethink your strategy. If you receive a notice from the bankruptcy court or a letter or phone call from your potential defendant or the potential defendant's attorney stating that he or she has filed for bankruptcy, do not, under any circumstances, file your lawsuit. If you do, you will be violating the law and could be fined substantially.

You should, however, file a Proof of Claim form with the bankruptcy court after you've received a notice from the court, within the time specified on the notice. Bankruptcy is a federal proceeding and the Proof of Claim form is an official form of the bankruptcy court.

If your claim is not satisfied in the bankruptcy court—and it probably won't be—there are only a few situations in which you can sue the potential defendant. You can sue if the bankruptcy case is dismissed, if the bankruptcy court gives you permission to sue in California Superior Court (called "lifting the automatic stay"), or if the particular debt you want to sue on is not erased ("discharged") by the bankruptcy court. Many debts arising from intentional acts, such as theft, embezzlement, or drunk driving, won't necessarily be erased in bankruptcy, but you need to take some steps to pursue such claims.

Suing for Libel or Slander

In Chapter 1, I recommended that you not represent yourself in a lawsuit for libel or slander. If, nevertheless, you want to handle your own lawsuit against a newspaper, radio station, television station for libel or slander (called a "defamation action"), be aware that before suing, you must serve the publisher or broadcaster with a demand for retraction within 20 days after you learn of the defamation. (Civil Code § 48(a).) If you don't serve this notice, your recovery of damages will be seriously limited.

Suing a Minor

If you plan to sue a minor (someone under age 18), understand that some underage persons will be treated as adults if they have been "emancipated," by marrying, serving on active duty in the military, or through a court order of emancipation.

Suing an unemancipated minor is rarely worth the effort unless the defendant has an insurance policy or some other way to pay you. The considerations vary depending on the type of case.

Breach of Contract Cases

Suing a minor for breach of contract is particularly hard. Minors can back out of most contracts they enter into before they turn 18. All they have to do is notify the other party to the contract that they want out before they turn 18 or within a reasonable period afterward.

This right, however, is not unlimited. A minor who is under the care of a parent unable to provide for him or her can't back out of a contract to pay for things necessary for the support of the minor or the minor's family (such as food, clothing, and housing). This means that if a minor lives away from his or her parents, or they live together but in poverty, the minor can't back out of a contract for these necessities.

Tort Cases

The vast majority of tort cases involving minors arise from vehicle accidents. If a minor is covered by automobile insurance, collecting a judgment if you win a tort lawsuit against the minor may be easy. Because it is illegal to drive without evidence of insurance in California, most people who have insurance will produce evidence of it for you or a police officer at the scene of the accident.

Even if a minor does not have insurance (or other substantial assets), there are other points to consider:

- Parents and legal guardians who have custody of a child are responsible for the willful—but not negligent—misconduct of the child. (The maximum amount that a parent may be liable for is $34,700, at the time this book went to press. However, in 2010 and every two years—the Judicial Council can increase the cap according to the rise in the cost of living.) For instance, if your daughter's 17-year-old boyfriend deliberately plows his car into yours because you insist that they not see each other, his parents are responsible. If he carelessly changes lanes on the freeway and hits you, they are not. The personal injury damage is limited to medical, dental, and hospital expenses. (Civil Code § 1714.1.)
- The Vehicle Code provides that with some exceptions, the person who signed a minor's application for a driver's license is liable for any damage or injuries caused by the minor's driving, whether negligent or intentional. (Vehicle Code § 17708.) By law, a minor's driver's license application must be signed by a parent, legal guardian, or other person having legal custody. The maximum liability for physical injuries is $15,000 per person, $30,000 per accident. Maximum property damage liability is $5,000 per accident. (Vehicle Code § 17709.)
- A parent or legal guardian who gives express or implied permission to drive to a licensed or unlicensed minor is liable in the same amounts as the person who signs the license application. In these cases, you sue both the minor and the minor's parents ("Jane Juvenile, a minor, and David and Mary Juvenile, her parents"). There is no limit

to liability if the minor was acting as the agent of the signer of the application (such as running an errand to the store) or if the minor has a learner's permit and the signer of the application failed to provide adequate supervision.

- A minor's employer may be responsible for an accident if the minor was driving in the course of her employment (Vehicle Code §§ 17706, 17707).

Even if the minor turns 18 while your lawsuit is pending, the parents remain liable for his or her acts as a minor.

If the Minor Used a Firearm, Painted Graffiti, or Shoplifted

If a parent or legal guardian lets a minor have a gun or access to a gun and someone is injured as a result, the parent or guardian can be liable up to $30,000 for personal injury for each person, not to exceed $60,000 total. (Civil Code § 1714.3, but see the description of parental liability caps above.)

Parents are liable up to $34,700 for any graffiti painted by their children. (Civil Code § 1714.1.) Parents and legal guardians of a minor who has shoplifted from a store or library are responsible, along with the minor, for up to $500 in damages, plus court costs and the value of any unreturned merchandise. A plaintiff may collect the entire sum from the parents. (Penal Code § 490.5.)

How to Proceed

If you sue a minor, the court will need to have an adult representative (called a "guardian *ad litem*") appointed to represent the minor in court. If you name the minor as a defendant and serve the papers on his or her parents—any minor over age 12 must be served as well—they'll most likely ask the court to be appointed guardians *ad litem*. If they don't and no one else asks for the appointment, you can ask the court to appoint a guardian *ad litem*. Instructions for this process are in Chapter 7.

Dealing With Unknown Defendants

If there's any possibility that you will add people as defendants after you investigate the matter a little more thoroughly, you'll want to name "Does." "Does" rhymes with "rows" and is derived from the practice of calling an unknown person "John Doe" or "Jane Doe." The Does in your complaint are placeholders for real people whose role you know but whose identity you don't yet know.

You may want to name a Doe, for example, if an Ajax Construction Company painter drops a can of paint on you, but you haven't been able to learn his name. You would sue the Ajax Construction Company and Doe One. As you conduct discovery (see Chapter 10) and learn the painter's name, you can file an amendment and substitute the correct name for Doe One. For now, just understand that to get a judgment against any particular defendant, you'll eventually need that defendant's name.

If you don't yet know the names of *any* defendants, you must do some investigating before suing. You shouldn't file a lawsuit and name only Doe defendants.

Making Sure You Can Sue in California

After reading through this chapter so far, you should have a clear idea about who will be the plaintiff or plaintiffs in your lawsuit and who will be the defendant or defendants. This information is fundamental in filling out the forms in Chapter 5 and elsewhere in this book. But before you can confidently proceed to the forms, you need to make sure that you can pull that defendant into a California court.

In order to sue in a California state court, at least one of your defendants must have some connection to California. How much of a connection is enough? Whole tomes have been penned on this subject (called "personal jurisdiction"), but for your purposes, it boils down to this:

- If your principal defendant lives in or does business in California, you should have no problem suing in California.
- If the defendant lives outside the state but did something in California that caused you damage or injury (for example, rear-ended you on I-5), you can sue here.
- If your defendant operates a business out of state, you still may be able to sue it in California if the defendant's connections with California are significant (the legal term is "continuous and systematic").

For example, suppose a New York mail order house sent you a catalog from which you ordered goods. They arrived and were defective. The mail order house won't refund your money. Even though the company is based in New York, you can sue it in California because it sent its catalog into the state for the purpose of doing business in the state.

CAUTION
Be aware that not all lawsuits belong in California state courts, even if the defendant meets the personal jurisdiction requirement. As explained in Chapter 1, if the incident you're suing over concerns federal law, or if you're suing an entity of the federal government, the suit must be heard in federal court. That process is outside the scope of this book.

Internet Disputes

Although online shopping is increasingly popular, there's one drawback that will vex shoppers sooner or later. How do you deal with a serious dispute that the customer relations department won't handle satisfactorily? For example, can you sue the online company located in Maine that sent you the bed that cost a fortune but doesn't fit together (and they won't refund your money)?

Whether you can pull the owners of an out-of-state website into a California court depends on the nature and quality of the site's commercial activity. Here are the rules:

- **Passive sites.** If an out-of-state website merely posted information on the Internet but didn't take the order online (perhaps you called the 800 number), it's unlikely that a California court would "exert jurisdiction"—that is, allow a suit against the defendant to proceed in California.
- **Repeated transmissions.** At the other end of the spectrum are out-of-state sites that repeatedly transmit computer files to residents of other states, by entering into contracts with them. California courts will almost certainly have jurisdiction over that business.
- **The interactive middle ground.** Some out-of-state websites fall in between the two extremes above. A site that allows you to exchange emails or download forms might not have enough connection to California to constitute a sufficient basis for jurisdiction.

When judges give reasons for their decisions to exert jurisdiction or not, they try to follow the rules mentioned above. But the fact is, there's a lot of room for discretion. If the nature of the website is offensive or if the business's conduct is disturbing, this may influence the judge's decision to exert jurisdiction. Businesses with websites that feature sexual content, involve gambling, or disparage religion may find themselves haled into court more easily than a more reputable defendant. Ditto for businesses that target children or those sued for an alleged consumer scam or for the sale of a product that causes injury. If your lawsuit involves one of these issues, your chances of being able to sue in California will go up.

Selecting the Right Court

If you've satisfied yourself that you can sue the defendant in a California court, you are ready for the next question: In which county's Superior Court may you file your suit? The answers to this question depend on factors like those you used when deciding whether a California court would hear the case.

Selecting the Right County

Each of California's 58 counties has a Superior Court that handles both limited and unlimited jurisdiction cases. Your first task is to decide in which county to sue. We'll deal with that question first. Then in some counties you are going to have to decide in which branch of the court you should sue. But one thing at a time—let's look at the following factors (I call them "determining factors") that affect where you should file your case:

- In general, you can sue in any county where any defendant resides. If one of the defendants lives in Ventura County and two live in Santa Barbara County, you can sue in either county's Superior Court.
- If your case is a tort case, you can sue where the injury to persons or property occurred. If the defendant lives in San Diego and the accident was in Fresno, you can sue in either county.
- If your case is a breach of contract case, you can sue where the contract was entered into or was to be performed (see "Where Is a Contract Entered Into?" below).
- If the defendant is a corporation or association, you may sue in the county where it has its principal place of business. If the business is located out of state (such as the New York mail order house), you can sue in any county in which it does business in California, such as the county in which you live.
- If a partnership or individuals own the business you are suing, you can choose any county where the partners or owners live.

Where Is a Contract Entered Into?

Figuring out where a contract is "entered into" can be tricky. If you and the defendant signed the contract face-to-face, it's obvious where it happened. But if the two parties entered into the agreement over the telephone and they were in different locations at the time, it's not so obvious.

The contract is considered entered into when the last act necessary for its making takes place. This last act is the "acceptance" of an offer. For example, if Jack in L.A. calls Wendy in San Francisco and offers to buy her dog and Wendy agrees, the contract is entered into when Wendy accepts. If an acceptance is by phone, as in our example, the contract is entered into in the place where the acceptor is located (San Francisco). If an acceptance is by mail, the contract is entered into in the place from which the acceptor mails her acceptance.

After reading the above list, write down all the possible counties in which you can sue. If you're not sure which county a particular town or unincorporated area is in, call the town clerk or sheriff's office.

Selecting the Right Courthouse

You're probably thinking that once you figure out the right county for your case, all you need do is go to that big courthouse in the county seat and file your papers. Unfortunately that is true only in counties that have just one court location. If that is the situation for your county, be thankful that you can avoid all of the complications chronicled between here and there. You are eligible for skipping these pages if you plan to sue in one of these counties: Alpine, Amador, Calaveras, Colusa,

Del Norte, Lassen, Marin, Mariposa, Modoc, Napa, Plumas, San Benito, Sierra, Sonoma, Sutter, Trinity, Tuolumne, Yolo, or Yuba.

Many Superior Courts are very insistent that you file in "the right branch." Why should they care as long as you pay your fee and file the right papers? The main reason has to do with convenience to the parties, and especially the defendant. For example, in Los Angeles, unless some boundaries are maintained, someone who was involved in an accident in Long Beach could file a case way up in Lancaster, in northern Los Angeles County, forcing a Long Beach defendant to drive for hours to get to court. Similar things could happen in mountain counties such as Placer, where the Auburn courthouse is more than an hour away from the branch in Tahoe City.

Choosing the Right Court in Populous Counties

Many California counties have courthouses in more than one location—which one is right for your case? Your best bet is to go first to the court's website, click "locations" or "courthouses," and look for a description for a branch that includes the words "limited jurisdiction." If you don't see a link like this, see what branches are described as handling "civil" cases. You can assume this means they do both limited and unlimited civil cases at that courthouse. If there are several branches that handle civil cases, take your case to any of your "determining factor" courthouses (where the defendant resides, where the contract was entered into, and so on). Some counties provide helpful information on this subject, including Butte, Contra Costa, Fresno, Kern, Madera, Mendocino, Monterey, Orange, Riverside, Sacramento, Tehama, and Ventura counties.

Here is information on specific counties in California's large population centers:

- **San Francisco** has three courthouses (Civil, Criminal, and Juvenile). Your limited jurisdiction case must be filed and heard in the Civic Center Courthouse because that is the only place the court handles civil cases.
- **Los Angeles** has more than 50 courthouses. An ingenious device on the court's website asks you to enter the zip code for the appropriate determining factor and click "Search." You're taken to a chart that tells you which of the more than 50 courthouses will accept your limited jurisdiction case. (If you don't have access to the Internet, you can get the same information by phoning one of the branch Los Angeles courts listed in the Government section of your phone book.)
- **Riverside** will accept the filing in any branch, but will transfer the case to a branch that complies with the court's rules. (Riverside brags that it is the only court in the state to do this, but my spies tell me there are others.) But since you will be dealing with a particular branch court for the remainder of your case, you might as well find out now where your case will wind up and start doing business there.
- **Santa Clara** (which has branches in Palo Alto, Sunnyvale, and Los Gatos) provides that limited jurisdiction cases can be filed and handled only at the main courthouse in San Jose, though if the "determining factor" is in South County, the case should be filed at the courthouse in San Martin.

Visit or Call a Court and Ask

If you don't have access to the Internet or if your court's website isn't helpful, you can try to break through to a real person on the court's telephone tree or go to one of the courthouses near you. On some telephone trees, hitting "O" in the middle of the recording will connect you to a person who can tell you what branch to use. If that doesn't work, you will just have to go to the civil filing counter in the clerk's office at any branch and ask for assistance.

Always Call Ahead

If you choose among several branches, try to confirm your choice by telephone before going to court. To find the number, go to the Government Pages of your phone book and look under "County Government Offices." The courts are normally listed under "Courts" or "Superior Court." If there is a listing for "Civil Division," so much the better. (If you are dealing with a court in a county other than yours, you may have to go to your main library, where you can find phone books for the whole state.) Many courts have phone listings on their websites, which you can locate by following the directions in "Finding the Law, on Paper and Online" in Chapter 1.

Once you have the number, try to use the answering system to reach the Civil Division and ask the person who answers something like this: "I want to file a limited jurisdiction suit about an automobile accident that happened in downtown Hawthorne. Is this the right branch for my case?" or "I want to file a limited jurisdiction suit about a contract I have with a defendant whose office is in Fontana. Is this the right branch for my case?"

Most court employees will answer these questions correctly. If a clerk tells you he or she isn't allowed to give legal advice, change your question a little and ask: "Is the city of Fontana in your court's district?" If you are told you are calling the wrong branch, ask the clerk to give you the number of the right branch.

Special Rules for Los Angeles

As with most things in the Golden State, Los Angeles is a special case. There are more than 50 courthouses and well over 600 judges and commissioners. The task of dividing up the work among all of these courtrooms is complex. Fortunately, the court's website gives you clear directions on how to choose the right courthouse for a case.

If you have a tort case, determine the zip code in which the accident occurred. If all you know is that it was somewhere on the Harbor Freeway, don't worry about the zip code for the accident—just find the zip for the defendant's home (on the police report) or, if the defendant is a business, for its main Los Angeles office.

Then, if you're using the Internet, follow the directions in Chapter 2 to find the website for the Los Angeles Superior Court. Under the heading "About the Court," click on "Locations" and then "Filing Court Locator." Enter the applicable zip code, click on "Search," and you will see one or more choices in the column "Limited Civil." This is where you must file.

If you're not using the Internet, phone any of the branch courts listed in the phone book and give the necessary information about the type of case and the locations involved. The clerk will run the Locator and tell you what your choices are.

For a contract case, follow the same pattern, but use the zip code of the place where the contract was entered into (see "Where Is a Contract Entered Into?" above), where it was to be performed, or where a defendant resided when it was entered into.

In any case, once you have chosen a branch (unless it is the Central Courthouse on North Hill Street), telephone that branch and confirm the information you received. The court requires you to fill out a special form showing how you picked your branch. I'll tell you more about it in the next chapter.

The Consequences of Picking the Wrong County or Branch

If you choose the wrong county or branch, most of the time you won't face serious consequences as long as you have a valid ground for suing in California (as explained above). You may lose some time and may have to refile, as explained below, but your case won't be thrown out.

Choosing the Wrong County

Technically, every Superior Court in the state has judicial power anywhere in California over any person or business that is located in the state, doing business in the state, or causing damage or injury in the state. In most situations, however, the right county will be evident, as explained above. If you don't choose it initially, the judge in the county you picked is likely to select the appropriate county for you (sometimes at the behest of the defendant).

For example, if you flew from California to Chicago and United Airlines lost your luggage, technically you can file your suit in any county in California. United can then ask that the case be transferred to the county where you bought the ticket, where you flew from, or where United has its principal California office.

Here's another example of what might happen if you file in the wrong county. If you present your papers to a clerk in Shasta County Superior Court to sue a defendant who lives in Orange County regarding an accident that occurred in yet a third county (Fresno), the clerk will take your papers and filing fee and file the case. But problems may arise after you serve the defendant. The defendant is likely to file a motion in Shasta County for a change of venue (the place of the trial). Because you filed your case in an inappropriate place, the judge who hears the motion will probably transfer the case to Orange County or Fresno.

If the Shasta County judge decides that your filing was done in "bad faith"—without a valid reason or to gain an unfair advantage—the judge may order you to pay the defendant's attorney fees and costs in filing the motion to transfer. You will also be charged a transfer fee, and you'll have to pay a filing fee in the new court. The sanction and fees together could exceed $650, so try to understand and follow the rules.

Choosing the Wrong Branch Court

Choosing the wrong branch of the correct county usually isn't such a big deal. Your case can be transferred easily to the appropriate branch. But choosing a branch other than the one where the defendant lives may be considered serious if you are a businessperson suing for repayment of an auto or retail loan. If you think this may apply to you, you'll want to be particularly careful to choose the correct branch. For more information, see "Path One: Cutting Off the Defendant's Ability to Answer," in Chapter 9.

Preparing the Complaint

Beginning Your Tort or Contract Complaint	70
General Tips on Preparing Forms	70
Select the Correct Complaint Form	71
The Caption	71
Tort Complaints: Personal Injury, Property Damage, and Wrongful Death	73
The "Complaint" Box on the Tort Complaint	73
Filling Out the Balance of the Complaint	73
Tort Cause of Action Attachments	79
Cleaning Up the Tort Complaint	91
Contract Complaints	92
Contract Cause of Action Attachments	96
Cleaning Up the Contract Complaint	107
Complaints for Other Types of Lawsuits	108
Find a Law Library	108
Research the Subject Area	108
Choose the Right Form	109
Local Rules	109
Prepare the Complaint	109
Preparing the Summons and Cover Sheet	110
The Summons	110
The Civil Case Cover Sheet	110
Preparing a Case Questionnaire	112
Requesting a Waiver of the Filing Fee	113
Preparing an Attachment	117

> **SKIP AHEAD**
>
> If you're a defendant, you can skip ahead to Chapter 8.

You're probably eager to start putting some words to paper. That's what this chapter is all about—creating the first documents you'll need to get your lawsuit moving.

These first documents are the cornerstone of your lawsuit. Judges and lawyers will refer to them constantly as your case develops. For this reason, pay close attention to the material in this chapter, especially the instructions for filling out the forms (the sample forms will be very instructive). I've seen otherwise good cases stopped in their tracks because the plaintiff neglected to prepare the initial papers correctly.

Beginning Your Tort or Contract Complaint

The basic document in which you lay out your lawsuit is called a Complaint. Fortunately, for tort and contract cases the Complaint is a simple check-the-box form furnished by the court.

A tort or contract Complaint has two parts. The first part contains general information about you and the parties you are suing. The second part consists of attachments describing your causes of action. (The cause of action is the official name for the legal theory under which you claim that what happened to you entitles you to relief from the court, such as an order that the defendant pay you money damages.) Later in this chapter, I'll tell you about the possible causes of action for your case.

General Tips on Preparing Forms

Remember, your Complaint will be studied by every defendant, and possibly each defendant's insurance company. Reading your forms will give these people a preliminary impression of how serious and competent you are. The conclusions they reach may significantly affect the amount of any settlement offer they make. Here are a few tips:

- All papers filed should be typewritten and neat. If you use handwriting to fill in the blanks on the Judicial Council printed forms in this book, the clerk cannot reject them for not being typed (Rules of Court 2.135). California's Rules of Court require that all filings be on recycled paper, but I have never heard of a court enforcing that rule. Printing must be clear and permanent, in type not smaller than 12 points on unglazed paper "of standard quality," 8½" x 11" in size. Each form must have two holes punched at the top and have its pages stapled together. The typeface must be "essentially equivalent to Courier, Times, or Helvetica" in blue-black or black. If you'd rather not type the papers yourself, see "Using a Professional Typing Service," below.

> **Using a Professional Typing Service**
>
> If you'd like help preparing your Complaint, look in the yellow pages under "Paralegals," "Legal Document Assistance," "Legal Clinics," "Typing Services," or "Secretarial Services." A service may be particularly helpful if, rather than using the forms in this book, you're preparing a Complaint from scratch in a type of case not covered in this book (discussed further below).
>
> Many people, especially in large cities, prepare forms for people who are representing themselves in court. Call one or two and ask what services they offer and at what price. Those listed under "Paralegals" probably offer their services principally to lawyers, but they may be willing to prepare forms for you for a fee. People listed under "Secretarial Services" may include former legal secretaries who lost interest in the 9-to-5 routine and started their own businesses.
>
> Some directories also contain listings under names such as "Legal Clinics" and "Legal Forms."

- To save yourself extra trips to the courthouse, make several photocopies of each blank form you intend to use before you begin to fill them out. This will let you prepare rough drafts and still have a clean copy to use for the final product.
- You are the plaintiff—always refer to yourself that way. Rather than saying, "I went to the store," say "Plaintiff went to the store." This may feel contrived, but—trust me on this one—it's the way it is done.
- If you run out of space on any printed form, you can finish the information on an attachment I'll explain how to prepare one later in this chapter.

Get the Current Form From the Web

In the appendix, you'll find all the forms the book covers. (Copies are supposed to be available at court clerks' office, but I have found that some courts' supplies are spotty or out of date.) These forms were current as of the date this book was published, but the Judicial Council, which writes the forms, changes them from time to time.

If you want to be super sure that you have the latest form, go to www.courtinfo.ca.gov. Click the heading "Forms" at the top of the Judicial Council page and choose to view all the forms by number. By scrolling down to your form's number, you can see when it was last revised (compare that date to the one on the form you have in hand). You can also view the form and download it.

If the form has changed, understand that our item-by-item instructions may no longer mesh completely with the new form's numbering and questions. Chances are, however, that the changes will be minor and not pose a problem.

The Silly World of Pleading Paper

As your case progresses, you may have to file papers that are not on preprinted forms. If so, you must use 8½" x 11" legal paper with a double vertical line on the left side of the page and numbers from 1 to 28 left of the line. The paper, which must be recycled and of at least 20-pound weight, is generally available at office supply and stationery stores. We've included a blank numbered sheet in the appendix. You can make photocopies and use them.

Many word processing programs provide all you need to create your own legal paper under the heading "Legal Pleadings" or something similar. In Microsoft Word, you can create legal pleadings by clicking "File," "New," "Legal Pleadings," and then "Pleading Wizard."

Select the Correct Complaint Form

Depending on what kind of case you have, tort or contract, you begin by choosing one of two Complaint forms. As you'll see from the samples in this chapter, Complaint forms in tort cases state on the bottom margin: "COMPLAINT—Personal Injury, Property Damage, Wrongful Death." Complaint forms in contract cases state on the bottom margin: "COMPLAINT—Contract."

The Caption

In both Complaint forms, the top portion (called "the caption") asks for exactly the same information. To get started, use the information you came up with in Chapter 4 about the name(s) of the plaintiff(s), the name(s) of the defendant(s), and the name and address of the court in which you are suing.

We'll start in the upper left-hand corner.

Attorney or Party Without Attorney: Type your name and the address at which you want to receive mail about the case. Fill in a phone number, including the area code, preferably where you can be reached during the day. Sometimes a clerk may try to reschedule a hearing by phone, so including a number where a message can be left for you will be helpful. If you aren't reachable at a phone number, don't put anything—you don't have to have a phone to file a lawsuit. The form asks for a State Bar number but you don't have to worry about that if you're not a California attorney. Next to the line that says "Attorney for (Name)," type "in pro per." In other words, you're representing yourself. If you change your address while the suit is pending, be sure you notify both the court and your opponent in writing.

Superior Court of California, County of: Here, type the name of the county where you are filing the lawsuit, and the address of the courthouse where you are filing, along with the branch name if applicable. I explained how to determine which courthouse you should select in Chapter 4. If there are several branches in your county, try to confirm your choice by calling the court clerk before you fill this in.

Plaintiff: In this box, fill in your name and the name of any coplaintiff joining with you in this suit. Identify any plaintiffs who are neither adults nor natural persons. (By "natural person" we mean an individual rather than a business entity.)

For example, let's say your name is Michael Smith and you operate a business called Michael's Sandwich Shop. If you plan to include your business's name here, handle it like this: "Michael Smith, dba Michael's Sandwich Shop." Dba stands for "doing business as." Include your business only if it's involved in the lawsuit—and be sure you've filed a fictitious business name certificate with the County Clerk (see "Selecting the Plaintiff(s)" in Chapter 4).

Defendant: Fill in the name(s) of the defendant(s). As with plaintiffs, identify any defendants who are neither adults nor natural persons. Here are some examples:
- Mitchell Davis, a minor
- Axel Construction Company, a corporation (although corporations cannot be pro per plaintiffs, you certainly can sue one)
- Tweedle Associates, a partnership
- John Dee and Frank Dum, partners in Tweedle Associates, a partnership
- Sidney Blue, individually and dba Blue Blood
- the County of Orange, a public entity.

For now, skip the "Does 1 to ___" box.

Complaint: This information depends on whether you have a tort or contract case. Leave it blank for now.

Jurisdiction: Type an "x" in the first box ("Action Is a Limited Civil Case") and in the applicable box below, depending on whether you are suing for more or less than $10,000. Your filing fee will differ, depending on which you pick. Leave the rest of this box blank.

Case Number: Leave this blank. The clerk will fill it in when you file your case.

> **Your Case Number**
>
> Once the clerk has given you a case number, be very careful when you type that number on subsequent court papers. An amazing number of documents get filed with the numbers transposed or otherwise wrong. As a result, the documents are placed in the wrong case file and can be lost forever.

SKIP AHEAD
If yours is a contract case, skip ahead to "Contract Complaints."

Tort Complaints: Personal Injury, Property Damage, and Wrongful Death

Now it's time to complete your basic three-page Complaint form with information that's specific to the facts of your dispute or case. You have already filled out most of the caption box as instructed above. The "Complaint" box, however, is still blank. The following section shows you how to complete this part.

FORM
The appendix contains a tear-out version of Form PLD-PI-001, *Complaint–Personal Injury, Property Damage, Wrongful Death*, and you can download one from the Judicial Council website at www.courtinfo.ca.gov. A filled-out sample is shown in this chapter.

The "Complaint" Box on the Tort Complaint

Use these guidelines to fill out the Complaint part of your tort Complaint.

Amended. Since you're filling out your first Complaint, you can leave this blank. If you need to amend, or change, the information in your Complaint, you can do so. "Demurrer" in Chapter 11 explains how to amend a Complaint.

Motor Vehicle. If your case arises out of a car or other motor vehicle accident, type an "x" in this box.

Other (specify). Type an "x" in this box if your case doesn't arise out of a motor vehicle accident. Then specify the type of case. Some possibilities include "dog bite," "slip and fall," and "assault and battery." (An assault is a threat to use force on another person; a battery is the willful and intentional use of force on another person.) Don't stew over the correct choice of words—this is not an especially important decision.

Property Damage. Type an "x" in this box if you're seeking compensation for damage to your house, yard, car, furniture, child's bicycle, or any other item of real or personal property that belongs to you.

Wrongful Death. If you follow my advice, you won't check this box. It's used when you sue because of the death of a close relative. Most wrongful death lawsuits are filed in the unlimited division because you'd normally ask for more than $25,000. If you want to bring a wrongful death lawsuit, consult a lawyer.

Personal Injury. Type an "x" in this box if you claim an injury to yourself or any coplaintiff. If you've been injured in a car accident, you'll check both "Motor Vehicle" and "Personal Injury."

Other Damages (specify). If you're asking for exemplary damages, type an "x" in this box and explain them. Exemplary damages, also called punitive damages, are available only if you are suing on an intentional, not negligent, act. I'll explain what that means in further detail below.

Again, don't stew over the exact language. Your lawsuit is ultimately controlled by what you say in the following pages of the form in the body of the Complaint. The boxes on this first page are intended to quickly give information about the nature of the case.

Filling Out the Balance of the Complaint

Now let's get into the body of the Complaint. Take the Complaint from the appendix, photocopy it (this will be your final copy), and use the original as a working copy. (You can also print multiple blank copies from the Judicial Council's website at www.courtinfo.ca.gov.) Follow along on your working copy of your Complaint as I go through the numbered questions (called "Items").

Item 1. Type the names of the plaintiff(s) and defendant(s).

Item 2. Skip this for now. You'll come back and enter the number of pages after you've completed the Complaint and the causes of action.

	PLD-PI-001
ATTORNEY OR PARTY WITHOUT ATTORNEY *(Name, State Bar number, and address)*: Sam Kim 421 Combes Lane Napa, CA 94559 　TELEPHONE NO: 707-555-1219　　FAX NO. *(Optional)*: E-MAIL ADDRESS *(Optional)*: 　ATTORNEY FOR *(Name)*: In pro per	FOR COURT USE ONLY
SUPERIOR COURT OF CALIFORNIA, COUNTY OF Napa 　STREET ADDRESS: 1125 Third Street 　MAILING ADDRESS: P.O. Box 880 　CITY AND ZIP CODE: Napa, CA 94559 　BRANCH NAME:	
PLAINTIFF: Sam Kim, dba Kim's Book Supplies DEFENDANT: Jenny Offer, Martin Myotic, and April Ruin, individually and dba ROMMOR BOOKS [X] DOES 1 TO ___5___	
COMPLAINT—Personal Injury, Property Damage, Wrongful Death 　[ ] **AMENDED** *(Number)*: **Type** *(check all that apply)*: [ ] **MOTOR VEHICLE**　[X] **OTHER** *(specify)*: assault and battery 　[X] Property Damage　[ ] Wrongful Death　lost business profits, 　[X] Personal Injury　[X] Other Damages *(specify)*: punitive damages **Jurisdiction** *(check all that apply)*: [X] **ACTION IS A LIMITED CIVIL CASE** 　Amount demanded　[ ] does not exceed $10,000 　　　　　　　　　　[X] exceeds $10,000, but does not exceed $25,000 [ ] **ACTION IS AN UNLIMITED CIVIL CASE** (exceeds $25,000) [ ] **ACTION IS RECLASSIFIED** by this amended complaint 　[ ] from limited to unlimited 　[ ] from unlimited to limited	CASE NUMBER:

1. **Plaintiff** *(name or names)*: Sam Kim
   alleges causes of action against **defendant** *(name or names)*: Jenny Offer, Martin Myotic, and April Ruin, individually and dba Rommor Books
2. This pleading, including attachments and exhibits, consists of the following number of pages: 3
3. Each plaintiff named above is a competent adult
   a. [ ] **except** plaintiff *(name)*:
      (1) [ ] a corporation qualified to do business in California
      (2) [ ] an unincorporated entity *(describe)*:
      (3) [ ] a public entity *(describe)*:
      (4) [ ] a minor [ ] an adult
         (a) [ ] for whom a guardian or conservator of the estate or a guardian ad litem has been appointed
         (b) [ ] other *(specify)*:
      (5) [ ] other *(specify)*:
   b. [ ] **except** plaintiff *(name)*:
      (1) [ ] a corporation qualified to do business in California
      (2) [ ] an unincorporated entity *(describe)*:
      (3) [ ] a public entity *(describe)*:
      (4) [ ] a minor [ ] an adult
         (a) [ ] for whom a guardian or conservator of the estate or a guardian ad litem has been appointed
         (b) [ ] other *(specify)*:
      (5) [ ] other *(specify)*:

   [ ] Information about additional plaintiffs who are not competent adults is shown in Attachment 3.

Item 3. If you and all your coplaintiffs are adult persons, skip Item 3 and go to Item 4 on the next page. If any plaintiff is a partnership, continue reading.

Item 3a. Type an "x" in box (2), "an unincorporated entity," if any plaintiff is a partnership. (You wouldn't check any of the other boxes in Item 3a because none of the types of plaintiffs listed—corporations, public entities, minors, etc.—can represent themselves without a lawyer.) Type the word "partnership."

If a second plaintiff is a partnership, complete Item 3b, which is identical to 3a.

Unnumbered box. Leave this box blank, unless you used up 3a and 3b and have more coplaintiffs who qualify. Then go on to page two.

Short Title. This is the name by which your case will be known. Type the last names (or the business names) of the first (perhaps only) plaintiff and the first (perhaps only) defendant, separated by a "vs." For example, "Brown vs. Black" or "Brown vs. Golden Bear Typing Service."

Case Number. Leave this blank. You won't be able to fill it in until you've filed your Complaint with the court clerk, who will give you a case number.

Item 4. Type an "x" in this box if you are suing in the name of your business. If you own a business as a sole proprietor, type your own name after "Plaintiff (name)" and type the fictitious business name on the next line after "(specify)." If your partnership does business under a fictitious name, type the partnership's name after "Plaintiff (name)" and type the fictitious business name on the next line after "(specify)."

Item 5. If all defendants are natural persons (not business entities or associations), skip all of Item 5.

Item 5a. If any defendant is a partnership, association, corporation, or government entity, place an "x" in the appropriate box. You are given four identical paragraphs, "a" through "d." For each defendant that falls into this category, put its name after "Except defendant (name)," and type an "x" in the applicable box underneath. You'll need to provide a description if you name an unincorporated entity (simply write "partnership" or "association") or public entity (such as "County of Santa Clara"). If more than four defendants fall into this category, continue on an attachment sheet.

Item 6a. If you have named unknown or "Doe" defendants—explained in Chapter 4—type an "x" in box a if you believe that one or more of the Doe defendants acted as an employee or representative of another defendant. For example, if you were in an auto accident with a delivery service truck, you may know the name of the truck company, but not the driver's name. In the blank you will name the appropriate number of Does, for example "Does 1 and 2."

Item 6b. If you have named other Doe defendants because you're not sure who's responsible and may discover the identity of those defendants later, put an "x" in this box. You'll also have to specify the number of Doe defendants that are unknown to you at this time—for example, "Does 3 through 7."

Item 7. Skip this item—it involves a complex legal situation you need not worry about. If you are curious, in some cases there is a party who is needed as a plaintiff but has refused to participate in the lawsuit. Code of Civil Procedure § 382 allows you to name this party as a defendant. If this is your situation, you'll need the help of a lawyer. (See Chapter 17.)

Item 8. To decide which box to check here, you may want to reread "Selecting the Right Court" in Chapter 4, where I discuss reasons for choosing to sue in a particular county. Type an "x" in the appropriate box. If you chose this county because a business defendant does business there, check the "other" box and type the reason (for example, "Defendant Construction Co. does business in this county"). Don't worry about explaining here which branch court within the county you may have picked. The form is concerned with why you chose the county, not the branch.

SHORT TITLE: Kim v. Offer	CASE NUMBER:

PLD-PI-001

4. [X] Plaintiff *(name):* Sam Kim
   is doing business under the fictitious name *(specify):* Kim's Book Supplies
   and has complied with the fictitious business name laws.

5. Each defendant named above is a natural person
   a. [X] **except** defendant *(name):* ROMMOR BOOKS
      (1) [X] a business organization, form unknown
      (2) [ ] a corporation
      (3) [ ] an unincorporated entity *(describe):*
      (4) [ ] a public entity *(describe):*
      (5) [ ] other *(specify):*

   c. [ ] **except** defendant *(name):*
      (1) [ ] a business organization, form unknown
      (2) [ ] a corporation
      (3) [ ] an unincorporated entity *(describe):*
      (4) [ ] a public entity *(describe):*
      (5) [ ] other *(specify):*

   b. [ ] **except** defendant *(name):*
      (1) [ ] a business organization, form unknown
      (2) [ ] a corporation
      (3) [ ] an unincorporated entity *(describe):*
      (4) [ ] a public entity *(describe):*
      (5) [ ] other *(specify):*

   d. [ ] **except** defendant *(name):*
      (1) [ ] a business organization, form unknown
      (2) [ ] a corporation
      (3) [ ] an unincorporated entity *(describe):*
      (4) [ ] a public entity *(describe):*
      (5) [ ] other *(specify):*

   [ ] Information about additional defendants who are not natural persons is contained in Attachment 5.

6. The true names of defendants sued as Does are unknown to plaintiff.
   a. [ ] Doe defendants *(specify Doe numbers):* _____ were the agents or employees of other named defendants and acted within the scope of that agency or employment.
   b. [ ] Doe defendants *(specify Doe numbers):* _____ are persons whose capacities are unknown to plaintiff.

7. [ ] Defendants who are joined under Code of Civil Procedure section 382 are *(names):*

8. This court is the proper court because
   a. [ ] at least one defendant now resides in its jurisdictional area.
   b. [ ] the principal place of business of a defendant corporation or unincorporated association is in its jurisdictional area.
   c. [X] injury to person or damage to personal property occurred in its jurisdictional area.
   d. [ ] other *(specify):*

9. [ ] Plaintiff is required to comply with a claims statute, **and**
   a. [ ] has complied with applicable claims statutes, **or**
   b. [ ] is excused from complying because *(specify):*

PLD-PI-001 [Rev. January 1, 2007]

COMPLAINT—Personal Injury, Property Damage, Wrongful Death

Item 9. Type an "x" in this box if at least one defendant is a government defendant—that is, you are suing the State of California, a county, city, school district, or other public entity. Before filing a lawsuit in court, you should have complied with the government claims procedure, discussed in "Suing the Government" in Chapter 4. If you have, type an "x" next to Item 9a. If you haven't complied with the claims procedure by now, you should consult a lawyer. There are ways to get around this process when suing a government entity, but they are complex and it's dangerous to rely on them. Now proceed to page three.

Short Title. Put exactly what you put at the top of page two.

Case Number. Leave this blank—again, the court clerk will assign you a case number when you file the Complaint.

> **If There's More Than One Plaintiff**
>
> If your case involves more than one plaintiff, you must use a different Page Three for each. You designate each plaintiff's damages and requests by putting a slash mark (/) after the word "plaintiff" in Items 11 and 14, and above the slash typing the name of the particular plaintiff whose damages and requests you're describing. Each plaintiff must have his or her name typed at the bottom of his or her page and must sign on the signature line.

Item 10. Skip this item for now. You'll fill it in after you prepare your "cause of action" forms (see below).

Item 11. Here you check off the various categories of damages you are claiming. Don't specify the amounts.

Item 11a. Type an "x" if you claim damages for lost salary or wages.

Item 11b. If your car, camera, or any other damaged item was in the shop being repaired for any length of time, or you had to do without it while looking for a replacement, type an "x" in this box. (Note that this is not the same as "property damage," another item in this list.)

Item 11c. Check if you claim any hospital or medical expenses.

Item 11d. "General damage" refers to pain and suffering. Anytime someone is physically injured, it is safe to assume he or she also had pain and suffering, so type an "x" in the box if you were injured. However, if you did not have physical injuries but want to recover for pain, suffering, or any other emotional damages, you should probably consult a lawyer for assistance. Such cases involve some complicated law. Note that you cannot recover for this category of damages if you were in a motor vehicle accident and you were not insured (Civil Code § 3333.4).

Item 11e. Type an "x" here if you claim any physical damage to anything you own, such as your house, yard, car, or a camera in the car that broke because of the accident.

Item 11f. If you anticipate a loss of future income because of work you'll miss or because you'll have to take a lower-paying job as a result of your injury, type an "x" in this box.

Item 11g. Type an "x" in this box if you have any damages not covered by one of the other boxes. The most common is punitive or exemplary ("to make an example") damages. You might want to ask for these damages if a defendant acted against you with the intent to cause you injury or with a conscious disregard of your rights or safety. You should note, however, that courts rarely award punitive damages.

Item 12. Skip this paragraph. A lawsuit over someone's death does not belong in the limited jurisdiction division.

Item 13. This statement is there just to remind you that by using this Complaint form and filing it in the limited jurisdiction division, you understand that you are limited to recovering $25,000.

Item 14. Despite the phrase "Plaintiff Prays," this item is not an inquiry into your religious beliefs. It asks you to state what you want out of the lawsuit. (In legalese, that request is called a "prayer.")

SHORT TITLE: Kim v. Offer	CASE NUMBER:

10. The following causes of action are attached and the statements above apply to each *(each complaint must have one or more causes of action attached)*:
    a. ☐ Motor Vehicle
    b. ☐ General Negligence
    c. ☐ Intentional Tort
    d. ☐ Products Liability
    e. ☐ Premises Liability
    f. ☐ Other *(specify):*

11. Plaintiff has suffered
    a. ☐ wage loss
    b. ☒ loss of use of property
    c. ☒ hospital and medical expenses
    d. ☒ general damage
    e. ☒ property damage
    f. ☐ loss of earning capacity
    g. ☒ other damage *(specify):* lost business profits, punitive damages

12. ☐ The damages claimed for wrongful death and the relationships of plaintiff to the deceased are
    a. ☐ listed in Attachment 12.
    b. ☐ as follows:

13. The relief sought in this complaint is within the jurisdiction of this court.

14. **Plaintiff prays** for judgment for costs of suit; for such relief as is fair, just, and equitable; and for
    a. (1) ☒ compensatory damages
       (2) ☒ punitive damages
       The amount of damages is *(in cases for personal injury or wrongful death, you must check (1))*:
       (1) ☒ according to proof
       (2) ☒ in the amount of: $ 24,000

15. ☐ The paragraphs of this complaint alleged on information and belief are as follows *(specify paragraph numbers):*

Date:

Sam Kim   ▶ *Sam Kim*
(TYPE OR PRINT NAME)   (SIGNATURE OF PLAINTIFF OR ATTORNEY)

COMPLAINT—Personal Injury, Property Damage, Wrongful Death

Item 14a. Put an "x" in the box (1) for compensatory damages and an "x" in box (2) if you are seeking punitive damages.

The amount of damages. The form erroneously doesn't have a "b," but this may be corrected in later editions. In any case, this asks you to specify the amount of money you are seeking in this suit. You should have arrived at that figure in Chapter 2. If you are suing for personal injury (and checked that box in the caption on page one), check box (1) only. If you are suing for something other than personal injury, check box (2) and fill in the amount you are asking for.

You can insert any number up to $25,000. But be reasonable. If your damages will never exceed $10,000, you may be embarrassed and at a disadvantage later if you write $25,000. In a jury trial, the jury might feel you were being greedy and outrageous. So use some common sense.

State a number that gives you a little room for unforeseen developments, but don't go too far. It is possible to amend your Complaint later if it turns out you didn't ask for enough originally.

Item 15. Skip this paragraph for now. You'll fill it out after you prepare your "cause of action" form or forms.

Signature. Type your name above the line in the lower left-hand corner and sign above the line on the right.

Congratulations! You've finished your first form. Now you must complete and attach at least one "cause of action" form to finish the preparation of your Complaint.

Tort Cause of Action Attachments

The forms that you'll attach to the Complaint you just finished will tell the Court and your opponent what "cause of action" you're asserting. As noted earlier, a cause of action is a statement of the legal theory you are using to ask the court for relief. Your Complaint must include at least one cause of action, but it certainly can include more.

The causes of action you use w[ill depend on the] facts of your case. For instan[ce, if you had an] automobile accident with a d[river who you] believe was intentionally try[ing to hit you,] you'd complete both a Motor V[ehicle Cause of] Action and an Intentional Tort Cause of Actio[n.]

The tort causes of action among which you can choose are set out the table, "Possible Tort Causes of Action," below. You'll need to read only the subsection below that pertains to your situation.

Possible Tort Causes of Action

Cause of Action Form	When Used
Motor Vehicle	All car and other motor vehicle accident cases
Premises Liability	If the claim happened on someone's property because of a condition the owner allowed to exist on that property
General Negligence	If the defendant acted negligently (carelessly), and the case does not involve a motor vehicle, premises liability, or a defective product
Intentional Tort	If your claim arose out of defendant's intentional, not merely negligent, act
Product Liability	If your claim arose out of a defective product
Exemplary Damages Attachment (technically not a cause of action, but the discussion is the same)	If your claim arose out of the defendant's malicious, oppressive, or fraudulent act—not merely a negligent act—and you wish to ask for exemplary (punitive) damages

Motor Vehicle Cause of Action

Use this form, *Cause of Action—Motor Vehicle*, Form PLD-PI-001(1), if you are suing because of a defendant's negligent use of a motor vehicle (car, truck, van, motorcycle, scooter, all-terrain vehicle, and the like). Use a separate form for each plaintiff.

FORM

The appendix contains a tear-out version of Form PLD-PI-001(1), *Cause of Action–Motor Vehicle*, and you can download one from the Judicial Council website at www.courtinfo.ca.gov. A filled-out sample is shown below.

Short Title: Type exactly what you typed in the box of the same name at the top of Page Two of the Complaint.

Case number. Leave this blank.

_____ **CAUSE OF ACTION—Motor Vehicle.** Type the word "First" in the blank, indicating this is the first attachment to your Complaint.

Attachment to. Type an "x" in the box for "Complaint."

Plaintiff (name): Type only one plaintiff's name. If there's more than one plaintiff, complete a separate form for each plaintiff. For each additional plaintiff, add one to the number in the blank preceding "CAUSE OF ACTION" ("Second," "Third," etc.) and to the page number at the bottom right corner.

MV-1. Type the date and place of the accident here. If you are not sure of the exact date, state something like "on or about September 5, 2010." If the accident didn't occur at an easily identifiable location, such as "the intersection of Third and Market Streets, San Francisco, California," do the best you can—for example, "approximately five miles north of Sea Ranch on State Route 1 in Mendocino County."

MV-2. Here you identify the defendants responsible for your damages arising out of the motor vehicle accident.

MV-2a. Type an "x" in this box and type the full names of all defendants whom you know or suspect drove vehicles involved in the accident. Normally there will be just one, but multicar accidents are not unusual. If you don't know the identity of a driver, check the "Does" box and name the appropriate number of Does, such as "Does 1 to 2."

MV-2b. If a driver was working at the time of the accident, check this item and type the names of the employer or employers. If you don't know the name of an employer, check the "Does" box and name the appropriate number of Does, such as "Does 3 to 4."

MV-2c. If a driver had permission to borrow someone else's vehicle at the time of the accident, type an "x" in this box and type the names of the owner or owners. Unless you have facts to the contrary, you can assume permission was granted. Granting of permission could have been expressly stated or it could have been implied from the situation. For example, if the owner of a car customarily let his roommates borrow it, his permission to use the car on the day of the accident will be implied. If you don't know the name of an owner, type an "x" in the "Does" box and name the appropriate number of Does, such as "Does 5 to 6."

MV-2d. Entrustment is a legal theory under which someone can be held responsible for an accident if that person let an incompetent, reckless, or intoxicated person use a vehicle. (Entrustment is described more fully in Chapter 4.) Someone who is responsible in the situations described in Items MV-2b or MV-2c is also responsible on an entrustment theory, so if you completed either of those items, put an "x" in this box and list the same information you listed there. In addition, under this theory a car dealer, a co-owner, or someone who gives a car as a gift might be held responsible for an accident. If you're unsure, refer back to Chapter 4. If you don't know the name of someone who entrusted the vehicle, fill in the "Does" box and name the appropriate number of Does, such as "Does 7 to 8."

MV-2e. In this item, identify any foremen or supervisors of the driver who had the accident in the course of employment. This will be relevant only if the employer doesn't have money or insurance coverage and you identify a foreman or supervisor who does. Because you aren't likely to have this information until after your lawsuit is filed, fill in the "Does" box and name several Does, such as "Does 9 to 12."

	PLD-PI-001(1)
SHORT TITLE: Brown v. White	CASE NUMBER:

___First___ **CAUSE OF ACTION—Motor Vehicle**
(number)

ATTACHMENT TO [X] Complaint [ ] Cross - Complaint

(Use a separate cause of action form for each cause of action.)

Plaintiff *(name):* Sandra Brown

MV-1. Plaintiff alleges the acts of defendants were negligent; the acts were the legal (proximate) cause of injuries and damages to plaintiff; the acts occurred
on *(date):* February 5, 20xx
at *(place):* The intersection of Dwight Way and San Pablo Avenue, Berkeley, California

MV-2. DEFENDANTS
    a. [X] The defendants who operated a motor vehicle are *(names):* William White
        3701 Fourth Street
        Oakland, CA 94700

    [ ] Does _____ to _____

    b. [ ] The defendants who employed the persons who operated a motor vehicle in the course of their employment are *(names):*

    [ ] Does _____ to _____

    c. [ ] The defendants who owned the motor vehicle which was operated with their permission are *(names):*

    [ ] Does _____ to _____

    d. [ ] The defendants who entrusted the motor vehicle are *(names):*

    [ ] Does _____ to _____

    e. [ ] The defendants who were the agents and employees of the other defendants and acted within the scope of the agency were *(names):*

    [ ] Does _____ to _____

    f. [ ] The defendants who are liable to plaintiffs for other reasons and the reasons for the liability are
        [ ] listed in Attachment MV-2f [ ] as follows:

[ ] Does _____ to _____   Page ___4___

Page 1 of 1

Form Approved for Optional Use
Judicial Council of California
PLD-PI-001(1) [Rev. January 1, 2007]

CAUSE OF ACTION—Motor Vehicle

Code of Civil Procedure 425.12
www.courtinfo.ca.gov

MV-2f. Type an "x" in this box only if an unemancipated minor was the driver of a vehicle that contributed to the accident. (For more on a minor's liability, and that of his parents, see "Suing a Minor" in Chapter 4.) To sue the parents or legal guardians for signing the minor's driver's license application, put an "x" in the "as follows" box and write something like: "Bruce and Suzanne O'Brien, the parents of Peter O'Brien, a minor, by reason of their having signed his application for a driver's license." If the minor was unlicensed, put an "x" in the "as follows" box and write something like "Bruce and Suzanne O'Brien, the parents of Peter O'Brien, a minor who was not licensed to drive."

Page. Add one number to the last page you completed and put that number here.

SKIP AHEAD
Your *Motor Vehicle Cause of Action* form is now complete. If you have no other tort claims, skip ahead to "Cleaning Up the Tort Complaint."

Premises Liability Cause of Action

Use this form, *Cause of Action—Premises Liability*, Form PLD-PI-001(4), if your accident and damages resulted from a dangerous condition that existed in a store, home, park, apartment, or other premises. Typical premises liability cases involve a landlord's failure to keep a rental property safe, a store owner's failure to warn of the risk of a slippery floor, or a business operator's neglect in allowing debris to collect on the floor or on the sidewalk in front of the business. Interestingly, you can sue under this theory even if you weren't specifically invited onto the premises, as long as you can prove that it was reasonably likely that you would be on the property and exposed to the concealed condition.

In general, a person will be liable for your damage or injury if you can prove that he or she:
- was legally obligated to watch out for your safety in this particular situation (lawyers refer to this as a "duty of care"). For example, a tenant can expect a landlord to provide a reasonably safe building, but normally cannot expect another tenant to provide that safety.
- was aware, or should have been aware, of a dangerous condition that created an unreasonable risk of harm to people coming on the property, and
- failed to warn about or repair a dangerous condition.

FORM
The appendix contains a tear-out version of Form PLD-PI-001(4), *Cause of Action–Premises Liability*, and you can download one from the Judicial Council website at www.courtinfo.ca.gov. A filled-out sample is shown below.

Short Title: Type exactly what you typed at the top of Page Two of the Complaint.

Case Number: Leave this blank.

_____ **CAUSE OF ACTION—Premises Liability.** If this is the first attachment to your Complaint—type "First" in the blank. If it is the second, use "Second," and so on.

Page. Add one to the number of the last page you completed and put that number here.

Attachment to. Put an "x" next to "Complaint."

Prem.L-1. Next to "Plaintiff (name):" type only one plaintiff's name. If there's more than one plaintiff, complete a separate form for each plaintiff. For each additional plaintiff, add one to the number in the blank preceding "CAUSE OF ACTION" ("Second," "Third," etc.) and the page number. After filling in the plaintiff's name, enter the date of the injury.

Next, the form asks for a description of the premises and the circumstances of injury. Begin by stating the address of the property where the injury occurred. Normally, a street and city address is sufficient. If the injury occurred in a multistory building or apartment house, add the floor number, apartment number, or room number.

		PLD-PI-001(4)
SHORT TITLE: Stewart v. Crusty Pizza		CASE NUMBER:

___First___ CAUSE OF ACTION—Premises Liability   Page ___4___
(number)

ATTACHMENT TO [X] Complaint   [ ] Cross - Complaint
(Use a separate cause of action form for each cause of action.)

Prem.L-1. Plaintiff *(name):* Ralph Stewart
alleges the acts of defendants were the legal (proximate) cause of damages to plaintiff.
On *(date):* February 5, 20xx   plaintiff was injured on the following premises in the following fashion *(description of premises and circumstances of injury):*
1002 5th Street, Albany, California; plaintiff was injured when Crusty's waiter dropped a hot, extra large pizza on her arm.

Prem.L-2. [X] **Count One—Negligence** The defendants who negligently owned, maintained, managed and operated the described premises were *(names):* Max Sommers, owner

[X] Does ___1___ to ___1___

Prem.L-3. [ ] **Count Two—Willful Failure to Warn** [Civil Code section 846] The defendant owners who willfully or maliciously failed to guard or warn against a dangerous condition, use, structure, or activity were *(names):*

[ ] Does _____ to _____
Plaintiff, a recreational user, was [ ] an invited guest [ ] a paying guest.

Prem.L-4. [ ] **Count Three—Dangerous Condition of Public Property** The defendants who owned public property on which a dangerous condition existed were *(names):*

[ ] Does _____ to _____
a. [ ] The defendant public entity had [ ] actual [ ] constructive notice of the existence of the dangerous condition in sufficient time prior to the injury to have corrected it.
b. [ ] The condition was created by employees of the defendant public entity.

Prem.L-5. a. [X] **Allegations about Other Defendants** The defendants who were the agents and employees of the other defendants and acted within the scope of the agency were *(names):*

[X] Does ___1___ to ___1___
b. [ ] The defendants who are liable to plaintiffs for other reasons and the reasons for their liability are
[ ] described in attachment Prem.L-5.b [ ] as follows *(names):*

CAUSE OF ACTION—Premises Liability

Then describe how you were injured, and specifically what the defendant did or did not do that caused your injury. Be concise; try to say what is necessary in 40 words or less. Also, refer to plaintiffs and defendants in the third person. This may feel contrived, but that's the way it's done. Here are some examples:

"Safeway store, 9356 Market Street, San Jose, California; plaintiff was injured when she slipped and fell as the result of a piece of fruit negligently left on the floor in the produce department."

"Apartment C, 3445 Elm Street, Santa Ana, California; plaintiff was injured when a defective knob on a faucet on the bathroom basin broke while she was turning it."

"Swimming pool, Central Park, Eighth and Park Streets, Long Beach, California; plaintiff was injured when a defective diving board collapsed while she was using it normally."

Prem.L-2. Put an "x" in this box and type the full names of all defendants you know or suspect owned, maintained, managed, or operated the property. If you don't know the identity of an owner or manager, check the "Does" box and name the appropriate number of Does, such as "Does 1 to 2."

Prem.L-3. This question has to do with injuries that happened while you were on the premises for recreational purposes (if this doesn't apply to you, skip the item). Under California law (Civil Code § 846), an owner who permits—as opposed to expressly invites—people to use his or her property for recreation without charge is not liable for injuries to those people unless that owner willfully or maliciously failed to protect or warn against a dangerous condition or activity. But this protection extends only to uninvited visitors. If you paid a fee to use the facilities, or if you were personally invited onto the premises (as opposed to a general permission extended to the public), the landowner won't escape liability.

If you do fit into one of the above categories, put an "x" in this box. Type the names of all of the defendants listed in Item Prem.L-2, including the Doe defendants. If you were an invited guest or a paying guest, check the applicable box, but you don't have to be either one to use this portion of the form.

Prem.L-4. Skip this item unless you were using property owned or operated by a government agency. And be sure that before filing this suit, you have complied with the government claims procedure discussed in Chapter 4.

If the property was owned or operated by a government agency, put an "x" in the box and type the full names of all defendants who owned the property. If there may be co-owners you haven't yet identified, check the "Does" box and state the same number of Does as there are unknown co-owners, such as "Does 3 to 4."

Then put an "x" next to Paragraph a or b, or possibly both. If you check "a," check both "actual" and "constructive." Actual means the agency actually knew about the dangerous condition; constructive means the agency should have known about it. Checking both gives you room to prove either one. Even if the agency didn't have actual notice, the court may well find it had constructive notice if a dangerous condition existed for some time and was obvious enough that a reasonable inspection would have disclosed it.

Prem.L-5a. If any defendants were agents or employees of the property owner or manager, put an "x" next to this item and type the names of the agents or employees. Include any foremen or supervisors who may have been responsible for the injury. For example, if a maintenance contractor worked for the owner and he contributed to the injury by his actions or by failing to take action, put his name here. If you don't know a name—or if you want to give yourself room in case a yet-unknown person emerges as responsible—check the "Does" box and name the number of Does that correspond to the number of unknown identities, such as "Does 5 to 7."

Prem.L-5b. Leave this blank. The reasons you would add defendants under subparagraph b are beyond the scope of this book.

SKIP AHEAD
The *Premises Liability Cause of Action* form is now complete. If you have no other tort claims, skip ahead to "Cleaning Up the Tort Complaint."

General Negligence Cause of Action

Use this form, *Cause of Action—General Negligence*, PLD-PI-001(2), if the defendant has committed a careless or negligent act (as opposed to an intentional act), substantially leading to damage or injury, in a situation other than a motor vehicle or premises liability accident.

Negligence cases crowd the dockets of courts throughout the nation. The term means doing something that a reasonably prudent person would not do, or failing to do something that a reasonably prudent person would do, under similar circumstances, substantially resulting in harm. Chapter 1 gave several examples of negligence cases; here are a few others:

- A window washer spills soapy water on your car, causing the car's finish to be eaten away.
- The owner of a ferocious dog lets it escape from her yard; the dog bites you.
- A restaurant owner serves you spoiled food; you get violently ill.
- Your lawyer, doctor, or other professional performs services for you in a manner that falls below the standard of the ordinary practitioner.

FORM
The appendix contains a tear-out version of Form PLD-PI-001(2), *Cause of Action–General Negligence*, and you can download one from the Judicial Council website at www.courtinfo.ca.gov. A filled-out sample is shown below.

Short Title: Type exactly what you typed at the top of Page Two of the Complaint.

Case Number: Leave this blank.

_____ CAUSE OF ACTION—General Negligence. If this is the first Cause of Action—and this is the first attachment to your Complaint—type "First" in the blank. If it is the second, use "Second," and so on.

Page. Add one to the number of the last page you completed and put that number here.

Attachment to. Put an "x" next to "Complaint."

GN-1. After "Plaintiff (name):" put only one plaintiff's name in the blank, and complete a separate form for each additional plaintiff. For each additional plaintiff, add one to the number in the blank preceding "CAUSE OF ACTION" ("Second," "Third," etc.) and the page number.

After "defendant (name):" type the full names of all defendants who are in any way responsible for your damage or injury in this cause of action. If you don't know the identity of a defendant, check the "Does" box and name the appropriate number of Does, such as "Does 1 to 4."

Next, type the date and place of the accident in the appropriate spaces. If you are not sure of the exact date, state something like "on or about September 5, 2010." If the accident didn't occur at an easily identifiable location, such as "1800 Main Street, Fresno, California," provide the best description of the location you can.

Next, the form asks for the reasons for liability. Describe how you or your property were injured, and specifically what the defendant did or did not do that caused the injury. Be concise; try to say what is necessary in 40 words or fewer. Also, refer to plaintiffs and defendants in the third person. This may feel contrived, but that's the way it's done. Here are some examples:

"Defendants negligently dropped a bucket of paint on plaintiff's computer, causing it to be damaged while plaintiff was pushing the computer across the sidewalk on a dolly below them."

"Defendants negligently left a gate on their property open and thereby allowed their dangerous German Shepherd dog to come onto plaintiff's property and bite him, which caused injury to plaintiff."

	PLD-PI-001(2)
SHORT TITLE: 　　Sanchez v. Moreno	CASE NUMBER:

　　　First　　　　**CAUSE OF ACTION—General Negligence**　　Page　4
　　(number)

ATTACHMENT TO　[X] Complaint　[ ] Cross - Complaint

(Use a separate cause of action form for each cause of action.)

GN-1. Plaintiff *(name)*: Gilbert Sanchez

　　　alleges that defendant *(name)*: Simon Moreno

　　　　[ ] Does _____ to _____

was the legal (proximate) cause of damages to plaintiff. By the following acts or omissions to act, defendant negligently caused the damage to plaintiff
on *(date)*: January 12, 20xx
at *(place)*: 785 First Street, Santa Monica, CA 94123

(description of reasons for liability):

Defendant allowed his dog to roam the streets unleashed. The dog chased and bit plaintiff, without provocation, injuring him.

CAUSE OF ACTION—General Negligence

Form Approved for Optional Use
Judicial Council of California
PLD-PI-001(2) [Rev. January 1, 2007]

Code of Civil Procedure 425.12
www.courtinfo.ca.gov

"Defendants negligently prepared an unsanitary meal in their restaurant and served it to plaintiff, who ate it and was thus caused to become violently ill."

"Defendant negligently prepared plaintiff's 2009 tax return and thereby caused taxing agencies to charge her penalties and interest." (Note that this scenario describes a claim of professional malpractice. You can use this form in a malpractice case, including medical malpractice and legal malpractice. But because malpractice cases are usually more complicated than other types of negligence cases, you should first research the subject area, as described below.)

You probably noticed a formula in these descriptions. Each description starts with a recital of something the defendants did negligently. Then the victim (plaintiff) is named. Finally, the plaintiff's injuries or damages are identified as having been caused by the defendants' action or inaction.

You can use the same formula to describe a bus driver who stopped too sharply, causing you to fall to the floor of the bus, or a delivery person who ran over your toes with a dolly. As long as you mention that the defendant's negligent act caused injury or damage to the plaintiff, you've described the reasons for liability just fine.

SKIP AHEAD
The *General Negligence Cause of Action* form is now complete. If you have no other tort claims, skip ahead to "Cleaning Up the Tort Complaint."

Intentional Tort Cause of Action

Use this form, *Cause of Action—Intentional Tort*, PLD-PI-001(3), if the defendant intentionally caused you injury or property damage. There are many types of intentional torts; the two most common kinds fortunately lend themselves to self-representation. They are:

- battery (a willful and unlawful use of force upon the body of one person by another), and
- conversion (theft, or the intentional and substantial interference with your possession of your personal property).

There are many more intentional torts—such as fraud, defamation (libel and slander), intentional infliction of emotional distress, false imprisonment, malicious prosecution, abuse of process, invasion of privacy, trespass, interference with prospective economic advantage, and inducing breach of contract. But you'll need some extra help if you plan to bring a lawsuit that falls into one of these categories. Read "Complaints for Other Types of Lawsuits" later in this chapter and consider getting some advice from a lawyer.

FORM
The appendix contains a tear-out version of Form PLD-PI-001(3), *Cause of Action–Intentional Tort*, and you can download one from the Judicial Council website at www.courtinfo.ca.gov. A filled-out sample is shown below.

Follow these instructions to complete your form. If you're suing more than one plaintiff, use a separate form for each.

Short Title: Type exactly what you typed at the top of Page Two of the Complaint.

_____ **CAUSE OF ACTION—Intentional Tort.** If this is the first Cause of Action, insert the word "First." If it is the second, use "Second," and so on.

Page. Add one to the number of the last page you completed and put that number here.

Attachment to. Put an "x" next to "Complaint."

IT-1. After "Plaintiff (name):" put only one plaintiff's name in the blank, and complete a separate form for each additional plaintiff. For each additional plaintiff, add one to the number in the blank preceding "CAUSE OF ACTION" ("Second," "Third," etc.) and the page number.

After "defendant (name):" type the full names of all defendants who committed an intentional

	PLD-PI-001(3)
SHORT TITLE: Warner v. Jones	CASE NUMBER

___First___ **CAUSE OF ACTION—Intentional Tort**   Page ___4___
   (number)

ATTACHMENT TO   [X] Complaint   [ ] Cross - Complaint

(Use a separate cause of action form for each cause of action.)

IT-1. Plaintiff *(name)*: John Warner

alleges that defendant *(name)*: Alex Jones

[ ] Does _____ to _____

was the legal (proximate) cause of damages to plaintiff. By the following acts or omissions to act, defendant intentionally caused the damage to plaintiff
on *(date)*: April 23, 20xx
at *(place)*: 1705 Hill Street, Anytown, CA 94123

(description of reasons for liability):

Defendant Jones removed plaintiff's Dell Laptop from plaintiff's living room, without plaintiff's permission, with the intent of interfering with his possession of said laptop and has not returned it.

CAUSE OF ACTION–Intentional Tort

Form Approved for Optional Use
Judicial Council of California
PLD-PI-001(3) [Rev. January 1, 2007]

Code of Civil Procedure, § 425.12
www.courtinfo.ca.gov

tort that damaged or injured you. If you don't know the identity of a defendant, check the "Does" box and name the appropriate number of Does, such as "Does 1 to 4."

Next, type the date and place of the accident in the appropriate spaces. If you are not sure of the exact date, state something like "on or about September 5, 2009." If the accident didn't occur at an easily identifiable location, such as "1800 Main Street, Fresno, California," provide the best description of the location you can.

Next, the form asks for reasons for liability. Describe how you or your property were injured and what the defendant did that caused the injury. Be concise—try to say what is necessary in 40 words or less. Also, refer to plaintiffs and defendants in the third person. This may feel contrived, but that's the way it's done. Here are some examples:

- In a battery case: "Defendant Robinson approached the table at which plaintiff was sitting in a restaurant and intentionally poured water over plaintiff's head and struck plaintiff in the face with his fist, causing her to become unconscious."
- In a conversion case: "Defendant Robinson came on to plaintiff's property and, without her permission, removed her Hyundai automobile with the intent of interfering with her possession of that automobile. He has not returned it."

Products Liability Causes of Action

If you intend to sue a manufacturer, supplier, or seller of a defective product that caused you physical injury, you should see a lawyer instead of representing yourself. If you're determined to represent yourself in a products liability lawsuit, see *California Forms of Pleading and Practice*, Volume 40, Chapter 460, which you'll find in major law libraries.

SKIP AHEAD
The *Intentional Tort Cause of Action* form is now complete. If you have no other tort claims, skip ahead to "Cleaning Up the Tort Complaint."

Exemplary (Punitive) Damages Attachment

Exemplary, or punitive, damages are awarded in tort cases when the court is convinced that a defendant acted outrageously. This damage award, which exceeds your out-of-pocket losses, is intended to punish or make the defendant an example to others.

You might want to ask for these damages if a defendant acted against you with the intent to cause you injury or with a conscious disregard of your rights or safety. Remember, however, that only a small percentage of people who believe they were victims of outrageous conduct are awarded punitive damages.

In legal terms, you will have to prove that the defendant acted out of malice, fraud, or oppression. These terms are defined in Civil Code § 3294 as follows:

- Malice means conduct that is intended by the defendant to cause injury to the plaintiff or despicable conduct that is carried on by the defendant with a willful and conscious disregard of the rights or safety of others.
- Oppression means despicable conduct that subjects a person to cruel and unjust hardship in conscious disregard of that person's rights.
- Fraud means an intentional misrepresentation, deceit, or concealment of a material fact known to the defendant, with the intention on the part of the defendant of depriving a person of property or legal rights or otherwise causing injury.

CAUTION
Don't ask for punitive damages unless they're warranted. Asking for exemplary or punitive damages in a case involving ordinary negligence (as

		PLD-PI-001(6)
SHORT TITLE: McConnel v. Wright	CASE NUMBER:	

Exemplary Damages Attachment   Page ___4___

ATTACHMENT TO   [X] Complaint   [ ] Cross - Complaint

EX-1. As additional damages against defendant *(name):* Sarah Wright

    Plaintiff alleges defendant was guilty of
    [X] malice
    [ ] fraud
    [X] oppression

as defined in Civil Code section 3294, and plaintiff should recover, in addition to actual damages, damages to make an example of and to punish defendant.

EX-2. The facts supporting plaintiff's claim are as follows: Defendant Wright is plaintiff's former wife. On November 11, 20xx, defendant waited for plaintiff to pass the corner of First and Cedar streets in the City of Santa Monica and when he approached, caused a large rock to fall through the windshield of his car, injuring him and damaging his car.

EX-3. The amount of exemplary damages sought is
    a. [X] not shown, pursuant to Code of Civil Procedure section 425.10.
    b. [ ] $

Page 1 of 1

Form Approved for Optional Use
Judicial Council of California
PLD-PI-001(6) [Rev. January 1, 2007]

Exemplary Damages Attachment

Code of Civil Procedure, § 425.12
www.courtinfo.ca.gov

opposed to deliberate, willful misconduct) is rarely a good idea. As a self-represented plaintiff, you want to look like a reasonable person who wants just compensation for your injuries, not like an aggressive, professional litigant who screams for exemplary damages for every minor affront you've suffered. Only if the defendant's conduct was really malicious, oppressive, or fraudulent should you claim exemplary damages.

FORM

The appendix contains a tear-out version of Form PLD-PI-001(6), *Exemplary Damages Attachment*, and you can download one from the Judicial Council website at www.courtinfo.ca.gov. A filled-out sample is shown above.

Follow these instructions when filling out your form. If there is more than one defendant from whom you are claiming exemplary damages, use a separate form for each.

Short Title: Type exactly what you typed at the top of Page Two of the Complaint.

Case Number: Leave this blank.

Page. Add one to the number of the last page you completed and put that number here.

Attachment to: Put an "x" next to "Complaint."

EX-1. After "defendant (name):" type the full name of a defendant who was guilty of malice, fraud, and/or oppression. Then check any of the three boxes that apply. For each defendant, complete a separate form and increase the page number by one.

EX-2. Set forth the facts that you claim establish that there was malice, fraud, or oppression. Examples of language that might be used in this item are:

"As described in the First Cause of Action, defendant hid in plaintiff's garage and then jumped on him without warning, knocking him to the ground and causing him to become unconscious."

"As described in the First Cause of Action, defendant fraudulently concealed from plaintiff the fact that there was no engine in the automobile he sold to plaintiff and that it was therefore worthless, thus causing plaintiff to be defrauded of the $7,000 he paid to defendant."

EX-3. Check box a and do not enter a number in box b.

Cleaning Up the Tort Complaint

Now is the time to complete the paragraphs you've skipped in the Complaint form—the first document you prepared.

Does 1 to ___. Count your Doe defendants; they should be numbered consecutively throughout all the causes of action you filled out. Enter the total in the third box from the top on the first page of the Complaint.

Item 2 (number of pages): Count your total number of pages—don't forget any attachment sheets—and insert the total.

Item 10 (causes of action attached): Put an "x" next to all that are applicable. If you completed an Exemplary Damages Attachment, check the "other" box and specify.

Item 15 (matters you are alleging on information and belief): To answer this question, you have to play lawyer for a moment. Read over the factual statements in the Complaint and the causes of action. If any statement is true, but you can't verify it based on your own knowledge—that is, you relied on something someone else told you—the statement is said to have been made "on information and belief." Common information and belief statements include:

- identifying a defendant as the employee or agent of someone else, and
- concluding that a driver who didn't own the car had the permission of the owner to drive it.

If any statements in the Complaint or causes of action fit this category, put an "x" in this box and type the paragraph number (such as "MV-1"). If there is more than one cause of action of the same kind (such as two motor vehicle causes of action), be sure to note both the paragraph number and the number of the cause of action. Do your best at this, but do not spend a lot of time worrying about it.

Review all your page numbers and Cause of Action headings. Be sure they are in order.

Contract Complaints

Now it's time to complete your Complaint form with information that's specific to the facts of your contractual dispute or case. Go back to "The Caption" in this chapter, where this portion of the form is explained for all cases. Use these instructions to fill in the caption at the top of the Contract Complaint and any other applicable forms you will be using in this book. You have already filled out most of the caption box. The "Complaint" box, however, is still blank. Put an "x" in the box next to "Complaint." Now we'll get into the body of the Complaint, dealing with the numbered items in sequence.

FORM
The appendix contains a tear-out version of Form PLD-C-001, *Complaint—Contract*, and you can download one from the Judicial Council website at www.courtinfo.ca.gov. A filled-out sample is shown below.

Follow these instructions to complete your Complaint:

Item 1. Insert the names of the plaintiff(s) and defendant(s).

Item 2. Skip this for now. You'll come back and enter the number of pages after you complete the Complaint and the causes of action.

Item 3a. If you and all your coplaintiffs are adult persons, skip this item. If any plaintiff is a partnership, continue reading.

First, put an "x" in the box next to "except plaintiff (name)." Then type the name of the partnership after "(name)."

Under that, put an "x" in the second of the three boxes, "an unincorporated entity (describe)," and then put "partnership." (You wouldn't check "a corporation" because a corporation must hire a lawyer to represent itself.)

Item 3b. Put an "x" in this box and deal with this item if any plaintiff is a partnership, an individual doing business under a fictitious name ("Wood's Pest Service"), or an individual engaged in a business that requires a license (such as a real estate broker, contractor, or chiropractor). Type that plaintiff's name after "Plaintiff (*name*)."

Remember that if you use a fictitious business name, you will need to have filed a certificate with the county clerk. If you have complied with this requirement, put an "x" in the box next to "has complied with the fictitious business name laws…." and type the fictitious name at the end of the line.

If you must have a license from the state to practice your occupation (a city business license doesn't count) and that occupation is relevant to the subject of the lawsuit (for example, you're a licensed real estate broker suing over unpaid fees), put an "x" in the box next to "has complied with all licensing requirements." At the end of the line, specify the type of license you have.

Item 3c. If one or more other plaintiffs are partnerships or sole proprietorships, you'll need the same information requested above in Items 3a and 3b.

Item 4. If all defendants are natural persons—individuals, not business entities or associations—skip all of Item 4.

Item 4a. If any defendant is a partnership, association, corporation, or government entity, complete this section. There are two identical paragraphs. For each defendant that falls into this category, put its name after "except defendant (*name*)," and check the applicable box underneath. You'll need to provide a description if you name an unincorporated entity (simply write "partnership" or "association") or public entity (such as "County of Santa Clara"). If more than two defendants fall into this category, continue on an attachment sheet.

If you don't know the form of the business (for example, whether it's a partnership or a

	PLD-C-001
ATTORNEY OR PARTY WITHOUT ATTORNEY *(Name, State Bar number, and address):* James Garcia 82 Southwest Drive San Mateo, CA 94404 TELEPHONE NO: 650-555-2044 FAX NO. *(Optional):* E-MAIL ADDRESS *(Optional):* ATTORNEY FOR *(Name):* In pro per	FOR COURT USE ONLY

SUPERIOR COURT OF CALIFORNIA, COUNTY OF San Mateo
STREET ADDRESS: 400 County Center
MAILING ADDRESS:
CITY AND ZIP CODE: Redwood City, CA 04063-1655
BRANCH NAME:

PLAINTIFF: James Garcia dba Flour Power

DEFENDANT: Anne Warren dba Anne's Pie Shop

☐ DOES 1 TO _____

CONTRACT
[X] **COMPLAINT** ☐ **AMENDED COMPLAINT** *(Number):*
☐ **CROSS-COMPLAINT** ☐ **AMENDED CROSS-COMPLAINT** *(Number):*

Jurisdiction *(check all that apply):*
[X] ACTION IS A LIMITED CIVIL CASE
  Amount demanded [X] does not exceed $10,000
           ☐ exceeds $10,000 but does not exceed $25,000
☐ ACTION IS AN UNLIMITED CIVIL CASE *(exceeds $25,000)*
☐ ACTION IS RECLASSIFIED by this amended complaint or cross-complaint
    ☐ from limited to unlimited
    ☐ from unlimited to limited
	CASE NUMBER:

1. **Plaintiff*** *(name or names):* James Garcia

   alleges causes of action against **defendant*** *(name or names):* Anne Warren

2. This pleading, including attachments and exhibits, consists of the following number of pages:
3. a. Each plaintiff named above is a competent adult
   [X] except plaintiff *(name):* Flour Power
      (1) ☐ a corporation qualified to do business in California
      (2) ☐ an unincorporated entity *(describe):*
      (3) [X] other *(specify):* sole proprietorship

   b. [X] Plaintiff *(name):* James Garcia
      a. [X] has complied with the fictitious business name laws and is doing business under the fictitious name *(specify):*
         Flour Power
      b. ☐ has complied with all licensing requirements as a licensed *(specify):*
   c. ☐ Information about additional plaintiffs who are not competent adults is shown in Attachment 3c.
4. a. Each defendant named above is a natural person
      ☐ except defendant *(name):*   ☐ except defendant *(name):*
         (1) ☐ a business organization, form unknown   (1) ☐ a business organization, form unknown
         (2) ☐ a corporation   (2) ☐ a corporation
         (3) ☐ an unincorporated entity *(describe):*   (3) ☐ an unincorporated entity *(describe):*
         (4) ☐ a public entity *(describe):*   (4) ☐ a public entity *(describe):*
         (5) ☐ other *(specify):*   (5) ☐ other *(specify):*

* If this form is used as a cross-complaint, plaintiff means cross-complainant and defendant means cross-defendant.

Form Approved for Optional Use
Judicial Council of California
PLD-C-001 [Rev. January 1, 2007]

COMPLAINT—Contract

Code of Civil Procedure, § 425.12

corporation), place a check next to "a business organization, form unknown." Now turn to Page Two of the form.

> **! CAUTION**
> **If there's more than one plaintiff, use a separate Page Two for each.** The caption and responses to Items 4b through 9 and 11 will be identical for all. Your answers to Item 10 should be specific to each plaintiff, as explained in the instructions for Item 10, below.

Short Title: This is the name by which your case will be known. Type the last names (or the business names) of the first (perhaps only) plaintiff and the first (perhaps only) defendant, separated by a "vs." For example, "Brown vs. Black" or "Brown vs. Golden Bear Typing Service."

Case Number: Leave this blank. You won't be able to fill it in until you've filed your Complaint with the court clerk, who will give you a case number.

Item 4b. If you have named unknown or "Doe" defendants—explained in Chapter 4—type an "x" in box a if you believe that one or more of the Doe defendants acted as an employee or representative of another defendant. For example, if a salesperson promised to provide you service on behalf of a company, you may know the name of the company but not the name of the salesperson. In the blank you will insert the appropriate number of Does, for example "Does 1 and 2."

Item 4c. This item needs to be checked and completed only if you ran out of space in 4a.

Item 4d. Skip this item—it involves a complex legal situation you need not worry about. (If you are curious, some cases involve a party who is needed as a plaintiff but who has refused to participate in the lawsuit. Code of Civil Procedure § 382 allows you to name this party as a defendant. If this is your situation, you'll need the help of a lawyer.)

Item 5. Type an "x" in this box if at least one defendant is a government defendant—that is, you are suing the State of California, a county, city, school district, or other public entity.

Item 5a. Before filing a lawsuit in court, you should have complied with the government claims procedure, discussed in Chapter 4. If you have done so, type an "x" in this box. If you haven't complied with the claims procedure by now, resist the temptation to choose Item 5b (where you give reasons you might be excused from following normal procedures) and consult a lawyer. There are ways to get around the claims process when suing a government entity, but they are complex.

Item 6. Complete this item only if your lawsuit involves one of two specific situations. Civil Code § 1812.10 is also known as the Unruh Retail Installment Sales Act. It applies to your case if your business sells goods or furnishes services, and you are suing a buyer concerning a retail installment contract under which the buyer is required to pay a finance charge.

Civil Code § 2984.4 is part of the Rees-Levering Motor Vehicle Sales and Finance Act. It applies to your case if your business sells or leases motor vehicles and you are suing a buyer regarding a conditional sales contract.

Businesses that sue under these laws normally use lawyers. Retail installment contracts and motor vehicle sales and leasing are highly regulated areas of the law. If your lawsuit is covered by either of these laws, check the appropriate box and be prepared to show that you have complied with the applicable laws when you get to trial. If you want to represent yourself, consider consulting a lawyer for help preparing your case.

Item 7. Check all boxes that describe why you are filing your lawsuit in this county.

If a defendant entered into a contract—including buying goods or services—in this county, check "a." If a defendant lived in the county when the contract was signed, check "b." If a defendant lives in the county now, check "c." If services, sales, or other terms of the contract were to be performed in the county, check "d." If a business defendant (corporation or association)

	PLD-C-001
SHORT TITLE: Garcia v. Warren	CASE NUMBER:

4. *(Continued)*
   b. The true names of defendants sued as Does are unknown to plaintiff.
      (1) ☐ Doe defendants *(specify Doe numbers):* _____ were the agents or employees of the named defendants and acted within the scope of that agency or employment.
      (2) ☐ Doe defendants *(specify Doe numbers):* _____ are persons whose capacities are unknown to plaintiff.
   c. ☐ Information about additional defendants who are not natural persons is contained in Attachment 4c.
   d. ☐ Defendants who are joined under Code of Civil Procedure section 382 are *(names):*

5. ☐ Plaintiff is required to comply with a claims statute, **and**
   a. ☐ has complied with applicable claims statutes, *or*
   b. ☐ is excused from complying because *(specify):*

6. ☐ This action is subject to ☐ Civil Code section 1812.10 ☐ Civil Code section 2984.4.

7. This court is the proper court because
   a. [X] a defendant entered into the contract here.
   b. ☐ a defendant lived here when the contract was entered into.
   c. ☐ a defendant lives here now.
   d. [X] the contract was to be performed here.
   e. ☐ a defendant is a corporation or unincorporated association and its principal place of business is here.
   f. ☐ real property that is the subject of this action is located here.
   g. ☐ other *(specify):*

8. The following causes of action are attached and the statements above apply to each *(each complaint must have one or more causes of action attached):*

   ☐ Breach of Contract
   ☐ Common Counts
   ☐ Other *(specify):*

9. ☐ Other allegations:

10. **Plaintiff prays** for judgment for costs of suit; for such relief as is fair, just, and equitable; and for
   a. [X] damages of: $ 8,456.17
   b. [X] interest on the damages
      (1) [X] according to proof
      (2) ☐ at the rate of *(specify):*   percent per year from *(date):*
   c. ☐ attorney's fees
      (1) ☐ of: $
      (2) ☐ according to proof.
   d. ☐ other *(specify):*

11. ☐ The paragraphs of this pleading alleged on information and belief are as follows *(specify paragraph numbers):*

Date:

James Garcia   ▶   *James Garcia*
(TYPE OR PRINT NAME)   (SIGNATURE OF PLAINTIFF OR ATTORNEY)

(If you wish to verify this pleading, affix a verification.)

COMPLAINT—Contract

has its principal place of business here, check "e." If your lawsuit has to do with real property that is located in this county, check "f." If you need help deciding, refer to "Complaints for Other Types of Lawsuits" in Chapter 4.

Item 8. Skip this for now; later you will need to describe the attachments, which are explained later in this chapter.

Item 9. Skip this.

Item 10a. Despite the phrase "Plaintiff Prays," this paragraph is not an inquiry into your religious beliefs. It asks you to state what you want out of the lawsuit. (In legalese, that request is called a "prayer.")

> **CAUTION**
> **If your case involves multiple plaintiffs, each should answer Item 10 individually.** Designate each plaintiff's requests by putting a slash mark (/) after the word "plaintiff" in Item 10, then write the name of the particular plaintiff whose requests you're describing above the slash. Each plaintiff must have his or her name at the bottom of his or her page and sign at the signature line.

Put an "x" in the first box for damages. After the "$," type the total amount of money you are seeking in this lawsuit. As discussed in Chapter 2, you can recover your out-of-pocket losses that reasonably could have been foreseen by the defendant. If you didn't get what you contracted for, you are entitled to the reasonable costs you incurred in acquiring it elsewhere, as well as any incidental expenses that reasonably could have been anticipated. (For more on this point, see "Breach of Contract Cases" in Chapter 2.)

Item 10b. You're entitled to interest on your award, starting from the time the defendant broke the contract. Put an "x" in this box. Also check Item 10b(1), "according to proof," *unless* your contract specified an interest rate that would apply if one party defaulted. In that case, put an "x" in Item 10b(2), next to "at the rate of" and type the interest rate. After "(date):" type the date the contract was broken. If you could reasonably argue that the contract was broken on any of several dates, choose the earliest one.

Skip the rest of the boxes in Item 10. They apply only if you use a lawyer.

Item 11. Skip this paragraph for now. You'll fill it out after you prepare your "cause of action" form or forms.

Date and signature. Type the date, then type your name above the line in the lower left-hand corner and sign above the line on the right.

The bottom line of the Complaint form says you can "affix a verification," but there is little to be gained by doing so. A verification is a form in which you swear under penalty of perjury that everything you say in these papers is true. You wouldn't normally put yourself in this position unless there was something to be gained by doing so—and in the past, a verified Complaint meant that the defendant had to verify the document filed in response, called the Answer. Plaintiffs might force the defendant into filing a verified Answer to scare the defendant or limit the response the defendant might make. Now, however, your verified Complaint may be met by an unverified Answer, so there's no reason to expose yourself to perjury charges.

Congratulations! You've finished your first form. Now you must complete and attach at least one "cause of action" form to finish the preparation of your Complaint.

Contract Cause of Action Attachments

As noted earlier, a cause of action is a statement of the legal theory you are using to ask the court for relief. Your Complaint must include at least one cause of action, but it can include more. For example, you may be suing for both breach of contract and breach of warranty. Use as many cause of action forms as apply to your case, even though they may ask for much of the same information.

CHAPTER 5 | PREPARING THE COMPLAINT | 97

> **SKIP AHEAD**
> Read only the sections below that pertain to your lawsuit.

Breach of Contract Cause of Action

Use this form, *Cause of Action—Breach of Contract*, Form PLD-C-001(1), in *every* contract action.

> **FORM**
> The appendix contains a tear-out version of Form PLD-C-001(1), *Cause of Action–Breach of Contract*, and you can download one from the Judicial Council website at www.courtinfo.ca.gov. A filled-out sample is shown below.

Short Title: Type exactly what you typed at the top of Page Two of the Complaint.

Case Number: Leave this blank.

_____ **CAUSE OF ACTION—Breach of Contract.** If this is the first cause of action, type "First" on the line above "number." If it's the second, type "Second," and so on.

Attachment to. Check "Complaint."

Item BC-1. If there is only one plaintiff, type the plaintiff's name here.

If there is more than one plaintiff, you need to determine whether the plaintiffs seek to receive a single sum of money as compensation or whether they are asking for separate relief. For example, if a repairperson does defective work on a house co-owned by two spouses, the spouses would seek to recover one amount to compensate for the expenses they incurred. On the other hand, if each plaintiff was supposed to receive something different under a particular contract and the defendant breaches the contract, each plaintiff has a separate Cause of Action.

If two or more plaintiffs are seeking to recover jointly, type both (or all) names after "Plaintiff (*name*)."

If the plaintiffs are seeking separate relief, type only one plaintiff's name here and complete a separate form for each plaintiff. For each additional form, add one to the number in the blank preceding "CAUSE OF ACTION" ("Second," "Third," etc.) and to the page number.

After "(*date*)," type the date the contract was made or entered into. This is normally the last date on which all parties signed a written contract or agreed to an oral one. If you're not sure of the exact date, state something like "on or about September 5, 2009."

Next, put an "x" in the box that describes the contract. If it was part oral and part written, put an "x" in both boxes. If the contract was neither oral nor written—that is, it was implied because of the past relationship between the parties or by the circumstances—check the "other" box and write the word "implied."

After "(*name parties to agreement*):" list the names of all people who were parties to the agreement, including businesses that were represented by agents. Include anyone who agreed—either in writing or orally—to be bound by its terms. If a defendant never orally or in writing agreed to its terms, but acted as if he or she agreed to them, put that person's name here also.

Next, you're asked to set forth the terms of the contract. If the entire agreement is written, type an "x" in the box next to "A copy of the agreement is attached…," mark a copy of the contract "Exhibit A," and attach it to this page. Keep the original contract in a safe place. You may need it later.

If your contract is part written and part oral, check the box that says a copy is attached, cross out the word "or," and add the parenthetical "(a portion is attached)." Mark a copy of the written part as "Exhibit A" and attach it to the page.

If the contract was entirely or partially oral, put an "x" next to "The essential terms of the agreement." Then, checking the appropriate box, either summarize the contract terms in the blank space or do so on a separate sheet that you designate as Attachment BC-1 and attach. Here are some examples of how terms of a contract might be summarized:

- "On or about September 30, 2008, plaintiff loaned defendant $11,000 at 4% annual interest compounded monthly. Defendant agreed to pay back half on November 4, 2009, and half on February 4, 2010."
- "Plaintiff paid defendant $17,500 in exchange for defendant's promise to deliver to plaintiff a vintage 1932 Ford Model A Roadster automobile in perfect order, except for the transmission, which had second gear missing."
- "Defendant agreed to perform competent legal services to plaintiff regarding plaintiff's proposed purchase of a restaurant business. Plaintiff agreed to pay $175 per hour for defendant's services and defendant agreed that after she had performed $5,000 worth of services, she would stop performing services and seek a further authorization."
- "Plaintiff agreed to purchase toys for resale from defendant at prices specified on an agreed-upon list. Defendant agreed to deliver the toys promptly upon receiving plaintiff's order and plaintiff agreed to pay defendant within 30 days of being billed. If, in plaintiff's opinion, the toys did not sell well with her customers, she had the right to notify defendant at any time. Defendant agreed that in such event, he would pick up the remaining toys and refund any money plaintiff had previously paid defendant for those remaining toys."
- "For over two years, plaintiff has ordered cosmetics from defendant by telephone. Defendant has delivered them to plaintiff's business without any C.O.D. or delivery charge, with payment due 30 days later. On September 5, 2009 plaintiff placed such an order with defendant, who said nothing about a change in payment or delivery terms."

(In a case in which the parties had a written rental contract for outdoor tents, but also agreed orally on terms allowing the contract to be canceled): "In addition to the writing, defendant Brown agreed orally that if it rained during the week of September 14, 2010 the entire transaction would be canceled and plaintiff's $15,000 would be returned within ten days."

Item BC-2. After "On or about (*dates*):" type the date the defendant broke the contract. Don't make the common mistake of using the date the contract was entered into. A contract is broken on the date that a party failed to do what he or she was supposed to do under the agreement. If you lent Jim money in January and he was to pay you back on April 18 and didn't, April 18 is the day the contract was broken. If he was to pay you back over six months—for example, in installments payable on April 18, May 18, June 18, July 18, August 18, and September 18—but never paid a cent, put in the first date it was broken (April 18) and add "and at various times thereafter."

Then, checking the appropriate box, summarize how the contract was broken—either in the blank space or on a separate sheet that you designate as Attachment BC-2 and attach this to your Cause of Action. Here are some examples of breach of contract descriptions:

- "Defendant failed and refused to pay plaintiff anything."
- "The second, third, and reverse gears in the automobile that defendant delivered to plaintiff did not work."
- "Defendant performed over 50 hours of work for plaintiff in a generally incompetent and unsatisfactory manner and failed to notify plaintiff when total services incurred had reached $5,000."
- "Plaintiff notified defendant that the line of toys was not selling well, and that she wanted defendant to remove them from her store and refund plaintiff the money she had paid defendant. Defendant failed and refused to remove the toys or refund the money."
- "Defendant instructed the delivery company that brought the cosmetics to plaintiff's place

	PLD-C-001(1)
SHORT TITLE: Garcia vs. Warren	CASE NUMBER:

First **CAUSE OF ACTION—Breach of Contract**
(number)

ATTACHMENT TO [X] Complaint   [ ] Cross - Complaint

(Use a separate cause of action form for each cause of action.)

BC-1. Plaintiff *(name):* James Garcia

alleges that on or about *(date):* January 8, 20xx
a [ ] written [X] oral [ ] other *(specify):*
agreement was made between *(name parties to agreement):* Jamie Garcia and Anne Warren

[ ] A copy of the agreement is attached as Exhibit A, or
[X] The essential terms of the agreement [X] are stated in Attachment BC-1 [ ] are as follows *(specify):*

Plaintiff delivered to defendant several hundred pounds of flour, baking soda, baking powder, shortening, and other wet and dry goods for use in baking pies. Defendant agreed to pay plaintiff $8,456.17 for said goods, one-quarter of said amount to be paid on January 15, February 15, March 15, and April 15.

BC-2. On or about *(dates):* January 15, 20xx and at various times thereafter
defendant breached the agreement by [ ] the acts specified in Attachment BC-2 [X] the following acts *(specify):* failing to pay anything to plaintiff

BC-3. Plaintiff has performed all obligations to defendant except those obligations plaintiff was prevented or excused from performing.

BC-4. Plaintiff suffered damages legally (proximately) caused by defendant's breach of the agreement
[ ] as stated in Attachment BC-4 [X] as follows *(specify):*

$8,456.17 and interest at 10% from each date for payment as alleged above.

BC-5. [ ] Plaintiff is entitled to attorney fees by an agreement or a statute
[ ] of $
[ ] according to proof.

BC-6. [ ] Other:

Page 3

Form Approved for Optional Use
Judicial Council of California
PLD-C-001(1) [Rev. January 1, 2007]

CAUSE OF ACTION—Breach of Contract

Code of Civil Procedure, § 425.12
www.courtinfo.ca.gov

of business not to deliver them until plaintiff paid its driver $10,413 for an unpaid account receivable plus the cost of the order and delivery charges. Because of an urgent need for the product, plaintiff was forced to pay this amount to the driver."

Item BC-3. This statement is there simply to remind you that you will eventually have to establish that you performed your part of the bargain.

Item BC-4. Specify exactly how you were damaged, using either the space provided or on a separate page that you designate as Attachment BC-4 and attach. Be sure to check the appropriate box. Here are some examples of how damages might be described:

- "$8,000 principal and interest at 4% from November 4, 2009 until paid in full."
- "The reasonable cost of the repair of second, third, and reverse gears in the amount of $6,250, plus loss of use of the vehicle for three months at a cost of $500 per month."
- "$10,789 for sums paid by plaintiff to defendant together with $500 per week for storage of the toys on plaintiff's shelves from October 1, 2007, when notice was given to defendant, until February 15, 2010, when the toys were picked up by defendant."
- "$2,018 for delivery charges and $4,212 for the loss of the use of the remaining funds during the normal maturity period."

Item BC-5. Skip this item. Attorney fees aren't relevant to the cases covered by this book.

Item BC-6. Skip this item.

Page. Add one to the number of the last page you completed and put that number here.

> **SKIP AHEAD**
> The *Breach of Contract Cause of Action* form is now complete. If you have no other contract claims, skip ahead to "Cleaning Up the Contract Complaint."

Breach of Warranty Causes of Action

The Breach of Contract Cause of Action form, discussed just above, will take care of most of the ordinary contract lawsuits you're likely to pursue. However, if you've bought or leased a product that has turned out to be defective, you might want to bring a breach of warranty suit as described in Chapter 4.

If the defective product in question cost $7,500 ($5,000 if you are suing on behalf of a business), you should file your case in Small Claims Court. But if the product was more expensive, such as an automobile, an air conditioning unit, or a sound system, a lawsuit in the limited jurisdiction division may be your best option for recovering your losses. (Note that a lawsuit over problems with a new car is covered by the state Lemon Law, Civil Code § 1793.22. Before you can sue, you must have complied with that law's specific provisions, discussed in Chapter 4.)

Review the discussion of breach of warranty in Chapter 4. Then become familiar with the law itself—the Song-Beverly Consumer Warranty Act in the Civil Code, beginning at Section 1790. You can find it in most law libraries or online at www.leginfo.ca.gov/calaw.html. Look particularly at Sections 1792 and 1793. Check the definition of "consumer goods" in Section 1791.

If your situation seems to fit within the Song-Beverly Consumer Warranty Act, it's a good idea to look a bit further in the code for additional provisions that may cover your case. The sections following 1793 deal with appliances, automobiles, mobile homes, service contracts, and other matters.

To sue for breach of warranty, use one of the cause of action forms that follow and attach it to your Complaint. The California Judicial Council, the body that created most of the court forms used in this book, has not prepared cause of action forms for breach of warranty—either warranty of merchantability or warranty of fitness. So we created some, and they should work just fine for a breach of warranty action, including a lawsuit brought under the Song-Beverly Consumer Warranty Act.

As discussed in Chapter 4, warranties can be either express or implied. An express warranty is a written document or pamphlet supplied by the manufacturer. An implied warranty isn't set out in writing; it's an unwritten guarantee that a product will do what it's supposed to. An implied warranty can be for "merchantability" or "fitness."

The first of these forms is for lawsuits claiming breach of implied warranty of merchantability. You can also use it if you're suing over breach of an express warranty. And it is possible to claim both breach of implied warranty and breach of express warranty in the same lawsuit.

Breach of Implied Warranty of Merchantability

The implied warranty of merchantability is the unwritten guarantee that your product is fit for the ordinary purposes for which it was designed (for example, that a lawn mower will cut grass) and conforms to the statements of fact on the container or label (for instance, that regular use of a drug will clear up your cold in two days).

FORM

The appendix contains a tear-out version of the form *Cause of Action—Breach of Implied Warranty (Merchantability)*. Note that this is not a Judicial Council form (you cannot download it from the Internet, so be sure to make extra copies before filling it out). A filled-out sample is shown below.

Short Title: Type exactly what you typed at the top of Page Two of the Complaint.

Case Number: Leave this blank.

_____ **CAUSE OF ACTION—Breach of Warranty (Merchantability).** If this is the first Cause of Action, type "First" in the blank. If it is the second, type "Second," and so on.

Page. Add one to the number of the last page you completed and put that number here.

Attachment to. Put an "x" next to "Complaint."

Item BWM-1. Enter the following information here:
- the name of a plaintiff (you must use a different form for each plaintiff who is requesting separate relief)
- the date you bought the goods
- the name of the defendant who sold you the goods
- a description of the goods, and
- the retail price you paid.

If you have a sales receipt or invoice, put an "x" in the box next to "A true copy of a memorandum …." Make a copy of the receipt or invoice, designate it as "Exhibit BWM-1," and attach the copy to the form.

Item BWM-2. If you believe the manufacturer may have caused the defect, type an "x" in this box. Skip the date request. Then type the name of the manufacturer. If you don't know who that is, use a Doe defendant ("Doe defendants" are covered in Chapter 4). If this is your first Doe defendant, type "Doe 1." Otherwise, add one to the number of the last Doe you used.

Item BWM-3. If you believe the distributor may have caused the defect or may have known about it, type an "x" in this box. Unless you know the date, skip the date request. If, for some reason, you know the name of the distributor, type it here. More than likely, you'll need to use another Doe defendant.

Item BWM-4. If you received a written warranty with the product, put an "x" in the box and fill in the manufacturer's name. Then make a copy of the warranty, designate the copy as "Exhibit BWM-4," and attach it to the form.

Item BWM-5. Type the names of the defendants listed in Items BWM-1 (seller), BWM-2 (manufacturer), and BWM-3 (distributor), including Doe defendants. Now go on to page two.

Short Title: Type exactly what you typed on the first page.

Case Number: Leave this blank.

Page. Add one to the number of the previous page.

SHORT TITLE: Goodman v. Hough	CASE NUMBER:

_____First_____ **CAUSE OF ACTION**—Breach of Warranty (Merchantability)   Page __3__
(number)

ATTACHMENT TO   [X] Complaint   [ ] Cross-Complaint

BWM-1.   Plaintiff *(name)*: Jane Goodman

     alleges that on or about *(date)*: August 12, 20xx
     defendant(s) *(seller)*: Ian Hough, dba Beds and Brass

     sold plaintiff *(quantity and description of goods)*: two double beds with brass headboards, four dressers, two mirrors, two chairs, and a rug
     at retail and plaintiff brought such goods from defendant(s) for a price of *(amount)*: $ 9,300 .
     [X] A true copy of a memorandum or contract regarding this sale is attached to this Cause of Action as Exhibit BWM-1.

BWM-2.   [X] On or about *(date)*:
     defendant(s) *(manufacturer)*: Better Bedroom Builders

     manufactured such goods for the purpose of their eventual sale to retail buyers.

BWM-3.   [X] On or about *(date)*:
     defendant(s) *(distributor)*: Does 1-3

     acquired such goods from defendant(s) manufacturer and distributed them to defendant(s) seller for eventual retail sale to consumers.

BWM-4.   [X] In the process, defendants *(name)*: Ian Hough

     appended to such goods a written warranty which is attached to this Cause of Action as Exhibit BWM-4.

BWM-5.   Such retail sale to plaintiff was accompanied separately and individually by the implied warranty that such goods were merchantable by defendant(s) *(name)*: Ian Hough, Better Bedroom Builders, & Does 1-3

SHORT TITLE: Goodman v. Hough	CASE NUMBER:

CAUSE OF ACTION—Breach of Warranty (Merchantability)   Page __4__

BWM-6. Defendant(s) breached their respective warranties implied in the sale in that (*describe*): The beds have fallen apart, dresser doors stick closed, mirrors are distorted, and the chairs and rug are moldy and smell bad

As a result of the breach by defendant(s), plaintiff did not receive merchantable goods as impliedly warranted by defendant(s).

BWM-7. Plaintiff discovered such breach of warranty on or about (date): September 15, 20xx

   a. ☐ On or about (date):

     plaintiff notified defendant(s) (*name*):

     ☒ By letter, a true copy of which is attached to this Cause of Action as Exhibit BWM-7.

     ☒ Other (*describe*): by telephone September 15, 20xx

BWM-8. As a legal result of such breach of the warranty of merchantability by defendant(s), plaintiff has been damaged in the amount $ 9,300 .

Item BWM-6. Describe the defect in the goods. Examples of defect descriptions are:
- "The transmission will not shift into second, third, or reverse gears."
- "The printer continually jams, unable to produce any legible pages."

Item BWM-7. In the first line, fill in the date you discovered the defect. Next, if you notified any of the defendants about the defect, put an "x" in box "a." Type the date(s) of the notification(s), list the names of the defendants you notified (such as the seller and the manufacturer), and check the box describing your means of notification. If it was by letter, attach a copy designated as "Exhibit BWM-7." If it was by phone or in person, check "other" and state the method.

Item BWM-8. Here you indicate the amount of your damages. In most cases, the damages begin with the purchase price of the defective goods. If you've tried to have repairs done but the goods could not be repaired satisfactorily, add to your purchase price the cost you incurred in trying to have the goods repaired. You can also add the value of your time (at about $10 per hour) in trying to get repairs made.

Breach of Express Warranty

If you received an express warranty—a guarantee in writing from the manufacturer—and the product didn't do what was promised, you can use the same cause of action form, Breach of Warranty (Merchantability). Many product warranties are cleverly written so that it's difficult for consumers to argue they've been breached. But if a product comes with a claim that it will never need maintenance or will reduce your electric bill, and that proves untrue, you have a valid breach of *express* warranty case.

The instructions immediately above will apply if you are suing for breach of express warranty. When you fill out Item BWM-4, it's essential to attach a copy of whatever warranty or written promise you claim the defendant has breached.

Breach of Implied Warranty of Fitness

The implied warranty of fitness applies when you tell a seller or manufacturer that you intend to use an item for a particular purpose and the seller or manufacturer recommends a particular model or product. (For a full explanation, see Chapter 4.) For example, suppose you told a dealer you needed an outboard motor to power a specific boat. If the motor he sold you turned out to be underpowered, you could claim he breached the implied warranty of fitness for that purpose.

FORM

The appendix contains a tear-out version of the form *Cause of Action—Breach of Implied Warranty (Fitness)*. Note that this is not a Judicial Council form (you cannot download it from the Internet, so be sure to make extra copies before filling it out). A filled-out sample is shown below.

Short Title: Type exactly what you typed at the top of Page Two of the Complaint.

Case Number: Leave this blank.

_____ CAUSE OF ACTION—Breach of Warranty (Fitness). If this is the first Cause of Action, type "First" in the blank. If it is the second, type "Second," and so on.

Page. Add one to the number of the last page you completed and put that number here.

Attachment to. Put an "x" next to "Complaint."

BWF-1. Enter the following information here:
- the name of a plaintiff (you must use a different form for each plaintiff who is requesting separate relief)
- the date you discussed your special requirements for the product in question with a dealer or manufacturer
- a description of the product
- a description of your special requirements, and
- the name(s) of the defendant(s) to whom you described your requirements. Be sure to

SHORT TITLE: Moran v. Sagarmatha Dream Co.	CASE NUMBER:

___First___ CAUSE OF ACTION—Breach of Warranty (Fitness)   Page __3__
(number)

ATTACHMENT TO   ☒ Complaint   ☐ Cross-Complaint

BWF-1. Plaintiff (name): Mae Moran

alleges that on or about (date): February 2, 20xx
plaintiff required (quantity and description of goods):

8,000 meters of new static 9 mm rope

for the particular purpose of (describe):

climbing the south face of Cho Oyo and the south face of Gyanchung Kang, two mountains in Nepal

To select and furnish suitable goods for such purpose, plaintiff relied on the skill and judgment of defendant(s) (name):

Sagarmatha Dream Co., Obadiah Walters and Does 1-4

BWF-2. ☒ On or about (date): February 1, 19xx
defendant(s) sold to plaintiff (quantity and description of goods):

8,000 meters of static 9 mm rope

and plaintiff bought such goods from defendant(s), in such reliance, for amount of (price paid): $ __8,000__

☒ A true copy of the memorandum or contract of the sale is attached to this Cause of Action as Exhibit BWF-2.

BWF-3. At the time of the retail sale of such goods, defendant(s) had reason to know the particular purpose for which the goods were required because plaintiff expressly communicated such purposes to defendant(s). Defendant(s) further knew plaintiff was relying on the skill and judgment of defendant(s) to select and furnish suitable goods; thus there was an implied warranty that goods were fit for such purpose.

SHORT TITLE: Moran v. Sagarmatha Dream Co.	CASE NUMBER:

CAUSE OF ACTION—Breach of Warranty (Fitness)   Page __4__

BWF-4. Defendant(s) breached such warranty in that plaintiff did not receive suitable goods and such goods were not fit for the particular purpose for which they were required in that (*describe failure*):
The ropes were needed to climb two steep, technical mountain sides. The ropes were used, and had cuts and weak spots. Some ropes were melted together. Many of the ropes broke when we tried to use them.

BWF-5. Plaintiff discovered such breach of warranty on or about (date): March 15, 20xx
    a. [X] On or about (date): March 20, 20xx
       plaintiff notified defendant(s) (*name*):

       [ ] By letter, a true copy of which is attached to this Cause of Action as Exhibit BWF-7.
       [X] Other (*describe*): by telephone

BWF-6. As a result of such breach of the warranty of fitness by defendant(s), plaintiff has been damaged in the amount $ 8,500 .

include Doe defendants if you don't yet have the identities.

BWF-2. Enter the following information here:
- the date you bought the product
- a description of the product, and
- the price you paid.

If you have a sales receipt or invoice, put an "x" in the box next to "A true copy of a memorandum…." Make a copy of the receipt or invoice, designate it as "Exhibit BWF-2," and attach the copy to the form.

BWF-3. You don't have to enter anything here. It's just a statement of the circumstances that create an implied warranty of fitness. Now go on to page two.

Short Title: Type exactly what you typed on the first page.

Case Number: Leave this blank.

Page. Add one to the number of the previous page.

BWF-4. Describe the defect in the product. Here's an example of such a description: "The tires on the dune buggy, which I needed for off-road and mountainous riding, punctured when I rode over stone and rocks."

BWF-5. In the first line, fill in the date you discovered the defect. Next, if you notified any of the defendants about the defect, put an "x" in box "a." Type the date(s) of the notification(s), list the names of the defendants you notified (such as the seller), and check the box describing your means of notification. If it was by letter, attach a copy designated as "Exhibit BWF-5." If it was by phone or in person, check "other" and state the method.

BWF-6. Here you indicate the amount of your damages. In most cases, the damages begin with the purchase price of the defective goods. If you've tried to have repairs done but the goods could not be repaired satisfactorily, add to your purchase price the expense of trying to have the goods repaired. You can also add the value of your time (at about $10 per hour) in trying to get repairs made.

Cleaning Up the Contract Complaint

Now is the time to fill in the paragraphs you've skipped in the "Complaint—Contract" form—the first document you prepared.

Defendant: Does 1 to ____. Count your Doe defendants—they should be numbered consecutively throughout all the causes of action you filled out. Enter the total in the appropriate blank.

Item 2 (total number of pages): Count your total number of pages—don't forget any attachment sheets—and insert the total.

Item 8 (causes of action attached): Put an "x" next to any Breach of Contract or any others that are applicable. (The "Common counts" box refers to a form that I don't recommend you use.) If you completed any breach of warranty causes of action, put an "x" next to "Other" and specify which ones.

Item 9. Leave this blank.

Item 11 (matters you are alleging on information and belief): Here you have to play lawyer for a moment. Read over the factual statements in the Complaint and causes of action. If any statement is true, but you can't verify it based on your own knowledge—that is, you relied on something someone else told you—lawyers and judges call that a statement made "on information and belief." For example, in a breach of contract case, a common information and belief statement is the identification of a defendant as the employee or agent of someone else.

If any statements in the Complaint or causes of action fit this category, put an "x" in this box and type the paragraph number, such as BC-2. If there is more than one cause of action of the same kind (such as two breach of contract causes of action), be sure to note the paragraph number and the number of the cause of action. Do your best at this, but do not spend a lot of time worrying about it. If you fail to include something in this item, the worst that can happen is that a lawyer for the defense may attempt to embarrass you with a picky objection. It would be very unusual for a judge to be concerned, however.

Review all your page numbers and Cause of Action headings. Be sure that the pages are numbered sequentially and that any "Does" you use are appropriately numbered.

Complaints for Other Types of Lawsuits

If you're going to sue without a lawyer in Superior Court, even in the limited jurisdiction division, your chances of success are best if you're bringing one of the standard types of tort or breach of contract actions discussed above. If you want to file a lawsuit based on grounds or causes of action other than these standard ones, you'll still find this book helpful, but you are going to have to do some legal research. Here are the steps I recommend you take.

RESOURCE

If you are not experienced in doing legal research, a good place to start is *Legal Research: How to Find & Understand the Law*, by Stephen R. Elias and Susan Levinkind (Nolo).

Find a Law Library

The state Constitution requires each California county to have a law library that is open to the public without charge. Unfortunately, some smaller counties comply with the law by providing only what they call "electronic access." In these counties, you'll have to go to a computer in the courthouse or perhaps in the public library, which is hooked up to a legal research service such as LexisNexis or Westlaw. You cannot access these services from your own computer.

To find out whether your county has a physical law library, go to the Judicial Council website at www.courtinfo.ca.gov. Click on the Self-Help icon in the upper left corner and then on the Ask the Law Librarian icon in the upper left corner. This will take you to a site where you may be able to do limited research, but more importantly, it also lists under the heading "Directory of California's public law libraries" what facilities, if any, each county has and where they are located. A clue as to how helpful they will be is in the line listing the number of volumes in the library. If it is only a few thousand, you probably should save your research issues and journey to a larger library in a nearby county. Larger libraries are staffed with librarians who will help you find books and materials. If you have a law school nearby, check to see if they permit public access to their library.

Research the Subject Area

Your law library will contain a multivolume set of loose-leaf books called *California Forms of Pleading and Practice* (published by Matthew Bender). These books contain a summary of California law on any area in which you might want to bring a lawsuit. They refer you to other sources that discuss the area and, perhaps most importantly, they provide numerous forms that you can adapt.

These books are written for lawyers and contain a fair amount of legalese. But if you are determined to sue on a subject not covered by the forms discussed earlier in this chapter, this is your best place to get help. Ask the librarian for help if the books' indexes, which are full of legal jargon, leave you stymied.

CAUTION

Get help if you're determined to bring a professional malpractice suit on your own. Even with the help of the forms in *California Forms of Pleading and Practice*, you'll need to consult with a lawyer willing to serve as your legal coach. You'll certainly need an expert witness, whose fees will likely be very high. The cost of bringing a professional malpractice suit (especially against a doctor) may eclipse any award you receive in a limited jurisdiction case.

Choose the Right Form

When you find the right subject area, look at the forms and choose the one that seems to come closest to your situation. In some cases, you can plug language from the book into one of the forms printed here.

Once you've become somewhat familiar with the pleading and practice books, you may end up using clauses from more than one form and creating your own. The books contain forms for many different areas but they do not cover all situations.

You'll see that the forms in the pleading and practice volumes are not like the ones in this book, which have many boxes that simply need to be checked off. Instead, they contain paragraphs of text you'll have to copy and retype. Don't let that scare you. It may take some time, but it isn't terribly complicated.

Most libraries won't let you check out the pleading and practice books, since they are used by many lawyers who don't want to spend thousands of dollars to buy a whole set for themselves. Bring lots of change and be ready to photocopy forms and instructions.

Local Rules

The Superior Court in every county has a set of local rules. These rules cover many minor and some major issues that the statewide rules don't concern themselves with, and sometimes the local rules vary or add to the statewide procedures. When you use the official forms we've provided in this book for most tort and breach of contract cases, you're not likely to run into any conflicts with local rules. However, if you're pursuing a different type of lawsuit, review the local rules to learn whether your county requires additional special forms or procedures.

It used to be difficult to find a copy of the local rules and often they were not kept up to date. Since all the courts have websites now, it is much easier to find them and the rules are kept current.

Prepare the Complaint

After you've gathered your sample forms and directions, you'll have to create your own Complaint, type it up and give it to the court clerk for filing. You need to pay careful attention to the requirements. But if you have some typing experience, you should be able to handle it on your own. If you'd prefer to have it done professionally, see "Using a Professional Typing Service" at the beginning of this chapter.

Use pleading paper—the paper with numbers down the left side. Looking at the sample motions in Chapter 10 will give you an idea of how this part of the Complaint should appear.

At line 1, in the left corner, type your name, address, and phone number single-spaced on three lines. Skip a line and then type "In Pro Per," which means you are representing yourself. For each additional plaintiff, repeat this information.

Then skip down to line 8. (If you have more than one plaintiff, you might be below line 8—that's fine.) On the center of the page on two lines, type the name of the court and the county, in all capital letters. You don't need to include the branch of the court or its address.

Move down to line 11 (or just below the court name, if you're already beyond line 11). Here you name the plaintiffs and the defendants. Everything must be kept on the left half of the page. In all capital letters, type the names of the plaintiffs. Then add the word "Plaintiff" or "Plaintiffs" just below and slightly indented. Skip a couple of lines and type "vs." (the abbreviation for the word "versus") at the left. Skip another couple of lines and, in all capital letters, type the names of the defendants, plus any "Does" you are suing. Then add the word "Defendant" or "Defendants," as you did with the plaintiffs. Finally, type a line out to the middle of the page.

To the right of the plaintiff's name, type "Case No." Leave it blank for now because you won't get that number until you file your Complaint with the court. On subsequent papers, however, be sure to include it.

In all capitals, immediately under "Case No.," describe the paper you're filing ("COMPLAINT"). Some local rules require you to say something further, such as "For Discrimination" or "For Nuisance." On a Complaint, you must also state the nature of the case. Great precision is not necessary. If you are suing on a civil rights violation, type "COMPLAINT—VIOLATION OF CIVIL RIGHTS."

Just below this, type in the words "Limited Jurisdiction" and below that "Amount exceeds $10,000" or "Amount does not exceed $10,000" (see California Rule of Court 2.111).

Now follow the form(s) you've copied from the law library books. Number your paragraphs and follow the instructions in the form book itself. When you get to the end, type your "prayer" (where you ask for money) and sign and date the form.

At the bottom of each page, add what the rules call a "footer," a brief description of what the document is, such as "Complaint." Center the information and include a page number (such as, "Page 3 of 5"), and separate the footer from the rest of the page by a horizontal line above it running the width of the page. (California Rule of Court 2.110 requires this.) The printed forms in this book include proper footers, but if you are preparing a form from scratch, review the rule and create your own footer.

Preparing the Summons and Cover Sheet

Every Complaint must have a Summons and Cover Sheet. The Summons is a document that you partially fill out and the court officially stamps. Once stamped, you must have it served on the defendants, notifying them that they are being sued and have 30 days to respond to contest the case. The courts use the Cover Sheets to gather statistics on the types of cases being filed in California.

FORM
The appendix contains tear-out versions of the *Summons, Form SUM-100*, and the *Civil Case Cover Sheet*, Form CM-010. You can download both from the Judicial Council website at www.courtinfo.ca.gov. If you are filing in Los Angeles County, be sure to use the cover sheet specifically for that county, discussed later (and also found in the appendix).

The Summons

Follow these directions to complete the Summons. First, under "Notice to Defendant:" type the names of all of the defendants exactly as you typed them on the Complaint. Under "You are Being Sued by Plaintiff:" type the names of all of the plaintiffs exactly as you typed them on the Complaint.

Below the box with bold-faced type, insert the name and address of the court. Use the full name and address, including any branch. Under the address, put your name, address, and phone number just as they appeared on the top of the Complaint form. Leave the Notice to the Person Served blank. In the NOTICE TO THE PERSON SERVED, check the applicable box (usually the first one) and enter the date of service at paragraph 4.

The Civil Case Cover Sheet

This Cover Sheet will have no bearing on the outcome of your case, but you must prepare and file one to get started. You do not serve a copy on the defendant. You really don't even need to keep a copy for your records.

All Cases

To fill out the Cover Sheet, go back to "The Caption" section at the beginning of this chapter for instructions on how to fill out the three boxes in the upper-left corner and the case number box. In the "Case Name" box, just enter the names of the first plaintiff and the first defendant: "William Freeman v. Henry Deadou." In the next box, check the "Limited" box. Do not put anything in the box to the right. The clerk will fill in the "Case Number" box, and, since you don't know who your judge will be yet, leave the box below blank. Now go down to the large box 1 and choose what seems to be the best description of your case. If your case arises from an automobile accident, check the "Auto" box under the "Auto Tort" heading. If concerns a broken contract, check the "Breach of contract/warranty" box under the "Contract" heading.

Don't lose any sleep over choosing the correct box—just do what seems to make sense. In item 2, check the "is not" box. In item 3, check "monetary" and add "punitive" only if you filled out the Exemplary Damages Attachment. Count up your causes of action and put that in item 4. Check "is not" in item 5. Finally, sign the form, date it, and print your name.

A few counties (including Kern, Los Angeles, Riverside, San Bernardino, Santa Clara, and Ventura) use additional Cover Sheets. They may be labeled "Certificate of Counsel," "Case Information Sheet," "Statement of Location," "Declaration for Court Assignment," or something similar. The courts' websites sometimes provide these forms, and you can always get them from the court clerk's office. If you haven't obtained one earlier, you'll find that these forms are fairly simple and you can fill them out quickly at the clerk's counter when you file your case.

The questions on these local forms elicit information that will enable the judge to determine whether you have filed in the correct branch of the county court. If you encounter a local form like this, you shouldn't have any difficulty answering the questions and justifying your choice of the branch you have picked.

Los Angeles Cases

If you're filing in Los Angeles, use their form (*Civil Case Cover Sheet Addendum* and *Statement of Location*) in addition to the Judicial Council form described above. Fill out the top of the form as you have done with all of the earlier forms. Just below the second box, circle the third "YES" after the words "LIMITED CASE." On the line asking for your estimate of time for trial, put in "less than one-half day" in most cases or, if you believe it is very likely to take longer, put in your estimate. (It's hard to predict the time you'll need for trial at this point because you don't know what action the defendant will take, so don't spend time worrying about this item.)

CAUTION
Other counties use this cover sheet too. Find out if yours is one of them by checking the website or calling the clerk. If you are required to use this form, you can download it and fill it out before filing your Complaint. But even if you don't learn it's required until you arrive at the courthouse to file your case, the form is fairly simple, and you should be able to fill it out in the clerk's office—just make sure you have a black or blue/black pen.

The instructions for limited jurisdiction cases direct you to skip to page 4. On page 4, fill in the boxes at the top of the page and then add the address you are using to justify the courthouse you have chosen (address of an accident, residence or place of business of the defendant, and so on.) To figure out which number to circle in the remaining box, go back to the first page and the ten alternatives printed in the box "Applicable Reasons for Choosing Courthouse Location." Pick out one of these reasons and circle its corresponding number on page 4. In Item IV, put in the name of the courthouse you have chosen. The districts are Central, North Central, Northeast, North Valley, North, Northwest, South, South Central,

Southeast, Southwest, and West. Pick the one that fits your courthouse and then date and sign the form at the bottom. Keep two copies of this form and the Civil Case Cover Sheet because Los Angeles requires they be served on the defendant with the Summons, Complaint, and Case Questionnaire.

> **FORM**
> The appendix contains a tear-out version of the *Civil Case Cover Sheet* and Statement of Location for Los Angeles County. You can download this form from the Los Angeles County Superior Court website at www.lasuperiorcourt.org. Choose the forms link in the Civil section.

Preparing a Case Questionnaire

To initiate a lawsuit in a limited jurisdiction case, you need only prepare and file a Summons, a Civil Case Cover Sheet, and a Complaint. But I recommend that you prepare another form: the Case Questionnaire–For Limited Civil Cases. It's a four-page form that the plaintiff fills in and delivers to the defendant along with a blank copy of the form. The defendant must fill out the blank form and return it to you when filing the defendant's answer to the Complaint. The Questionnaire is designed to get all the facts of the case out in the open as quickly as possible so as to encourage settlement before trial. If you don't use it at this point, you lose the right to do so (though you can of course settle the case at any time).

You don't file the Case Questionnaire with the court. Instead, you deliver it ("serve" in legalese) to the defendant with the Summons and Complaint after you file your case. Thus, you should prepare it now.

Only plaintiffs can initiate the Case Questionnaire exchange. If you are a defendant, be prepared to receive your opponent's Questionnaire, along with a blank form for you to fill out. Both plaintiffs and defendants should do a draft of their answers before doing the final. Get together with your Sounding Board as I suggested in Chapters 1 and 2 and discuss your answers. Ask if your answers are easily understood and sound like the unvarnished truth. If your advisor thinks something sounds exaggerated or unnecessarily hostile, make some changes. And remember—when you sign the form, you'll do so under penalty of perjury.

> **FORM**
> The appendix contains a tear-out version of Form DISC-010, *Case Questionnaire–For Limited Civil Cases*, and you can download one from the Judicial Council website at www.courtinfo.ca.gov.

At the top of the page, in the first blank after the words "COUNTY OF," insert the name of the county you are suing in. Leave the case number blank for now; you'll get it when you file your Summons and Complaint (this number must go on all four pages).

After PLAINTIFF, type the name of the first plaintiff and, if there is more than one plaintiff, the words "et al." (this must go on all four pages). For the DEFENDANT, type the name of the first defendant and, if there is more than one, the words "et al." (this must go on all four pages). The "Requesting Party" is you. The "Responding Party" is the defendant. Enter those names. If there's more than one defendant, do a separate Case Questionnaire for each.

Once you fill in the top, read the instructions. They explain most of what you need to know to complete the form. In general, you should give the most positive and optimistic view of your case that you can truthfully state. Don't worry about legal language or sounding like a lawyer. Just factually tell your story without exaggeration or insults. Your job is to convince the other side that when you tell the court what happened, you will win.

Most of the questions are self-explanatory. Here are instructions for those few that are not self-explanatory:

Item 1c. Use descriptive, not argumentative language, to explain what happened, for example:

"At approximately 8:15 p.m. August 15, 20xx, plaintiff was driving her 2000 Pontiac car east on Market Street in Lynwood just west of Ninth Street, at approximately 30 mph. The traffic light in her direction was green. As she entered the intersection of Ninth Street, defendant, who was driving north on Ninth Street at approximately 40 to 50 mph, also entered the intersection. The traffic signal in his direction was red. Defendant depressed his brakes as he entered the intersection, creating four skid marks of approximately 35 feet. Then the front right of his car struck plaintiff's car to the right of the rear passenger side door. The force of the collision caused both cars to spin through the intersection and come to rest against buildings in the area."

"On December 13, 20xx, defendant promised plaintiff that for the sum of $10,000, he would place a permanent plaque on the floor of plaintiff's restaurant commemorating an important event in plaintiff's life. On January 6, 20xx, plaintiff paid defendant the $10,000 and accepted defendant's offer. Defendant has since failed and refused to place the plaque."

Item 1d. List every witness you might use. Include eyewitnesses, doctors, police officers, tow truck drivers, repairpeople, the payroll person from your job, and the like.

Item 1e. Be sure to include contracts, letters, photographs, and the like.

Item 1f. Keep in mind that physical evidence is any object (such as a damaged car) or mark (such as a skid mark or mark on the side of a building) or drawing that is relevant.

Item 2. Answer these questions only if you are bringing a tort case.

Items 2c–g. Use the calculations you came up with in "How Much Should You Sue For?" in Chapter 2.

Item 3. Answer these questions only if you are bringing a contract case.

Verification and signature. Type your name above the left line and sign above the solid line on the right. Because this form is "verified," you are swearing that what you have said is true. If you've exaggerated—or lied—you could be embarrassed and possibly discredited if you have to explain yourself to a judge or jury.

Requesting a Waiver of the Filing Fee

When you file your Complaint, you will have to pay a filing fee, somewhere in the area of $205–$330. There's a second fee for each additional plaintiff. But if you have a very low income, you do not have to pay court fees and costs if you obtain court approval. People currently receiving TANF, Food Stamps, County Relief, General Relief, General Assistance, SSI, or SSP qualify for a fee waiver. You will also qualify if your family gross income (the monthly amount you get before any deductions are taken) is less than the amount shown in "Information Sheet on Waiver of Court Fees and Costs," reproduced below. If you do not qualify under this schedule, it's still possible to receive a waiver by explaining why you cannot pay the fees.

To obtain a fee waiver, you'll need to complete an application where you give information about your financial situation, offer supporting documents, and request that fees be waived (Form FW-001).

FORM

The appendix cont... Form FW-001, *Request t...* can download one from www.courtinfo.ca.gov. Th FW-001-INFO, which gives fee waivers. Other forms n... are referred to in some of th

FW-001	Request to Waive Court Fees		CONFIDENTIAL

Clerk stamps date here when form is filed.

If you are getting public benefits, are a low-income person, or do not have enough income to pay for household's basic needs and your court fees, you may use this form to ask the court to waive all or part of your court fees. The court may order you to answer questions about your finances. If the court waives the fees, you may still have to pay later if:
- You cannot give the court proof of your eligibility,
- Your financial situation improves during this case, or
- You settle your civil case for **$10,000** or more. The trial court that waives your fees will have a lien on any such settlement in the amount of the waived fees and costs. The court may also charge you any collection costs.

Fill in court name and street address:

① **Your Information** *(person asking the court to waive the fees):*
Name: _____

Street or mailing address: _____

Fill in case number and name:

City: _____ State: _____ Zip: _____

Case Number:

Phone number: _____

② **Your Job,** if you have one *(job title):* _____

Case Name:

Name of employer: _____

Employer's address: _____

③ **Your lawyer,** if you have one *(name, firm or affiliation, address, phone number, and State Bar number):*
_____
_____

a. The lawyer has agreed to advance all or a portion of your fees or costs *(check one):* Yes ☐ No ☐
b. *(If yes, your lawyer must sign here)* Lawyer's signature: _____

If your lawyer is not providing legal-aid type services based on your low income, you may have to go to a hearing to explain why you are asking the court to waive the fees.

④ **What court's fees or costs are you asking to be waived?**
☐ Superior Court (See *Information Sheet on Waiver of Superior Court Fees and Costs* (form FW-001-INFO).)
☐ Supreme Court, Court of Appeal, or Appellate Division of Superior Court (See *Information Sheet on Waiver of Appellate Court Fees and Costs* (form APP-015/FW-015-INFO).)

⑤ **Why are you asking the court to waive your court fees?**
a. ☐ I receive *(check all that apply):* ☐ Medi-Cal ☐ Food Stamps ☐ SSI ☐ SSP ☐ County Relief/General Assistance ☐ IHSS (In-Home Supportive Services) ☐ CalWORKS or Tribal TANF (Tribal Temporary Assistance for Needy Families) ☐ CAPI (Cash Assistance Program for Aged, Blind and Disabled)
b. ☐ My gross monthly household income (before deductions for taxes) is less than the amount listed below. *(If you check 5b you must fill out 7, 8 and 9 on page 2 of this form.)*

Family Size	Family Income	Family Size	Family Income	Family Size	Family Income	
1	$1,128.13	3	$1,907.30	5	$2,686.46	*If more than 6 people at home, add $389.59 for each extra person.*
2	$1,517.71	4	$2,296.88	6	$3,076.05	

c. ☐ I do not have enough income to pay for my household's basic needs *and* the court fees. I ask the court to *(check one):* ☐ waive all court fees ☐ waive some of the court fees ☐ let me make payments over time *(Explain):* _____ *(If you check 5c, you must fill out page 2.)*

⑥ ☐ Check here if you asked the court to waive your court fees for this case in the last six months. *(If your previous request is reasonably available, please attach it to this form and check here:* ☐ *)*

I declare under penalty of perjury under the laws of the State of California that the information I have provided on this form and all attachments is true and correct.

Date: _____

▶

Print your name here _____ *Sign here* _____

Judicial Council of California, www.courtinfo.ca.gov
Rev. July 1, 2009, Mandatory Form
Gov. Code, § 68633
Cal. Rules of Court, rules 3.51, 8.26, and 8.818

Request to Waive Court Fees

FW-001, Page 1 of 2

Your name: _____

Case Number: _____

*If you checked 5a on page 1, do not fill out below. If you checked 5b, fill out questions 7, 8, and 9 only. If you checked 5c, you **must** fill out this entire page. If you need more space, attach form MC-025 or attach a sheet of paper and write Financial Information and your name and case number at the top.*

⑦ ☐ Check here if your income changes a lot from month to month. Fill out below based on your average income for the past 12 months.

⑧ **Your Monthly Income**
  a. Gross monthly income (before deductions): $ _____
     List each payroll deduction and amount below:
     (1) _____ $ _____
     (2) _____ $ _____
     (3) _____ $ _____
     (4) _____ $ _____
  b. Total deductions (add 8a (1)-(4) above): $ _____
  c. Total monthly take-home pay (8a minus 8b): $ _____
  d. List the source and amount of *any* other income you get each month, including: spousal/child support, retirement, social security, disability, unemployment, military basic allowance for quarters (BAQ), veterans payments, dividends, interest, trust income, annuities, net business or rental income, reimbursement for job-related expenses, gambling or lottery winnings, etc.
     (1) _____ $ _____
     (2) _____ $ _____
     (3) _____ $ _____
     (4) _____ $ _____
  e. Your total monthly income is (8c plus 8d): $ _____

⑨ **Household Income**
  a. List all other persons living in your home and their income; include only your spouse and all individuals who depend in whole or in part on you for support, or on whom you depend in whole or in part for support.

Name	Age	Relationship	Gross Monthly Income
(1) _____	___	_____	$ _____
(2) _____	___	_____	$ _____
(3) _____	___	_____	$ _____
(4) _____	___	_____	$ _____

  b. **Total monthly income of persons above:** $ _____

Total monthly income *and* household income (8e plus 9b): $ _____

To list any other facts you want the court to know, such as unusual medical expenses, family emergencies, etc., attach form MC-025. Or attach a sheet of paper, and write Financial Information and your name and case number at the top. Check here if you attach another page. ☐

Important! **If your financial situation or ability to pay court fees improves, you must notify the court within five days on form FW-010.**

⑩ **Your Money and Property**
  a. Cash -------------------------------- $ _____
  b. All financial accounts (List bank name and amount):
     (1) _____ $ _____
     (2) _____ $ _____
     (3) _____ $ _____
     (4) _____ $ _____

  c. Cars, boats, and other vehicles

Make / Year	Fair Market Value	How Much You Still Owe
(1) _____	$ _____	$ _____
(2) _____	$ _____	$ _____
(3) _____	$ _____	$ _____

  d. Real estate

Address	Fair Market Value	How Much You Still Owe
(1) _____	$ _____	$ _____
(2) _____	$ _____	$ _____
(3) _____	$ _____	$ _____

  e. Other personal property (jewelry, furniture, furs, stocks, bonds, etc.):

Describe	Fair Market Value	How Much You Still Owe
(1) _____	$ _____	$ _____
(2) _____	$ _____	$ _____
(3) _____	$ _____	$ _____

⑪ **Your Monthly Expenses**
(Do not include payroll deductions you already listed in 8b.)
  a. Rent or house payment & maintenance $ _____
  b. Food and household supplies $ _____
  c. Utilities and telephone $ _____
  d. Clothing $ _____
  e. Laundry and cleaning $ _____
  f. Medical and dental expenses $ _____
  g. Insurance (life, health, accident, etc.) $ _____
  h. School, child care $ _____
  i. Child, spousal support (another marriage) $ _____
  j. Transportation, gas, auto repair and insurance $ _____
  k. Installment payments (list each below):
     Paid to:
     (1) _____ $ _____
     (2) _____ $ _____
     (3) _____ $ _____
  l. Wages/earnings withheld by court order $ _____
  m. Any other monthly expenses (list each below). $ _____
     Paid to: How Much?
     (1) _____ $ _____
     (2) _____ $ _____
     (3) _____ $ _____

Total monthly expenses (add 11a –11m above): $ _____

Request to Waive Court Fees

FW-001-INFO

INFORMATION SHEET ON WAIVER OF SUPERIOR COURT FEES AND COSTS

If you have been sued or if you wish to sue someone, or if you are filing or have received a family law petition, and if you cannot afford to pay court fees and costs, you may not have to pay them in order to go to court. If you are getting public benefits, are a low-income person, or do not have enough income to pay for your household's basic needs *and* your court fees, you may ask the court to waive all or part of your court fees.

1. To make a request to the court to waive your fees in superior court, complete the *Request to Waive Court Fees* (form FW-001). If you qualify, the court will waive all or part of its fees for the following:
   - Filing papers in superior court (other than for an appeal in a case with a value of over $25,000)
   - Making and certifying copies
   - Sheriff's fee to give notice
   - Court fees for telephone hearings
   - Giving notice and certificates
   - Sending papers to another court department
   - Having a court-appointed interpreter in small claims court
   - Reporter's daily fee *(for up to 60 days after the grant of the fee waiver, at the court-approved daily rate)*
   - Preparing, certifying, copying, and sending the clerk's transcript on appeal.

2. You may ask the court to waive other court fees during your case in superior court as well. To do that, complete a *Request to Waive Additional Court Fees (Superior Court)* (form FW-002). The court will consider waiving fees for items such as the following, or other court services you need for your case:
   - Jury fees and expenses
   - Fees for court-appointed experts
   - Reporter's daily fees *(beyond the 60-day period after the grant of the fee waiver, at the court-approved daily rate)*
   - Fees for a peace officer to testify in court
   - Court-appointed interpreter fees for a witness
   - Other necessary court fees

3. If you want the Appellate Division of Superior Court or the Court of Appeal to review an order or judgment against you and you want the court fees waived, ask for and follow the instructions on *Information Sheet on Waiver of Appellate Court Fees, Supreme Court, Court of Appeal, Appellate Division* (form APP-015/FW-015-INFO).

IMPORTANT INFORMATION!

- **You are signing your request under penalty of perjury. Please answer truthfully, accurately, and completely.**

- **The court may ask you for information and evidence.** You may be ordered to go to court to answer questions about your ability to pay court fees and costs and to provide proof of eligibility. Any initial fee waiver you are granted may be ended if you do not go to court when asked. You may be ordered to repay amounts that were waived if the court finds you were not eligible for the fee waiver.

- **If you receive a fee waiver, you must tell the court if there is a change in your finances.** You must tell the court within five days if your finances improve or if you become able to pay court fees or costs during this case. (File *Notice to Court of Improved Financial Situation or Settlement* (form FW-010) with the court.) You may be ordered to repay any amounts that were waived after your eligibility came to an end.

- **If you receive a judgment or support order in a family law matter:** You may be ordered to pay all or part of your waived fees and costs if the court finds your circumstances have changed so that you can afford to pay. You will have the opportunity to ask the court for a hearing if the court makes such a decision.

- **If you win your case in the trial court:** In most circumstances the other side will be ordered to pay your waived fees and costs to the court. The court will not enter a satisfaction of judgment until the court is paid. (This does not apply in unlawful detainer cases. Special rules apply in family law cases. (Government Code, section 68637(d), (e).)

- **If you settle your civil case for $10,000 or more:** Any trial court waived fees and costs must first be paid to the court out of the settlement. **The court will have a lien on the settlement in the amount of the waived fees and costs.** The court may refuse to dismiss the case until the lien is satisfied. A request to dismiss the case (use form CIV-110) must have a declaration under penalty of perjury that the waived fees and costs have been paid. Special rules apply to family law cases.

- **The court can collect fees and costs due to the court.** If waived fees and costs are ordered paid to the trial court, the court can start collection proceedings and add a $25 fee plus any additional costs of collection to the other fees and costs owed to the court.

- **The fee waiver ends.** The fee waiver expires 60 days after the judgment, dismissal, or other final disposition of the case or earlier if a court finds that you are not eligible for a fee waiver.

- **If you are in jail or state prison:** Prisoners may be required to pay the full cost of the filing fee in the trial court but may be allowed to do so over time.

Judicial Council of California, www.courtinfo.ca.gov
Revised July 1, 2009
Government Code, §§ 68630–68640
California Rules of Court, rule 3.51

Information Sheet on Waiver of Superior Court Fees and Costs

chapter. If they apply to your financial condition, you can get them on the Judicial Council's website, www.courtinfo.ca.gov.

By law, you can file your Complaint and Application for Waiver of Court Fees and Costs at the same time, without paying a filing fee. An inexperienced clerk might tell you that you'll have to wait a few days for a judge to grant the fee waiver before you can file your papers. If this happens, be polite but firm. Tell the clerk that you are entitled to file your papers now under Rule 3.51 of the California Rules of Court.

If you file your documents in person, you may have to take the fee waiver application to be reviewed and filed by a clerk in a different department or courtroom from the court's filing desk. You may be required to meet with a financial hearing officer who is entitled to ask you to verify the statements made in your application.

Once your fee waiver application has been filed, the court must decide on the request within five days. If the court doesn't deny your request within that time, your fees are automatically waived.

If your request is granted, the court sends you a document so stating. If your fee waiver request is denied, however, the *Order on Application for Waiver of Court Fees and Costs* will be marked and sent to you and you'll have to pay court fees within ten days. If you don't get any notification from the court within a week after you file your fee waiver documents, call the clerk to find out whether your fees were waived.

Preparing an Attachment

People often run out of space when filling out Judicial Council forms. Use Form MC-025, *Attachment to Judicial Council Form*, to complete your answer. Instructions follow.

FORM
The appendix contains a tear-out version of Form MC-025, *Attachment to Judicial Council Form*, and you can download one from the Judicial Council website at www.courtinfo.ca.gov.

Short Title: This is the name by which your case will be known. Type the last names (or the business names) of the first (perhaps only) plaintiff and the first (perhaps only) defendant, separated by "vs." For example, "Brown vs. Black" or "Brown vs. Golden Bear Typing Service."

Case Number: If you've filed your Complaint with the court clerk, you'll have a case number and you should enter it here. Leave it blank if the Attachment goes with the Complaint.

Attachment (Number) and Page. Number the Attachment "1" if it is your first for this pleading; "2" if there are two attachments, and so on. If you need more than the single side, number the first page "1 of 2," or "1 of 3," and so on.

The body of the Attachment. The rest of the form is blank. At the top of this space, type the Item or question from the form that the Attachment belongs to. For example, "Attachment for Item 4." Then, type the information you want to add. If you need additional space, use another MC-025 form.

CAUTION
If the item or question on the main form that the Attachment belongs to is made under penalty of perjury, the statements in the Attachment are also made under penalty of perjury. In other words, even though there are no words like "I declare under penalty of perjury that the foregoing is true and correct ..." on this Attachment, if this phrase appears on the main form, you're bound here, too.

Filing the Papers

Call the Clerk's Office 120
Photocopy Your Documents 120
Filing the Papers 121
    Filing the Papers in Person 121
    Filing the Papers by Mail or Fax 122

...ong way toward getting ...re a judge or jury—you've ...ummons, the Cover Sheet, ...ur next step is to file these ...erk. This chapter will guide you through these mechanical steps. Compared to the tedium of filling out your forms, you'll find this part easy.

Call the Clerk's Office

Before you physically visit the clerk's office, call the office and ask the following questions, which will help you prepare for your trip to the courthouse. (You may not get through to a live person—in these tight budget times, many counties have eliminated their help lines.)

- **How many extra copies of my documents should I bring?** As explained in the next section, you normally need a copy for each defendant and one for yourself. But some courts, especially branch courts, require an extra.
- **How much is the filing fee?** Limited Jurisdiction filing fees are currently $205 to $330, depending on whether you are suing for over or under $10,000. You can usually pay in cash or by check, unless you have bounced a check on the court in the past. If you can't afford the filing fee, you may qualify for a waiver, as discussed in Chapter 5.
- **What hours is the office open to the public?** Most open at 8:00 or 8:30 a.m. and close to the public at 4:00 or 4:30 p.m. A few close for lunch from 12:00 to 1:00 p.m.

Photocopy Your Documents

You will need to make photocopies of the following documents that you've already prepared:
- Complaint
- Summons
- Case Questionnaire, and
- Application for Waiver of Court Fees and Costs (and the Order on Application for Waiver of Court Fees and Costs), if applicable to your case.

Unless printed off the Judicial Council website, many Judicial Council forms have printing on the back. The backside is printed upside down (court files are attached at the top of the page, so that when you flip the page up, you can read the back side without turning the file upside down). For double-sided forms, you can make single-sided copies (one for the front, one for the back). If you have access to the proper equipment, you can make two-sided copies, but be sure that the backside is, like the original, upside down. Also, the originals of all forms filed with the court have to be double-hole punched at the top. Here's how many copies to make:

- **Complaint.** The original gets filed with the court; make one copy for each defendant and two for yourself. Obviously, if the court needs an extra, make one.
- **Summons.** Make one copy of the Summons for each defendant and two for yourself. Unlike the Complaint, you don't file a Summons when you file the Complaint. Instead, the clerk stamps the Summons, hands it back to you and you will have a copy of it served on the defendants. (See Chapter 7.)
- **Case Questionnaire.** You'll keep the original Questionnaire, so make one copy for each defendant and one copy for yourself (in case you misplace the original). Don't bring these documents to the clerk's office when you file the Summons and Complaint.
- **Cover Sheet.** The original is all you need, except in Los Angeles and several other counties (discussed in Chapter 5), where you must serve a copy on each defendant (and don't forget to use the Los Angeles Civil Case Cover Sheet Addendum and Statement of Location, also).
- **Application for Waiver of Court Fees and Costs, and Order on Application for Waiver of Court Fees and Costs.** You'll use these if you have a low income and are applying for a fee

waiver, as discussed in Chapter 5. You file the originals with the court. Make two copies of each for yourself.

Filing the Papers

You have at least two and possibly three options for filing your papers:
- file them in person
- file them by mail, or
- file them by fax (in most but not all courts).

Many people prefer to file in person, since they can get some instant feedback about any problems that the clerk spots. However, if time, distance, or transportation is an issue, filing by mail or fax are commonly used options.

Filing the Papers in Person

The first step to filing your papers in person is to find the Superior Court clerk's office. This is usually located in the courthouse. That address is on your Complaint. The civil division is the one you want (the other major divisions are criminal and, in larger courts, small claims and traffic). In small counties, the civil division will be combined with the criminal division.

When you enter the building, look for a directory or information desk. Then locate or ask where the civil division clerk's office is. If you can't find a directory or information desk, look for a deputy sheriff or someone who looks like a lawyer. They'll know where the office is.

TIP
Bring plenty of change! If there are problems with your paperwork, you may be able to fix them on the spot or in a nearby law library. But you may need to make new copies, so bring plenty of quarters.

When you get to the clerk's office, look for a sign showing where new cases are filed. In the larger courts there may be separate windows for limited and unlimited jurisdiction cases. Be prepared to wait in line a while.

When it's your turn, walk to the counter and immediately tell the clerk that you are a pro per plaintiff filing a new action and that you've never done this before. Often the clerk will become quite helpful. Believe me, this works much better than pretending you are an old experienced litigator who knows the ropes.

Hand the clerk all your documents. Put the original Cover Sheet and Complaint on top, followed by the copies of the Complaint, the original Summons, and its copies. If you're applying for a fee waiver, place those documents on the bottom. The clerk will first review the Complaint to see if it meets the requirements for filing.

If the Clerk Rejects Your Forms

It is unlikely this will happen, but if the clerk rejects your forms, be sure you understand exactly what you did wrong. Write down what the clerk tells you and repeat it back. Sometimes the clerk will point out that you have failed to check a box or to fill in a blank. Ask if you can take care of the problem now by checking the box or writing in what is needed. In most cases this will be permitted.

Don't argue with the clerk—establishing a bad relationship at the outset could cause you problems throughout your lawsuit. If the clerk is hostile and tells you to hire a lawyer, politely ask to talk to the supervisor. You're entitled to represent yourself and to be treated courteously, and most supervising clerks will want to solve any problems that come up.

There is a growing realization in California that courts should provide some self-help resources in the courthouse for pro pers having problems navigating a system built by lawyers for lawyers. Substantial progress has been made—54 of 58 counties have self-help programs in place (the exceptions are Kings, Plumas, Siskiyou, and San

Bernardino counties). Ventura County has a splendid program that is a model for anything I have seen anywhere in the United States.

To determine whether your court has a Self-Help Center, ask your clerk's office or go to the website courtinfo.ca.gov and click the Self Help icon in the upper left corner. Then click "Free and Low Cost Legal Help" and then "Help From Your Court." Scroll down the page to the chart to see whether there is an SHC (Self-Help Center) there. Centers called "Facilitators" are restricted to helping people in family law cases.

If you're not applying for a fee waiver, the clerk will ask you to pay the filing fee. A personal check is acceptable in most circumstances. You'll get a receipt, which you should keep. If you have requested a fee waiver and you have something that shows you receive SSI or public assistance, the clerk may approve the waiver right there. If you don't receive public assistance, a judge or hearing officer must approve your application. The clerk will tell you how to find out the judge's decision.

The clerk will stamp a case number and other information on the originals and copies of the Summons and Complaint. Then the clerk will sign the original Summons and place the official seal of the court in the lower left corner. Ask the clerk if you can use his or her stamp to fill in the case number on the copies of the documents where you left it blank. If you forget to do this, you can fill in the numbers by hand later.

In many courts, you'll be handed the stamping device and allowed to place the official court stamp on as many copies as you wish. If you'd prefer not to stand at the desk stamping your papers, you can photocopy the forms with the official court stamp on them. A photocopy of a court stamp is as good as the original on everything other than the Summons.

The clerk will hand you back all the copies of the Complaint (unless local rules require the clerk to keep a copy), plus the original and copies of the Summons. You may feel strange walking off with the original Summons, but because it is the official notice to the defendant that he or she is being sued, you keep it. (When served, the defendant gets a copy of the Summons.) If a defendant doesn't respond within the time required, you can go back to the court and take a "default judgment" (a judgment you get because the other side didn't contest your case). That's when you file the original Summons. This material is covered in detail in Chapters 7 and 9.

The clerk may also give you an ADR (alternative dispute resolution) brochure for each defendant. If so, you must serve this on each defendant along with the Summons and the Complaint. In some counties (such as Santa Clara), the clerk will give you other documents, including a "Notice to Litigants" that tells the parties when and where they must attend a Case Management Conference (more on this in Chapter 12). It also instructs them to file a Case Management Statement before the conference (a blank statement, which each party will fill out and file, comes with the Notice).

If you have gotten this far without a hitch, congratulations! Many new lawyers make several trips to the clerk's office before their first papers pass muster. If you need to fix something, take care of it and file again.

Filing the Papers by Mail or Fax

You can file the papers by mail instead of in person. The disadvantage in filing by mail is that if you have made even a minor mistake in filling in the blanks, the court will probably return your papers to you by mail for correction. There may be delays of more than a few days as the processing takes place. Many mistakes can be corrected quickly at the counter if you have taken your papers there personally. This said, you can file by mail in any court and in some courts you can file by fax. Although filing electronically is authorized as described in California Rule of Court 2.250 and following, it has not really taken off yet, except for small claims cases, where it is available in several counties.

If you decide to file by mail, send your papers to the same court (branch or main) that you would have gone to if you'd decided to file in person. Enclose a note asking the clerk to

- file the original Complaint
- issue the Summons
- file-stamp the papers (put the court's stamp, with the date the papers were filed, on each document), and
- return the extra copies to you. The clerk will probably file-stamp only one copy. If that happens, make copies of the file-stamped papers and use those when serving the defendants.

Be sure to include a check for the filing fee (or your Application and Order for a Waiver) and a large self-addressed, stamped envelope with enough postage to mail the forms back to you. If your envelope isn't large enough to hold the papers or doesn't have enough postage, the clerk may not mail the papers back to you.

Fax filing is described beginning at California Rule of Court 2.300. The simplest way to use it is to use a private fax filing agency, which will accept your papers by fax and then file them personally in the clerk's office. Your local clerk's office can tell you if there is such an agency doing business with the court. A few courts allow you to do direct fax filing without an intermediary. If you wish to use this procedure, check the court's website for procedures, which will include the preparation of a special cover page (MC-005) that is available in the forms section at www.courtinfo.ca.gov. Read over California Rule of Court 2.304 for a description of general procedures. Fees (including an extra $1.00 per page) can be paid by credit card.

CHAPTER 7

Serving the Papers on the Defendants

Completing the Summons	126
Serve Your Papers by Mail	126
Selecting a Process Server	128
Serving the Summons and Complaint	128
Getting More Time to Serve Your Papers	129
Serving Defendants Who Aren't Natural Adults	129
Serving Minors	130
Completing the Proof of Service	130
Serving Other Papers as the Case Proceeds	134

Once you file your papers with the court, your next task is to let the defendant know you have brought the lawsuit. You do this by serving the defendant with certain legal papers. "Serving" means delivering papers to the defendant in one of the methods permitted by law.

The defendant must be served with the following documents:
- a copy of the Summons (be sure to keep the original)
- a copy of the Complaint (make sure it has either an original or a photocopy of the court's stamp on it)
- a copy of your completed Case Questionnaire
- a blank Case Questionnaire
- any alternative dispute brochure supplied by the court, and
- any other forms your court requires by local rules.

This chapter will explain the steps you need to take to assemble the papers, select a person to do the serving, and then present proof to the court that you have complied with the service requirements. It also explains how to accomplish service at other times during the lawsuit, which you may need to do.

Completing the Summons

To prepare to serve the defendant, paper-clip together one complete set of the documents (make one set for each defendant), putting the copy of the Summons on top. Before the defendant can actually be served, you must complete the box at the bottom portion of the Summons form. If you have more than one defendant, you must complete a Summons form for each.

- **Box 1.** Check this box if you are suing an adult person in his or her own name, such as Jonathan Walton.
- **Box 2.** Check this box if you are suing an adult person who does business using a fictitious business name (for example, Joe Smith operates as Racafrax Tile Imports). Type the business's fictitious name after "(specify:)." Also, check the box if you're suing an unknown defendant—type the name and identifying number, such as "Doe 4" after "(specify):"
- **Box 3.** Check this box if you are suing a corporation, a limited liability company (LLC), a defunct corporation, an association or partnership, a government agency, a minor, or a person subject to a conservatorship. Specify the name of the defendant and check the applicable sub-box. If you are suing a government agency, use the "Other" Box.
- **Box 4.** It isn't necessary to check box 4.

If you are suing a particular defendant in more than one capacity—such as an individual who does business under a fictitious name, or an officer of a corporation who is being sued as an individual and as the corporation's representative—check all boxes that apply.

Serve Your Papers by Mail

The cheapest and easiest way to serve your papers on the defendant is to mail them, using the "Notice and Acknowledgement of Service" form. It is also very simple—you mail copies of the documents you have filed with the court to the defendant, along with two copies of a simple court form for the defendant to sign to acknowledge receipt, and a stamped return envelope addressed to you. The defendant has 20 days to complete the process and return the form to you. The service is deemed complete ten days after the defendant's dated signature.

Serving your papers by mail lets you avoid the hassle and cost of finding and hiring a process server. It may also be tactically advantageous to you. You'll save the defendant the embarrassment of being served in a possible inconvenient or uncomfortable situation—for example, at work in front of colleagues, or at home in front of children or family members. If you are interested in settling the matter (and I truly hope you are, as I explain in Chapter 13), it's wise to begin your lawsuit on a more sensitive note than you'll set with the use of a process server. Additionally, the defendant will save money if he or she returns the forms and you win (normally, the defendant will pay your cost of service if you win).

There is one disadvantage to serving by mail—you stand to lose some time. When you use personal service through a process server, the defendant's time to contest your suit begins immediately upon being served. The Mail and Acknowledgement method extends the defendant's response date by up to 20 days. And, suppose the defendant doesn't sign the form? In that event, the case will be delayed even further because you'll have to start over with a process server.

Some defendants think they can dodge the whole matter by refusing to sign and return the form. This is a short-sighted approach. If you have to hire a process server, you can ask the court to reimburse your costs, as long as you can convince the court that you properly sent the Mail and Acknowledgment forms to the defendant—even if you ultimately lose the case. Because so many defendants don't understand that they stand to lose some money by playing games, it's a good idea to enclose a letter, like the one below, explaining the consequences of refusing to return the form.

FORM
The appendix contains a tear-out version of the form POS-015, *Notice and Acknowledgement of Receipt–Civil*. We do not include a filled-out sample because the form is quite straightforward.

Follow these directions to fill out your Mail Notice and Acknowledgment of Receipt form.

Top Three Boxes: Fill out these boxes exactly as you did in the Complaint in Chapter 5.

TO: Type in the name of the defendant being served. If there is more than one defendant, use a separate form for each.

Date of mailing and Signature: This form must be sent by someone other than you, who is over the age of 18. Type in the date of mailing and the name of the person who is going to put it in the mail. That person should sign on the right.

Acknowledgement of Receipt: This is where the defendant is asked to sign. Check Box 1 and Box 2. After the word (specify): in Box 2, add the names of the other documents you are mailing, including any Alternative Dispute Resolution package, a filled-out copy of the Case Questionnaire–For Limited Civil Cases, and a blank copy of the Questionnaire. Remember to also include a postage-paid envelope addressed to the person who signed above. Remember that you should send a copy of the Summons, not the original, which you should hold onto for the time being.

Signature: Type the name of the defendant. If it is a business or governmental entity, put that in the line on the left. Leave the line on the right blank for the signature. If the person is signing on behalf of an entity and you know what his or her title is, type that below the line. For example: "Designated Agent for Service of Process for Ajax Company" or "President of General Plumbing, Inc."

The sender should mail two copies of the Acknowledgement form and the other documents mentioned above to the defendant. It's a good idea to include a letter from you, explaining the process. A sample copy of such a letter is shown below.

Sample Letter Accompanying Notice and Acknowledgment Service

October 10, 20xx

Ms. Edith Samuels, President
General Plumbing, Inc.
14 Central Street
Ukiah, CA 84790

Dear Ms. Samuels:

Enclosed are some legal papers related to the lawsuit I have filed against General Plumbing. If you will sign and date the Notice of Acknowledgment and Receipt and return it in the enclosed stamped envelope within 20 days, we will avoid having a process server deliver the papers to you personally. As it says on the Summons, you then have 30 days to file an Answer with the court.

Your participation in this process will save you some money. If you don't return the form on time and I am forced to hire a process server, the court may order you to pay for the cost of the process server.

Thank you for your cooperation.

Sincerely,
Norma Perry
Norma Perry

Selecting a Process Server

If you decide not to use the Notice and Acknowledgment method of service discussed above (or are not able to), you need to select someone to do the actual serving. This person is called a "process server." You have several options, but doing it yourself is not one of them—court papers must be served by someone age 18 or over who is not a party to the case.

You can use a friend or a professional process server. You can also use a sheriff if you need to serve the paper in a county where the sheriff's office still provides the service. (Budget cutbacks have forced many of them to eliminate it.) You'll have to pay the sheriff about $30; a professional process server will charge closer to $50.

Even though you may be tempted to ask a friend to serve your papers, I recommend against doing so. Friends have not been trained in the rules of proper process serving and often make mistakes. In addition, if a dispute arises over whether the defendant was served—or served correctly—friends are less likely to be believed than are sheriffs or professional process servers. Finally, the law presumes that a sheriff or professional process server's statement that service was correct is true. (Evidence Code § 647.) This law doesn't apply to friends.

I recommend that you hire a professional process server. Not only do professional process servers know the rules of proper service better than anyone else, they get paid when they accomplish service and thus will usually work hard to find and serve the defendant. Sheriffs have less incentive to complete the task—they're paid by the county whether they successfully serve the defendant or not. Professional process servers are listed in the telephone yellow pages under "Process Serving." Make sure you know the fee before you hire someone.

You may need the server some day to testify to making the service, so the safest thing to do is to use an established agency. Those who serve court papers more than occasionally must register and post a bond with the county where they work. In turn, they receive a certificate of registration that you should ask to see if you have any question about reliability.

Serving the Summons and Complaint

If you use a sheriff or professional process server, you don't have to worry about how to actually serve the defendant. That's why you've hired someone to do the job. If you use a friend, however, the rules of proper service are important—though not all that complicated. While you may have seen process servers in the movies or on television act as though they have to touch the defendant with the papers, that's Hollywood hype. In truth, the process server needs only to:

- identify the defendant ("Are you Morton Kaifu?")
- state his or her purpose ("These are legal documents I am serving on you"), and
- leave the documents in the presence of the defendant.

The process server doesn't have to physically hand the papers to the defendant or see the defendant pick them up. The process server can simply place them on a counter or desk in front of a defendant, leave them under the windshield wiper of a car in which the defendant is sitting, or even push them under a door after the process server has identified the defendant as being on the other side.

Getting More Time to Serve Your Papers

Statewide Rules of Court give you 60 days after you've filed the lawsuit to serve the papers. If you are going to need more time, ask the court for an extension *before* the deadline has expired. There is no printed form for an extension, so you'll have to adapt the form in " Ask for More Time" in Chapter 8. Simply change the last word of the title "Request and Order for Extension of Time to Plead" to "Serve Summons and Complaint." In the first paragraph, explain why you have not been able to serve a defendant. Change the wording of the Order from "to answer" to "serve the Summons and Complaint."

Take the signed form to the Clerk's office, where you may be directed to take it to a particular department of the court. Leave it with the appropriate clerk with a stamped, self-addressed envelope so that it can be mailed to you after a judge has processed it.

If you have a complicated service problem, check out the Continuing Education of the Bar Action Guide, "Handling Service of Process," available at your local law library or for sale on the CEB website at www.ceb.com or by calling 800-232-3111.

Serving Defendants Who Aren't Natural Adults

The rules above are all you need to know if the defendant is an adult and is a real person. But if the defendant is something else (a business, for example), the process server must follow special rules.

- **Corporations and LLCs.** All corporations (for-profit and nonprofit alike), limited partnerships, limited liability companies (LLCs), and limited liability partnerships (LLPs), must file with the California Secretary of State the names and addresses of their officers and any other person (known as a designated agent) whom they've chosen to accept legal papers. Your process server can serve the designated agent or any officer or general manager of the corporation or partnership.
- **Partnerships or unincorporated associations.** To serve a partnership or unincorporated association, your process server may serve the papers on any general partner, officer, or general manager. Service on a limited partner won't fly. If this person is being sued in his or her individual capacity as well, the process server should mark the lower box on the Summons appropriately and leave two copies of the papers.
- **Government agencies.** Before suing the government, remember that you must file an administrative claim, described in Chapter 4. After the claim is rejected and you prepare and file the court papers, your process server can simply deliver them to the clerk of the governing body.

- **Doe defendants.** So long as you have taken care of Box 2 at the bottom of the Summons, you serve a Doe just as you would any adult.

Serving Minors

To serve a minor, you must serve the minor's parent or guardian. If the minor is 12 or older, your process server must also serve the minor personally.

When a minor is sued, the parents or guardians normally take some action to have the court appoint them to handle their child's defense to your lawsuit. If the parents don't take this action, you will have to do it for them. The process is called asking for an "appointment of a guardian *ad litem*" (this means that the court appoints the parent or guardian as a special guardian for the purposes of this lawsuit only). You'll need to fill out the form sometime after the minor and/or the minor's parents have been served with your Summons and Complaint. Follow the instructions below to complete the form.

FORM

The appendix contains a tear-out version of Form CIV-010, *Application and Order for Appointment of Guardian Ad Litem–Civil*, and you can download one from the Judicial Council website at www.courtinfo.ca.gov.

Caption. Fortunately, you already know how to fill out the top portion of the form because you have had exactly the same task in Chapter 5.

Item 1. Fill in your name (check the "ex parte" box) as "Applicant." Check Box d ("a party to the suit").

Item 2. Fill in the name of and information regarding the minor's parent or a responsible adult who can supervise the defense.

Item 3. Enter the name and other information about the minor.

Item 4. Check the first box. The minor's date of birth should be on any police report. If it isn't or if there is no police report, just put "unknown."

Item 5a. Skip this and go to the next page.

Item 5b. Check this box and skip the next two boxes.

Items 6 and 7. These are self-explanatory.

Date and sign the form. Leave the consent section blank. In the Order section, fill in the name of the proposed guardian and the minor and leave the rest of the form blank.

Make several copies of the form and file the originals with the clerk of the court. The clerk will present it to a judge for signature. Leave a self-addressed envelope so that a copy can be mailed to you when it has been signed. Mail a copy of the form to the proposed guardian when it is filed and again after it has been signed by the judge.

Serving Elusive Defendants

If a defendant is evading service—for example, not answering the door—there are a few special methods a process server can use to effect service. For instance, after several unsuccessful attempts, the process server can leave the papers with a coresident at a home or with a person in charge of a business, then mail a copy to the defendant. (Code of Civil Procedure § 415.20.) These methods are intricate and, if necessary, should not be attempted by anyone other than a professional process server.

Completing the Proof of Service

After serving the defendant, the process server must fill out a form called a Proof of Service of Summons, which describes how and when service was accomplished. A professional process server or sheriff will complete the form and give it to you.

If you ask a friend or acquaintance to do the service, that person will have to complete a Proof of Service of Summons as well. This can be done using the back page of the original Summons. If more than one defendant was served, the process server should fill out the a separate proof of service for each one. Follow the instructions below for completing the Proof of Service of Summons.

It's a good idea to fill out this form right away. You'll need it to prove the defendant got your papers if the defendant doesn't respond and you want to go ahead and obtain a judgment (called a "default judgment," as described in Chapter 9). If the defendant follows the instructions on the Summons and files a pleading with the court within the time allowed, you may never need this form. It is up to you whether you fill this out now or wait to see whether the defendant responds. Follow the directions below to complete the form.

FORM

The appendix contains a tear-out version of Form POS-010, *Proof of Service of Summons,* and you can download one from the Judicial Council website at www.courtinfo.ca.gov. A filled-out sample is shown below.

Caption. This calls for the same routine you have already followed. Put in the case number assigned by the court, but leave the Ref. No. box blank.

Item 2. Check the boxes for what was served. This will normally be the first three boxes and Box f, where you will type in the words "blank and filled-out copies of Case Questionnaire–For Limited Civil Cases" and a description of any local forms you were required to serve.

Item 3a. If you served an individual defendant, enter that person's name here. If you served a business or government entity, enter the name of that organization here just as it was listed on the Summons.

Item 3b. If you served an individual defendant, repeat that name here and check the first box. If you served a person on behalf of an organization, check the second box and put that person's name here, specifying what position that person holds with relation to the organization named above. And example would be "Ralph Rizzo, President of Ajax Construction, Inc." or "Phyllis Ongaro, agent for service of process on Fairfax Enterprises."

Item 4. Enter the address where the defendant was served.

Item 5a. If the documents were served personally on a named defendant, enter the date and time of the service.

Item 5b. This section is for substituted service, a complex procedure with a number of requirements that normally should not be attempted by anyone other than a professional process server. As explained in "Serving Elusive Defendants," above, I suggest hiring a professional server if you encounter this situation (the professional will complete the form). The rest of you should go on to page 2 and fill in the boxes at the top of the page.

Item 5c. As previously explained, service by mail is the best and most economical method of service. If you have chosen this method and received the "acknowledgement" back in the mail, check this box and fill out the line below for the date and city from which you mailed. Depending on whether you sent it in or out of the state, check box (3) or (4).

Item 5d. Leave this blank.

Item 6. Copy here what you placed on the bottom portion of the front of the Summons.

Item 7. If you used the Acknowledgement of Receipt of Summons method, fill out lines a, b, and c using information on the person who mailed the package of documents. If the person who made service was a friend of yours, your friend should answer in the same way and not claim a fee for the service, so leave d blank and check e(1).

Item 8. Check this box.

Item 9. Leave this blank.

Date. The person who served the papers should enter the date on which the person signs this form.

Name and signature. Type the server's name on the left. The server should sign on the line on the right.

Once you have the completed Proof of Service of Summons—from the sheriff, professional process server, or your friend—make two copies of it. If

	POS-010
ATTORNEY OR PARTY WITHOUT ATTORNEY *(Name, State Bar number, and address)*: John Burns 37 5th Street Napa, CA 94559 TELEPHONE NO.: 707-555-1234 FAX NO. *(Optional)*: E-MAIL ADDRESS *(Optional)*: ATTORNEY FOR *(Name)*: In pro per	FOR COURT USE ONLY
SUPERIOR COURT OF CALIFORNIA, COUNTY OF Napa STREET ADDRESS: 1125 Third Street MAILING ADDRESS: P.O. Box 880 CITY AND ZIP CODE: Napa, CA 94559 BRANCH NAME:	
PLAINTIFF/PETITIONER: John Burns DEFENDANT/RESPONDENT: Sam Smith	CASE NUMBER:
PROOF OF SERVICE OF SUMMONS	Ref. No. or File No.:

(Separate proof of service is required for each party served.)

1. At the time of service I was at least 18 years of age and not a party to this action.
2. I served copies of:
   a. [X] summons
   b. [X] complaint
   c. [X] Alternative Dispute Resolution (ADR) package
   d. [ ] Civil Case Cover Sheet *(served in complex cases only)*
   e. [ ] cross-complaint
   f. [X] other *(specify documents)*: blank and filled-out copies of Case Questionnaire—For Limited Civil Cases
3. a. Party served *(specify name of party as shown on documents served)*: Sam Smith

   b. [ ] Person (other than the party in item 3a) served on behalf of an entity or as an authorized agent (and not a person under item 5b on whom substituted service was made) *(specify name and relationship to the party named in item 3a)*:

4. Address where the party was served: 271 Shady Lane, Apt. 4, Napa, CA 94559
5. I served the party *(check proper box)*
   a. [ ] **by personal service.** I personally delivered the documents listed in item 2 to the party or person authorized to receive service of process for the party (1) on *(date)*:   (2) at *(time)*:
   b. [ ] **by substituted service.** On *(date)*:   at *(time)*:   I left the documents listed in item 2 with or in the presence of *(name and title or relationship to person indicated in item 3)*:

      (1) [ ] **(business)** a person at least 18 years of age apparently in charge at the office or usual place of business of the person to be served. I informed him or her of the general nature of the papers.

      (2) [ ] **(home)** a competent member of the household (at least 18 years of age) at the dwelling house or usual place of abode of the party. I informed him or her of the general nature of the papers.

      (3) [ ] **(physical address unknown)** a person at least 18 years of age apparently in charge at the usual mailing address of the person to be served, other than a United States Postal Service post office box. I informed him or her of the general nature of the papers.

      (4) [ ] I thereafter mailed (by first-class, postage prepaid) copies of the documents to the person to be served at the place where the copies were left (Code Civ. Proc., § 415.20). I mailed the documents on *(date)*:   from *(city)*:   or [ ] a declaration of mailing is attached.

      (5) [ ] I attach a **declaration of diligence** stating actions taken first to attempt personal service.

Form Adopted for Mandatory Use
Judicial Council of California
POS-010 [Rev. January 1, 2007]

PROOF OF SERVICE OF SUMMONS

Code of Civil Procedure, § 417.10

PLAINTIFF/PETITIONER: John Burns	CASE NUMBER:
DEFENDANT/RESPONDENT: Sam Smith	

5. c. [X] **by mail and acknowledgment of receipt of service.** I mailed the documents listed in item 2 to the party, to the address shown in item 4, by first-class mail, postage prepaid,

    (1) on *(date)*: August 10, 20xx   (2) from *(city)*: Napa, CA

    (3) [X] with two copies of the *Notice and Acknowledgment of Receipt* and a postage-paid return envelope addressed to me. *(Attach completed* Notice and Acknowledgement of Receipt.) (Code Civ. Proc., § 415.30.)

    (4) [ ] to an address outside California with return receipt requested. (Code Civ. Proc., § 415.40.)

  d. [ ] **by other means** *(specify means of service and authorizing code section)*:

    [ ] Additional page describing service is attached.

6. The "Notice to the Person Served" (on the summons) was completed as follows:
    a. [X] as an individual defendant.
    b. [ ] as the person sued under the fictitious name of *(specify)*:
    c. [ ] as occupant.
    d. [ ] On behalf of *(specify)*:
        under the following Code of Civil Procedure section:
        [ ] 416.10 (corporation)   [ ] 415.95 (business organization, form unknown)
        [ ] 416.20 (defunct corporation)   [ ] 416.60 (minor)
        [ ] 416.30 (joint stock company/association)   [ ] 416.70 (ward or conservatee)
        [ ] 416.40 (association or partnership)   [ ] 416.90 (authorized person)
        [ ] 416.50 (public entity)   [ ] 415.46 (occupant)
                                                [ ] other:

7. **Person who served papers**
    a. Name: Judy Jones
    b. Address: 75 Creekside Lane
    c. Telephone number: 707-123-4567
    d. **The fee** for service was: $
    e. I am:
        (1) [X] not a registered California process server.
        (2) [ ] exempt from registration under Business and Professions Code section 22350(b).
        (3) [ ] a registered California process server:
            (i) [ ] owner [ ] employee [ ] independent contractor.
            (ii) Registration No.:
            (iii) County:

8. [X] **I declare** under penalty of perjury under the laws of the State of California that the foregoing is true and correct.

    or

9. [ ] **I am a California sheriff or marshal and** I certify that the foregoing is true and correct.

Date:

    Judy Jones   ▶ *Judy Jones*
    (NAME OF PERSON WHO SERVED PAPERS/SHERIFF OR MARSHAL)   (SIGNATURE)

PROOF OF SERVICE OF SUMMONS

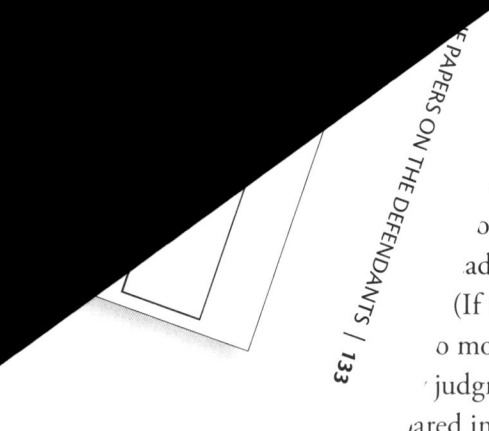

e the case when
ed), make two
o wait to see if the
adings and moves
(If the defendant
o move ahead to enter
judgment.) Hold on
ared in this chapter and

Serving Other Papers as the Case Proceeds

As the case progresses, you will need to serve other documents on your opponent. This service is much easier than serving the Summons and Complaint—it all can be done by mail. Like the personal service of the Summons and Complaint, serving by mail must be done by someone over 18 who is not a party to the lawsuit. You can certainly use a friend, relative, or business associate. You can prepare the documents and even address the envelope—but your helper must physically do the mailing.

To serve papers by mail, your server must prepare a Proof of Service by First-Class Mail—Civil for each person being served. The form is very simple and the Judicial Council even provides an Information Sheet on how to complete it. I will spare you instructions on how to fill it out line by line because I have supreme confidence that if you have gotten this far in this book, filling it out will be, as they say, a piece of cake.

FORM

The appendix contains a tear-out version of form POS-030, *Proof of Service by First-Class Mail–Civil*, and you can download one from the Judicial Council website at www.courtinfo.ca.gov.

CAUTION

Your opponent is entitled to a served copy of everything the court gets—and you're about to begin filing a lot of documents with the court. When you prepare a document for filing with the court, you should also:

- Make at least two copies of the document that's going to the court (one for each defendant and one for yourself).
- Fill out the Proof of Service by First-Class Mail and ask the person who will be mailing the documents to the defendant to sign it (remember, this can't be you). Make a copy for each defendant and one for yourself.
- Attach the original Proof of Service to the original document going to the court, and file them together.
- Attach a copy of the Proof of Service to the copy of the document you filed in court, and send both to your opponent
- Keep the second copy for yourself.

CHAPTER 8

Lawsuits from the Defendant's Point of View

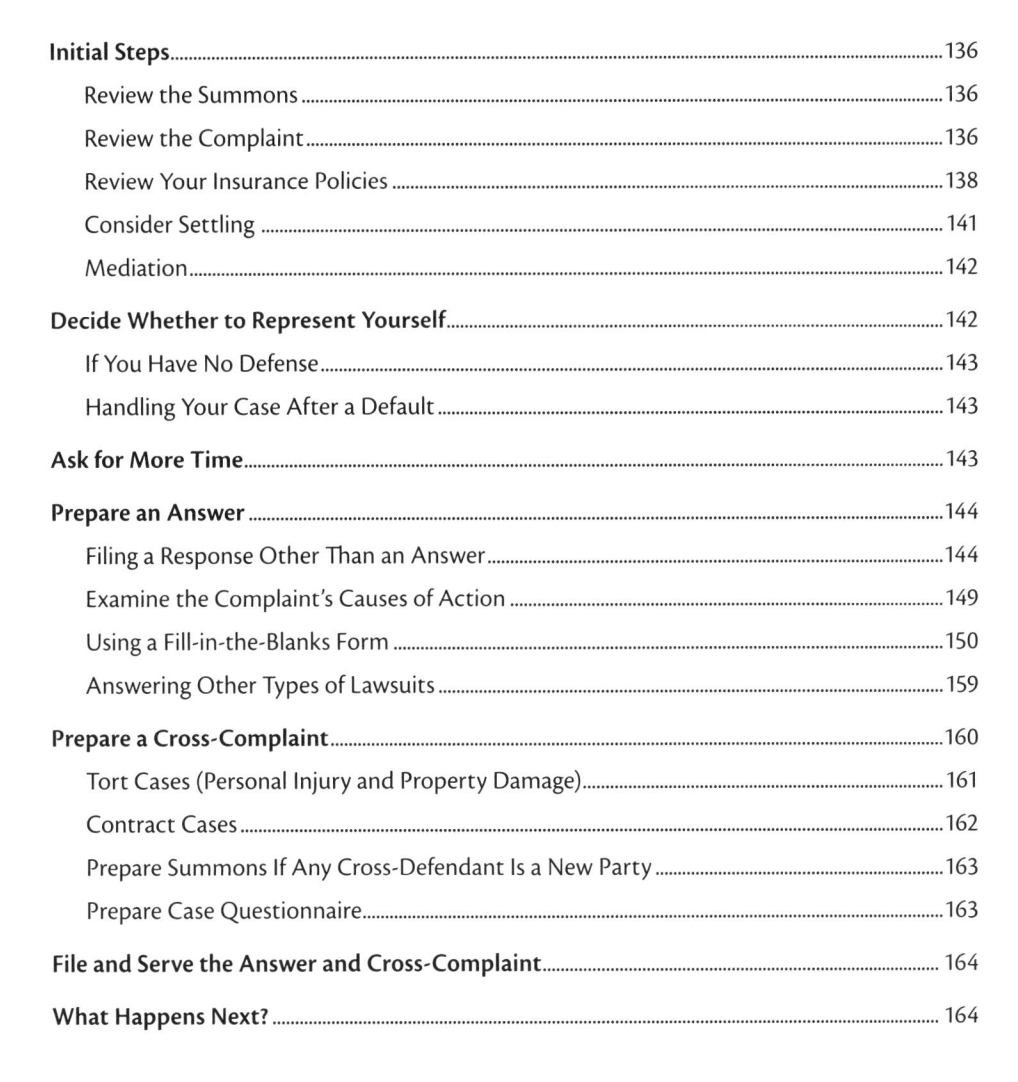

Initial Steps 136
    Review the Summons 136
    Review the Complaint 136
    Review Your Insurance Policies 138
    Consider Settling 141
    Mediation 142

Decide Whether to Represent Yourself 142
    If You Have No Defense 143
    Handling Your Case After a Default 143

Ask for More Time 143

Prepare an Answer 144
    Filing a Response Other Than an Answer 144
    Examine the Complaint's Causes of Action 149
    Using a Fill-in-the-Blanks Form 150
    Answering Other Types of Lawsuits 159

Prepare a Cross-Complaint 160
    Tort Cases (Personal Injury and Property Damage) 161
    Contract Cases 162
    Prepare Summons If Any Cross-Defendant Is a New Party 163
    Prepare Case Questionnaire 163

File and Serve the Answer and Cross-Complaint 164

What Happens Next? 164

Up to now, most of this book has been devoted to considering things from the viewpoint of the person suing. This makes sense given that the plaintiff is the initiator of the legal contest. But if you're being sued, you are surely ready for a sympathetic and understanding word. I hope to provide it here.

Being sued is not fun. You may feel it's unfair for the plaintiff to sue you. Your initial reaction may be rage, followed closely by fear and panic. But remember that all it takes to sue someone is a typewriter and a filing fee (and even the fee can be waived). No government official had to approve the suit for fairness before it was filed. Of course, lots of lawsuits that lack any merit are tossed out later.

Being sued doesn't mean you're a bad person. Most businesspeople know that being sued every so often is more or less the cost of doing business. So get control of your emotions and get to work deciding how best to deal with the legal action that has been thrust upon you.

Your first order of business is to put this matter at the top of your "to do" list. Responding late can severely compromise your ability to defend yourself and may even cost you the lawsuit. For example, if you don't file the paper called an Answer within 30 days, the plaintiff can go to court and get what's called a "default judgment"—essentially, a proclamation that the plaintiff won because you chose not to respond. Some plaintiffs do this as soon as the court opens on day 31. If you miss the deadline, there are methods to get the case reopened, but they are time-consuming and not always successful. And this can be true even if you feel you were not properly served with the papers.

Initial Steps

When you are sued, your first task is to figure out why you've been sued and what the plaintiff wants. Only when you clearly understand this can you figure out what to do about it. If you have jumped into this book at this chapter, go back and read Chapters 1, 2, and 3. They explain what lawsuits are and how to analyze the papers you were served with.

Review the Summons

One of the papers that was served on you is called the Summons. As soon as you get it, write down the date on which you were served (it's fine to do it right on the Summons). If you don't remember, call the plaintiff's attorney (or the plaintiff, if he or she is self-represented) and ask the date you were served. Within 30 days of that date, you must file a formal paper with the court or, if you need more time, you must make a written agreement with the plaintiff (or the plaintiff's lawyer) extending your time to respond. The law limits the amount of extra time the plaintiff can allow you to 15 days, but you can usually get at least one short extension.

In counting the 30 days you are allowed, don't count the day you were served. Start on the next day and include holidays, Saturdays, and Sundays. If the 30th day falls on a weekend or court holiday, your time is extended to the next day the court is open.

TIP
Don't waste time and money contesting the manner in which you were sued. If you've read Chapter 7, you know what the plaintiff was supposed to do when serving you with the Summons and Complaint. If the plaintiff got it wrong, technically you can contest the service. I advise against it—in most cases, it isn't worth the hassle of filing a motion with the court and appearing at a hearing. If you win, the now-educated plaintiff will just serve you again and you'll be back to where you started—you need to file an Answer.

Review the Complaint

The most important paper served on you is the Complaint, which tells you what the lawsuit is about. The plaintiff can use one of two types of Complaints:

- a simple, check the boxes, fill-in-the-blanks form supplied by the court (explained in detail in Chapter 5); or
- a traditional legal document prepared on plain white paper that contains numbers down the left side (called "pleading" paper).

Form Complaints

If the plaintiff used a fill-in-the-blanks form, take a look the list of topics on first page of Chapter 5 to locate the form you received. Each of the paragraphs on the form is explained there and you should be able to get a general view of what the suit is all about.

Pleading Paper Complaints

If a lawyer represents the plaintiff, you probably received a Complaint on traditional pleading paper. For some reason (perhaps because it takes more time to write one than simply checking boxes on a prepared form), some lawyers prefer using the old-fashioned approach.

Complaints written on pleading paper tend to be very repetitive, because the lawyer is presenting the lawsuit in the traditional legal way that glories in saying everything several times. Even more confusing will be the lawyer's language (pure legalese). For help deciphering the jargon, consult www.nolo.com. On the home page, click "Law Dictionary" and enter the word that that concerns you.

How Are You Named?

If your name or the name of your business isn't listed in the caption at the top of the first page of the Complaint, you are probably being sued as an unidentified defendant or, in legalspeak, a "Doe" (see "Dealing With Unknown Defendants" in Chapter 4.) Look at the bottom of the Summons to see if the plaintiff has identified you as someone sued by a fictitious name (a "Doe").

Plaintiffs normally identify defendants as Does when, at the time they prepare their initial papers, they don't know the defendant's name or involvement in the lawsuit. If the plaintiff checked the box on the front of the service saying that you are served as a Doe, the service is just as legal as if the plaintiff had used your correct name. Take it seriously, get an Answer on file with the court and refer to yourself by your real name, "served herein as Doe 17" (or whatever number follows your Doe name).

The Causes of Action in the Complaint

Most Complaints are divided into several causes of action, each of which is supposed to stand on its own as a separate legal reason or theory for the suit. For instance, if you are being sued because of a defect in a product you sold to the plaintiff, the complaint may include one cause of action for breaching what the plaintiff claims was the contract of sale and a second cause of action for a breach of a warranty. Similarly, if you were in an automobile accident with a plaintiff who feels you were driving very aggressively, there may be one cause of action for negligence in your operation of your car and another for having intentionally caused the crash.

The opening paragraph of all causes of action after the first one will usually incorporate paragraphs from previous causes of action to save endless repeating of basic facts. You'll have to flip back and forth from one to the other to get the full picture, but once you see how this works, it should be easy. If there is more than one defendant, note as you go through the Complaint that some paragraphs are directed against only some of the defendants. You can disregard those that don't name you by your name or as a Doe. After the preliminaries, there will be a paragraph or two describing what the plaintiff claims you did to justify the lawsuit. This material may be loaded up with legal language, for which you should consult Nolo's dictionary, as described above. There may be references to statutes (such as the Civil Code or Motor Vehicle Code). To read these online or at a library, follow the directions in "Finding the Law, on Paper and Online" in Chapter 1.

If the plaintiff is suing in one of the areas dealt with in Chapter 1, check Chapters 2, 4, and 5 for indications of possible weaknesses in the Complaint. If the lawsuit concerns another area of the law, go to your county law library and find the applicable section of the set of books titled *California Forms of Pleading and Practice* (discussed in "Complaints for Other Types of Lawsuits" in Chapter 5). If you are still confused, consider buying an hour of a lawyer's time for a consultation.

> **If You're a Plaintiff Who's Received a Cross-Complaint**
>
> Sometimes a defendant not only answers a Complaint, but also files a lawsuit against the plaintiff. This is called a Cross-Complaint. If you're a plaintiff who was served with a Cross-Complaint, this chapter tells you how to respond. The only difference is that if you were served with the papers by mail, you have 35, not 30, days from the date of mailing to respond.

The Prayer, or Request, for Relief

No matter what kind of Complaint you've been given, when you get to the end you'll find the plaintiff "praying for" certain relief. In a form Complaint, the prayer is at the end of the form entitled "COMPLAINT," before the Cause of Action forms. In a pleading paper Complaint, the prayer comes at the very end. The prayer is not a religious plea. It's a summary of what the plaintiff is asking for. Usually it's a sum of money. Don't panic over the dollar amount, however. It is often arbitrary and exaggerated. What the plaintiff wants and what a court will award are frequently far apart.

> **When the Complaint Asks for More Than $25,000**
>
> If the plaintiff is asking for more than $25,000, the suit belongs in the Unlimited Division of the Superior Court, not the Limited Division which is, of course, the subject of this book. All of the cautions above about taking action as soon as you are served still apply, but the need to consult with a lawyer becomes greater both because more money is involved and because you'll face more complicated court procedures.
>
> If you don't have insurance coverage, can't make arrangements with a lawyer, and can't convince the plaintiff you haven't got the kind of money he or she is seeking, you will probably want to file an Answer within the 30-day limit on your own. Preparing a fully competent Answer in an Unlimited Jurisdiction case is beyond the scope of this book. That said, if you do a little manicuring of one of the Answer forms printed later in this chapter, you may be able to prevent the judge entering a default against you, thus at least buying a little more time to negotiate.

Review Your Insurance Policies

If you have homeowner's, renter's, or another umbrella liability coverage, your insurance company may cover your defense (and perhaps a settlement or verdict, too) in a number of situations that aren't immediately obvious. Read your policies and, if you're having trouble decoding the language, get help from your agent or a lawyer coach to figure out the coverage. You'll find a more detailed discussion about dealing with insurance companies and many other important issues in *How to Win Your Personal Injury Claim,* by Joseph L. Matthews (Nolo).

Homeowner's and Renter's Policies

Homeowner's and renter's policies cover most situations in which you are sued for negligent bodily injury or property damage suffered by another person, as long as there's no motor vehicle involved. If someone visiting your home is injured, you are probably covered. Even if someone claims he was injured as a result of your careless act *away* from your home, you are also probably covered by a homeowner's or renter's policy. The act that led to the injury or damage must have been unexpected and accidental, not intentional. For example:

- Your child runs across a playground and collides with another child. Your homeowner's policy provides coverage because your child is covered under your policy and the act was careless, not intentional.
- You buy some ten-foot 2x4s at the lumberyard, drive home, and lift them out of the car and onto your shoulder. You stop to talk to your neighbor for a minute and then turn toward your backyard, thereby swinging the 2x4 squarely in your neighbor's eye and causing serious damage. It's a negligent act and you are covered.

Not all cases are so clear-cut, however. The legal newspapers are full of cases involving insurance companies' refusals to represent their insureds in close cases—sometimes they win, and sometimes the courts insist that the companies step up and at least defend the lawsuit, if not also pay for settlements or verdicts. The following scenarios illustrate close cases:

- The house that you've just sold had slide problems, but you forgot to tell the buyer before selling the house. The house slips some more and the buyer sues you for fraud. As long as you can convince your insurance company that your failure to reveal the slide problem was due to forgetfulness and was not

Coverage for Persons Who Do Work at Your House

If someone who was doing work at your home has sued you, you'll want to get in touch with your insurance agent right away. Here are the common scenarios and the relevant rules:

- **Occasional workers doing low-level work.** These people will be covered under your policy as long as they are not considered your employees (and are not doing work that must by law be done by an independent contractor, as explained below). For example, suppose you hire the neighborhood kid to mow the lawn every Saturday. He trips in a gopher hole and twists his ankle. Your policy will probably cover this accident.
- **Housekeepers or other domestic help who are your employees (or who would be considered employees regardless of how you designate them).** Since 1977, California law requires insurance companies to cover "residence employees" within a homeowner's policy. (Calif. Ins. Code § 11590.) However, during the 90 days preceding the accident, your employee must have actually worked at least 52 hours and been paid at least $100 in wages.

- **Independent contractors injured on the job.** People who have their own businesses and perform work for many clients are independent contractors. The owners should have workers' compensation policies for their employees, which will cover accidents on the job (the owners themselves may or may not have their own, personal policies). If a contractor's employee is injured and the contractor does not have workers' comp coverage, you may be liable. Whether your homeowner's policy will cover you is a complicated question that depends on many factors. Get help from a lawyer if you find yourself in this situation.
- **Unlicensed people (who are not independent contractors) whom you hire to do work that must, by law, be done by a licensed contractor.** By law, many types of work must be performed by a licensed contractor, including roofing, tree work, and electrical work. If you nevertheless hire someone who is not licensed and that person is injured while on the job, you may be liable—and your homeowner's policy may not cover you. Again, if you are in this position, see a lawyer.

intentional, the company may agree to defend you.

- You and some guy you've never met get into a little argument around the pool table in a local bar. The argument gets more heated and suddenly the other guy is bleeding and claiming you punched him. If his lawyer includes a cause of action for a negligent act (and your insurance company buys your report that if you caused any injury, it was a careless, not intentional act), you are covered.

The lesson to be learned here is that it always pays to read the policy and ask whether you are covered. If you are unsure, file a claim anyway and see what happens. Keep in mind that the insurance company's duty to defend you is broader (applies in more situations) than their duty to pay out if you lose, so at the very least you might get defense help. You can always decide to live with a denial of coverage, but if the case is close, you may want to pursue it. Convincing an insurance company to cover you is beyond the scope of this book and will usually require the help of a lawyer.

CAUTION
Don't rely on a homeowner's or renter's policy if the incident that caused the claim involved your business. You'll need commercial liability insurance for these claims, unless you've obtained a separate endorsement to your homeowner's policy.

Motor Vehicle Policies

If you're being sued over a car accident, by all means refer the policy to your insurance company unless you are convinced that there are good reasons to handle it on your own—such as the desire not to rack up another claim against your policy. But understand that even if you don't tell your insurance company about the accident, they will find out about it if the person suing you reports it to his or her insurance company.

Dealing With Your Insurance Company

If it's at all possible that your insurance will cover the case, contact your insurance agent or a claims adjuster immediately. Ask for an appointment and make copies of the papers you were served with. Deliver the copies to your agent and have the agent sign a note acknowledging receipt. Ask if the insurance company will defend you (and therefore file a response within 30 days). The agent may respond in one of three ways—a waffle, a denial, or an acceptance of the claim.

The Waffle

The agent may tell you that the company will take care of the matter, but then refuse to say so in writing. In this case, write the agent a letter confirming what he or she said, and send it "return receipt requested." Instead, you could send the same letter to the regional or home office of your insurance company.

The Denial

The insurance company may refuse to defend you. If you disagree, reread your policy to learn what the insured (that's you) must do to contest a "denial of coverage." Comply with these provisions. Also, write the company a letter similar to the Sample Letter Protesting Denial of Coverage, below.

If the company still denies coverage, seek some advice on whether to pursue your claim against the company further. A good insurance broker not connected with the dispute is likely to have a valuable opinion, and this advice won't cost anything if the broker thinks you may change policies in the future.

You can also consult a lawyer. Some lawyers specialize in insurance coverage situations, but it's a challenge to find the right lawyer who will charge an affordable fee (see Chapter 17). The yellow pages contain an attorney subcategory entitled "Insurance Law." If you don't have any other leads, call several of these listings to see if you can work out a reasonable fee for a consultation.

Sample Letter Protesting Denial of Coverage

December 10, 20xx

Helpful Hands Insurance Company
349 West Fifth Street
Los Angeles, CA 90013

Re: Homeowner's Policy 345 678 989

To Whom It May Concern:

On November 15, 20xx I delivered to your agent Ralph Rizzo a Complaint naming me as a defendant in Los Angeles Superior Court action 445 786, which was served upon me November 12, 20xx. You have informed me that you are denying coverage because the above policy does not cover the matters addressed in the suit.

As a result of your action, I will be forced to hire an attorney or represent myself without legal assistance. This letter is notice that when the lawsuit is resolved, I will bring an action against your company for your failure to defend me.

Sincerely,
Will Reconwith
Will Reconwith

The Acceptance

The insurance company may, of course, agree to defend you. If it does, it should give you a letter to that effect. The letter may be one of two kinds.

- **An agreement to defend and cover any settlement or judgment.** The insurance company agrees that the incident is covered and defends the case. This means it will also pay any settlement or judgment obtained by the plaintiff, as long as it's within your policy limit.
- **An agreement to defend only.** The insurance company may believe that the incident really isn't one of the types of occurrences that your policy is designed to cover, but it may also realize that it doesn't know enough yet to make that decision. In this situation, the company will agree to provide you with a lawyer, but won't commit to paying any settlement or judgment obtained by the plaintiff. The letter (called a "reservation of rights" letter) will state that the company will make this final decision as more facts develop. If this happens to you, meet with the insurance company's lawyer at once. If you feel comfortable and the lawyer agrees to consult with you and keep you informed about the status of the case, you probably want to accept this defense from the insurance company. But if you are not comfortable with the lawyer and are not convinced you'll be kept informed, consider hiring your own lawyer to work with the insurance company's lawyer and see that you are getting the defense you are entitled to.

Consider Settling

When you are sued, you should always consider settling with the plaintiff. Just because the plaintiff "prays" for $25,000 in the complaint doesn't mean $5,000 in settlement won't be accepted. Remember—most people use arbitrary and inflated numbers in the Complaint.

> **EXAMPLE:** Oliver borrowed $12,000 from Kate, but can't pay her back. Kate sues him for the $12,000 plus interest and the cost of collection. Oliver scrapes together $8,000 and offers that amount to settle the whole thing. Kate accepts, knowing that the costs and delays of a lawsuit make a healthy discount worthwhile. She also realizes that because Oliver is in poor financial shape, having the cash now is preferable to trying to collect a judgment later.

If you want to try to settle the case, read Chapter 3 and consider its tips on how to negotiate. If you do settle the case, be sure to file (or to have the plaintiff file) a Request for Dismissal, which is explained in "Taking Care of the Details" in Chapter 3.

Ways to Settle an Expensive Lawsuit Fast

If you don't have the money or energy to fight a battle with the plaintiff, you may want to try to settle fast. One way is to contact a law firm and find out what it would cost to have one of its attorneys write a letter stating, "This firm represents Mr. Evans in this matter and intends to engage in a vigorous defense of the lawsuit you have filed." Some plaintiffs (especially those representing themselves), faced with the prospect of a major battle, will decide to settle for a reasonable sum.

If your financial position is such that it's unlikely you'd be able to pay the plaintiff a large judgment anytime soon, you may use this information to try and get a quick settlement too. Some plaintiffs will be interested in a quick settlement and guaranteed payment, rather than the hassle of a lawsuit and a drawn out recovery.

> **EXAMPLE:** Bruce, an uninsured driver, is blinded by the sun while going through a stoplight and hits Jennifer's car. Jennifer has a whiplash injury and is treated by a chiropractor for several weeks. The police give Bruce a citation. Jennifer acts as her own attorney and serves Bruce with a complaint. He sends her the following letter:

October 12, 20xx

Dear Ms. Brown:

I am anxious to settle with you regarding the damages you claim as a result of the collision between our cars last month. Unfortunately, I am in terrible financial shape and cannot offer much money. I was laid off from my job in July and am now living on unemployment insurance. I have enclosed a copy of my most recent check to verify this. I have no insurance. Since being laid off, I have exhausted the small savings account I had. A copy of my most recent bank statement is enclosed.

My parents have agreed to lend me $4,500 to settle this matter and I hereby offer that sum to you in exchange for a complete release from all damages you have suffered. I believe I could get you the money within ten days if you indicate it is acceptable and that you will sign a release prepared by my father.

Sincerely,
Bruce Nosum
Bruce Nosum

Mediation

Every day in California, mediation sessions settle more disputes than the court system resolves in a month. Mediation is not only inexpensive, it's relatively quick and far less stressful than being involved in a contested lawsuit. The process is described in Chapter 3, along with hints on how to find a mediation center in your area.

Should you doubt mediation will be effective to settle your dispute, you should understand that professional mediators have gone through extensive training on how to break an impasse between parties who just can't seem to agree. Since retiring, I have done a number of successful mediations with divorcing parties who at the outset couldn't even stand to be in the same room with each other. In short, mediation can and does frequently work to help resolve even seemingly intractable disputes.

Decide Whether to Represent Yourself

The balance of this chapter describes the procedures to follow if you represent yourself in defending the lawsuit. Defending yourself in a court system designed for lawyers can be stressful, time-consuming, and frequently frustrating. But it can also be rewarding, self-empowering, and, of course, often necessary if you can't afford to hire a lawyer. The pros and cons are covered in Chapter 1.

If You Have No Defense

If you decide to represent yourself and you have no defense, you should still take steps to protect your interests. At the very least, you should file an Answer and show up for the court date. If you don't file an Answer, you'll lose the case by default (the process is explained in Chapter 9) and you won't be informed of any future court dates, nor will you have a chance to check over the plaintiff's evidence. Don't depend on the judge to do this for you—nobody is very concerned about the rights of someone who can't bother to come to court.

There's an almost unlimited list of horrors that attend the entry of a default judgment. The plaintiff may submit medical bills that don't relate to your accident or falsely claim lost time from work. You'll miss a possible chance to reduce the plaintiff's award—for example, if you explain your side of the story, the judge might conclude that the plaintiff caused part of the accident and thus reduce the plaintiff's award.

> **EXAMPLE:** Don borrowed $9,000 from a bank, which sues him for failing to repay it. When Don borrowed the money, he signed a contract letting the bank recover costs and attorney's fees if it had to sue him. At trial, the bank's lawyer claims that those fees (the lawyer's bill and a collection agency's bill) total $6,000. Don filed an Answer and attended his trial, where he protests those amounts as excessive. The judge agrees and sets them at $2,000. Had Don not been in court, it might have cost him $4,000.

Another advantage of filing an Answer and attending the trial, even if you expect to lose, is that it gives you an opportunity to ask the court to let you pay the judgment in monthly payments. (Code of Civil Procedure § 582.5.) In the above example, Don might have gone on to convince the judge to let him pay $300 a month. So long as he makes the payments, the other side can't garnish his wages or take other aggressive collection actions. But if Don hadn't answered and appeared in court, the entire judgment would be payable immediately. This would enable the creditor to set up a wage garnishment, attach Don's bank accounts, and place a lien on his house.

Handling Your Case After a Default

In the event you are reading this after judgment has already been entered in your case, all is not lost. The court can order installments at any time before the judgment has been paid. The problem is that if you want to arrange for payment terms after a judgment has been entered, you must file a motion in the court, serve the plaintiff with a notice of the motion, and appear in court to make your request. To prepare such a motion, take a look at the forms in "File a Motion to Compel" in Chapter 10, and simply change the title to Motion to Order Payment of Judgment by Installments (Code of Civil Procedure § 582.5). Follow the instructions preceding the forms for getting your motion set for hearing.

Ask for More Time

You might need more than 30 days to file your response—for example, if discussions with your insurance company (over whether it will defend you) or with potential lawyers have taken up most of that time. If so, call the plaintiff (or the plaintiff's lawyer) and ask for a 15-day extension for you to file an Answer. The Case Management rules explained in Chapter 6 limit the amount of time the plaintiff can give you, but most (lawyers, at least) will agree to an extra week or two. If the plaintiff agrees to extend your time, send a confirming letter immediately, as shown by the Sample Letter Confirming Time Extension, below.

Sample Letter Confirming Time Extension

September 23, 20xx

John Tweedle, Esq.
Tweedle, Dee, & Dum
405 14th Street
Oakland, California 97001

Re: *Solomon vs. Sucherman*, case # 890 765

Dear Mr. Tweedle:

This letter confirms our phone conversation today, in which you agreed that I may have until October 19, 20xx, to answer or otherwise plead in this case. If you believe this is not our agreement, please contact me immediately.

Sincerely,

Monica Sucherman

Monica Sucherman

If the plaintiff or the plaintiff's lawyer won't agree to an extension of time (most lawyers will), you can ask the court for one. Be sure to do so before the 30 days has expired. The Request must be accompanied by a declaration under penalty of perjury explaining why you need more time. The declaration must also state that by at least 10 a.m. on the prior court day, you informed the plaintiff that you would be requesting an extension of time.

To get your extension, you will need to prepare a form called a "Request for Extension of Time to Plead." This is not a fill-in-the-blanks form, but one that you must type on numbered legal paper. An example is shown below. When you prepare your own, of course, you'll give the reason that corresponds to your situation. Keep your explanation clear and brief. You'll also need to prepare a document called an order—it's for the judge to sign if your request is granted. On a separate sheet of paper with a heading just like the one on the Request, type the word "Order" in place of "Request for Extension." A sample appears below. If the judge grants your request, he or she will fill in the appropriate date, then sign and date the order.

Deliver the Request and Order, along with two copies of each and a stamped, self-addressed envelope, to the court clerk. The judge will usually consider the issue without scheduling a hearing. Ask when and how you will know whether the judge has granted your request. Once you get the signed Order back, be sure to keep one copy for your records and send another copy to the plaintiff or the plaintiff's lawyer.

Prepare an Answer

By filing an Answer, you establish that you're contesting the case and requiring the plaintiff to prove the case at trial to win. This section guides you through the form that most defendants will use. First, however, I'll explain some alternate or simultaneous motions that a few defendants may find useful.

Filing a Response Other Than an Answer

The law requires that you "respond" to the complaint within 30 days. Your response does not necessarily have to be an Answer. Lawyers frequently spend hours filing "motion" papers objecting to a Complaint before they ever file an Answer (or at the same time as filing an Answer). This is the litigation game. Usually, all it does is delay the inevitable (filing an Answer if you haven't yet done so) and make the lawyer's wallet thicker. Nevertheless, here are some of the grounds for filing one of those other possible responses.

The Plaintiff Filed in the Wrong State

It's possible that you should have been sued in a state other than California. To raise this defense, you must file a document called a "General Demurrer." If you now live in California, however, you'll gain very little by objecting. The lawsuit may

MONICA SUCHERMAN
1818 Euclid Avenue
San Francisco, CA 94111
415-555-7777
Defendant In Pro Per

SUPERIOR COURT OF CALIFORNIA—LIMITED JURISDICTION

CITY AND COUNTY OF SAN FRANCISCO

LITTLE PEN SHOPPE,)	
)	
Plaintiff,)	Case No. 4443-9000
)	
vs.)	REQUEST FOR EXTENSION
)	OF TIME TO PLEAD
MONICA SUCHERMAN,)	
)	
Defendant.)	

Defendant cannot afford to hire a lawyer to represent her in this case and is undertaking the research to represent herself. She needs and requests an additional 20 days to complete the necessary work.

Monica Sucherman   3-17-xx
Signature   Date

MONICA SUCHERMAN
1818 Euclid Avenue
San Francisco, CA 94111
415-555-7777
Defendant In Pro Per

SUPERIOR COURT OF CALIFORNIA—LIMITED JURISDICTION

CITY AND COUNTY OF SAN FRANCISCO

LITTLE PEN SHOPPE,	))
Plaintiff,	) Case No. 4443-9000)
vs.	) ORDER GRANTING DEFENDANT'S MOTION) FOR EXTENSION OF TIME TO PLEAD
MONICA SUCHERMAN,	))
Defendant.	)

ORDER

It is hereby ordered that defendant may have until _____ to answer in this matter.

_____   _____
Judge of the Superior Court   Date

be thrown out and then refiled in a different state, where it will probably be very inconvenient for you to defend. Chapter 4 explains how to analyze a case to determine whether it has been properly brought before a California court.

The Plaintiff Filed in the Wrong County

It's also possible that you've been sued in the wrong county—you can find out for sure by reviewing "Selecting the Right Court" in Chapter 4. If so, you can request that the case be moved by filing a Motion for Change of Venue when you file your Answer. It's not terribly complicated, but it does require that you compose and type several documents. Unless the county where the suit has been filed is truly inconvenient, it's probably best to ignore the problem.

If it is terribly inconvenient, consider hiring a lawyer to help you prepare a pro per Motion for Change of Venue. The lawyer prepares the papers that are filed in your name, and you argue the motion in court without the lawyer. To prepare the forms yourself, see *California Forms of Pleading and Practice*, Volume 50, Chapter 571, pages 105–117.

The Plaintiff Filed in the Wrong Branch

As explained in Chapter 4, many Superior Courts have branches within their county. Some will allow a plaintiff to file a complaint in the main courthouse or in any branch. Others require the plaintiff to show a good legal reason to file in any particular branch. If you are sued in an inappropriate branch and want to get the case transferred to the main courthouse or one of the other branches, consider carefully whether it is worth making a big fuss over the problem.

In many instances it won't be worth the trouble it takes to raise this technical challenge. However, in some counties it can mean a drive of an hour or more to get from one outlying branch to another closer to you. In that case, I recommend a letter to the judge in the branch where the case was filed (with a copy to the plaintiff), explaining the problem and asking for a transfer (judges have the power to do this without a motion being filed). A Sample Letter Asking for Change of Venue is shown below. If the judge tells you you'll have to file a formal motion, follow the procedure in the last section. You may decide to skip it and suffer the long drive.

Sample Letter Asking for Change of Venue

Hon. Peter H. Norell, Presiding Judge
San Bernardino Superior Court
172 W. Third Street
San Bernardino, CA 92415

Re: *Somers vs. Black*, case no. SC 987 376

Dear Judge Norell:

I am the defendant in the above case involving an automobile accident that occurred last year in Needles, which is where my home is located. Plaintiff has filed this case in the Rancho Cucamonga Branch of the court, which I believe is very close to where she resides. As I am sure you know, Needles and Rancho Cucamonga are over 200 miles apart. The Mapquest program on my computer estimates the driving time between these two cities is over three hours. I operate my own business in Needles and traveling all the way to Rancho Cucamonga for hearings would be very expensive and time-consuming for me.

I respectfully request you transfer this case from the Rancho Cucamonga branch of the court to the Needles branch.

If such a transfer is not convenient for the court, the Barstow branch would be acceptable, but even that would leave me with a drive of over two hours.

Respectfully,

Andrew Black

Andrew Black

cc: Martha Somers

The Plaintiff Filed in an Inconvenient County

You can file a Motion for Change of Venue if the county in which the case was filed will be inconvenient for the people who will be called as witnesses. You don't have to file this Motion with the Answer, but be sure to file it soon thereafter. Again, you'll probably be best off having a lawyer draft the Motion for you to file but arguing it yourself.

Improper Service

You may have been served incorrectly with the Summons and Complaint (the rules are explained in Chapter 7). For example, the papers may have been shoved under your door when you weren't home. You can contest it by filing a Motion to Quash Service. You'd probably need the help of a lawyer, and normally would accomplish very little—the plaintiff will simply have you served again—most likely on the day you show up in court to fight the initial improper service! Again, in most cases it's probably best to ignore the problem.

Legal Defects in the Complaint

You can challenge some types of legal defects in a Complaint by filing a General Demurrer (the same document you'd file if the plaintiff sued you in the wrong state) or a Motion to Strike a portion of the prayer (where the plaintiff states what he or she is asking for) of the Complaint. For example, if the Complaint does not include all of the necessary allegations (such as a negligence complaint that never states that you acted negligently), you could file a Demurrer. But this procedure is not worth your time, especially given that even if you're successful, the plaintiff will usually file an Amended Complaint correcting the technical defect and the case will continue.

In your perusal of the law books, you may also encounter a legal pleading called a "special demurrer." Special demurrers are not allowed in limited jurisdiction cases. (Code of Civil Procedure § 92c.)

> **Verified Complaints**
>
> Occasionally a plaintiff may sign the bottom of a Complaint verifying that the contents are true and given under penalty of perjury. This is called a "verified complaint." It used to be that if served with a verified complaint, a defendant's answer also had to be verified. But that's no longer true in a limited jurisdiction case, so even if the plaintiff's Complaint is verified, your Answer doesn't have to be.

File Your Alternate Response on Time

Be sure that your response is filed on time. This means within 30 days of the date you were served with the Summons and Complaint (or whatever extension you arranged). If you file a General Demurrer or Motion to Strike after the proceedings are finished, the court will tell you how long you have to file an Answer.

If you don't make the 30-day deadline, it may not be too late to file, since the clerk will accept your response for filing any time until the plaintiff files a Request to Enter Default (described in Chapter 9). If the plaintiff has delayed filing this Request, you might slip in under the wire.

If you attempt to file your response *after* the plaintiff has taken a judgment against you by default, the clerk will refuse to accept it. You'll need to quickly get the help of a lawyer (or represent yourself) to ask the court to "set aside the default." Your right to do this normally expires six months after the default was entered. The decision is up to the judge, who may not be very sympathetic, especially if you let several months go by without a good excuse. In short, just because you have six months doesn't mean you should ever wait six months. The longer you wait, the more difficult it may be to set aside a default.

Examine the Complaint's Causes of Action

Now it's time to turn to the Complaint itself. The Complaint may be divided into several Causes of Action (First Cause of Action, Second Cause of Action, and so on). Each cause of action contains numbered paragraphs. These Causes of Action are often different ways of stating the same facts under different legal theories. Sometimes, one Cause of Action incorporates by reference paragraphs from another Cause of Action.

In your Answer, you must state which of the plaintiff's assertions you agree with and which you dispute. To do this, you must respond to every paragraph containing an allegation. For each paragraph, your choices will be to:
- admit the allegation
- deny the allegation
- deny the allegation on information and belief
- deny the allegation because you don't have enough information at this time to make certain denial, or
- when faced with a complaint on pleading paper (not a fill-in-the-box form), skip any paragraph that simply incorporates earlier paragraphs.

Let me explain each of these options one at a time.

> **Typing an Attachment Sheet**
>
> If you run out of space on any printed form, you can finish the information on another official form, called an Attachment. See "Preparing an Attachment" in Chapter 5 for instructions on how to use this form.

Admitting the Allegations

For each paragraph where you agree absolutely with everything said (such as "Market Street and Van Ness Avenue intersect in the City and County of San Francisco"), write "admit" next to it. If you admit a statement, the plaintiff won't have to prove it. Thus, admit only those statements you have absolutely no argument about. But don't refuse to admit something obviously true just to make it hard for the plaintiff. Forcing a plaintiff to prove that Market Street is in San Francisco will anger a judge who is trying to sort out the real disputes in the case and avoid wasting time. But if you honestly don't know if a statement is true or you agree with only part of it, don't admit it.

Denying the Allegations

Write "deny" near each paragraph in which you deny all *or part* of what was said. For instance, suppose a paragraph says, "Defendant was speeding and driving recklessly on Elm Street." If you agree that you were on Elm Street but deny that you were speeding or reckless, deny the whole paragraph.

Denying on Information and Belief

If you are not sure what the truth is, but you believe the plaintiff's statement is probably more false than true, write "deny on information and belief." For instance, if the plaintiff has alleged that the accident happened at night, but you think—and aren't completely sure—it was in the late afternoon, use this designation.

Denying Because You Lack Sufficient Information

You may have no idea whether or not an allegation in a paragraph is true, especially if the allegation concerns your opponent. For example, a paragraph saying that the plaintiff was on the job performing his duties as a delivery person when the accident happened may be true or not—most of the time, you'll have no way of knowing. In these situations, write "deny because no information."

TIP
Don't obsess about which type of denial to use. The distinctions among the different types of denials

can be vague. Don't spend a lot of time worrying about which is precisely appropriate. As long as you use one of them, you are protected.

Responding to Allegations in Pleading Paper Complaints

If the Complaint is on pleading paper (instead of a fill-in-the-blanks form) and has more than one Cause of Action, it probably will have a paragraph at the beginning of the second, and each subsequent Cause of Action, incorporating paragraphs (often referred to as allegations) from other Causes of Action. This is an accepted way for the plaintiff to avoid repeating the same information (for example, that the accident occurred at Market Street and Van Ness Avenue in San Francisco). It may read something like this: "Plaintiff incorporates paragraphs 1-7 of his First Cause of Action and makes them a part of this Second Cause of Action." Because you've already responded to the earlier allegations, you don't need to put a designation next to the incorporating paragraphs. Start your admitting or denying process with the next paragraph.

Using a Fill-in-the-Blanks Form

You can use a fill-in-the-blanks form to respond to contract Complaints and those dealing with injuries to people and property (torts). (If you don't know what a contract or tort is, see Chapter 4.) Use these forms even if the plaintiff wrote a Complaint on pleading paper. There is no reason to draft your own Answer from scratch. Save your creative energies for the trial, where you'll have plenty of opportunities to exercise them.

TIP
Use the contract or tort form to respond to other types of Complaints, too. Cross out the words "Personal Injury, Property Damage, Wrongful Death" or "Contract" in the title and substitute whatever the plaintiff called the suit in this part of the Complaint.

SKIP AHEAD
If your case involves a contract or anything other than a tort case, skip ahead to "Contract Cases."

Tort Cases (Personal Injury and Property Damage)

Use the form *Answer–Personal Injury, Property Damage, Wrongful Death* to answer a Complaint based on these claims. Make several photocopies of the form and fill one in with pencil as a rough draft before you type it. The instructions below guide you through the parts of the form.

FORM
The appendix contains a tear-out version of Form PLD-PI-003, *Answer–Personal Injury, Property Damage, Wrongful Death*, and you can download one from the Judicial Council website at www.courtinfo.ca.gov. A filled-out sample is shown below.

Attorney or Party Without Attorney (Name and Address): Write your name and the address at which you want to receive mail about the case. Include a phone number, preferably where you can be reached during the day. If you aren't reachable at a phone number, don't put anything—you don't have to have a phone to defend a lawsuit. Put "Defendant in pro per" after the line that says "Attorney for (Name):"

Insert name of court, judicial district or branch court, if any, and post office and street address: Copy this information from the Complaint.

Plaintiff: Fill in the names of the plaintiffs exactly as they appear on the Complaint.

Defendant: Fill in the names of the defendants, exactly as they appear on the Complaint, even if your name is misspelled.

Complaint of (name): Check this box and type in the name(s) of the plaintiff(s) whose Complaint you are answering, unless you are a plaintiff answering a defendant's Cross-Complaint. In either case, just below the name, type (in all capital letters) the words, "LIMITED CIVIL CASE." Adding this phrase is necessary because the form is behind the times and has not caught up with the advent of limited jurisdiction cases in Superior Court.

Cross-Complaint of (name): Skip this box, unless you are a plaintiff answering a defendant's Cross-Complaint.

Case Number: Type in the case number that's on the Summons and Complaint. Make sure you type the number correctly.

Item 1. Skip this for now. You'll come back to it.

Item 2. Defendant or Cross-Defendant (name): Don't enter any information following the line that reads "DEFENDANT OR CROSS-DEFENDANT (name)." An old law allows you, in some cases, to check the box that follows, but it's not worth the hassle. Just leave that box blank.

Item 3. Here you make use of the "admit" and "deny" notations you made above.

Item 3a. Check this box if you wrote "deny" for any paragraphs in the Complaint. Next, list the numbers of all the paragraphs you denied. If the Complaint has only one Cause of Action, simply type the corresponding paragraph numbers (for instance, "3, 5, 7, and 9"). If the Complaint has several Causes of Action, type your answers to each separate Cause of Action (such as "First Cause of Action—paragraphs 3, 5, 6, 7, and 8; Second Cause of Action—paragraphs 1, 2, 5, 7, and 9").

Item 3b. Follow the instructions for Item 3a for all paragraphs next to which you wrote "admit."

Item 3c. Follow the instructions for Item 3a for all paragraphs next to which you wrote "deny on information and belief."

Item 3d. Follow the instructions for Item 3a for all paragraphs next to which you wrote "deny because no information."

Item 3e. This is repetitive of the information above and you do not need to put anything here.

Short Title: Put the last names (or the business names) of the first (perhaps only) plaintiff and the first (perhaps only) defendant, separated by a "vs.," such as "Brown vs. Black" or "Brown vs. Golden Bear Typing Service."

Case Number: Copy it from the Complaint.

Item 3f. Skip this item.

Item 3g. You should check the box and add some silly legal words to cover an ancient legal principle called a "negative pregnant." Negative pregnant is the theory that if you deny that you owe the plaintiff $7,000, you are not denying that you owe him a sum less than $7,000, such as $6,999. To cover the possibility that you're admitting that you owe the plaintiff anything, I suggest you use the language set out below. If it seems ridiculous, that's because it is. I could probably invent a humorous story about this name, but I doubt you are much interested in jokes, so just check the box and type:

"In denying the allegations of the Complaint above, defendant denies not only the specific numbers and amounts alleged by plaintiff, but all other numbers and amounts claimed."

Items 4, 5, and 6. In these items, you raise any affirmative defenses you have. An affirmative defense goes beyond simply denying the facts and arguments in the plaintiff's Complaint. It sets out new facts and arguments that support your version of what happened. If you prove your affirmative defense, even if what the plaintiff's Complaint states is true, you will win, or at least reduce the amount the plaintiff is entitled to recover against you.

Item 4. Use this affirmative defense if you believe that the plaintiff was completely or partially at fault concerning the event described in the Complaint. This legal concept is called comparative fault and is explained in "Tort Cases" in Chapter 2. If it applies, check the box and put in the name of the plaintiff(s) who were at fault. Then describe the fault, with something like "Plaintiff's negligence legally contributed to his damages and injuries in that he:

		PLD-PI-003
ATTORNEY OR PARTY WITHOUT ATTORNEY *(NAME AND ADDRESS)*: Bonnie Rose 1406 Silverspoon Circle San Jose, CA 95100 ATTORNEY FOR *(NAME)*: defendant in pro per	TELEPHONE NO.: 408-555-6290	FOR COURT USE ONLY
Insert name of court, judicial district or branch court, if any, and post office and street address: Superior Court, County of Santa Clara San Jose Facility 200 W. Hedding St. San Jose, CA 95110		
PLAINTIFF: Daniel Woods		
DEFENDANT: Bonnie Rose, Does 1-5		
ANSWER—Personal Injury, Property Damage, Wrongful Death [X] **COMPLAINT OF** *(name)*: Daniel Wood [ ] **CROSS-COMPLAINT OF** *(name)*:	CASE NUMBER: RW843-2	

1. This pleading, including attachments and exhibits, consists of the following number of pages: __2__

DEFENDANT OR CROSS-DEFENDANT *(name)*:

2. [ ] Generally **denies** each allegation of the unverified complaint or cross-complaint.

3. a. [X] DENIES each allegation of the following numbered paragraphs:

   8, 10, MV-1, MV-2

   b. [X] ADMITS each allegation of the following numbered paragraphs:

   1, 5, 11

   c. [X] DENIES, ON INFORMATION AND BELIEF, each allegation of the following numbered paragraphs:

   2, 3, 4

   d. [X] DENIES, BECAUSE OF LACK OF SUFFICIENT INFORMATION OR BELIEF TO ANSWER, each allegation of the following numbered paragraphs:

   6, 7, 9

   e. [ ] ADMITS the following allegations and generally denies all other allegations:

Page 1 of 2

Form Approved for Optional Use
Judicial Council of California
PLD-PI-003 [Rev. January 1, 2007]

ANSWER—Personal Injury, Property Damage, Wrongful Death

Code of Civil Procedure, § 425.12
www.courtinfo.ca.gov

SHORT TITLE: Woods vs. Rose	CASE NUMBER: RW843-2

PLD-PI-003

ANSWER—Personal Injury, Property Damage, Wrongful Death

    f. ☐ DENIES the following allegations and admits all other allegations:

    g. ☒ Other *(specify)*:
        In denying the allegations of the complaint, above, defendant denies not only the specific numbers and amounts alleged by plaintiff, but all other numbers and amounts claimed.

AFFIRMATIVELY ALLEGES AS A DEFENSE

4. ☒ The comparative fault of plaintiff or cross-complainant *(name)*:
    as follows:
    Plaintiff's negligence legally contributed to his damages and injuries in that he ran a stop sign, sped, and made an illegal left turn.

5. ☒ The expiration of the Statute of Limitations as follows:
    Plaintiff failed to file this action within two years of his personal injury.

6. ☐ Other *(specify)*:

7. DEFENDANT OR CROSS - DEFENDANT PRAYS
    For costs of suit and that plaintiff or cross-complainant take nothing.
    ☐ Other *(specify)*:

_____   _____
Bonnie Rose   *Bonnie Rose*
(Type or print name)   (Signature of party or attorney)

- "failed to drive with due caution, was speeding and ran a red light."
- "ignored barriers and signs warning all pedestrians that the sidewalk was under construction."
- "knew there was an angry dog on the other side of the gate, but nevertheless opened the gate and walked into the yard."
- "had his head buried in a newspaper while ascending the stairs and failed to see an obvious hazard."
- "placed the ladder on which he was working against an obviously rotten pole."

Don't raise any affirmative defense that is ridiculous. For example, don't allege that a pedestrian who was walking calmly across the street in a crosswalk was somehow partly at fault when you ran a red light and hit her. If you can't come up with a rational theory of why the plaintiff contributed to the incident, don't say anything.

Item 5. Use this affirmative defense if you believe that the plaintiff didn't file the lawsuit within the time allowed by the law, called the statute of limitations. "Is Your Case Fresh Enough?" in Chapter 2 describes the applicable time limits. If the plaintiff hasn't complied, check the box and describe the problem, such as:

- "Plaintiff failed to file this action within two years of his personal injury."
- "Plaintiff's suit was not filed within three years after his alleged property damage."

Item 6. Check this box only if one or more of the following special defenses applies. Then describe the defense.

Bankruptcy. If you listed this matter in a bankruptcy in which you were discharged, write, "any obligation plaintiff claims defendant owes was discharged in bankruptcy on _____ in case number _____."

Self-defense. If the plaintiff claims you deliberately injured him or her, but you believe you were protecting yourself, type something like "At all times and in all of the actions described in the Complaint, defendant was defending himself from plaintiff's unjustified and unprovoked attack."

Assumption of risk. "Assumption of risk" means that before being injured or damaged, the plaintiff knew (or should have known) that there was a risk of injury or damage in the activity and is therefore responsible for any reasonably foreseeable accident that caused personal injury, even if it was caused by a negligent act of the defendant. If you are sued, you can claim that plaintiff assumed the risk in situations that resemble the following examples, and let the judge decide what the law is on this subject:

- You run wild river rafting expeditions and you had the plaintiff passenger sign a release before the trip started, acknowledging that rafting is dangerous and that there is a possibility that passengers will be injured.
- Plaintiff rents a horse named Tequila from your riding stable, after you tell her that the horse is very spirited and sometimes hard to control. Plaintiff tells you she is an experienced rider and that she is sure she can handle Tequila.
- You and your best friend are playing an informal game of touch football on the lawn in front of your house—something you have done many times before. While looking into the sky in anticipation of fielding a punt, you accidentally run into your best friend, who is waiting to tag you, and you break her hand, eventually causing a finger to be amputated.
- The wooden bridge over the stream in front of your house becomes rickety and you can't afford to fix it for a while. You place a large sign at its entrance, stating "Dangerous Bridge, Do Not Enter." Your mailbox is on the other side of the bridge. Your mailman ignores the sign and attempts to cross. The bridge collapses and he is badly injured.

Workers' compensation remedy. If you are the plaintiff's employer and the plaintiff sustained an injury while acting within the scope of employment, he or she should be covered by your workers' compensation insurance policy. If so, check this box and write, "Plaintiff's claim is barred by the Workers' Compensation Act." This Act requires an employee injured on the job to file a form titled "Employee's Claim for Workers' Compensation Benefits" with the worker's employer.

Someone working as an independent contractor, rather than as an employee, is not barred by the Workers' Compensation Act from suing the hiring person or business. Also, an employee injured on the job can sue any person who may be responsible for the injuries, other than the employer. Because these distinctions are sometimes hazy, raise this defense any time an employee sues you unless it is clear that the injury had nothing to do with the job.

Miscellaneous. Several tort suits that are not covered by this book have rules regarding affirmative defenses if you are sued for libel, slander, inducing another person to breach a contract, or for interfering with another person's prospective advantage, but they are so rare that they don't merit discussion here. If you suspect you may have such a case, consult a lawyer or the set of books described below.

Other defenses to be aware of in any case where you are sued include:
- plaintiff has signed a release as part of a settlement
- there's another lawsuit pending between these parties over the same matter
- plaintiff is a corporation that has had its corporate powers suspended for not paying taxes, and
- plaintiff is an out-of-state corporation not qualified to do business in California.

RESOURCE
For more information on affirmative defenses, see *California Procedure*, 4th edition, by Bernard Witkin, Vol. 5, Pleading §§ 1027–1079.

Item 7. Skip this item.

Signature line. Type your name above the first line on the left and sign above the signature line. Also, go back to Item 1 and fill in your total number of pages. This will probably be two, but remember to count any attachments, such as a written agreement signed by the plaintiff.

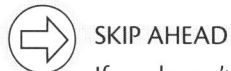

SKIP AHEAD
If you haven't been sued on a contract case, skip to "Prepare a Cross-Complaint."

Contract Cases

To respond to a contract Complaint, use the form Answer–Contract. Use this form even if the Complaint is typed on legal paper from scratch. Make several photocopies of the form and fill one in with pencil as a rough draft before you type it.

FORM
The appendix contains a tear-out version of Form PLD-C-010, *Answer–Contract*, and you can download one from the Judicial Council website at www.courtinfo.ca.gov. A filled-out sample is shown below.

Top Half of Page 1. Fill in these boxes following the instructions in "Tort Cases (Personal Injury and Property Damage)," above.

Item 1. Skip this for now. You'll come back to it.

Item 2. Fill in your name and the name of your business or partnership if it is named in the Complaint. If your spouse is being sued as well, type in both names. Any other defendant should prepare and file a separate Answer.

Item 3a. An old law allows you to check this box in some cases, but it's not worth the hassle. Just leave it blank

Item 3b. Check this box. This item is where you make use of your "admit" and "deny" notations.

PLD-C-010

ATTORNEY OR PARTY WITHOUT ATTORNEY (NAME AND ADDRESS): TELEPHONE:	FOR COURT USE ONLY:
Joan McCoy 805-555-0862 P.O. Box 11178 Santa Barbara, CA 93111	
ATTORNEY FOR (NAME): defendant in pro per	

Insert name of court, judicial district or branch court, if any, and post office and street address:
   Superior Court, County of Santa Barbara
   Santa Barbara Judicial District
   111 E. Figueroa St.
   Santa Barbara, CA 93101

PLAINTIFF:
   A-1 Corporation

DEFENDANT:
   Joan McCoy, individually and dba McCoy's, and Does 1-8

ANSWER—Contract	CASE NUMBER:
[X] TO COMPLAINT OF (name): A-1 Corporation [ ] TO CROSS-COMPLAINT (name):	300045

1. This pleading, including attachments and exhibits, consists of the following number of pages: ___2___

2. DEFENDANT (name): Joan McCoy, individually and dba McCoy's
   answers the complaint or cross-complaint as follows:

3. Check ONLY ONE of the next two boxes:
   a. [ ] Defendant generally denies each statement of the complaint or cross-complaint. *(Do not check this box if the verified complaint or cross-complaint demands more than $1,000.)*
   b. [X] Defendant admits that all of the statements of the complaint or cross-complaint are true EXCEPT:
      (1) Defendant claims the following statements are false *(use paragraph numbers or explain)*:

         3,4,6,9,10,11

         [ ] Continued on Attachment 3.b.(1).
      (2) Defendant has no information or belief that the following statements are true, so defendant denies them *(use paragraph numbers or explain)*:

         5,7,8

         [ ] Continued on Attachment 3.b.(2).

If this form is used to answer a cross-complaint, plaintiff means cross-complainant and defendant means cross-defendant.

Page 1 of 2

Form Approved for Optional Use **ANSWER—Contract** Code of Civil Procedure, § 425.12
Judicial Council of California www.courtinfo.ca.gov
PLD-C-010 [Rev. January 1, 2007]

	PLD-C-010
SHORT TITLE: A-1 Corporation vs. McCoy	CASE NUMBER: 300045

ANSWER—Contract

4. [X] AFFIRMATIVE DEFENSES Defendant alleges the following additional reasons that plaintiff is not entitled to recover anything:

   Plaintiff's lawsuit is barred by Code of Civil Procedure Section 337.

   [ ] Continued on Attachment 4.

5. [X] Other

   In denying the allegations of the Complaint, above, defendant denies not only the specific numbers and amounts alleged by plaintiff, but all other numbers and amounts claimed.

6. DEFENDANT PRAYS
   a. that plaintiff take nothing.
   b. [X] for costs of suit.
   c. [ ] other *(specify)*:

Joan McCoy
(Type or print name)

Joan McCoy
(Signature of party or attorney)

PLD-C - 010 [Rev. January 1, 2007]   ANSWER—Contract   Page 2 of 2

Item 3b(1). Find all the paragraphs next to which you wrote "deny." If the Complaint has only one Cause of Action, simply type the corresponding paragraph numbers (for instance, "3, 5, 7, and 9"). If the Complaint has several Causes of Action, type your answers to each separate Cause of Action (such as "First Cause of Action—paragraphs 3, 5, 6, 7, and 8; Second Cause of Action—paragraphs 1, 2, 5, 7, and 9"). Use attachment pages if necessary.

Item 3b(2). List the paragraphs next to which you wrote "deny on information and belief" or "deny because no information." Then turn to page two of the form.

Short Title: Put the last names (or the business names) of the first (perhaps only) plaintiff and the first (perhaps only) defendant, separated by a "vs.," such as "Brown vs. Black" or "Brown vs. Golden Bear Typing Service."

Case Number: Copy it from the Complaint.

Item 4. Here you raise any affirmative defenses you have. An affirmative defense goes beyond simply denying the facts and arguments in the plaintiff's Complaint. It sets out new facts and arguments. If you prove your affirmative defense, even if what the plaintiff's Complaint states is true, you will win, or at least reduce the amount the plaintiff is entitled to recover against you. Raise all of the following that apply:

Statute of limitations. Use this affirmative defense if the plaintiff didn't file the lawsuit within the time allowed by the law (called the statute of limitations). "Is Your Case Fresh Enough?" in Chapter 2 describes the applicable time limits, which depend on whether the contract is written or oral. If the plaintiff hasn't complied, check the box and write:

- "Plaintiff's lawsuit is barred by Code of Civil Procedure Section 337" (written contract); or
- "Plaintiff's lawsuit is barred by Code of Civil Procedure Section 339" (oral contract).

Statute of frauds. Use this affirmative defense if the contract should have been in writing but wasn't. (See "Breach of Contract Cases" in Chapter 1 for a brief discussion of the statute of frauds.) Check this box and write, "Plaintiff's claim is barred by the Statute of Frauds—Civil Code Section 1624."

Contract signed because of force, fraud, or the pressure of someone in a confidential relationship. Use this affirmative defense if you signed the contract because of the plaintiff's physical force, threats, or fraud. Fraud is the intentional lying or concealing of an important fact in order to induce you to sign the contract. For example, if you loaned a friend $10,000 based on his written statement that the Food and Drug Administration had approved a drug he had developed but, in fact, FDA approval had been denied, the inducement for the loan would have been fraudulent.

This affirmative defense also applies when one member of a confidential relationship puts inappropriate pressure on the other, resulting in a contract that forms the basis of the "heavy's" lawsuit. A confidential relationship is one between two people who have gained each other's confidences and who purport to act with the other's interests in mind. These people have a duty to act toward each other with good faith and honesty. Spouses, agents and principals, business partners, attorneys and clients, and guardians and wards are in confidential relationships. Car dealers and customers are not.

RESOURCE
To learn more about these and other affirmative defenses, consult *California Procedure*, 4th edition, by Bernard Witkin, Vol. 4, Pleading, 505-512, §§ 508–511.

Situations involving force, fraud, or pressure from someone in a confidential relationship are usually complicated and require the help of a lawyer unless you're willing to do considerable legal research. If you want to at least raise the defense in your Answer, check the box and type something like, "The contract that is the subject of this lawsuit is invalid because defendant's agreement to its terms was obtained as a result of plaintiff's threats to injure defendant if defendant did not sign it."

Mistake of fact. Use this affirmative defense if you signed the contract because you were mistaken about a material fact. A material fact goes to the core of the contract—for example, you bought a racehorse believing it was a one-year-old, when in fact the horse was five. It does not include minor terms of the contract, such as that the horse was born in May, not June as stated in the contract. This defense can be complicated and require a lawyer's help unless you want to do some legal research. Again, if you are willing, see *Witkin, Summary of California Law,* 10th edition, Vol. 1, Contracts, §§ 256–271. If you want to at least raise the defense in your Answer, check the box and type something like, "The contract that is the subject of this lawsuit is invalid because defendant's agreement to its terms was obtained under a mistake of a material fact in that the parties believed that the horse was a one-year-old when in fact the horse was five."

Contracts signed by a minor. Use this affirmative defense if you entered into the contract before you turned 18 and you have since changed your mind. Check the box and type: "At the time defendant entered into the contract alleged by plaintiff, defendant was a minor. Defendant subsequently disaffirmed the contract under Family Code Section 6710."

Before using this defense, read Family Code §§ 6700 through 6929 for exceptions, which may apply. These exceptions generally bar you from canceling contracts for medical care and for the purchase of items necessary for your support or the support of your family, or contracts relating to show business or sports that have been approved by a court.

Miscellaneous. Several other legal defenses can be raised if they apply, but they involve complicated issues such as the formation of a contract and are beyond the scope of this book. Some defenses to be aware of include:

- plaintiff has signed a release as part of a settlement
- there's another lawsuit pending between these parties over the same matter
- plaintiff is a corporation that has had its corporate powers suspended for not paying taxes, and
- plaintiff is an out-of-state corporation not qualified to do business in California.

RESOURCE

For information on additional affirmative defenses, see *California Procedure* (4th edition), by Bernard Witkin, Vol. 5, Pleading, §§ 1015–1026.

Item 5. Check the box and add some silly legal words to cover an ancient legal principle called a "negative pregnant." A negative pregnant is a theory that if you deny that you owe the plaintiff $7,000, you are not denying that you owe a sum less than $7,000, such as $6,999. To cover the possibility that you're admitting that you owe the plaintiff anything, I suggest you use the language set out below. If it seems ridiculous, that's because it is.

"In denying the allegations of the Complaint above, defendant denies not only the specific numbers and amounts alleged by plaintiff, but all other numbers and amounts claimed."

Items 6a-c. Check Item 6b.

Now, type your name above the dotted line and sign above the solid line. Also, go back to Item 1 and fill in your total number of pages. This will probably be two, but remember to count any attachment pages.

Answering Other Types of Lawsuits

The Judicial Council has prepared check-the-box Answer forms only for tort and contract cases. But in limited jurisdiction cases, you can use another form as an Answer, called a General Denial. You cannot use a General Denial if you are being sued by a collection agency for more than $1,000. In other nontort, noncontract cases, you can use this form, but be certain not to miss any affirmative defenses in paragraph 2. The principles listed there regarding a Complaint apply to your situation here.

The research resources listed there will help you in determining if there are affirmative defenses that should be listed in paragraph 2 here.

CAUTION
For some strange reason, the General Denial form includes a Proof of Service as a second page. As explained in Chapter 7, an Answer may be served by mail. The person doing the mailing (who cannot be you) should fill in Items 2b, c, and d, and sign below.

FORM
The appendix contains a tear-out version of Form PLD-050, *Answer–General Denial*, and you can download one from the Judicial Council website at www.courtinfo.ca.gov.

Prepare a Cross-Complaint

A Cross-Complaint allows a defendant to sue a plaintiff. In some cases, a defendant may also use a Cross-Complaint to sue a third person who is not yet a party to the lawsuit. Although a Cross-Complaint is technically an independent legal action, it has the same case number as the original lawsuit and travels with it in the court system to avoid piecemeal disposition of the legal battle.

If your claim arises out of the same transaction, occurrence, or series of transactions or occurrences as the plaintiff's lawsuit, you must file a Cross-Complaint with your Answer or give up the claim forever. If your claim arises from a different transaction, occurrence, or series of transactions or occurrences as the plaintiff's lawsuit, bringing a Cross-Complaint now is optional.

Fortunately, this is a situation where you don't need to mire yourself in technical rules to make a decision. If you have any claim against the plaintiff, law or practicality dictates that you file a Cross-Complaint now.

EXAMPLE 1: Ted sues Naomi for an automobile accident that she believes was mostly his fault. She was injured in the accident and her car was damaged. She must cross-complain now if she wants to recover for her loss. But if Naomi and Ted were in an accident in March (over which Ted has sued) and another one in June (in which Naomi was injured), Naomi legally does not have to cross-complain now, though as a practical matter she should.

EXAMPLE 2: Ed sues Ida for the bill she never paid him for repairing her front porch. Ida has a claim against Ed for tearing up her front yard with his truck while he was working on the porch. Ida must cross-complain now. If, however, Ida's claim against Ed was for failing to pay back a loan she made him two years ago or for an auto accident that happened six months back, she isn't required to file a Cross-Complaint now, but she might as well.

> **Naming a New Party**
>
> With the Cross-Complaint, you can name someone not named by the plaintiff (a "third party") in the lawsuit. For example, say you were in a car accident and the plaintiff sued only you. You, however, believe a third car that clipped your rear just before your impact with the plaintiff caused the accident. You can add this new third party as a cross-defendant and proceed as if he had been a party from the start.
>
> The discussions below on preparing a tort and contract Cross-Complaint include instructions on adding a third party.

Preparing a Cross-Complaint is very similar to preparing a Complaint, so you'll want to read Chapter 5 before starting. Bear in mind that Cross-Complaints introduce new terminology. The defendant in the original suit who files a Cross-

Complaint is now called the "cross-complainant" (but still the defendant for purposes of the original suit). The original plaintiff against whom the Cross-Complaint is filed is now called the "cross-defendant."

Tort Cases (Personal Injury and Property Damage)

If your Cross-Complaint is based on a personal injury or damage to your property (torts), use the *Cross-Complaint–Personal Injury, Property Damage, Wrongful Death* form. Follow the instructions below to fill out the form. Use a separate form for each cross-defendant.

FORM
The appendix contains a tear-out copy of Form PLD-PI-002, *Cross-Complaint–Personal Injury, Property Damage, Wrongful Death*; and you can download one from the Judicial Council website at www.courtinfo.ca.gov.

Top two boxes. Follow the instructions in "The Caption" in Chapter 5.

Short Title: Put the last names (or the business names) of the first (perhaps only) plaintiff and the first (perhaps only) defendant, separated by a "vs.," such as "Brown vs. Black" or "Brown vs. Golden Bear Typing Service."

Cross-Complainant: That's you. If the plaintiff misspelled your name on the Complaint, type it correctly here.

Cross-Defendant: Type the names of all possible cross-defendants. Be sure to identify those cross-defendants who are neither adults nor natural persons. Here are some examples:
- "Mitchell Davis, a minor"
- "Axel Construction Company, a corporation" (although corporations cannot be pro per plaintiffs, you certainly can sue one)
- "Tweedle Associates, a partnership"
- "John Dee and Frank Dum, partners in Tweedle Associates partnership"
- "Sidney Blue, dba Blue Blood"
- "the County of Orange, a public entity"
- "Does 1, 2, 3, and 4." Doe defendants are people you sue but whose identity you are not sure of.

Cross-Complaint. Check all applicable boxes as follows:

Apportionment of Fault. Check if a cross-defendant was partially or totally at fault for the incident that is the subject of the complaint.

Declaratory Relief. Check if a cross-defendant was partially or totally at fault for the incident that is the subject of the complaint.

Indemnification. Skip this, since it involves circumstances beyond the scope of this book. If you think this may apply to your situation, consider hiring a lawyer.

Other. Check if you are seeking money from this cross-defendant for your injuries or property damages. After checking "Other," type "for damages" after the colon.

Jurisdiction: If you are seeking $25,000 or less in your Cross-Complaint, check the first box and the "is not" box below. If you are seeking more than that, check the second box and the "is" box below. If you checked the "is" box, your case will probably be transferred to the unlimited division and you should expect complications that aren't covered in this book. (See Code of Civil Procedure §§ 403.010 and following.)

Case Number: Type in the case number that's on the Summons and the Complaint.

Item 1. Cross-Complainant (name): Type your name and the cross-defendant's name. (Remember, you must complete a different Cross-Complaint for each cross-defendant.)

Item 2. Leave this for now; we'll come back to it later.

Item 3. Check the first and third boxes if any cross-complainant is suing as a member of a partnership. (None of the other listed cross-complainants can sue in pro per.) Type in the name of the partnership after the first box, then state whether it is a partnership or association after the third box. If you need more room, check the appropriate box and use an attachment sheet. Then go on to page two.

Short Title: Put the last names (or the business names) of the first (perhaps only) plaintiff and the first (perhaps only) defendant, separated by a "vs.," such as "Brown vs. Black" or "Brown vs. Golden Bear Typing Service."

Case Number: This is the number that's on the Summons and the Complaint.

Item 4. If all cross-defendants are natural persons (adults or minors), skip all of Item 4.

Items 4a and b. If any cross-defendant is a partnership, association, corporation, or government entity, check the box and complete this section, which contains two identical paragraphs. For each cross-defendant that falls into this category, put its name after "Except cross-defendant (name)," and check the applicable sub-box. You'll have to add a description for an unincorporated entity (such as a "partnership" or "labor union"), and a public entity (such as the "County of Santa Clara").

Item 5. You don't need to do anything here.

Item 6. Check this box if you are suing the State of California, a county, city, school district, or other public entity.

Item 6a. You should have complied with the claims procedure within six months of the incident involved (this is discussed in detail in Chapter 4). If you have, check this box.

Item 6b. If you haven't complied with the claims procedure, you should see a lawyer. There are ways to get leave to file a late claim, but they are complex and pursuing them on your own is dangerous.

Item 7. Skip this. It is beyond the scope of this book.

Item 8. If you believe that this cross-defendant was partially or totally at fault and should be required to pay for the damages the plaintiff has asked for in the original complaint (or if the cross-defendant is the plaintiff and should be declared at fault), check this box and type in "First" in the blank line. Now go on to page three.

Short Title and Case Number: Enter what you typed on page two.

Item 9. If you checked Item 8, check this box and type "Second" in the blank line. Then check the "as follows" box and write, "Cross-defendant was the legal cause of any injuries and damages sustained by plaintiff and therefore should be responsible for paying any sums recovered in this action by plaintiff."

Item 10. If you or your property was injured, check this box and enter "First" in the blank line if you did not check Items 7 and 8; or "Third" if you did. After "(Specify)," type "Cross-complainant claims damages as alleged in the attached Cause of Action forms."

Item 11. Now return to Chapter 5 ("Tort Cause of Action Attachments"). Read the whole section and decide which of the forms applies to what you are requesting. Follow the instructions there and fill out the forms and attach them to your Cross-Complaint. Then check the applicable boxes.

Don't worry about using the terms "cross-complainant" and "cross-defendant" on those forms. As the note on the form at Item 11 states, consider yourself to be the plaintiff and the cross-defendant the defendant. Be careful numbering the Causes of Action if you completed Items 8, 9, or 10.

Item 12. If you are asking for damages in Item 10 above, check box d and then (2) beneath it, adding the amount you are seeking up to $25,000. If you checked Item 8 above, check Box b here. If you checked Item 9 above, check Box c here.

Now, type your name above the line on the left and sign above the signature line. Also, go back to Item 1 and fill in your total number of pages. Remember to count all Cause of Action forms and their attachments.

Contract Cases

Here are a few examples of when you might bring a Cross-Complaint in a contract case:

- You're a repairperson sued for doing defective work, but the responsibility lies with a supplier or a subcontractor who provided defective materials or substandard work.
- You're a merchant sued for supplying defective merchandise, but the responsibility lies with the manufacturer or the supplier.
- You borrowed money from your uncle and didn't repay, and now he is suing you. In the meantime, your uncle became indebted to you because he's refused to share the proceeds of a winning lottery ticket you bought together.

To prepare a contract Cross-Complaint, use the contract Complaint form described in Chapter 5. The form states at the very bottom in small print that if the form is used as a Cross-Complaint (rather than a Complaint), the term "plaintiff" means cross-complainant (you) and "defendant" means cross-defendant.

Follow the instructions in Chapter 5. Bear in mind that on the form, you are the plaintiff and the defendants are the cross-defendants. Make only the following minor changes:

The CONTRACT box. Check the **Cross-Complaint** box.

The Jurisdiction box. If you are seeking damages of $25,000 or less in your Cross-Complaint, check the first box and the appropriate sub-box. If you are seeking more than $25,000, check the next two boxes as well as the first sub-box. Your case will probably be transferred to the unlimited division and you should stand by for action from the court that this book doesn't cover. (See Code of Civil Procedure §§ 403.010 and following.)

Page Two, Case number box. Copy the number from the Summons.

Items 1-6. Follow the instruction in Chapter 5 for these entries.

Item 7. Skip this item.

Items 8-9. Follow the instruction in Chapter 5 for these entries.

Item 10. Follow the instructions in Chapter 5 for the first three parts of this item. If you're asking that a new party (the new cross-defendant) be responsible for any damages the plaintiff is awarded, check the "other" box and type: "a judicial determination that defendants are legally responsible for any injuries and damages sustained in this action and a complete or partial indemnification by cross-defendants for any sums of money rendered against me in this action."

Prepare Summons If Any Cross-Defendant Is a New Party

If you named a new party to the lawsuit in your Cross-Complaint, fill out a Summons as described in Chapter 5, with the following changes:

- After the word "Summons" at the top of the page, type "On Cross-Complaint."
- Where the form says, "Notice to Defendant," put a slash (/) after the "to" and write "Cross-" above the slash.
- Where the form says "You Are Being Sued by Plaintiff," cross out "Plaintiff" and type "Cross-Complainant."
- Where the form says "name, address, and telephone number of plaintiff's attorney or plaintiff without an attorney," cross out the word "plaintiff" and substitute "cross-complainant."

Prepare Case Questionnaire

As you may remember from Chapter 5, if the plaintiff served you with a Case Questionnaire, you will have to serve the plaintiff with a completed Questionnaire along with your *Answer*. Instructions for filling it out are on the cover sheet. Some suggestions on how to approach the task are in Chapter 5. If the plaintiff didn't serve one on you, you can't, however, serve one on the plaintiff.

If you are filing a Cross-Complaint, you should use this excellent tool even if the plaintiff didn't serve one on you. Even if you think the plaintiff may abandon the suit, serve the Case Questionnaire now. If you don't serve it with the Cross-Complaint, you lose the right to use it forever.

File and Serve the Answer and Cross-Complaint

You should now have the following completed forms ready to go:
- Answer
- Cross-Complaint (if applicable)
- Summons, if you are naming new parties in your Cross-Complaint
- Case Questionnaire, if you are filing a Cross-Complaint, and
- answers to plaintiff's Case Questionnaire, if you were served with one.

> **CAUTION**
> **File your papers promptly.** Your Answer and any Cross-Complaint must be filed within 30 days of the date you were served with a Complaint—or by whatever date you were allowed as a formal extension (usually an additional 15 days). If you miss this deadline, the plaintiff has the right to obtain a default judgment against you. (See Chapter 9.)

Photocopy two sets of your documents plus one set for each person named as a plaintiff or cross-defendant. If anyone is named in both capacities, you need only one set of the documents for that person. To serve the plaintiff, follow the instructions for service by mail in Chapter 7.

After serving the plaintiff—and while you're still within your filing deadline—file your original papers with the court. Get an extra, stamped copy for yourself and each cross-defendant. Attach the declaration of mailing to the original. You'll need to pay a filing fee for the Answer—which will be between $205 and $330 per defendant. If you can't afford the fee, see Chapter 5 for information about obtaining a fee waiver.

Most courts accept checks. The clerk will file the original Answer and Cross-Complaint and issue the Summons to be served on any cross-defendant. The Case Questionnaire is not filed with the court. Instructions for filing documents are in Chapter 6.

Have a copy of the issued Summons, Cross-Complaint, and Case Questionnaire personally served on each cross-defendant, following the instructions in Chapter 7.

What Happens Next?

By filing your Answer, you've taken steps to ensure that your side of the dispute will be heard in court. And if you filed a Cross-Complaint, you've preserved your right to possibly recover money. If you're in no particular hurry to resolve this headache called a lawsuit, sit back and see what, if anything, the court or plaintiff does to move it forward.

An amazing number of lawsuits never progress beyond this spot. Perhaps the plaintiff never expected you to fight back. Maybe the plaintiff lost interest in the suit, perhaps because a personal life change now means that this lawsuit has low priority. Whatever the reason, unless you want a resolution, do nothing.

Dismissing the Case If No One Takes Action

If the plaintiff doesn't take steps to bring the case to trial within your court's case management limit, the court will dismiss the case. If, somehow, the court never becomes aware that the plaintiff has missed the limit, the court must dismiss the case five years after it was filed. A court will do this on its own or in response to a motion you file.

If you don't want to wait five years, you can file a motion after two years asking the court to dismiss the case if the plaintiff hasn't taken any steps to move the case along. Unlike the five-year motion, which is mandatory, this motion is discretionary with the judge and you'll probably need the help of a lawyer. (See Rules of Court 3.1340 and 3.1342.)

Of course, you may want the case to move along, especially if you've filed a Cross-Complaint to recover money. You may also want the case to progress because having a lawsuit filed against you is likely to affect your credit rating. No matter what the reason, you can move the case along by conducting discovery, filing motions, and complying with the case management papers you will receive from the court. All these procedures are described in this book.

You should also consider the possibility of reopening settlement discussions. You have just fired a shot across the plaintiff's bow that indicates that this litigation is going to be a battle. If you believe that you and the plaintiff can't negotiate productively between yourselves, suggest the possibility of mediation.

Even if you prefer to sit back, the plaintiff may not let you, instead serving you with discovery requests requiring your response, or even filing a Motion for Summary Judgment. I'll explain what these things mean in the following chapters.

CHAPTER 9

If Defendant Doesn't Respond

Taking the Defendant's Default 168
  Path One: Cutting Off the Defendant's Ability to Answer 169
  Path Two: Suing for Money Owed on a Specific Date 172
  Path Three: Going After the Default and Judgment Now 173

Applying for a Judgment 174
  Path One: Finish the Process to Obtain a Judgment 174
  Path Two: Suing for Money Owed on a Certain Date 174
  Path Three: Getting the Default and Judgment Now 175

Court Hearings on Your Default 180

Setting Aside a Default Judgment 181
  Grounds for Setting Aside a Default 182
  Minimizing the Chances of a Late Set-Aside 182
  Responding to a Motion to Set Aside 183

When going to court (or fighting any battle), it's sensible to anticipate that your opponent will put up a tough fight. After you've gone through all the rigors described in Chapters 4, 5, 6, and 7, it will probably be a shock (albeit a very welcome one) if the defendant doesn't file an Answer or other responsive document. This chapter describes what happens if the defendant fails to file a response within 30 days of service of process, or whatever date you agreed to extend the time to answer.

> ### How to Count to 30
>
> To decide when you can take the defendant's default, you need to know when the 30 days to answer runs out. To compute this, you don't count the day service is made, but begin counting to 30 on the following day. Count Saturdays and Sundays. If the 30th day falls on a weekend or court holiday, the defendant has until the clerk's office closes for the next court day (normally a Monday).

> ### Defendant Equals Cross-Defendant
>
> If you were the defendant in the original case and filed a Cross-Complaint against the plaintiff (who is now the cross-defendant), this chapter applies to you. As you read along, just substitute the word "cross-defendant" for the word "defendant" and the word "cross-complainant" for the word "plaintiff."

Sometimes a defendant fails to answer because he or she can't afford a lawyer and doesn't dare go to court alone. More commonly, however, the defendant doesn't answer because he or she has no defense, owes you money, and figures that fighting the case will do little good. This may be a mistake on the defendant's part. A judge might let the defendant pay off money owed on a monthly payment plan, or object if you asked for more damages than you were entitled to. But of course, it's up to the defendant to show up in court.

Taking the Defendant's Default

Once the 30-day response deadline has passed, you can go to the court and ask that judgment be entered for you. This is known as "taking the defendant's default." Getting a judge or, in some types of contract cases, a court clerk to declare that you won because the defendant didn't show up is a somewhat picky process, but it certainly can be done without a lawyer. Obtaining the default judgment involves two steps:

- First, entering the default with the clerk's office, and
- Second, having a judgment entered.

There are three different ways, or paths, to complete steps one and two, depending on the nature of your case and on your situation:

- **Path One.** If you want to act fast and prevent a tardy defendant from filing an Answer before you file your request for default, you'll choose "Path One."
- **Path Two.** If you are suing over a written contract for the payment of money on a certain date, take "Path Two."
- **Path Three.** Many of you won't be worried about beating the defendant to the clerk's office (Path One) and don't have a case that fits within Path Two. If you want to get your default and the judgment accomplished in one step and are willing to do all the paperwork now, you'll follow "Path Three." All of these paths are explored more fully below.

TIP
There are benefits to filing your default in person. You may want to hand carry the papers to the courthouse, so the defendant doesn't beat you to the clerk's office and file an Answer before the default papers arrive in the mail. Also, going in person usually gives you

the opportunity to interact with the clerk, who can tell you if there are any errors on your Request for Entry of Default—sometimes you can fix them right there.

Path One: Cutting Off the Defendant's Ability to Answer

As explained at the beginning of this chapter, you can enter the defendant's default any time after the 31st day from the date he or she was served—*unless* the defendant shows up late and files an Answer (or, once in a great while, some other technical motion) before you manage to file your default. Or, put another way, if you haven't gotten around to filing a request for entry of default and the defendant comes into court with an Answer even though it's late, the clerk will accept it and file it and you will have lost your chance for obtaining a quick judgment. You don't have unlimited time to file your default, either—the California Rules of Court provide you must file for default within ten days of the defendant's failure to file an Answer on time. The Rule also requires that after you enter the default, you must obtain a judgment within the next 45 days. These requirements are not scrupulously enforced, but they are an additional reason to move this procedure along.

One way to avoid this unfortunate turn of events is to be vigilant and file your request on the 31st day. However, not everyone is so prompt; and if you wake up and realize that there may be a race to the courthouse, you'll want to get there first with the minimum advance preparation. If this describes your situation, choose this method, which involves requesting a default now and coming back later to get a judgment. As long as your request is on file, the defendant should be foreclosed from filing an Answer, at least temporarily. Coming back later involves more paperwork and an extra trip to court, but it's worth it if you don't want to take the time now to prepare default *and* judgment papers. However, judges are pretty liberal about vacating a default and allowing the defendant to file an Answer if the defendant presents a good reason for missing the deadline.

FORM
The appendix contains a tear-out version of Form CIV-100, REQUEST FOR ENTRY OF DEFAULT, and you can download one from the Judicial Council website at www.courtinfo.ca.gov. A sample is shown below.

TIP
Speak up if the clerk accepts the defendant's Answer after you enter a default. Once in a while the clerk won't be aware that your request for default has been filed and will mistakenly accept the defendant's Answer. If you immediately call this error to the clerk's attention, the Answer should be rejected.

To take defendant's default in this situation, start by completing the boxes at the top of the request form, as you have done on other forms. Check only the Entry of Default box and follow these instructions:

Case Number: Copy this from the Complaint.

Item 1a. Type the date on which the Complaint (or Cross-Complaint) was filed with the clerk. The clerk stamped the date in the upper right-hand corner of the Complaint when you filed it.

Item 1b. Type the names of all plaintiffs.

Item 1c. Check the box and type the names of all defendants who have missed the 30-day deadline. Skip the rest of Item 1 and all of Items 2 and 3.

Date and signature. Fill in the date, type your name above the first line, and sign on the second line. Fill in the box on the top of page two.

Item 4. Check the "did not" box unless you paid a legal document assistant to help you with this form.

Item 5. This item is designed to eliminate a practice once used by some merchants and collection agencies that purposely sued lower-income persons for unpaid bills by filing their suit

	CIV-100
ATTORNEY OR PARTY WITHOUT ATTORNEY (Name, State Bar number, and address): Donna Goodwill 9888 North Broadway Oakland, CA 94610 TELEPHONE NO.: 510-555-4644 FAX NO. (Optional): E-MAIL ADDRESS (Optional): ATTORNEY FOR (Name): In pro per	FOR COURT USE ONLY

SUPERIOR COURT OF CALIFORNIA, COUNTY OF Alameda
STREET ADDRESS: 600 Washington Street
MAILING ADDRESS: 600 Washington Street
CITY AND ZIP CODE: Oakland, CA 94607
BRANCH NAME:

PLAINTIFF/PETITIONER: Donna Goodwill
DEFENDANT/RESPONDENT: Allen Jones

REQUEST FOR (Application)	☐ Entry of Default ☐ Clerk's Judgment ☐ Court Judgment	CASE NUMBER: 0051717

1. TO THE CLERK: On the complaint or cross-complaint filed
   a. on (date): June 4, 20xx
   b. by (name): Donna Goodwill
   c. [X] Enter default of defendant (names):
      Allen Jones
   d. [X] I request a court judgment under Code of Civil Procedure sections 585(b), 585(c), 989, etc., against defendant (names):
      Allen Jones

   (Testimony required. Apply to the clerk for a hearing date, unless the court will enter a judgment on an affidavit under Code Civ. Proc., § 585(d).)

   e. ☐ Enter clerk's judgment
      (1) ☐ for restitution of the premises only and issue a writ of execution on the judgment. Code of Civil Procedure section 1174(c) does not apply. (Code Civ. Proc., § 1169.)
          ☐ Include in the judgment all tenants, subtenants, named claimants, and other occupants of the premises. The *Prejudgment Claim of Right to Possession* was served in compliance with Code of Civil Procedure section 415.46.
      (2) ☐ under Code of Civil Procedure section 585(a). *(Complete the declaration under Code Civ. Proc., § 585.5 on the reverse (item 5).)*
      (3) ☐ for default previously entered on (date):

2. **Judgment to be entered.**

	Amount	Credits acknowledged	Balance
a. Demand of complaint	$ 11,250	$ 0	$ 11,250
b. Statement of damages *			
(1) Special	$	$	$
(2) General	$	$	$
c. Interest	$ 715	$ 0	$ 715
d. Costs (see reverse)	$ 109	$ 0	$ 109
e. Attorney fees	$	$	$
f. **TOTALS**	$ 12,074	$ 0	$ 12,074

   g. **Daily damages** were demanded in complaint at the rate of: $ per day beginning (date):
   (* Personal injury or wrongful death actions; Code Civ. Proc., § 425.11.)

3. ☐ *(Check if filed in an unlawful detainer case)* **Legal document assistant or unlawful detainer assistant** information is on the reverse *(complete item 4)*.

Date: August 1, 20xx

Donna Goodwill   ▶ *Donna Goodwill*
(TYPE OR PRINT NAME)   (SIGNATURE OF PLAINTIFF OR ATTORNEY FOR PLAINTIFF)

FOR COURT USE ONLY
(1) ☐ Default entered as requested on (date):
(2) ☐ Default NOT entered as requested (state reason):

Clerk, by _____, Deputy

Page 1 of 2

Form Adopted for Mandatory Use
Judicial Council of California
CIV-100 [Rev. January 1, 2007]

REQUEST FOR ENTRY OF DEFAULT
(Application to Enter Default)

Code of Civil Procedure,
§§ 585–587, 1169
www.courtinfo.ca.gov

PLAINTIFF/PETITIONER:	Donna Goodwill	CASE NUMBER:	
DEFENDANT/RESPONDENT:	Allen Jones	0051717	

CIV-100

4. **Legal document assistant or unlawful detainer assistant (Bus. & Prof. Code, § 6400 et seq.).** A legal document assistant or unlawful detainer assistant ☐ did ☒ did **not** for compensation give advice or assistance with this form. *(If declarant has received **any** help or advice for pay from a legal document assistant or unlawful detainer assistant, state)*:

   a. Assistant's name:
   b. Street address, city, and zip code:
   c. Telephone no.:
   d. County of registration:
   e. Registration no.:
   f. Expires on *(date)*:

5. ☐ **Declaration under Code of Civil Procedure Section 585.5** *(required for entry of default under Code Civ. Proc., § 585(a))*. This action
   a. ☐ is ☐ is not on a contract or installment sale for goods or services subject to Civ. Code, § 1801 et seq. (Unruh Act).
   b. ☐ is ☐ is not on a conditional sales contract subject to Civ. Code, § 2981 et seq. (Rees-Levering Motor Vehicle Sales and Finance Act).
   c. ☐ is ☐ is not on an obligation for goods, services, loans, or extensions of credit subject to Code Civ. Proc., § 395(b).

6. **Declaration of mailing (Code Civ. Proc., § 587).** A copy of this *Request for Entry of Default* was
   a. ☐ **not mailed** to the following defendants, whose addresses are **unknown** to plaintiff or plaintiff's attorney *(names)*:
   b. ☒ **mailed** first-class, postage prepaid, in a sealed envelope addressed to each defendant's attorney of record or, if none, to each defendant's last known address as follows:
      (1) Mailed on *(date)*: August 1, 20xx
      (2) To *(specify names and addresses shown on the envelopes)*:
         Allen Jones
         493 Cedar Street
         Emeryville, CA 94732

I declare under penalty of perjury under the laws of the State of California that the foregoing items 4, 5, and 6 are true and correct.
Date:

Donna Goodwill ▶ *Donna Goodwill*
(TYPE OR PRINT NAME) (SIGNATURE OF DECLARANT)

7. **Memorandum of costs** *(required if money judgment requested)*. Costs and disbursements are as follows (Code Civ. Proc., § 1033.5):
   a. Clerk's filing fees .... 90 ...... $
   b. Process server's fees ...... 19 ...... $
   c. Other *(specify)*: .... $
   d. .... $
   e. **TOTAL** .... 109 ...... $
   f. ☐ Costs and disbursements are waived.
   g. I am the attorney, agent, or party who claims these costs. To the best of my knowledge and belief this memorandum of costs is correct and these costs were necessarily incurred in this case.

I declare under penalty of perjury under the laws of the State of California that the foregoing is true and correct.
Date:

Donna Goodwill ▶ *Donna Goodwill*
(TYPE OR PRINT NAME) (SIGNATURE OF DECLARANT)

8. ☐ **Declaration of nonmilitary status** *(required for a judgment)*. No defendant named in item 1c of the application is in the military service so as to be entitled to the benefits of the Servicemembers Civil Relief Act (50 U.S.C. App. § 501 et seq.).

I declare under penalty of perjury under the laws of the State of California that the foregoing is true and correct.
Date: August 1, 20xx

Donna Goodwill ▶ *Donna Goodwill*
(TYPE OR PRINT NAME) (SIGNATURE OF DECLARANT)

Civ-100 [Rev. January 1, 2007] **REQUEST FOR ENTRY OF DEFAULT**
(Application to Enter Default)

in courthouses far from the defendant's home. You should check the three "is not" boxes unless you are suing a buyer to collect what you are owed on a sale of goods (including motor vehicles) or services. If you suspect you might meet this definition, read the code sections referred to in the item to be sure. If you check one of the "is" boxes, you probably will be required to supply a declaration that establishes you have sued the defendant in a courthouse that is near where he or she lives or where your contract was entered into. If, back when you first filed your case, your court required you to file a local form to show you filed in the right courthouse, a further declaration won't be required.

Item 6. Before you file this form with the clerk, you must mail a copy of it to the defendant or the defendant's lawyer, by first class mail. If you have no address for the defendant or the lawyer, check Box a. Otherwise, check Box b, and below the (2), type the applicable address. Be sure to use an address that's as exact and current as you can. After you mail the form, enter the date next to (1).

Date and Signature. Fill in the date, type your name above the first line, and sign above the second line. Again, always use the exact version of your name that appears on the Complaint.

Path One users are now done with this form. Take or mail these forms to the court clerk. Now skip ahead to "Applying for a Judgment" for the next step.

Path Two: Suing for Money Owed on a Specific Date

If you are suing on a written or oral contract that clearly specifies an amount of money that is due on a particular date, you may choose this somewhat expedited path to a judgment. To follow this path, you must have alleged in your Complaint that you have a contract that clearly shows the amount you claim due without requiring the clerk to make any calculations or resolve any uncertainties. Cases that fall into this category are not that common, but if you have a promissory note or a clear agreement to pay you something that you have sued on because it wasn't paid, you may follow this path.

In this situation, use the same form as Path One, complete all of the boxes and items called for above in Path 1 and also check the Clerk's Judgment box at the top of page one. Also check Box 1e and 1e(2).

Item 2a. Turn to the prayer, Item 10 of your Complaint. In the first column, enter the dollar amount you requested in your Complaint next to "damages." If the defendant has paid any money since you filed the lawsuit (miracles do happen!), put the amount of the payment in the second column. Enter the balance in the third column.

Item 2b. Leave this blank.

Item 2c. Enter the amount of interest to which you are entitled. Unless the contract contains a provision for interest, this must be calculated from the date the contract was broken—not the date it was signed. If the defendant made any payments, you must take this into account when calculating interest. If your contract provides an interest rate, you may calculate from the date the contract was signed and use that rate unless it is so high it violates the usury law. (See "Breach of Contract Cases" in Chapter 1.) If the contract is silent (or violates the usury law), use the rate of 10% simple interest per year. List any credits (unlikely) in column two. Enter the balance in the third column. Now skip ahead to Item 7.

Item 7. Here you list your filing fees and process server's fees, which may be added to the judgment. Type your name and sign on the blank below.

Item 2d. Refer back to Item 7 and enter the total costs (Item 7e) in the first column. List any credits (again, unlikely), and enter the balance in the third column.

Item 2e. Leave each of these columns blank unless your contract specifically provides that you are entitled to attorney fees and you consulted—and paid—an attorney to assist you in this lawsuit. Unless these fees were provided for in your contract and you specifically prayed for them in your Complaint, you probably won't be awarded them.

Item 2f. Total up each of the three columns.

Item 2g. Skip this. It applies to eviction cases.

Fill in the date, and then type and sign your name on the blanks provided. Fill in the two familiar boxes at the top of page two.

Item 3. Leave this blank.

Item 4. Check the "did not" box unless you paid a legal document assistant to help you with this form.

Item 5. Read the explanation regarding this item above in Path One. The same instructions apply here.

Item 6. Before you file this form with the clerk, you must mail a copy of it to the defendant or the defendant's lawyer, by first class mail. If you have no address for the defendant or the lawyer, check Box a. Otherwise, check Box b, and below the (2), type the applicable address. Be sure to use an address that's as exact and current as you can. After you mail the form, enter the date next to (1). Type and sign your name.

Item 8. Here, you or someone with personal knowledge must state that the defendant is not on active military service. If you know the defendant and have never had any indication that he or she is an active member of the military, check the box. Then date and sign this declaration yourself. If you don't know, ask around. Call the defendant and ask.

If the defendant is on active military duty and has not responded to your Complaint, the court must appoint an attorney to represent the defendant before the case can proceed. Now go on to "Applying for a Judgment."

Path Three: Going After the Default and Judgment Now

If you want to complete the whole process for judgment now and you don't qualify for the expedited procedure described in Path Two, you will have to complete additional work. Fill in the boxes at the top of the same form you used above, much as you have done before, but in the "Request For" box, check the "Entry of Default" and "Court Judgment" boxes. In Item 1, fill in sub a, b, and c as in Path One. Then check 1d and enter the names of the relevant defendants. Next, fill in Item 2 as described in Path Two. Skip Item 3 and sign at the bottom of the page. Then complete Items 4, 5, 6, 7, and 8 on page 2, signing each time in the blank provided. Instructions for completing these items are contained in Path Two.

> **Papers the Clerk Will Need for Processing Your Default**
>
> Regardless of whether you are following Path One, Two, or Three, you must gather several documents together to take to the clerk's office to get your request for default processed. They are:
> - the original and one copy of the completed Request for Entry of Default
> - the original and one copy of the signed Proof of Service of Summons
> - the original and one copy of the Summons
> - a large self-addressed envelope with sufficient postage for the clerk to return your copies to you, and
> - if you are mailing this to the clerk, a letter asking that the default be entered and that endorsed copies of the Request for Entry of Default, Proof of Service, and Summons be returned to you.
>
> You may want to file the papers in person, so the defendant doesn't beat you to the courthouse and file an Answer before the default papers arrive in the mail. Also, by filing in person, often the clerk can tell you if there are any errors on your Request for Entry of Default, and sometimes you can fix them right there. If you file in person, you don't need the envelope or the letter, unless the clerk tells you that the papers can't be processed while you wait.

Applying for a Judgment

To obtain a judgment, you'll use a simple Judgment form. Your use of the form will vary depending on which of the three paths above you are following.

FORM
The appendix contains a tear-out version of Form JUD-100, *Judgment*, and you can download one from the Judicial Council website at www.courtinfo.ca.gov. Because the same form is used differently depending on what Path you've chosen for your default, I haven't included a filled-out sample. You'll find the instructions adequate.

Path One: Finish the Process to Obtain a Judgment

If you are following this plan, you will have already processed your Request for Entry of Default and the clerk will have entered the defendant's default. Now to obtain a judgment, you will first have to fill out a new copy of the same Request for Entry of Default form described above. Begin by filling out the boxes at the top of the form just as you did earlier. In the "Request For" box, check only the Court Judgment box. Then fill out Item 1a and b and d. You won't check c because you already have the default entered. Then go back to the instructions above for Path Three in "Taking the Defendant's Default" and complete Items 4 through 8. Mail a copy of the Request for Entry of Default form to the applicable defendants.

Next, you will have to prepare the Judgment form referred to above, number JUD-100. Follow the instructions for Path Three below for completing that form. Then mail or take an original and at least two copies of the Request for Entry form and the Judgment form to the clerk's office for processing.

Path Two: Suing for Money Owed on a Certain Date

You will need to mail or take the papers described in "Papers the Clerk Will Need for Processing Your Default," along with the contract or statement of account you are relying on and the Judgment form, to the clerk's office. Here are instructions on how to fill out the Judgment form:

Boxes at the top. Fill these out exactly the same as you did the Request for Entry of Default.

Judgment. Check the By Clerk and By Default boxes.

Item 1. Check this box and Box d below. Now skip to page two and fill in the boxes at the top.

Item 4. Skip this.

Item 5a. Enter your name and that of any other plaintiffs who are entitled to judgment. Do the same as to any defendants who have defaulted.

Item 5b. Skip this.

Item 5c. Use this only if you are a defendant taking a default on your Cross-Complaint.

Item 6a. Check the box and then enter the figures you used in the Request for Entry of Default form at Item 2.

Item 6b. Use this only if you are a defendant taking a default on your Cross-Complaint.

The signature lines are for the court—leave them blank. Now gather the papers listed in "Papers the Clerk Will Need for Processing Your Default" and mail or take them to the clerk's office for processing. Checking your forms may take some time and probably won't be done while you wait.

The clerk may decide that you belong on Path Three instead of Path Two. If so, you may get a notice telling you to appear before a judge for a hearing on your request. This is not unusual and should not alarm you. Some judges want to personally review all requests for judgment in some categories.

Path Three: Getting the Default and Judgment Now

You will have to take or mail the papers from the list, "Papers the Clerk Will Need for Processing Your Default," along with a completed Judgment form, to the clerk's office. Here are instructions on how to fill out the Judgment form:

Boxes at the top. Fill these out exactly as you did on the Request for Entry of Default.

Judgment. Check the "By Court" and "By Default" boxes.

Item 1. Check this box and Boxes e and (2) below. Now skip to page two and fill in the boxes at the top. Check the "THE COURT" box.

Item 5. Skip this.

Item 5a. Enter your name and that of any other plaintiffs who are entitled to judgment. Do the same as to any defendants who have defaulted.

Item 5b. Skip this.

Item 5c. Use this only if you are a defendant taking a default on your Cross-Complaint.

Item 6a. Check the first box. As to Item (1) in the larger box, you can follow one of two courses. If the amount of money you are seeking is pretty definite and you are feeling confident the judge will award it to you, put in the amount you seek. If the number includes damages for pain and suffering or other less tangible amounts, you can leave this blank and let the judge fill in whatever he or she thinks is appropriate. You'll have an opportunity to describe the circumstances in a document I will describe below. On Items (2) through (5), enter the figures you used in Item 2 of the Request for Entry of Judgment. Leave the rest of the form blank.

You are also required to enclose several additional documents with your proposed Judgment form. These may avoid the necessity of having to appear in court for your Judgment. They will at least shorten any hearing the judge decides is necessary to rule on your request for judgment. The additional documents are:

- a brief summary of the case identifying the parties and what the case is all about
- declarations under penalty of perjury and any other original items of evidence that support the judgment you are requesting, and
- a dismissal of all parties against whom a judgment is not sought.

I recommend that you use form MC-030, a Declaration form, to satisfy the requirement of the first two items listed.

FORM
You'll find a tear-out copy of Form CIV-110, *Request for Dismissal*, in the appendix. You can download one from the Judicial Council website at www.courtinfo.c.gov.

FORM
The appendix contains a tear-out version of Form MC-030, *Declaration*, and you can download one from the Judicial Council website at www.courtinfo.ca.gov. Two samples are shown below.

You know by now how to fill out the boxes at the top of the page. The rest of the form is blank space, in which you'll write your statement. I suggest you begin as shown in the first sample Declaration, below. It is followed by a declaration for a contract case.

If there are other defendants named in your lawsuit, you must execute a dismissal of the case against them or explain to the judge why you should not have to do so. A form for a dismissal is available in the appendix or on the Internet, as described in Chapter 4. Check the box that says you are dismissing them "without prejudice" (which will allow you to bring a subsequent lawsuit if there is any chance you may need to sue them based on the same fact situation).

All of the papers in "Papers the Clerk Will Need for Processing Your Default," above, plus the Judgment form and the attached declarations, need to be delivered to the clerk with any dismissals that may be required.

		MC-030
ATTORNEY OR PARTY WITHOUT ATTORNEY *(Name, State Bar number, and address):* Earl Jones 2222 Nolo Drive Folsom, CA 95810 TELEPHONE NO.: 510-555-1110 FAX NO. *(Optional):* E-MAIL ADDRESS *(Optional):* ATTORNEY FOR *(Name):* In pro per	FOR COURT USE ONLY	
SUPERIOR COURT OF CALIFORNIA, COUNTY OF Sacramento STREET ADDRESS: 670 Ninth Street MAILING ADDRESS: CITY AND ZIP CODE: Sacramento, CA 94514 BRANCH NAME: Downtown Courthouse		
PLAINTIFF/PETITIONER: Earl Jones DEFENDANT/RESPONDENT: Ralph Proscetti		
DECLARATION	CASE NUMBER: 03-02150	

Earl Jones declares as follows:

Brief Summary of My Case: We are suing Ralph Proscetti for damages my wife and I sustained January 5, 20xx, as a result of an automobile accident in the city of Folsom, California. The accident was caused by the defendant's negligence and caused us damages in doctor and hospital bills, repair of our car, time lost from work, and pain and suffering. A true copy of the California Highway Patrol accident report is attached to this declaration and marked Exhibit A.

Declaration in Support of Judgment: If sworn as a witness, I can testify competently to the facts stated in this declaration. All of the matters stated herein are of my own personal knowledge. Each of the original bills attached hereto as Exhibits B through F was personally received by me through the mail from the indicated provider and is either due and payable from me or paid by my personal insurance (in which case the insurance company is entitled to be reimbursed).

As indicated on Exhibit A, I was driving our 2000 Lexus SUV east on Carmichael Lane at about 30 miles per hour at a few minutes before 5 p.m. on January 5, 20xx. There were no obstructions to my view and the weather was clear.

I declare under penalty of perjury under the laws of the State of California that the foregoing is true and correct.

Date: March 15, 20xx

Earl Jones	*Earl Jones*
(TYPE OR PRINT NAME)	(SIGNATURE OF DECLARANT)

☐ Attorney for ☒ Plaintiff ☐ Petitioner ☐ Defendant
☐ Respondent ☐ Other *(Specify):*

Form Approved for Optional Use
Judicial Council of California
MC-030 [Rev. January 1, 2006]

DECLARATION

		MC-031
PLAINTIFF/PETITIONER: DEFENDANT/RESPONDENT:	Jones vs. Proscetti	CASE NUMBER: 03-02150

DECLARATION

(This form must be attached to another form or court paper before it can be filed in court.)

Without warning, Mr. Proscetti drove his 1998 Volkswagen van from a dirt strip behind some bushes just off to my right smack into the side of my car, knocking me across both lanes of the road. Mr. Proscetti approached our car after the accident and said, "I am really sorry I did that, but I was changing the station on my radio and I just didn't think there was any traffic approaching." He was cited by the Highway Patrol for violating our right of way.

My wife and I were taken to Lake View Hospital by ambulance (bill attached as Exhibit B) and received the treatment described in the attached hospital bill marked Exhibit C. In addition, we received follow-up care from our personal doctor as described in Exhibit D. Our car required repairs as a result of the accident, as shown on Exhibit E. We had a car rental bill during the repairs, as shown on Exhibit F. I lost two days of work at the State Prison where I am a correctional officer, at a cost of $500, and my wife lost three days of pay as an elementary school teacher at a cost of $475. Copies of applicable pay stubs are attached as Exhibits G and H.

My injuries were cervical strain and bruised left shoulder. I had considerable pain from each of the injuries for over two weeks and had trouble sleeping during that time. My wife's injuries were a bruised forehead and cervical strain. She was not able to concentrate on her work for almost a week and had pain and difficulty sleeping for two weeks. I believe she is entitled to $5,500 for her pain and suffering and that I am entitled to an award of $6,000 for my pain and suffering.

Based on the above, we believe I am entitled to a total judgment of $12,617 and that she is entitled to $10,789.

I declare under penalty of perjury under the laws of the State of California that the foregoing is true and correct.

Date: March 15, 20xx

Earl Jones	*Earl Jones*
(TYPE OR PRINT NAME)	(SIGNATURE OF DECLARANT)

☐ Attorney for [X] Plaintiff ☐ Petitioner ☐ Defendant
☐ Respondent ☐ Other *(Specify):*

Form Approved for Optional Use
Judicial Council of California
MC-031 [Rev. July 1, 2005]

ATTACHED DECLARATION

		MC-030
ATTORNEY OR PARTY WITHOUT ATTORNEY *(Name, State Bar number, and address)*: Jennifer Peabody 456 Ferndale Avenue Corona, CA 92282 TELEPHONE NO.: 510-555-2220 FAX NO. *(Optional)*: E-MAIL ADDRESS *(Optional)*: ATTORNEY FOR *(Name)*: In pro per		FOR COURT USE ONLY
SUPERIOR COURT OF CALIFORNIA, COUNTY OF Riverside STREET ADDRESS: 505 S. Buena Vista Avenue MAILING ADDRESS: CITY AND ZIP CODE: Corona, CA 02282 BRANCH NAME: Corona Branch		
PLAINTIFF/PETITIONER: Jennifer Peabody DEFENDANT/RESPONDENT: HGY Contractors		
DECLARATION	CASE NUMBER: 03-02150	

Jennifer Peabody declares:

Brief Summary of My Case: I contracted with HGY Contractors, Inc., on January 3, 20xx, to build an addition to my solely-owned home at 456 Ferndale Avenue, Corona, California. They failed to complete the job and did major parts of the work incorrectly, causing me damages of $15,678, which I spent to have the job completed as provided in the contract.

Declaration in Support of Judgment: If sworn as a witness, I can testify competently to the facts stated in this declaration. All of the matters stated herein are of my own personal knowledge. Exhibit B was personally received by me from the contractor and has been paid by me. I had plans for a dining room addition to my home in Corona drawn by John Frykman, a licensed architect. I have a set of plans in my possession and can furnish them to the court if requested. I had several contractors bid on the plan and finally entered into a contract with Joseph Hilty, who was a superintendent at HGY Contractors, Inc. The original contract is attached as Exhibit A. The contract calls for all work to be completed no later than May 29, 20xx. HGY started the work April 10, 20xx, and continued until May 20, the day they left the job, never to return. Despite my calls and letters, they have never explained why they did not finish the job. I request judgment in the amount of $15,678 for the breach of our agreement.

I declare under penalty of perjury under the laws of the State of California that the foregoing is true and correct.

Date: December 13, 20xx

Jennifer Peabody
(TYPE OR PRINT NAME)

Jennifer Peabody
(SIGNATURE OF DECLARANT)

☐ Attorney for [X] Plaintiff ☐ Petitioner ☐ Defendant
☐ Respondent ☐ Other *(Specify)*:

Form Approved for Optional Use
Judicial Council of California
MC-030 [Rev. January 1, 2006]

DECLARATION

PLAINTIFF/PETITIONER:	Peabody vs. HGY Contractors	CASE NUMBER:
DEFENDANT/RESPONDENT:		03-56789

MC-031

DECLARATION

(This form must be attached to another form or court paper before it can be filed in court.)

I subsequently hired Reliable Contractors, Inc., of Folson to complete the job. Their original bill for the work is attached as Exhibit B. All of the work on Exhibit was incurred solely in bulding the dining room addition to the requirements of the Frykman plans.

I declare under penalty of perjury under the laws of the State of California that the foregoing is true and correct.

Date: December 13, 20xx

Jennifer Peabody
(TYPE OR PRINT NAME)

Jennifer Peabody
(SIGNATURE OF DECLARANT)

☐ Attorney for [X] Plaintiff ☐ Petitioner ☐ Defendant
☐ Respondent ☐ Other *(Specify):*

Form Approved for Optional Use
Judicial Council of California
MC-031 [Rev. July 1, 2005]

ATTACHED DECLARATION

Page 1 of 1

> **Dismiss Your Does!**
>
> No matter which "path" you've chosen for your default, if you named Doe defendants in your complaint as suggested in "Dealing With Unknown Defendants" in Chapter 4, you will have to dismiss any Does whose identities you never determined and any defendant who was not served with the Summons and Complaint. Do this by using the Request for Dismissal form in Chapter 3. You have had practice filling out the boxes at the top of the form and I assume you'll breeze right through that. Follow these instructions for the rest of the form:
>
> **Item 1a.** Check the (2) box "Without Prejudice." That might preserve your right to sue someone on the facts of this case in the future in the unlikely event you locate a missing defendant or discover new evidence.
>
> **Item 1b.** Check the box for Complaint. Skip the next three boxes and in box (6) type "as to Does ____ to ____ ," listing the numbers of any remaining Does and add any other unserved defendant. Date and sign the form. Leave the rest of it blank.
>
> **Page 2.** This section applies only if you requested and were granted a fee waiver (Chapter 5).
>
> Send this form along with your Request for Entry of Default. Failure to include it will usually result in the rejection of your Request, because the court doesn't want this sliver of your case remaining alive after judgment has been entered against one or more defendants.

Your papers will be reviewed by a clerk and then by a judge. Either one of them may decide they want more information in declaration form or that they need some of your documents authenticated. In that case, you will get a notice telling you what they want. This is generally a sign that the judge feels that with a little more information he or she can probably give you a judgment without a court hearing.

You may instead get a notice that a court hearing is necessary before a judgment can be granted. A time and place for the hearing will be provided. This should not concern you. Judges differ on the amount of scrutiny they feel is appropriate in a default situation. Because a default has been entered, the defendant will not be given notice of this hearing and will not be allowed to testify if he or she shows up. If, at the court hearing, the judge says more evidence will be necessary, you should request a date for an additional hearing so you can supply what the judge suggests, which may mean, for example, producing a declaration from a witness the judge wants to hear from. If the witness won't sign a declaration, obtain a subpoena from the court clerk's office to force the witness to attend the hearing.

> **Default Clerks**
>
> The default clerk has one of the most responsible positions in the clerk's office and usually has quite a bit of influence on how your request for a judgment will be handled. Handle a request for further documentation from the default clerk in a cooperative manner. This is not the time to get pushy, ask to talk to a supervisor, or complain to the judge. Judges and the clerks they work with on a regular basis (courtroom clerks, default clerks, and supervising clerks) usually have a good relationship and the word that you are a "difficult person" can result in slowing the processing of your case.

Court Hearings on Your Default

If the judge has scheduled a hearing on your request for a default, I suggest that you get to the courtroom early on that day. If the judge is already on the bench, quietly take a seat. Assuming the judge is not on the bench yet, check in with the clerk, who will be sitting at a table near the front of the courtroom. When your case is called, go forward to the table in front of the judge.

Remember to call the judge "Your Honor" and state that you wish to "prove up" your default.

The judge may ask you questions or listen to your explanation—or may do both. If the judge just tells you to proceed, you should tell the important facts of your case in a form similar to the declaration at the beginning of this section.

EXAMPLE: Elliot sued the defendant for failure to pay for photographic services Elliot performed. At the default hearing, the judge says, "Proceed." Elliot replies, "On April 11, the defendant called me at my studio and asked what I would charge to photograph his wedding and produce five albums of 50 photos. I told him the price was $6,500. He hired me. I photographed his wedding and supplied the five albums on May 20. I also gave him a bill for $6,479 on that day. He has not paid me anything."

EXAMPLE: Austin was struck by a board falling off a construction project and sues the construction company. When the judge tells him to proceed, he says: "On June 4 at about 4 p.m. I was walking west down the north side of Comstock Street between Fifth and Sixth Avenues. There were several men putting up a scaffold on a five-story building on my right and I walked carefully around the base of the scaffold as I passed underneath them. There was no temporary wall or other structure to guard against falling objects. I heard someone on the scaffold yell, "Damn, I missed it!" and the next thing I knew I was flat on the ground and dizzy. A man with a name badge on his uniform came over and apologized. His badge said "Albuquerque Construction, James Bradley, Supervisor." I was taken to the hospital by an ambulance and took the next day off from work because of a headache. I have written several letters to the construction company and had them served with my complaint, but nobody has ever answered me. My damages are as follows:

"Ambulance (here is the bill)	$ 210
Emergency Room (this is the bill I received)	$1,100
Replace damaged clothing (this is the bill and I have the damaged clothing here in this bag)	$1,012
One month's lost income (here is last year's tax return showing my annual income)	$3,200
Pain and suffering	$5,000

"I request judgment against Albuquerque Construction in the amount of $10,522. Thank you, Your Honor"

At the end of your presentation, the judge will probably announce the amount of the judgment awarded to you. You have a Judgment form that has already been submitted to the court when you filed your Request for Entry of Judgment. If the clerk and the judge don't seem to be aware of that, say something like, "Your Honor [or "Madam or Mister Clerk"], I submitted a proposed Judgment form to the clerk's office when I filed my Request for Entry of Judgment."

TIP
Minimize the chances that the defendant will undo your victory. If the judge enters your judgment, you've won—unless the defendant comes in later and successfully asks to set aside the default. Read the next section to understand how this process works and what you can do to head the defendant off at the pass.

Setting Aside a Default Judgment

Under some circumstances, a defendant can show up after a default judgment has been entered and file a motion asking the court to "set it aside." If the court allows it, the defendant can then file an Answer and contest the case.

Grounds for Setting Aside a Default

You will first hear about the defendant's attempt to set aside your judgment when you receive a Motion to Set Aside in the mail. It will give you a time and place to appear to oppose the motion. The defendant must accompany his or her motion with a proposed Answer or other pleading to be filed if the motion to set aside the default is granted.

Read the motion carefully to see why the defendant failed to file the appropriate papers on time. Judges grant motions to set aside for these two reasons:

- the defendant failed to file due to inadvertence, surprise, mistake, or excusable neglect, or
- the defendant's attorney has accepted responsibility for the late or nonexistent filing.

Excusable Neglect

Under Code of Civil Procedure § 473(b), a defendant who can prove that his or her failure to file was excusable is entitled to have the default set aside. Courts tend to be pretty liberal in granting this sort of relief because of a public policy that favors deciding cases based upon the merits, rather than because of a procedural mistake by one of the parties. If the defendant's failure to file was the result of intervening forces beyond his or her control, the judge will probably set aside the order.

However, not all motions to set aside are full of winning arguments. A surprising number of defaulted defendants lose their motions because they appear to be people who just couldn't be bothered to follow the rules or take care of annoyances like lawsuits. And some propose "excuses" that are flimsy or unsupported. A few cases that might be helpful to you in resisting such a motion are *Gorman v. California Transit Co.* (1926) 199 Cal. 246 (holding that mere forgetfulness is not sufficient excuse), *Bellm v. Bellia* (1984) 150 Cal.App.3d 1036 (being overburdened with business is not a sufficient or excusable reason), and *Davis v. Thayer* (1980) 113 Cal.App.3d 892 (unsubstantiated poor health or not having funds to hire an attorney are not sufficient excuses).

When the Lawyer Takes the Blame

If the defendant's attorney will admit that the papers were not filed due to the attorney's negligence, the defendant has a very good shot at having the default set aside. Under Code of Civil Procedure § 473(b), the court is required to grant the motion under these circumstances, but you should ask the court to award you the penalty provided for in section (c)(1).

Minimizing the Chances of a Late Set-Aside

A defendant who tries to set aside a default must act within six months after it has been entered (filed). If the six months has elapsed, the default won't get set aside unless the defendant can show that he or she did not actually know about the lawsuit. If the defendant can convince the judge of this, that buys up to two years to set aside a default judgment. For instance, if you served the complaint by some legal means other than handing the papers over, for example by mailing them, it is possible that the defendant never actually learned of your lawsuit, even though you followed the rules for nonpersonal service to the letter.

To prevent the defendant from plausibly claiming no actual knowledge of your lawsuit, notify the defendant by certified letter, return receipt requested, as soon as you obtain the judgment. Assuming the defendant signs for the letter, he or she will have a hard time claiming no knowledge of the lawsuit. It also probably shortens the two-year limit to 180 days after receipt of your letter (Code of Civil Procedure § 473.5 (a)). If you want to make sure that the defendant will have only 180 days instead of two years, deliver the letter according to the rules of personal service, as described in Chapter 7. Doing so will clearly shorten the time to 180 days, but is also more likely to jar the defendant into action.

Responding to a Motion to Set Aside

It's not worth putting up a big defense to one of these motions unless it is clear that the defendant's case is very weak. If you or some other person has some evidence that bears on the question of the defendant's neglect, put it in the form of a Declaration on the court form (MC-030) that appears above. In the body of the declaration, you might say something like the following:

"Plaintiff David Schwarz declares: As demonstrated by the Proof of Service on file herein, the Defendant Michael Lyon was served by my process server April 10, 2010. On April 11, he phoned me and said, "You'll never be able to collect anything from me, so I am not going to file any papers in this case. All of the things you said in your papers are lies, but I just don't have time to argue about it, so go ahead and do whatever you want in court."

At any rate, if you lose the motion, point out to the court what work you have had to do because of the defendant's motion and explain the delay that has been caused. Ask for the penalty (not to exceed $1,000) provided for in Code of Civil Procedure § 473(c)(1).

Discovery

Types of Discovery 186

Discovery Rules and Limits 187
    Limits on Time..187
    Limits on the Number of Discovery Requests 188
    Limits on Taking Depositions 188
    Getting More Discovery 188

Doing Your Own Discovery 188
    Written Interrogatories 189
    Request for Production of Documents or Things 189
    Request for Admissions 191
    Depositions 191

Responding to Discovery 193
    Depositions 193
    Interrogatories 195
    Request for Production of Documents and Other Items 197
    Request for Admissions 197

Less-Used Methods of Discovery 198

Failing to Respond to a Discovery or Case Questionnaire Request 199
    Write a Letter 199
    File a Motion to Compel 200
    Argue Your Motion 200

Discovering Doe Defendants 203

CHAPTER 10

procedures
...in from the
...nts, and
...er side's
...very is
...holding,
...ore trial.
...ry is often used to
...other side or to delay the
...one party becomes disgusted
...ss than he or she is entitled to.
...ormation is discoverable if it is relevant
...e subject matter of the lawsuit and is either admissible as evidence or reasonably calculated to lead to the discovery of admissible evidence ("A Short Course in the Rules of Evidence" in Chapter 13 discusses admissibility). Also, through discovery you can get information about the monetary limit of any insurance policy held by the other side if the policy is related to the lawsuit.

The unsavory side of discovery—its use as a weapon to wear you down—often appears when a lawyer is hired to bring or defend a case against someone who is self-represented. Answering discovery requests can be tricky, especially with the form called "Request for Admissions," dealt with below, and many lawyers can't resist the opportunity to take advantage of untrained pro pers. Recently I saw a case involving two pro per defendants who had no idea how to appropriately respond to eight pages of questions. Their tangle of answers ended up legally admitting that everything in the Complaint was true! And to add insult to injury, they were also fined over $500 by an unsympathetic judge for their failure to comply with correct procedures. If they had been able to follow the instructions in this chapter, none of this would have happened.

RESOURCE

For an in-depth discussion of discovery—how to use it and respond to it—see *The Lawsuit Survival Guide,* by Joseph Matthews (Nolo), and *Represent Yourself in Court,* by Paul Bergman and Sara Berman (Nolo).

Types of Discovery

The discovery methods most often used in limited jurisdiction cases are:

Depositions. These are proceedings in which a witness or party is asked to answer questions orally, under oath, at a location away from the court, such as an office or private meeting room. The lawyers for each side ask questions or, if there is no lawyer, the party asks them. A court reporter records the answers and prepares a written transcript of the entire proceeding.

Interrogatories. These are written questions sent by one party to the other. The receiving party answers them under oath.

Requests for production of documents or things. These are demands from one party to the other to hand over certain documents or items for inspection and copying.

Subpoena duces tecum. This Latin phrase refers to an order telling a witness to bring certain documents to a deposition. Parties can also use this procedure to get documents to a trial.

Requests for admissions. These are requests from one party to the other to admit or deny certain allegations in the lawsuit.

Other discovery methods used less frequently in limited jurisdiction cases include:

Requests for physical examination. These may be used when a party's health is an issue in the case. They are requests by one party that a specified doctor examine the other party.

Witness list. This is a request by one party to the other to turn over the list of witnesses that the party plans to use at trial.

> **Don't File Your Discovery Documents With the Court**
>
> To begin any discovery using the methods described above, you'll serve original documents on the opposing party, along with the Proof of Service (described in Chapter 7). The opposing party furnishes the information or objects, and keeps copies of the requests (and the Proof of Service showing the date you served them) and his or her answers (and the date sent). When you get them back, don't file them in court. Instead, keep the originals in a safe place in case a controversy develops over their contents (or, if you manage to avoid discovery fights, keep them for six months after the case is over).
>
> If your opponent serves you with discovery requests, you'll send answers or objections back to your opponent, keeping copies of everything and recording the dates you received the requests and the date you sent your answers or objections. You'll also need to send copies of your answers to any other defendants who have filed an answer or other pleading with the court. Keep the Proof of Service. Your opponent should keep this original in a safe place for at least six months after the case is over. It will be needed only if there are disputes

- **Depositions.** The Code of Civil Procedure (C.C.P.) §§ 2025.010 through 2027.010 covers depositions.
- **Interrogatories.** The rules for interrogatories are found in C.C.P. §§ 2030.010 through 2030.410.
- **Requests for Admissions.** You'll find the rules in C.C.P. §§ 2033.010 through 2033.080.

The C.C.P. is available online, as explained in Chapter 1, and you'll find it in all law libraries and many large public libraries.

> **Complying With Discovery Rules**
>
> As you read the discovery rules, remember that they are primarily designed for lawsuits in the unlimited division of the Superior Court—cases that may involve millions of dollars. Your lawsuit, for $25,000 or less in the limited jurisdiction division, doesn't need the benefit (or burden!) of these complicated, detailed rules. In most cases, if you've not followed the precise procedures but you made a good faith effort to comply with the rules and you admit that you are a novice, a judge who may be called on later to review a discovery issue will often be sympathetic.
>
> Don't count on an understanding judge, however, if you have unreasonably failed to follow discovery rules or have attempted to use discovery to harass or intimidate your opponent. In that event, the judge can fine you (up to thousands of dollars), order other penalties (such as prohibiting you from introducing certain evidence at trial), or may, in extreme cases, dismiss your lawsuit outright.

Discovery Rules and Limits

Any information that is relevant to the case and is admissible as evidence (or likely to lead to admissible evidence) can be obtained through discovery. You can make discovery requests of any party in the lawsuit, as long as that party has filed an answer or other pleading with the court. Discovery, however, is not an endless fishing expedition. Be sure to read the discovery rules, set out below, before attending or scheduling a deposition, sending or answering interrogatories, or requesting or responding to admissions.

Limits on Time

Discovery must be completed 30 days before the date of the trial (Code of Civil Procedure § 2024.020). You can serve interrogatories ten days after service of summons, and a notice of deposition 20 days after service. The deposition itself may take place ten days after service of the notice.

Limits on the Number of Discovery Requests

The biggest limitation on discovery is the number of requests each side can make to the other. In limited jurisdiction cases, each side is limited to a total of 35 items of discovery directed to each adverse party in the case, whether the items are written interrogatories, requests for production of documents, or requests for admissions (Code of Civil Procedure § 94). If a question or request is divided into subparts, each subpart counts toward the total.

For example, if you use one sentence in a request for production of documents to ask the other party to produce three documents, that counts as three requests. Or, if the defendant gives you a written question asking you to list, for each place you've lived in the past 20 years, the address, names of all persons with whom you resided, the date you moved in and the date you moved out, that's probably four requests. And if you ask the defendant to admit to driving 40 miles an hour and running a stop light, that's two requests for admissions. Because it's tedious to keep track of subparts, judges don't like them. If you have questions or requests within requests, make each one a separate entity.

Limits on Taking Depositions

Just as you can't send adverse parties unlimited numbers of written discovery requests, you are also limited to the number of depositions you can take in limited jurisdiction cases. Each party can take as many depositions as there are adverse parties in the case. So, if you are the plaintiff and there are three defendants, you can take three depositions. If you are the defendant and there are two plaintiffs, you can take two depositions.

Getting More Discovery

If you want to serve the other side with more notices of depositions, interrogatories, requests for admissions, or requests to produce documents or things than are allowed by law, you'll have to file a formal motion before a judge. Judges rarely grant additional discovery, especially in small cases where the expense of lawyers and a court reporter can easily mount into thousands of dollars.

Doing Your Own Discovery

My aim throughout this book is to guide you to a quick and simple resolution of your lawsuit. Discovery cuts against that goal—it complicates and slows down the pace of the litigation. It often gives rise to side battles over the appropriateness of certain questions and whether penalties should be imposed for foot dragging, all of which can require frequent trips to the court where both sides argue over esoteric points of discovery law. Lawyers love it. You'll hate it.

Thus, my general advice is to avoid doing your own discovery if possible. If you are the plaintiff (or a cross-complainant), you should have a basic outline of the defendant's defense from the answers to your Case Questionnaire, which usually makes discovery unnecessary. What to do if the defendant hasn't answered the Case Questionnaire is covered in "Failing to Respond to a Discovery or Case Questionnaire Request," below.

There are, however, a few situations in which conducting limited discovery may be worth your while. If you have no idea what the other party's version of the dispute is, you may want to ask a few written questions (interrogatories). This approach may be especially helpful if you are a defendant in a case where the plaintiff did not use a Case Questionnaire.

Also, if your opponent is showing signs of planning to lie about your dispute, a skillfully phrased question during discovery can help you determine which lie he or she will tell at the trial.

This should give you an opportunity to prepare to disprove it.

EXAMPLE: The defendant states in her answer to interrogatories that she first saw the plaintiff's car approaching from her left a few seconds before the accident. Several months later, at the trial, she testifies that she never lost sight of the plaintiff after she first saw him approaching from several miles away. The plaintiff might respond to this discrepancy at the trial by asking "Were you telling the truth when you answered the interrogatories or are you telling the truth now?"

You can conduct discovery by using written interrogatories—which are much cheaper than a deposition—but they tend to be less effective because the other side won't answer spontaneously. Instead, since the answers are given in writing, the party answering will have ample time to avoid a straight answer to the question or concoct an answer that doesn't damage his or her position. The sections that follow outline how discovery techniques work.

Written Interrogatories

Written questions or interrogatories are the easiest form of discovery for a pro per to undertake. Use the standard form that has prewritten questions, which most lawyers use, too.

FORM
The appendix contains a tear-out version of Form DISC-004, *Form Interrogatories–Limited Civil Cases*, and you can download one from the Judicial Council website at www.courtinfo.ca.gov.

Make a few photocopies of the form. Review it carefully, and make a list of the questions you want to ask. In a personal injury or property damage case (called a tort case), you probably want to ask many of the questions in Sections 104 to 120. In a contract case, focus on the questions starting with Section 150.

In either type of case, you can add questions of your own if something you want to ask isn't on the form. Remember that along with requests for admissions and requests for production of documents and things, you can't exceed 35 questions. Don't waste any of your limited number of interrogatories asking questions that have already been answered in the response to your Case Questionnaire (which doesn't count as part of the 35).

Once you know what questions you want to ask, fill out the form. Copy the information requested at the top from the Complaint. Check the boxes for the questions you want answered and add any of your own—type them onto a piece of pleading (numbered) paper. Then have a friend serve the interrogatories on the defendants by mail. (See Chapter 7 for instructions on service.)

Request for Production of Documents or Things

If the other side has a document, account, letter, photograph, or other tangible item he or she won't voluntarily show you, you can use discovery to request that it be produced. Upon receiving your request, the other side must produce the items for you to inspect, copy, or photograph. You can also request that you or your agent (such as an inspector or engineer) be allowed to enter land or a house or building to inspect, measure, or take a sample.

EXAMPLE: Wally fell on a slippery painted surface in Grace's store. Wally wants an engineer to conduct some tests to determine just how slippery the surface is. Grace is not being helpful about arranging a time for the testing. Wally prepares and sends Grace a Request for Inspection, specifying when he will be there with his engineer.

One good overall discovery strategy is to first send written interrogatories designed to help you narrow the scope of your inquires and guide

ALICE MCMANN
98 Morton Road
Sunnyvale, CA 95000
408-555-8989
Defendant In Pro Per

SUPERIOR COURT OF CALIFORNIA—LIMITED JURISDICTION

COUNTY OF SANTA CLARA

CYNTHIA WONG and HAROLD WONG,
    Plaintiffs,

vs.

ALICE MCMANN,
    Defendant.

Case No. SC-90909

REQUEST FOR PRODUCTION OF DOCUMENTS AND OTHER ITEMS

Pursuant to Code of Civil Procedure § 2031.010, defendant, Alice McMann, hereby requests that plaintiffs produce for inspection and copying as follows:

Time: 10:00 a.m.

Date: September 21, 20xx

Place: Copy Cat Office, 990 Silver Street, Sunnyvale, California

Documents: (1) work order for repair of 1989 Volkswagen automobile, license 2MUN132 at German Garage June 3, 20xx; and (2) canceled check showing payment for that work order.

_____
Alice McMann

Defendant's Request for Production of Documents   Page 1

you toward objects that go to the very heart of the matter. Once you get the answers, you will hopefully have enough information or tips to figure out what documents or items you need to go after.

For example, if you were rear-ended on the freeway by someone who appeared to have bad brakes—the police report noted that his brake pedal went to the floor without resistance—you might ask in an interrogatory when and where he last had his brakes inspected by a car repairperson. Then ask him to produce a copy of the work order or invoice for that inspection.

In a dispute with a store owner over a defective product, ask the store to produce the form used to order the item from the manufacturer, the invoice received from the shipper, and any notices—including recall or defect notices—received about the item.

The courts have not produced a required form for a production request. To prepare your own, use pleading paper and follow the format of the sample shown above.

Subpoena Duces Tecum

If you want to obtain documents that are in the custody or control of someone who is *not* a party to the lawsuit, you must serve that person with a subpoena duces tecum. Because using a subpoena duces tecum can be complicated, I recommend that you hire a paralegal to do the paperwork. Paralegal services can be found in the yellow pages under "Attorneys' Service Bureaus" or "Typing Services." Call and ask if they prepare and serve subpoenas duces tecum.

Request for Admissions

A Request for Admissions is simple enough for a pro per to undertake, but normally in a small case, interrogatories are easier and more practical. Remember that along with interrogatories and requests for production of docu[ments,] you can't exceed 35 requests.

FORM

The appendix contains a tear-out v[ersion of] Form DISC-020, *Request for Admissions,* and you [can] download one from the Judicial Council website a[t] courtinfo.ca.gov.

If you want to send a Request for Admissions to the other party, photocopy the form. You'll see that there are two main parts, giving you an opportunity to request that the party admit:
- the facts that you list (Part 1), and
- that the original of certain attached documents (you attach the copies to the Request) is genuine (Part 2).

Write down on a piece of paper the requests you want to make. Here are some examples of statements of facts you might list in Part 1:
- "The windshield wipers on your automobile were not in use at the time of your collision with plaintiff's automobile."
- "You did not inspect the contents of the carton containing the A-2550 computer before you removed it from defendant's store."
- "Between 8 a.m. and noon on April 3, 2010, John Guillory was the employee in charge of sweeping the produce section of your store."
- "You stated on March 19, 2010 words to the effect that you would be able to repay the loan from plaintiff within six months."

In Part 2, you attach a copy of an important document that you want the other side to admit is genuine. For example, you could attach a copy of a bill of sale. An admission by the other party will establish that the original is in fact the bill of sale that the two of you signed.

Depositions

For a deposition, you pick the date, time, and location of the proceeding. You also must hire a

fiasco. No referee is present to maintain order or insist upon fair conduct. The court reporter simply records what happens. If you're treated unfairly, your only remedy is to file a motion in court and ask the judge to read the transcript and fine the other side.

There are, of course, cases where taking a deposition is an invaluable tool in preparing for trial or arbitration or in just convincing the other side that their case has problems that should motivate them to settle. It may be that you want to take the deposition of the other party to pin them down on what they would say at trial. Or there may be a police officer or low-level employee of a business who just won't talk to you voluntarily about what happened at a significant time.

If this is your situation, *Nolo's Deposition Handbook*, by Paul Bergman and Albert Moore,

Preparing for a Deposition

These tips can help you prepare for a deposition.

Tell the truth. This is the cardinal rule. Tell the truth even about little details that might be embarrassing or seem trivial to you.

Listen to the question carefully. Your job is to answer the question that is asked, not a question you wish had been asked. Concentrate on every word of the question and wait until it's been completely stated before you start to answer.

If you don't hear or understand the question, ask that it be repeated or explained. If you don't hear the question because the lawyer drops his or her voice or someone coughs while the question is being stated, ask that it be repeated. If the lawyer asks a long or convoluted question, don't answer until you're sure you know what is being asked. If the lawyer uses a word you're not familiar with, say that you don't understand. Don't be embarrassed—it's important that you know what's being asked before you answer.

Answer briefly and only the question asked. If the question can be answered with a "yes," "no," "I don't know," or "I don't remember," give that answer. If you want to explain further, keep it short and to the point. Don't make a speech or volunteer information. If the lawyer allows silence after you give an answer, resist the temptation to talk. People who are inexperienced at these legal games rarely gain anything by volunteering information.

Don't guess. If you're pretty sure of an answer, but not positive, say so. If you would have to guess to answer a question, state that you don't know.

Don't argue with your opponent's lawyer. If a question makes you angry, don't argue. Just answer it. If you argue, you'll only lose in the long run. Be courteous—but on guard—at all times.

Don't let a lawyer trick you. Your opponent's lawyer may try to trick you into thinking you've given a wrong or stupid answer by asking a question over and over again with slight variations. The lawyer may smirk and ask if you *really* meant what you just said— probably just trying to get you to change your answer. Stick to your answer, even if you begin to sound like a broken record.

will be an invaluable tool. Chapter 4 of the book, "Responding to Questions," is a complete guide for anyone who is about to take a deposition or be subject to one. In fact, read this material again before you go to trial. You'll find the book at most law libraries and many public libraries and it can be purchased from Nolo at www.nolo.com.

Responding to Discovery

Whether you are a plaintiff or a defendant, if your opponent has a lawyer, you will probably receive discovery requests—sometimes for no other reason than to try to teach you not to mess with the legal system.

Depositions

The purposes of a deposition are to:
- obtain information to help prepare for a settlement or trial
- find out what you or the witness will say at the trial, and
- trap you or a witness into saying something that will hurt your case or embarrass you at the trial.

Within the rules of evidence, relevant portions of a deposition can be—and frequently are—read out loud to the judge or jury during the trial.

Scheduling a Deposition

If you get a Notice of Deposition, review it carefully. Depositions are usually conducted at a lawyer's office, and you may be asked to bring relevant documents or tangible objects. The other side must give you at least ten days' notice (15 if the notice was mailed) and can't make you travel more than 75 miles (150 if the deposition will take place in the county where the lawsuit was filed).

If these distance or time requirements haven't been met, write the other side immediately and explain that you won't be at the deposition because you haven't been given sufficient notice or are being asked to travel too far. Be sure to keep a copy of your letter.

If you can't make the deposition at the time proposed, call the other side's attorney (or the other side, if unrepresented) and try to reschedule. Lawyers usually cooperate in rescheduling depositions. If you arrange a new time, send a letter stating your understanding of the new time. Keep a copy for yourself. If the other side won't cooperate, send a letter stating that you can't make the deposition (explain your conflict), that you asked for it to be rescheduled, and that the other side refused. Be sure to keep a copy.

If the other side goes ahead with the deposition and you don't show up, your opponent will probably file a motion with the court to "compel" you to appear at a deposition. The court can also fine you for not showing up. But if you had a good reason not to show and hand the judge your letter, the court will probably excuse you for refusing to appear.

If the other side is taking the deposition of a witness who is not a party to the case, usually your opponent will issue a subpoena to the witness, which forces the witness to show (in some cases the person will appear voluntarily). For example, the plumber who repaired the contractor's botched attempt to install your hot tub will normally not be delighted at the prospect of spending a few hours being grilled by a lawyer, and may not appear unless a subpoena shows that the power of the court is behind the invitation. You are entitled to (and should) attend.

Preparing for the Deposition

Below are some brief suggestions on how to behave at a deposition. You'll find far more thorough information in *Nolo's Deposition Handbook*, mentioned above. If the other side is taking your deposition, read that material. These suggestions were prepared by lawyers to instruct their clients. As you'll see from reading the material, not everything will apply to you. But enough will, so study it carefully.

TIP
Don't fall prey to a lawyer's tricks. There are far more of them than I can expose here. Consult Nolo's *Deposition Handbook* for the full story.

Attending the Deposition

For moral support, you can take your Sounding Board to the deposition and occasionally take short breaks to confer with him or her. If you whisper during the deposition, a truly aggressive lawyer representing your opponent might object, claiming that the Sounding Board was practicing law without a license. But if you do all the audible talking and the Sounding Board doesn't make speeches, ignore the objection.

The deposition itself may begin with the other side asking you to agree to "the usual stipulations." It's best to state that you do not agree to anything other than what is provided in the Code of Civil Procedure. Next, the court reporter will administer an oath ("Do you swear to tell the truth, the whole truth and nothing but the truth?") to you or the witness being deposed.

Then the lawyer who scheduled the deposition takes over. The lawyer's job is to ask questions. Many are routine and harmless, but some are designed to wear you down or trap you or the witness into an inconsistency. For example, in an automobile accident case, a lawyer might first ask you what you saw when you were 100 yards from the point of impact, 50 yards, 20 yards, ten yards, and then five yards. Then he or she will ask you what speed you were traveling at each point. Finally, the lawyer will ask how hard you were applying your brake pedal at each point.

You probably won't be able to give a precise answer to these questions. So adopt a standard reply and parrot it over and over if the lawyer tries to wear you down. In the above situation, you might say, "I can't answer that precise question, but I can tell you that the yellow car appeared from out of the alley going very fast when I was about half a block from the point of impact." If the lawyer gets angry and loud, don't worry about it. Some lawyers think that discovery was created to intimidate people.

What you say in the deposition can be read to the judge or jury during the trial. So if it is at all possible, frame your answer in a light that's positive to your case. If the lawyer asks, "Ms. Davis, the rain was coming down quite hard at the time of the accident, wasn't it?" A good answer, if it were true, would be, "Yes, it was, but I grew up in Seattle and am very accustomed to driving in the rain and observing what is going on."

If the lawyer asks if you are sure you told the service manager at the car repair shop that your car had stalled in the fast lane at 5:00 p.m., answer, "Yes, and I remember he said that it sounded like a defective fuel pump that he could fix it quickly and easily."

Objecting to Deposition Questions

As pointed out earlier, a discovery request can seek information related to the lawsuit if it would be either admissible as evidence or is reasonably calculated to lead to admissible evidence. Discovery can also seek the monetary limits of any insurance policy that may cover the lawsuit. You shouldn't have to answer (nor should you draft) questions and requests that don't fit within this description of proper discovery.

When the other side asks improper questions, it's time to object. You can make several different types of legal objections to deposition questions asked of you or another witness, but it is best to limit yourself to the following grounds:

- **The question or request seems far afield.** If a question doesn't seem to have anything to do with the issues in your case, say, "Objection, the question does not appear to be reasonably calculated to lead to the discovery of admissible evidence."

TIP
Don't waste your breath over irrelevant but harmless questions. You can answer irrelevant questions

if you're sure the answer won't hurt you, but take a stand if the question calls for private information. For example, if your car was totaled while it was legally parked at a curb and you're asked if you have ever been under a psychiatrist's care, object and refuse to answer it. Or, if in a breach of contract case you're asked about the time you shoplifted when you were 17, refuse to answer.

- **The questioner is acting rudely or asking intrusive questions.** If the lawyer badgers you or the witness, say "Objection, the question calls for material that is unduly intrusive, harassing, or embarrassing to the witness. Under the provisions of Evidence Code Section 765 and Code of Civil Procedure Section 2023.010, I decline to answer it (or I recommend to the witness that he or she not answer it)."

EXAMPLE: Blake is involved in an automobile accident on his way to work in the morning. At his deposition, the lawyer wants to know whom he slept with the night before. Blake objects and refuses to answer.

It's a good idea to keep your objections to a minimum so you can get the deposition completed peacefully. If the lawyer asks the same questions over and over, or becomes insulting, bullying, or extremely objectionable, warn that if these practices continue, you'll terminate the deposition and leave the premises. If the lawyer still doesn't stop, state for the court reporter why you are leaving, and leave. The law does not require you to stay put while you're being harassed. If a witness being deposed is harassed, remain at the deposition and make your objections until the witness leaves.

Interrogatories

If you receive written questions, you should have little trouble responding. Begin by reading the "Instructions to the Answering Party" on the first page of the form interrogatories in the appendix. Be careful to observe your time deadline. Even if the other side didn't use form interrogatories, these instructions are helpful. Then write down the number of each question asked of you on a sheet of paper and write out your answers. Review your answers with your Sounding Board. Finally, consult the format of the sample Answer to Interrogatories, below, when you prepare your answers.

Your answers should be a responsible attempt to give information, not an effort to be cute and avoid the subject. But you have no responsibility to give more information than what you've been asked. For instance, if you're a store owner asked how many lawn mowers you sold in May, answer "Nine." Don't say, "I sold as many lawn mowers as there were people paying for them." At the same time, don't give sales for April or June or the names and addresses of the buyers.

When you've completed the form, have a friend serve (by mail) the answers to the requesting party. (See Chapter 7, for instructions on service.)

Objecting to an Interrogatory

Remember, as long as it is relevant, a discovery request can seek information related to the lawsuit if it is either admissible as evidence or is reasonably calculated to lead to admissible evidence. Discovery also can seek the monetary limits of any insurance policy that may cover the lawsuit.

If an interrogatory calls for information not within the scope of the lawsuit—such as events that occurred long ago or private details unrelated to this case—you can object by writing "Plaintiff (or defendant) objects to interrogatory number ___ and refuses to answer. It is outside the scope of discovery provided in Code of Civil Procedure § 2017.010."

Before objecting, talk it over with your Sounding Board. Ask if the question could be related to the lawsuit. Be imaginative (the judge who may decide the question will be). If the question is at all possibly related, answer it.

ALICE MCMANN
98 Morton Road
Sunnyvale, CA 95000
408-555-8989
Defendant In Pro Per

SUPERIOR COURT OF CALIFORNIA—LIMITED JURISDICTION

COUNTY OF SANTA CLARA

CYNTHIA WONG and HAROLD WONG,	))	Case No. SC-90909
Plaintiffs,	))	DEFENDANT ALICE MCMANN'S ANSWER TO INTERROGATORIES
vs.	))	(SET NO. _____)
ALICE MCMANN,	))	
Defendant.	)	

Defendant, Alice McMann, hereby answers the first *(or appropriate number)* set of interrogatories propounded by plaintiffs.

(Type your answers in the numerical order in which they were requested; don't repeat the question you are answering.)

I declare under penalty of perjury the foregoing is true and correct.

Signed at Sunnyvale, California, November 3, 20xx.

_____

Alice McMann

Defendant's McMann's Answer to Interrogatories, Set _____

Request for Production of Documents and Other Items

If you are sent a Request for Production, produce the item before or at the time specified. If you can't comply on time, write to your opponent giving a date and time with which you can comply. If you don't have the documents or items asked for, write to your opponent and explain. To make it clear to the recipient that you are serious and telling the truth, end with a "penalty of perjury" paragraph, as illustrated in the "Sample Letter Objecting to Request for Production of Documents and Other Items," below.

You may also receive requests for items that have nothing to do with the issues in the case—requests for irrelevant items. If you don't believe the request is within the proper scope of discovery (admissible as evidence or reasonably calculated to lead to admissible evidence), send a letter explaining why you object. If the letter doesn't settle the matter, prepare a document on legal pleading paper, similar to the one you use to answer interrogatories, and explain the situation as to each request. End your document with a "penalty of perjury" provision (like the sample letter shown below) and sign it.

Requests for Admissions

Requests for Admissions can be used to avoid having to prove certain facts that are not really in dispute (for example, that there is a traffic light at the corner of First and Washington). But they also are frequently used by lawyers attempting to prepare to file a Motion for Summary Judgment, which is an attempt to end a lawsuit before a trial by showing that the facts are not in dispute and the legal issues are clearly in favor of the party making the motion (summary judgment motions are explained in detail in Chapter 11). So be very careful in answering the requests and be sure to answer on time. If you fail to deny requests for admissions on time, the court will consider them admitted, a potentially disastrous result for your

---

Sample Letter Objecting to Request for Production of Documents and Other Items

November 11, 20xx

Mr. Robert Dewey, Esq.
Dewey and Dewey
324 Downey Street
Los Angeles, CA 90012

Re: Harkins v. Blake,
       Los Angeles Superior Court 963-278-4

Dear Mr. Dewey:

I have received your Request for Production of the foreign material found in my carburetor after it caused my car to stall in the middle of the Harbor Freeway at 5:15 p.m. August 10 of this year. I would be happy to produce the material, but it has been seized by the Los Angeles Police Department as part of their manslaughter investigation. If you wish me to produce a formal legal document responding to your request, I will prepare one, but I hope that can be avoided.

I declare under penalty of perjury the foregoing is true and correct.

Executed at Los Angeles, California, November 11, 20xx.

/s/ *Harry Harkins*

Harry Harkins

---

case. Next to each statement, write one of the following notations:

Admit. For each statement where you agree with absolutely everything said, write "Admit" next to it. If you admit a statement, the other side won't have to prove it in court. Thus, admit only those statements you can't argue about. If you honestly don't know if a statement is true or if you agree with only part of it, don't admit it.

Deny. Write "Deny" near each statement in which you deny all or part of what was said. For instance, if a statement says, "In June, Defendant refused to sign a paper modifying the contract" and you deny it, say so. If part of it is true, answer something like, "The statement is only partly true. I refused to sign the paper on June 7 and June 20, but I offered to sign it June 28." If you deny something that the other party later shows that you should have admitted, the judge may require you to pay the cost of whatever the other party had to go through to prove it.

> ### Be Careful When Denying the Obvious
>
> Don't cavalierly deny a request just to make the other party prove the issue at trial—it could cost you. It's one thing to deny a statement over which there is a real dispute—for example, if the request says "Between 8 a.m. and noon on April 3, 2005 John Guillory was the employee in charge of sweeping the produce section of your store," the answering party (probably the store owner or manager) may have good reason to dispute that John was "in charge" of sweeping the produce section (perhaps he was a clerk in training and not in charge of much of anything). In that event, a denial of the request by the owner would simply leave the question open, and you would have to prove the statement at trial if you thought it necessary to your case. Even if you eventually proved the point, there would not be any negative consequences for the owner, despite having denied the statement's truth.
>
> But suppose John was clearly in charge of this task—his job title, the task assignment sheet in the produce room, and even his own admissions easily establish that that's his job. When there's really no dispute concerning the facts in a request, a denial by the person answering the question is risky. If a judge decides that a particular issue never was subject to a real dispute and the denial required a party to prove it in court, the judge can order the other party to pay the costs of proving the nonissue. The chances of getting reimbursed go up if that person had to spend a lot of time and money proving what should have been admitted during discovery.

Deny on information and belief. If you are not sure what the truth is, but you believe the plaintiff's statement is probably more false than true, write, "Deny on information and belief." For instance, if the plaintiff has alleged that the accident happened at night, but you think—and aren't completely sure—it was late on a winter afternoon, use this designation.

Deny because no information. If you have no idea whether the allegation in a statement is true—for example, a statement saying that the plaintiff was on the job performing his duties as a delivery person—write, "Deny because no information."

Prepare your answers to these Requests by using pleading paper and copying the format shown for answering interrogatories, as shown in the sample in "Interrogatories," above.

Less-Used Methods of Discovery

There are other discovery methods available to litigants in the limited division of the Superior Court, but they are appropriate for only certain kinds of cases. They are:

Request for physical examination. This is a request by one party that a doctor examine the other party. The request can be for a physical or mental exam. It's appropriate only if the person's health is an issue in the case. For example, if your leg broke during an accident you claim was the defendant's fault, the defendant is entitled to have his or her doctor examine your leg. If you claim severe mental distress as a result of the accident, the defendant can request that a psychiatrist, psychologist, or similar medical professional examine you.

Although medical examinations are not used much in limited jurisdiction cases—the examination is expensive and not worth the cost unless an injury claim appears suspicious—cooperate with any reasonable request. But be aware that anything you say to the doctor during the examination can be used against you in the case. No matter how friendly the doctor may seem, you should not treat the doctor as your friend. The doctor was hired by the other side to explore anything suspicious about your injury claim. You are allowed to have a tape recorder present during the examination and you are entitled to a copy of the resulting report.

TIP
Read the rules before you submit to an examination. The rules regarding mental and physical examinations are in Code of Civil Procedure §§ 2032.220–2032.610.

Expert Witness List. If you want a lot of information about experts your opponent plans to call at trial, you can get it following the complex procedures in Code of Civil Procedure § 2034.210. But don't do so lightly. Unless your case has complicated technical issues where expert testimony will be important, I recommend you skip this procedure. This said, if a preview of your opponent's testimony is vitally important to you, read the code section above and follow its directions. If you get such a request from your opponent, read the section and comply.

Failing to Respond to a Discovery or Case Questionnaire Request

The other side may not respond to your discovery request or Case Questionnaire. Some lawyers are not familiar with the Case Questionnaire and may ignore the requirement to answer it. And sometimes your discovery requests will be blown off or forgotten. If you get no response to either a discovery request or a Questionnaire, you can follow a two-step process to get some action.

Write a Letter

Your first step is to send the other side (or the other side's lawyer) a letter demanding compliance. The law requires you to informally try, in good faith, to resolve any discovery dispute by letter or telephone before heading for court. If you go to court without first trying to resolve the matter informally, a judge can impose penalties. Write a letter like the "Sample Letter Demanding Compliance With Discovery Request or Case Questionnaire," below.

Sample Letter Demanding Compliance With Discovery Request or Case Questionnaire

Gregory Dailey
Dailey and Weakly
2323 Mason Street
Santa Barbara, CA

July 5, 20xx

Re: Vincent vs. Higgins Superior Court Case # 497 233

Dear Mr. Dailey:

I am the plaintiff in the above-referred case. Per the rules in Code of Civil Procedure § 93, your client, Ms. Higgins, was served with a Case Questionnaire when she was served with the Summons and Complaint on May 21, 20xx, 45 days ago. Although you have filed an Answer on her behalf, you have not responded to the Questionnaire.

This letter asks you to please respond to the Questionnaire by July 12, 20xx. If I do not receive it, I will file a motion in court to obtain compliance and sanctions as provided by Code of Civil Procedure §§ 93 (e) and 2023.010.

Yours truly,

Sandra Vincent
Sandra Vincent

File a Motion to Compel

If you still don't receive a response to your discovery request or Case Questionnaire and you want to force the issue, you will have to file a paper called a Motion to Compel a (Further) Response with the court. This motion is authorized by Code of Civil Procedure § 93(e) (Case Questionnaire) and Code of Civil Procedure §§ 2023.010 to 2023.040 (discovery). If the other side only partially answered your questions, the motion is to compel a further response.

One of my favorite judges spends a lot of time hearing these discovery disputes. She describes the average motion to compel as "a sandbox fight between well-dressed lawyers who act like children." She thinks the lawyers need a playground director, not a judge. And the poor client (who may be much poorer by the end) has frequently paid upwards of $250 an hour for lawyers to think up questions other lawyers are sure to object to. If the dispute goes to court, the client also pays for the lawyer to sit around a courtroom waiting to fight in the sandbox.

If you still want to file your motion, call the clerk's office. Tell the clerk that you plan to file a Motion to Compel a Response to a Case Questionnaire or to your discovery. Ask the clerk what day and time, and in what courtroom (department) of the court, you should schedule your motion for a hearing by a judge. Ask what the fee is to file a motion. Then, using numbered pleading paper, type up the motion like the samples below. File the original with the court. Have a friend serve the papers by mail. (See Chapter 7.)

Many times, in response to your filing a motion, the other side will offer to comply if you will drop the motion. This is often because lawyers know that if a judge decides that they wrongfully withheld discovery, a penalty in the amount of $250 or more is not unusual (referred to as a sanction, the penalty also may be ordered against a party who makes an unsuccessful motion to compel further answers). Don't agree to drop the motion until you actually receive an adequate Case Questionnaire or response. If the court will permit it, you can agree to postpone (continue) the hearing on your motion to a later date, but you should not commit on promises of future compliance.

TIP

Demand a Case Questionnaire only if you need it. In some situations, when you don't know what kind of a story your opponent is going to tell at trial, it will be very important to receive Case Questionnaire answers so that you can prepare. But in other situations, where you already know a lot about the defendant's case, it often isn't worth the time and stress to go through a motion to compel discovery.

Argue Your Motion

If you decide to pursue the matter, read over California Rules of Court 3.110, 3.1345, and the following sections for a detailed description of the required procedures. At the hearing, dress appropriately (business attire is best if you have it, but going to court is not an event for which you should buy new clothes). Be sure to arrive at court on time.

Bring a copy of the Case Questionnaire, discovery question or admission that has not been responded to, the letter you sent, and the papers you filed (Notice of Motion and Motion to Compel a (Further) Response, and the Proof of Service by Mail). If the judge isn't yet in the courtroom when you arrive, check in with the courtroom clerk who sits near the judge's bench.

When the judge announces your case, stand before one of the tables in front of the judge. When the judge asks you to speak, simply explain what has happened: "Your honor, I served the Case Questionnaire (or discovery request) on the defendant and she did not respond within the time required. I attempted to get the defendant to comply by sending a letter, but she still has not responded."

ANDREW CHU
44 West Ellison Avenue
Chico, CA 95000
916-555-8989
Plaintiff In Pro Per

STATE OF CALIFORNIA

BUTTE COUNTY SUPERIOR COURT—LIMITED JURISDICTION

ANDREW CHU,	) Case No. 3847562
Plaintiff,	) NOTICE OF MOTION AND MOTION
	) TO COMPEL RESPONSE TO
vs.	) CASE QUESTIONNAIRE
	)
MAUREEN TAKAHASHI,	)
Defendant.	)

Notice is hereby given that at 9 a.m. on November 23, 20xx, *(be sure this date is at least 16 court days plus five calendar days after the date you will mail this notice)* in Department ____ of the above court, plaintiff will move C.C.P. § 93 to compel defendant Maureen Takahashi's responses to plaintiff's Case Questionnaire. Pursuant to C.C.P. § 93(e), plaintiff will further move that sanctions be imposed against defendant for failing to provide a [completed] Case Questionnaire as required by § 93.

This motion will be based upon the fact that plaintiff served his Case Questionnaire on defendant on September 2, 20xx, that defendant filed an Answer to plaintiff's Complaint on October 3, 20xx, but defendant has not filed her Case Questionnaire [or defendant has provided incomplete answers to questions: *(list number of each incomplete question and why answer is incomplete)*]. Sanctions are requested.

Andrew Chu   3-17-xx
Andrew Chu   Date

1	ANDREW CHU
	44 West Ellison Avenue
2	Chico, CA 95000
	916-555-8989
3	Plaintiff In Pro Per
4	
5	
6	
7	
8	STATE OF CALIFORNIA
9	BUTTE COUNTY SUPERIOR COURT—LIMITED JURISDICTION

10	ANDREW CHU,	)	Case No. 3847562
	Plaintiff,	)	NOTICE OF MOTION AND MOTION
11		)	TO COMPEL RESPONSE TO
	vs.	)	INTERROGATORIES [OR REQUEST
12		)	FOR PRODUCTION OF DOCUMENTS
	MAUREEN TAKAHASHI,	)	OR REQUEST FOR ADMISSIONS]
13	Defendant.	)	

14

15   Notice is hereby given that at 9 a.m. on November 23, 20xx, in Department _____ of the

16 above court, plaintiff will move pursuant to C.C.P. § 2030.290 [for interrogatories; for requests for

17 production, C.C.P. § 2031.300; for request for admissions, § 2033.250] to compel defendant Maureen

18 Takahashi's responses to plaintiff's interrogatories [or Requests for Production or Request for

19 Admissions]. Pursuant to C.C.P. § 2023.010 to 2023.040, plaintiff will further move that sanctions be

20 imposed against defendant for failing to [completely] respond to the same.

21   This motion will be based upon the fact that plaintiff served his interrogatories [or Request for

22 Production of Documents or Request for Admissions] on defendant on September 2, 20xx, and

23 that defendant has not served any response [or defendant has provided incomplete answers to

24 questions: *(list number of each incomplete question and why answer is incomplete)*]. Sanctions are

25 requested.

26

27 _Andrew Chu_   _3-17-xx_
   Andrew Chu   Date

28

Plaintiff's Motion to Compel   Page 1

Also, briefly tell the judge how much time you've spent on writing the letter, preparing the motion, and appearing in court. Explain that if you were a lawyer, you'd ask for $175 an hour for that time, but because you are a pro per, you'd like an award of sanctions of $60 an hour.

The judge will usually issue his or her ruling while you are in court. If the judge orders the other side to comply (usually within a certain amount of time) and you still get no response, reread § 93 or § 2023.010 of the Code of Civil Procedure. The other side may be uncooperative just because you are a pro per and they may think that you will be unable to cope with the obnoxious behavior. Consider consulting an attorney for possible limited assistance.

If You Didn't Comply With a Discovery Request

If you've failed to comply with discovery—for example, you left in the middle of a deposition because you were being harassed—and the other side files a Motion to Compel you to respond, you should go to court on the day of the hearing and explain to the judge what happened. You may want to buy a copy of the transcript from the reporter at the deposition so you can show the judge exactly what happened.

Discovering Doe Defendants

During discovery, you may learn the name of a defendant whom you have been identifying as a Doe. Up until now, you may have been identifying him as the owner of the other car that caused your accident, the parents of a juvenile driver, the employer for whom another defendant was working at the time of the accident, the owner of a building where you were injured as a result of a defect, the general contractor on a job where you were injured by a subcontractor, a salesman who made a misrepresentation about a product he sold you, or a foreman or supervisor who was responsible for the employee who injured or otherwise damaged you. Now that you have learned who this person is, you may want to officially name the individual as a defendant.

Converting a Doe defendant to a real defendant involves a fair amount of paperwork and can delay your trial date. Thus, you won't want to convert unless it will add something of value to your case. One value of bringing in a Doe may be that he or she has substantial assets to contribute toward paying a judgment or settlement you obtain. Another reason to make a Doe a named party is strategic—as a party (and not a mere witness), the person must appear at and participate in discovery and will usually appear at trial without your having to issue a subpoena.

The easiest way to turn a Doe defendant into a real defendant is to modify the Los Angeles form, *Amendment to Complaint (Fictitious/Incorrect Name)* (of course, if you are suing in Los Angeles, you can just go ahead and use it without any modifications). Strangely, the Judicial Council has developed hundreds of forms but as far as I can tell, they don't have one for this particular purpose.

This form is straightforward, so I haven't included a sample here. The first box on the form is self-explanatory (ignore the STATE BAR NUMBER box, and be sure to write "In Pro Per" after ATTORNEY FOR (Name)). In the second box, you will have to make a change that is not "fillable." Manually cross out the words "Los Angeles" (unless that is where you are suing) and above it, write in the name of the county in which you are suing. Then check the box "FICTITIOUS NAME" and in the box below type "Doe 1" or whatever Doe you are converting.

In the box "TRUE NAME," type the name of your new defendant. Then fill in the date, your name, and your signature under the heading "SIGNATURE OF ATTORNEY." You can cross out the word "attorney" if it will make you more comfortable. Then, attach a declaration of your having mailed a copy to the defendants and file the original with the court, getting back an endorsed copy.

If your new defendant (formerly Doe 1) was previously served with the original summons (with a check in the appropriate place indicating he or she is served as a Doe) and the complaint as described in Chapter 7, you need only serve the new defendant now with the Amendment. If the new defendant hasn't been served before, use personal service for the Amendment, the original Complaint, a Case Questionnaire, and a Summons.

FORM

The appendix contains a tear-out version of the Los Angeles form *Amendment to Complaint (Fictitious/Incorrect Name)*, and you can download one from the Los Angeles Superior Court website reached as described in "Finding the Law, on paper and Online" in Chapter 1. On the home page, click "Forms" under the "Civil" heading. Then scroll down to the form title. Just as with the Judicial Council forms, it is "fillable" on your computer.

This Doe defendant is now a real defendant, has 30 days to file an Answer, and 45 days to file a Case Questionnaire.

CHAPTER 11

The Opposition Gets Nasty: Summary Judgment and Other Motions

Motion for Summary Judgment 206
    Time Restrictions for an MSJ 207
    Review the Papers You Receive 208
    Prepare Your Opposition to the Summary Judgment Motion 209
    Prepare Your Supporting Declarations 214
    Defending Against the MSJ in Court 217
    Asking for Sanctions 217

Motion for Summary Adjudication of Issues 217

Motion for Judgment on the Pleadings 218

Other Motions: Demurrers, Motions to Quash, and Motions to Strike 218
    Demurrer 218
    Motion to Strike 219
    Motion to Quash 219

Demand for Bill of Particulars 219

A lawsuit doesn't have to take very long. As you know by now, the plaintiff files a Complaint, the defendant has 30 days to respond, and then the matter can be set for trial. Under the case management rules of many courts, this can all happen in six months. But few cases are resolved that quickly. One or both parties may want to conduct some discovery, explained in Chapter 10. Or one side may play "the litigation game" and file some motions.

Motions, which are formal written requests to the court to take some action, are the bread and butter of many attorneys. In fact, so many lawyers file motions that, in many large California counties, several judges are designated the "law and motion" judges. All these judges do, day after day, is hear motions.

Many motions have nothing to do with the merits of the case. For example, in response to a Complaint, a defendant may file—instead of an Answer—a Motion to Strike, Motion to Quash, or a Demurrer. These are written, technical objections complaining about something the plaintiff put in the Complaint or about the method used to serve the papers on the defendant. Usually, all they really do is delay the inevitable—the filing of an Answer by the defendant. Later on in a case, attorneys file motions to avoid disclosing—or to compel the disclosure of—certain information in discovery. Attorneys also file motions to keep certain evidence out of a trial.

A few motions, however, do address the merits of the case. That is, if you lose the motion, you lose the case, or major issues in the case. This chapter covers these motions. However, I do not recommend that you file these motions yourself. Not only do they involve another layer of procedural complexity, but you can normally get the result you want faster and cheaper by going to trial. For this reason, this chapter covers defending against—not filing—motions.

Motion for Summary Judgment

Like discovery, the Motion for Summary Judgment (called an "MSJ" by lawyers) is another legal reform invented with the best of intentions that now has run amok because of lawyers' excesses. The motion was designed to weed out weak lawsuits early on so that parties wouldn't have to spend time and money to get ready for an expensive trial. Sadly, because of the way lawyers have bent the process, the cost of preparing or defending such a motion in a complex case can wind up costing as much as a trial. This doesn't seem to bother some lawyers, who happily prepare gargantuan motions that sometimes amount to several pounds of paper.

Most judges dislike reading complex MSJs filed by large law firms employing legions of young lawyers whose main task seems to be to prepare them. A judge must search through often 50 pages of documents to decide a very technical legal question. And more often than not, the judge denies the motion.

How does all of this relate to your limited jurisdiction action? If your opponent files an MSJ in your case, it's not likely to run more then ten pages but, even so, when used against a pro per, an MSJ is rarely a good faith effort to get rid of a frivolous lawsuit. It is likely to be much more akin to the neighborhood bully putting tough moves on the new kid on the block.

If you were a pro per trying to win your lawsuit without the help of this book, you might well lose your case at this stage. Many years ago when I was a Municipal Court judge, I saw entirely too many of these motions brought against pro pers who had no idea how to respond. But if you follow the procedures I set out here, you can normally beat this sort of motion and perhaps in the process educate your opponent that you can't be scared into giving up your case.

To understand how an MSJ works, you must know that in a trial, two kinds of issues are resolved—issues of fact and issues of law. An issue of fact is one that can (or cannot) be verified by a witness, including you—such as the color of a traffic light at the time of an accident. In a jury trial, only the jury can decide factual issues.

Issues of law are different. They are for the judge and only the judge to decide, even in a jury trial. Issues of law arise when lawyers try to persuade a judge that, based on statutes and cases, the law means one thing or another. For example, a few years ago the California Supreme Court considered a motion for summary judgment brought by the defense in a case where a woman, the plaintiff, had sued for the emotional distress she suffered while being held at gunpoint by a robber at a Kentucky Fried Chicken store. She argued that her injuries resulted from the store employees failing to move quickly enough to open the cash register and give the robber the contents. The trial judge granted the motion, and was upheld when the Supreme Court agreed with his decision that the store had no duty to obey the robber's demands quickly. As a result the case was dismissed and no trial was held.

In an MSJ, the moving party—the party bringing the Motion—asks the judge to:
- declare that there are no important issues of fact in dispute and that the facts all support the moving party's argument
- review the legal issues, and
- decide the issues of law so as to make the moving party the winner.

EXAMPLE 1: Rick sues Mindy for colliding with his car in an intersection. Mindy's lawyer files an MSJ, claiming that because Mindy was to Rick's right and because the law gives the right-of-way to the driver most to the right when two cars approach an intersection at the same time, no issues of fact remain and she should win. Rick raises an issue of fact—he claims he was halfway through the intersection and therefore had the right-of-way. The judge denies the motion because this issue of fact is in dispute.

EXAMPLE 2: Molly hired Paula, a contractor, to build a fence for Molly. Molly never paid and Paula sued. Molly filed an MSJ, saying, "I agreed to pay plaintiff $1,800 to build a new fence in my yard. She never finished the job, so I owe her nothing." In opposition, Paula asserted, "I built the fence to specifications and finished the job." The judge denied the Motion for Summary Judgment because Paula established that there was an issue of fact in dispute.

To defeat a Motion for Summary Judgment, the responding party must show not only that there *is* a dispute over a fact in the case, but that the dispute concerns a significant ("controlling") fact, not a minor detail. For instance, suppose a plaintiff claims he was sitting at the intersection of Fifth and Market Streets, waiting for the light to change, when you roared up behind him in a red Porsche and crashed into his car. The plaintiff files a Motion for Summary Judgment. If your response states, "My Porsche was not red, it was orange," you have failed to show that there is a dispute over a controlling issue of fact. If this were the only material fact you opposed, you'd lose the motion and the case. On the other hand, if you had said, "I was proceeding through the green light in a westerly direction on Market Street, when plaintiff approached from the south, violated a red light, and struck my car," you'd have created a dispute over a controlling issue of fact and the motion should be denied. Beating the other side's MSJ does not mean you've won the case. It just means that, like Frodo Baggins, you have survived another peril and can go forward to trial.

Time Restrictions for an MSJ

Once you understand the difference between issues of fact and law, you should familiarize yourself with the relatively complex statute that governs summary judgment motions (Code of Civil Procedure § 437c.) This and all statutes referred to in this book can be read online, as explained in "Finding the Law, on Paper and Online" in Chapter 1.

It's also a good idea to check the rules on your court's website to see if any local rules affect MSJs. As far as state law is concerned, here are the rules that relate to the motion's timing:

- It may not be filed with the court earlier than 60 days after the "appearance" of the party against whom the motion is directed. (The party's appearance is the first time he or she filed a pleading in connection with this case.)
- It cannot be scheduled for hearing within 30 days of the trial.
- If the papers are sent to you by mail (normally they are), they must have been mailed at least 80 days before your scheduled hearing.

Review the Papers You Receive

If an MSJ is filed against you, the opposing lawyer should send you the following paperwork:

1. Notice of Motion, telling you when and where the motion will be heard by a judge
2. Separate Statement of Undisputed Material Facts
3. Written declarations made by a party or witness to support the motion
4. Answers to interrogatories, admissions of facts, or portions of depositions that your opponent will rely on.

Items 1, 3, and 4 are not complicated and you will understand what they are by what we have covered already. Item 2 should look something like the example below.

As you can see, this Statement is a summary of the position of the moving party (the defendant here), attempting to show the judge that there is no factual issue to be decided by the court. If your opponent sent you Requests for Admissions (discussed in Chapter 10) that you have not previously denied, they will be deemed admitted

---

Separate Statement of Undisputed Material Facts in Support of Defendant Dawson's Motion for Summary Judgment

Undisputed Material Facts	Supporting Evidence
1. Plaintiff Prior and Defendant Dawson agreed that Prior would construct a front porch for Dawson in exchange for $8,500. They agreed construction would be completed by March 11, 20xx.	Agreed in Plaintiff Prior's Complaint, paragraph III. Copy of contract attached as Exhibit 1.
2. Dawson and Prior agreed to plans for the work.	Declaration of Dawson (attached as Exhibit 2), paragraph 8. Plans attached as Exhibit 3.
3. Prior stopped all work March 9, 20xx, and contends that she has completed the work satisfactorily.	Deposition of Prior (attached as Exhibit 4), page 34, lines 10–23.
4. The work does not comply with the plans.	Declaration of Angelo Russo, City Building Inspector (attached as Exhibit 5), page 1, lines 19–23.
5. It will cost Dawson $2,500 to have the work completed by a competent contractor.	Declaration of Russo (attached as Exhibit 5), page 4, lines 2–23.

and used against you here. Because you will not be filing an MSJ (if you follow my advice), but will instead be presenting your case at trial, you need not worry about preparing this Statement. But you may be unlucky enough to have to respond to an MSJ, so read on.

Prepare Your Opposition to the Summary Judgment Motion

At least 14 days before the hearing date, you must file with the court and deliver to the moving party these items (Code of Civil Procedure § 437c(b)(2) and (3)):

1. Opposition to Motion for Summary Judgment
2. Separate Statement Responding to the Moving Party's Statement of Disputed and Undisputed Facts
3. Declarations, answers to interrogatories, admissions, or other material you will rely upon in your opposition.
4. If your opponent relied on hearsay or other inadmissible evidence to support the motion, an objection to that specific piece of evidence. Look to California Rule of Court 3.1354, which explains the required format for such an objection.

A sample Opposition to Motion for Summary Judgment and the required separate statement, which are based on the case described in the Separate Statement, above, are shown below. Your Opposition should read something like these, but should of course reflect the facts of your case.

In the sample Opposition papers, the plaintiff has:

- agreed to items that are not disputed, and
- presented the declaration of Felt, which says that the work was done satisfactorily. The declaration of Felt should be enough by itself to defeat the motion, because it demonstrates there is an issue of fact in the case—whether or not the porch was done satisfactorily.

Lawyers and Their Compliance With the Law

I spend a lot of time in this chapter explaining how to comply with laws and legal procedures. In some cases I suggest you read tedious code sections that have deadlines and requirements that are very specific. When you get your first motion or declaration from a lawyer that doesn't seem to even begin to comply with the law I told you to obey, you're going to wonder if we are all operating by the same rules.

We are, and I have been telling you what the rules require. But some lawyers don't seem to read the rules or care about complying with them. They just go on slapping together a motion and filing it, hoping their opponent won't object or that the judge will somehow excuse their noncompliance.

Don't despair. The party that follows the rules is usually rewarded. Sloppy lawyers disturb judges and embarrass the majority of lawyers who do things right. If your opponent is a lawyer who dresses expensively, acts pompously, and doesn't follow the law, tell the court at the hearing that you object to the papers filed by the opposition for their failure to comply with the rules. Ask the court for sanctions. You have the right to have your opponent follow the same rules you do.

BLAZE PRIOR
444 Dry Creek Road
Palm Desert, CA 91999
619-555-2285
Plaintiff In Pro Per

SUPERIOR COURT OF CALIFORNIA—LIMITED JURISDICTION

COUNTY OF RIVERSIDE

INDIO BRANCH

BLAZE PRIOR,
        Plaintiff,
 	
vs.
 	
PHILIP DAWSON, DBA
DESERT VIEW RESTAURANT,
        Defendant.
	Case No. 844-3994-2
	
	PLAINTIFF'S OPPOSITION TO
	DEFENDANT'S MOTION FOR
	SUMMARY JUDGMENT
	
	Hearing: Sept. 5, 20xx
	Department 23

    Plaintiff, Blaze Prior, opposes Defendant's Motion for Summary Judgment set for hearing as indicated above and requests that the motion be denied on the following grounds:

    1. The motion was not filed according to the time schedule provided by Code of Civil Procedure Section 437c. [*Use if the motion was filed earlier than 60 days after you filed the Complaint (if you're plaintiff) or Answer (if you're defendant), if you were not given at least 75 days' notice of the hearing (80 if the papers were served by mail), or if the hearing date is not at least 30 days before the date of the trial.*]

    2. The moving party's motion is not supported by a Separate Statement of Undisputed Facts which sets forth the basis for such motion plainly and concisely. [*Use if the moving party has not filed a plain and concise Separate Statement of Undisputed Facts similar to the one presented above.*]

    3. As demonstrated by plaintiff's attached declaration, facts essential to justify opposition to the motion exist but cannot be presented at this time. [*Use if you feel confident you could produce facts in opposition to the motion if you had more time to investigate or do discovery, but that for good*

Opposition to Motion for Summary Judgment   Page 1

reason you have not yet been able to develop those facts. Good reasons might be that you've recently been hospitalized or need a month to raise enough money to take your opponent's deposition.]

4. The motion is based upon the declaration of a witness who was the sole witness to a material fact relied upon by the moving party. [*Use if the motion is based on the declaration of only one person who has the ability to control the outcome of the case by his or her statement. The court is not bound to deny the motion on this ground, but can in its discretion.*]

Plaintiff requests sanctions be imposed upon defendant for filing this motion in bad faith and for purpose of delay. In support of the request, plaintiff points out that defendant must have realized that in attaching only his own declaration and that of a building inspector, it would be highly unlikely for the court to grant the motion and further, that defendant was relying upon plaintiff's pro per status to result in her inability to successfully oppose such a motion.

In considering sanctions against the defendant, the court should consider Plaintiff has spent 23 hours researching and preparing this opposition, and therefore requests sanctions of $460. In addition, plaintiff has incurred $175 consulting an attorney and $55 to have these documents typed.

Executed at Palm Springs, California, August 20, 20xx. I declare under penalty of perjury the factual statements contained above are true and correct.

Blaze Prior
Blaze Prior

BLAZE PRIOR
444 Dry Creek Road
Palm Desert, CA 91999
619-555-2285
Plaintiff In Pro Per

SUPERIOR COURT OF CALIFORNIA—LIMITED JURISDICTION

COUNTY OF RIVERSIDE

INDIO BRANCH

BLAZE PRIOR,
      Plaintiff,
RESPONDING SEPARATE
vs.

PHILIP DAWSON, DBA
DESERT VIEW RESTAURANT,
      Defendant.

Case No. 844-3994-2

STATEMENT OF DISPUTED AND
UNDISPUTED FACTS IN OPPOSITION
TO MOTION FOR SUMMARY JUDGMENT

Plaintiff Prior submits this separate statement responding to defendant's statement of undisputed and disputed facts herein:

DEFENDANT'S MATERIAL FACTS:	PLAINTIFF'S RESPONSE:
1. Prior and Dawson agreed that Prior would construct a front porch for Dawson in exchange for $8,500. It was agreed construction would be completed by March 11, 20xx.	Undisputed.
2. Prior and Dawson agreed to plans for the work.	Undisputed
3. Prior stopped all work March 9, 20xx, and contends that she completed the work satisfactorily.	Undisputed.

Plaintiff's Separate Statement   Page 1

4.	The work does not comply with the plans.	Disputed. Declaration of Steve Felt, (attached as Exhibit C), page 2, lines 1-25 [*See "Prepare Your Supporting Declarations," below, for help on declarations.*]
5.	It will cost Dawson $2,500 to have the work completed by a competent contractor.	Disputed. Prior contends that the work was done satisfactorily; this is irrelevant.

ADDITIONAL DISPUTED FACTS	SUPPORTING EVIDENCE
Whether defendant agreed to substitute pine lumber for the cedar specified in the plans.	Plaintiff's declaration filed herewith

Executed at Palm Springs, California, August 20, 20xx. I declare under penalty of perjury the factual statements contained above are true and correct.

Blaze Prior
Blaze Prior

Prepare Your Supporting Declarations

In your Opposition, you can rely on written legal documents called declarations or statements made in answers to interrogatories, depositions, or the Case Questionnaire. A written declaration must state clearly that it is made from personal knowledge of you or someone else with knowledge of the dispute. The content must be admissible under the rules of evidence. (See "A Short Course in the Rules of Evidence" in Chapter 13.) In addition, it must state that the person making the declaration "is competent to testify in court to the facts stated therein," which means that the person is able to express themselves in a way that can be understood directly or through an interpreter and that they understand a witness's duty to tell the truth. A child is not required to be of any certain age to meet these tests. Below is a sample. If you wish, you can put this declaration on the printed form shown at "Applying for a Judgment" in Chapter 9.

Your papers in opposition must be filed at the court at least 14 days before the hearing and delivered to your opponent at the same time. (See Chapter 7.) The person who serves the papers must file a Proof of Service with the court. Your opponent may file a reply to your Opposition at least five days before the hearing, but you don't have to respond in writing to that reply.

The Tentative Ruling System

When you file your response to a motion brought by your opponent (probably an attorney), inquire at the clerk's office as to whether the court has a "tentative ruling system." If it does, you will be instructed to phone a particular phone number at a specified time to find out what the judge's tentative ruling is on the motion based upon the papers that have been filed.

In addition to informing you of the tentative ruling, the telephone tape explains that unless one of the parties calls the court and requests a live hearing, the tentative ruling will become the permanent ruling. If you or the other side wants to argue the matter before a judge, you must notify both the court and the other side of this fact. Otherwise, the scheduled hearing will be canceled.

If the tentative ruling is in your favor and the other side requests a hearing, your wisest course at the hearing is to say nothing unless the judge asks you to respond to the other side's arguments. I have had winners inadvertently talk me out of a tentative decision in their favor. If the phone call indicates a ruling against you, you will have to decide whether to accept the ruling or to try to change the judge's mind at the scheduled hearing.

BLAZE PRIOR
444 Dry Creek Road
Palm Desert, CA 91999
619-555-2285
Plaintiff In Pro Per

SUPERIOR COURT OF CALIFORNIA—LIMITED JURISDICTION

COUNTY OF RIVERSIDE

INDIO BRANCH

BLAZE PRIOR,
      Plaintiff,

vs.

PHILIP DAWSON, DBA
DESERT VIEW RESTAURANT,
      Defendant.

Case No. 844-3994-2

DECLARATION OF STEVE FELT IN SUPPORT OF OPPOSITION TO MOTION FOR SUMMARY JUDGMENT

Steve Felt declares as follows:

The following facts are matters of my own personal knowledge and, if sworn, I could testify competently to them in court.

I am a contractor licensed by the State of California and have done general construction work including remodeling for 17 years in the Palm Springs area.

On July 17, 20xx, I was contacted by Plaintiff, who I did not know before that date, and was asked to examine certain plans for a porch construction job and then to inspect the construction work at 895 Lawton Street, Palm Desert, California.

I am very familiar with construction plans and use them daily in my work. I carefully looked at the plans (attached to this declaration as Exhibit A) on July 18, 20xx. On July 19, 20xx, I visited 895 Lawton Street, Palm Desert, and inspected what appeared to be a newly constructed front porch of a restaurant.

Declaration of Steve Felt   Page 1

I found each item specified as a repair, replacement, or new construction on the plans to have been done in a superior workmanlike manner. In my opinion, the work specified in the plans has been completed.

Executed in Palm Springs, California, August 10, 20xx. I declare under penalty of perjury the foregoing is true and correct.

Steve Felt
Steve Felt

Defending Against the MSJ in Court

Arrive a little early and check the bulletin board in front of the court to make sure your case is listed there. It is always possible that your motion has been transferred to a different judge in another courtroom. If so, head for that courtroom.

> **TIP**
>
> **Don't be intimidated by big players.** In some courts, limited jurisdiction law and motion matters are heard in the same courtroom and at the same time as big, complex unlimited jurisdiction cases. Your motion may be heard in between a million-dollar accident case and a fight over the huge estate of a very well-to-do person. In many courts, judges have realized that this is a bit intimidating and have arranged to have limited jurisdiction cases heard separately.

Once you're in the correct courtroom, and assuming you are early and the judge is not yet present, check in with the clerk, who sits just in front of the judge's bench. If court is in session when you arrive, do not go up to the clerk until there is a recess. Once you've checked in (or are waiting to check in), take a seat. Don't leave the room without the clerk's okay.

When the clerk announces or "calls" your case's name, walk to the table and stand before the one labeled "plaintiff" or "defendant," depending on what you are. The judge will usually call on the party who has initiated the motion to talk first. You can sit down, and be sure not to interrupt your opponent while he or she is talking.

When you are called upon to reply, stand up and point out that your papers counter what the moving party has said. If the judge seems to be siding with your opponent (horrors!) and you see that additional written statements (declarations) by people familiar with the facts of the case could help, ask the judge for ten days to file additional declarations. Point out that you are in pro per because of the high cost of hiring a lawyer, that § 437c of the Code of Civil Procedure is very complicated, and that you have done the best you could under the circumstances. Often this approach will succeed, especially if you make it clear to the judge what you expect your new declarations will say and why this new information should carry the day.

Asking for Sanctions

If the motion was filed in bad faith or for the purpose of delay, the court can award you monetary sanctions (a fine). If you believe you're dealing with a bully who is just attempting to exploit your status as a pro per, be sure to ask that be considered in awarding sanctions. If you spent money getting the advice of a lawyer to help you oppose the motion, ask for those fees also. Don't request sanctions unless it's clear that there's little chance the motion would have been granted as long as you filed some opposition.

Motion for Summary Adjudication of Issues

A Motion for Summary Adjudication of Issues is the child of the Motion for Summary Judgment. Here, the moving party wants the judge to resolve certain, but not all, legal issues, because it's obvious that a Motion for Summary Judgment would not succeed, but the moving party thinks the case will be simpler if one or two issues are decided before trial.

In a case between a homeowner and a plumber over a less-than-perfect repair job, for example, the plumber (the defendant) might file a Motion for Summary Adjudication to determine whether a written invoice he left on the job site, or a later phone conversation quoting a price, determined his fee. Other issues, such as whether the job was professional, would have to be proved at trial.

A Motion for Summary Adjudication is often made when a case involves a substantial amount of money. The motion is rarely made in limited jurisdiction cases because, even if the moving party wins, he or she still must prepare and pay for a trial. If your opponent files a Motion for Summary Adjudication, you should respond in exactly the same way you respond to a Motion for Summary Judgment, as explained above.

Motion for Judgment on the Pleadings

A Motion for Judgment on the Pleadings is, like the Motion for Summary Judgment, a way to end the lawsuit short of going to trial. In the former motion, the moving side asks for victory on the grounds that there are no genuine disputes as to the facts. In a Motion for Judgment on the Pleadings, the moving side alleges that there is a fatal defect in the other side's opening papers (either the Complaint or the Answer). To decide on the Motion, the judge will:

- look at the Complaint and Answer
- assume everything alleged in both papers is true, and
- grant judgment for the moving party if the other side left something important out of its Complaint (or Answer).

A Motion for Judgment on the Pleadings is rarely filed in limited jurisdiction cases and even more rarely granted. If you used the preprinted Judicial Council forms and answered every relevant item, a Motion for Judgment on the Pleadings should fail. If you constructed a Complaint or Answer from one of the form books I recommended, the motion is still likely to fail, provided you followed the author's directions. If your opposition tries to scare you with one of these Motions, simply show up in court and point out that you followed all of the instructions when filling your forms. The judge will normally need little else to dispatch it.

Other Motions: Demurrers, Motions to Quash, and Motions to Strike

The motions covered above are the major motions filed in limited jurisdiction cases. There are a few others you may encounter, and I've covered them elsewhere in this book:

- Motions regarding discovery matters are covered in Chapter 10.
- Motions to file before your jury trial begins, to keep certain evidence out, are covered in Chapter 15.

Once in a great while, however, your opponent may file a Demurrer, Motion to Quash, or Motion to Strike. Defendants normally file these to simply slow down or harass the plaintiff. Because they are fairly rare, I'll cover them quickly.

Demurrer

In a demurrer, which can be filed only by the defendant (or the cross-defendant), the defendant asserts that the plaintiff has failed to allege all of the elements necessary to state a potentially successful legal theory of recovery (called a Cause of Action). The moving party must state what was left out of the Complaint. For example, in a case involving a motor vehicle accident, maybe the plaintiff failed to state that at the time of the accident the defendant was actually driving the car responsible for the accident.

If you've used the preprinted Complaint forms explained in Chapter 5, it's unlikely you'll be hit with a demurrer. These forms were designed to include all of the elements necessary to state a Cause of Action for which they apply. It is difficult to imagine a successful General Demurrer against one of these forms.

If you're served with a demurrer, read it over and decide if the objection has any merit. If it does and you could correct the Complaint easily before the hearing, retype your Complaint. Simply retitle it on the first page, "First Amended Complaint." Make the corrections and file it with the clerk, following the steps in Chapter 6. You're allowed to file one Amended Complaint without the court's permission. (Code of Civil Procedure § 472.)

Have a friend serve the Amended Complaint by mail on the defendant (see Chapter 7 for instructions on service). When the judge sees that you have properly amended your Complaint voluntarily, the Demurrer will be overruled (denied).

Motion to Strike

In a Motion to Strike, the moving party asks the court to eliminate some of the language you have placed in your Complaint.

In limited jurisdiction cases, parties may use a Motion to Strike only to attack the "prayer" portion of a Complaint. (Code of Civil Procedure § 92.) The prayer is where you tell the court how much money (or what other relief) you are asking for. If your opponent believes you've asked for something the court can't give, he or she could file a Motion to Strike. But Motions to Strike are rarely filed, and then usually as a delaying tactic. If you used the printed forms in this book, a Motion to Strike should not succeed. If you have drafted your own Complaint and asked for some form of esoteric relief, however (such as an injunction against the governor), the motion may fly.

Motion to Quash

A Motion to Quash attacks the method the plaintiff used to serve the Summons and Complaint. Accordingly, defendants (or cross-defendants) make this motion. This is a pretty silly motion to bring if the defendant is nearby and not hard to locate—the plaintiff can simply re-serve the defendant, doing it right.

If the defendant files a Motion to Quash against you, you have a choice. You can:
- hire a professional process server (see Chapter 7) and serve the defendant over again; or
- file a declaration with the court explaining how the service took place and ask the judge to declare it valid. If you used a professional server, he or she can probably prepare the declaration for you and, for a fee, come to court on the hearing day to answer any questions the judge may have.

Defendants occasionally use Motions to Quash to object to a court's jurisdiction over a particular defendant, such as an out-of-state corporation with no offices in California that claims not to do business here. If the defendant files such a motion, you'll need the help of a lawyer (see Chapter 17).

Demand for Bill of Particulars

A Demand for a Bill of Particulars is a motion that defendants bring in lawsuits over an unpaid account. Defendants can bring the motion when the allegedly unpaid bill is on an open account, and when the plaintiff did not attach a copy of the account to the Complaint. (Code of Civil Procedure § 454.) In this motion, the defendant asks the plaintiff to send a detailed itemization of the account.

Responding is simple. Within ten days after receiving the demand, the plaintiff should prepare, on numbered pleading paper, a "Response to Demand for Bill of Particulars" (see the sample "Response to Demand for Bill of Particulars," below). Attach a copy of the bill to the Response. You don't have to file it with the court. If your normal bill does not include a detailed list of charges showing when and for how much you furnished goods or services, prepare such a bill now.

Alice McMann
98 Morton Road
Sunnyvale, CA 95000
408-555-8989
Plaintiff In Pro Per

SUPERIOR COURT OF CALIFORNIA—LIMITED JURISDICTION

COUNTY OF SANTA CLARA

ALICE MCMANN,	)	Case No. SC-90909
Plaintiff,	)))	RESPONSE TO DEMAND FOR BILL OF PARTICULARS
vs.	))	
DREW SORENSEN,	))	
Defendant.	)	

Attached is plaintiff's Bill of Particulars.

Dated: November 3, 20xx.

Alice McMann
Alice McMann

CHAPTER 12

Moving Your Case to Arbitration and Trial

Meeting With Your Opponent	222
Completing the Case Management Statement	223
Arbitration or Mediation?	227
Mediation	227
Arbitration	227
The Difference Between Arbitration and a Trial	227
Choosing an Arbitrator	228
Scheduling Your Arbitration	228
Preparing for the Arbitration Hearing	228
Introducing Evidence Without Witnesses	229
Telling Your Opponent About Your Evidence	229
Objecting to Your Opponent's Proposed Evidence	230
Attending the Arbitration Hearing	231
The Arbitration Decision	232
Deciding Whether to Reject the Award and Go to Trial	232
Demanding a Trial	233

Whether you are a plaintiff or a defendant, you're probably tired of playing procedural games and would like to have this chapter of your life behind you. The way to do that is to get a trial date.

The judge will usually initiate the date-setting by sending you a notice four to six months after the case was filed. The name and content of the notice will be somewhat different from county to county but, at a minimum, it will inform each party that they are required to:

- meet and confer with each other about the issues in their case, and
- file a Case Management Statement with the court.

Normally, after the Statements are received, a judge will review them and do one of the following:

- require the parties to come to court for what's called a Case Management Conference
- refer the case to a court mediation or arbitration program, or
- set a date for trial.

This chapter guides you through these steps and applies equally to plaintiffs and defendants.

Meeting With Your Opponent

The notice you receive from the court may state that all of the parties or their lawyers must meet and confer in person or by telephone to discuss a number of issues, which will be set forth in the notice. You and your opponent will arrange this meeting outside of court and without any supervision by the court. The two of you must discuss the following issues:

- whether all of the parties have been served and filed an Answer
- if there is any outstanding discovery, such as depositions or interrogatories
- whether either party desires arbitration
- what issues in the case are disputed and which are agreed upon
- possible settlement, and
- how long a trial is expected to take.

If you receive such a notice, you should contact the other party by letter or telephone and arrange a time to discuss the issues. If the other side has an attorney, you probably won't have any trouble making arrangements to meet. But some pro pers (and a few attorneys) won't answer or, if they do, will be so hostile or uncooperative that there is nothing to be gained by pursuing the matter. In the event you can't arrange a satisfactory conference, send the other party (or attorney) a letter similar to the Sample Letter Regarding Uncooperative Opponent, shown below.

Sample Letter Regarding Uncooperative Opponent

Mr. Gregory Dailey
2323 Mason Street
Santa Barbara, CA

Re: Superior Court Case Number 345 987

Dear Mr. Dailey:

This letter is to confirm that I attempted to phone you three times after receiving the court's notice that we were required to meet and confer. I received no answer to the messages I left at your office. On the fourth attempt on July 27, 20xx, you came to the phone and called me a string of bad names. I asked you to calm down and follow the court's directions. You refused to do that and I eventually terminated the phone call. If you wish to comply with the court order in a calm and noninsulting manner, contact me.

Sincerely,

Michael Stanley
Michael Stanley

If, on the other hand, you do have a productive conference, promptly write a letter to the other party with a copy to the court, as illustrated in the Sample Letter Confirming a Productive Meet & Confer, Numbers 1 and 2, below. The point here is to confirm what was agreed to before memories fade and, if necessary, to request the court to take action.

Sample Letter #1
Confirming a Productive Meet & Confer

> Mr. Gregory Dailey
> 2323 Mason Street
> Santa Barbara, CA
>
> Re: Superior Court Case Number 345 987
>
> Dear Mr. Dailey:
>
> This letter is to confirm that according to the court's instructions, we conferred by telephone July 15, 20xx about our lawsuit. We agreed:
>
> - all of the parties have been served and filed Answers
> - there is no outstanding discovery that has not been answered
> - the only issues in the case are who caused the subject automobile accident and what their damages are
> - we want a trial before a judge without a jury and are not interested in arbitration
> - we believe we could complete the trial in three hours of a judge's time.
>
> If you disagree with any of the above, please let me know.
>
> Sincerely,
> *Michael Stanley*
> Michael Stanley

Sample Letter #2
Confirming a Productive Meet & Confer

> Mr. Gregory Dailey
> 2323 Mason Street
> Santa Barbara, CA
>
> Re: Superior Court Case Number 345 987
>
> Dear Mr. Dailey:
>
> This letter is to confirm that according to the court's directions, we conferred over lunch at the Side Track Café about our lawsuit. We agreed that we wish the court to refer the case to arbitration as soon as possible.
>
> Sincerely,
> *Michael Stanley*
> Michael Stanley

Completing the Case Management Statement

If you are directed by the court to prepare a Case Management Statement, it will tell the court the important facts the judge needs to consider to schedule a trial. If you and the other party are cooperating, it's best to file the form jointly. If that isn't possible, file the form by yourself. Following are instructions on how to complete the form.

FORM
The appendix contains a tear-out version of Form CM-110, *Case Management Statement*, and you can download one from the Judicial Council website at www.courtinfo.ca.gov.

Boxes at the top. These should be familiar to you by now and can be copied from any of the other forms you have completed in Chapters 5 and 8. Check the Limited Case box.

Case Management Conference. If the notice you receive from the court directs you to appear for a conference, fill in that information here.

Item 1. Indicate whether this is one party's statement or a joint statement.

Item 2. Fill in the dates requested.

Item 3. These items are for plaintiffs and cross-complainants to answer. Check ≈ a unless:

- you have sued two or more defendants *and*
- one of them has not been served with your Complaint and has not been dismissed by you.

If you don't check Box a, you'll have to explain to the court why the case should be delayed for you to finish serving your Complaint. The judge will not want to try the case twice (once now and then again when the other defendant appears), so the judge will probably attempt to persuade you (or might require you) to dismiss any absent defendant.

> **CAUTION**
> **Defendants shouldn't attempt to stall a case by filing a Cross-Complaint and deliberately failing to serve the cross-defendant.** This ploy worked at one time, but doesn't work any more. (California Rule of Court 3.110(c).)

Item 3b. Check Box b if one of the subparts applies.

Item 3c. If you are hoping to add other defendants, you should check Box c, but, again, it is going to be difficult to persuade the judge to delay a trial for this purpose.

Item 4a. Here, the court asks you to explain what the case is about in the most general terms. Just a few words (which are descriptive but not extreme) are all that's required. Depending on the circumstances, brief descriptions such as "automobile accident," "contract for construction," "warranty action regarding automobile," or "slip and fall accident" will work just fine. Now go on to page two.

Box at the top. Insert the plaintiff's name, the defendant's name, and the case number assigned by the court clerk.

Item 4b. Give a longer description of the dispute here. Cover both what happened and the amount of your claimed loss. This is not the place to describe the strength or your case or the outrageousness of your opponent's position (if you avoid adjectives and adverbs, you'll be on the right track). Something like the following will do in a simple case: "Intersection accident, fault is disputed, plaintiff claims cervical sprain, broken elbow, medical expenses of $7,890, estimated future medical of $5,000, lost earnings of $1,456, no estimated future wage loss. Plaintiff also seeks general damages for pain and suffering."

In a more complicated case, you may need to say more and use an attachment sheet.

> **EXAMPLE: Item 4b.** Defendant is my uncle. In April 2010, he asked me to lend him $10,000 to fund a new business he was starting to import llamas from Peru for use in a tourist excursion business in Northern California. I lent him the money and he prepared a contract that we both signed, stating that the money would be used for purchasing the llamas and that I would be paid $1,000 each time any of the imported llamas was taken on a paid excursion, until I had been repaid my loan plus 10% interest. On April 1 of this year he told me he would not pay me back because the government would not allow him to import the llamas and that he had spent all of my money fighting the government. I have since learned from a copy of a letter another family member gave me that defendant had been denied permission to import the llamas over a year prior to our contract. My damages are the loss of my money and interest thereon. I am also seeking punitive damages for his fraud.

Item 5. This is where you make a request for a jury, if you want one. I suggest that you not request a jury—it is difficult enough to effectively present a case to a judge alone. Selecting and then convincing 12 jurors that you are right is very difficult—not to mention nerve-wracking—for a person without experience. Check the nonjury box.

Item 6. You normally will check b and then should cross out the "12" and put in some much lower number, such as "7" if you are ready now, or "9" if you need a little more time. (This form is also used for complex unlimited cases, which explains the use of 12 months.)

Item 6c. If there are dates when you are not available in the next few months, list them here.

Item 7. Trials for most limited jurisdiction cases should take less than half a day. If you are able to specify five or fewer hours, you are likely to be given preference on the court calendar, which means that your case will be scheduled sooner than cases with longer trial times. Resist the temptation to optimistically (but unrealistically) estimate too little time—if you do not complete the trial in close to the time you announced, the judge may declare a mistrial and make you start over again months later.

Estimating the time needed for trial is hard to do, and you are not expected to be precise. If you anticipate that just you and the other side will testify, put "one hour." If you expect a total of three or four witnesses (for both sides) to testify, five hours might be appropriate. If five to eight witnesses will give brief testimony, state "one day." Anything more than that, type "one day plus."

Item 8. Check the first box and insert a slash mark (/) after the word, "party." Then write "plaintiff in pro per" or "defendant in pro per" just above the slash mark. You can also use the term "self represented." Just be sure that you recognize the Latin when you see it and know that it refers to self-represented litigants.

Items 8a–8g. Ignore Items 8a and 8b; then for Items 8c through 8f, enter the address and so on that you are using for this lawsuit (be sure to consistently use this information; don't switch from your home to your office address, for example). If you don't have a fax or email, just leave these spaces blank. Under Item 8g, write "self." Ignore the final box.

Item 9. Several kinds of cases are supposedly entitled to preference on the court's trial calendar, giving them an earlier trial date than they normally would have had they waited their turn with all the other cases. An example is Code of Civil Procedure § 36, which says such a preference must be given to unhealthy 70-year-olds and children under 14 who are seeking damages for personal injury or wrongful death of a relative. Terminally ill persons are dealt with in Section 36(d). I've seen fewer than ten preference cases in over 25 years of judging, so my advice is not to be concerned with preferences unless you fit into one of the categories mentioned above.

Item 10a. Since you are not "counsel," you should skip this item. (Alternative Dispute Resolution is described in Chapter 3.)

Items 10b-d. Check the applicable box if the parties agree or have agreed in the past to any of these forms of alternative dispute resolution. In many courts, this will be the court's first invitation to take your case to mediation or arbitration. As pointed out in Chapter 3, mediation is appropriate when both parties can sit down civilly and discuss resolving their differences with a mediator who is experienced in helping people find a compromise. Arbitration is described in more detail in the rest of this chapter. If you would prefer arbitration over a trial, I recommend you check Box d (2) or (4). If both parties agree to arbitration, the court will normally refer you to an arbitrator. If only one or neither of the parties agree, the court has the power to order nonbinding arbitration.

Item 11. A limited jurisdiction case is not likely to get an early settlement conference, but I'd recommend checking this box just in case there's a judge willing to try to help you settle. As to "when," write, "At the court's convenience."

Item 12a. If you have an insurance policy that covers any part of the matter you are suing on, disclose the name of the company here. If there is an insurance company that may put some money into a settlement of the case, this will normally have a major effect on the chances of an agreement being reached. The court may order a representative of the insurance company to attend a settlement conference.

Items 12b and c. These items are relevant only to cases that involve—or could involve—your insurance company. Suppose you're sued by someone who was hurt on your property, and you have asked your homeowners' insurance carrier to defend you. If your insurance company steps up and provides counsel, then you won't have to worry about this form—the lawyer hired by the insurance company will file it for you and handle the litigation. On the other hand, sometimes insurance carriers suspect that, when all the facts are in, they won't have to cover any settlement or award. For example, they might suspect that the plaintiff's injuries were the result of your deliberate actions, not your negligence (insurance won't cover you if you deliberately hurt someone). In this event, the company will still defend you, but will do so under "reservation of rights," which means they reserve the right to argue about whether they'll need to pay up if you lose.

Item 13. Check the first box if any party is currently involved in a bankruptcy.

Item 14. This question asks whether you and the opposing parties are involved in any other cases that relate to the subject matter of this lawsuit. It's very unlikely that this is so, which means that most of you should leave these boxes blank.

Item 15. Now and then, a party to a lawsuit will ask the judge to try the case in two parts (for example, one part to try the issue of who was at fault or "liable," the second to determine damages, if liability has been found). It's very unlikely that you would find yourself in this situation, so leave this box blank.

Item 16. If you plan a motion to try to compel the other party to answer a question in the Case Questionnaire, which you believe has not been answered fully and fairly, indicate that here. Now go on to page four, and complete the boxes at the top as you have done for previous pages.

Item 17. The court wants to know if discovery is over. You'll get to trial more quickly if you can check Box a.

Item 18. Check Box a only.

Item 19. Although it isn't required, it would be a good idea to indicate now whether you request a court reporter for your trial. Theoretically, the advantage of having a court reporter is that if you lose at trial and decide to appeal, you can have the reporter transcribe the notes. The transcript will accompany your appellate brief and will (hopefully) back you up as you endeavor to show an appellate judge how the trial judge was wrong.

In most limited jurisdiction civil cases, however, it probably isn't worth the expense of hiring a reporter, because these cases are rarely overturned on appeal. The reason for this low reversal rate is that most of the time, appeals can only consider questions of law—not fact—and judges rarely make significant legal mistakes in small cases.

There may, however, be other, more sensible reasons to hire a reporter. Some experienced trial lawyers think that the cost of a reporter is worth it because everyone (including the judge) will be more likely to stay on their best behavior when a verbatim record is being made of everything that's said.

Be aware that reporters aren't cheap. As far as I can tell, every court in the state now charges several hundred dollars for a half-day's use of a court reporter. The amount must be paid before the trial and may well be more than your budget will allow. If you ask for a transcript, that will cost more. However, if you win the case, you can recover these fees from the other side.

Item 20a. Check this box if you have already met. If there are still parties to be served or discovery is pending, explain.

Item 20b. If you have reached some agreements, explain.

Item 21. Note the total number of attachment pages, if you've used them.

File the original and a copy of this completed form with the court, along with a declaration of mailing to all other parties in the case, as described in "Completing the Proof of Service" in Chapter 7. If the notice you received from the court specified a judge who would supervise the review of your case, mail it directly to that judge.

> **Getting Your Court Costs Waived**
>
> If your case goes to trial, you may be able to get some of the costs associated with trial waived if you have a low income and can't afford them—such as the costs of a court reporter and jury fees. To qualify for this waiver, you will have to file a supplemental waiver request form, available from the clerk's office. California Rules of Court, Rules 3.50–3.58, describes how to get the waiver. After the case is over, the court may attempt to recover any fees that were waived, particularly if you won a money recovery.

Arbitration or Mediation?

Individual courts have a great deal of freedom in the procedures they use to attempt to settle a case without the formalities of a full trial before a judge. The choices are compulsory mediation or compulsory arbitration. Courts set up their own programs with local rules and volunteer mediators or arbitrators, some of whom are paid a relatively small fee and some who are volunteers.

Mediation

In the courts that require mediation, the judge will tell you and the other side to meet with a attorney-mediator at a particular place and time. The mediator, most likely a volunteer lawyer experienced in settling cases, will attempt to arrive at a settlement. If you don't show up at the mediation meeting, you'll likely be fined.

The mediator will normally open by asking each party to tell the mediator about their case. Prepare ahead for this with a ten or 15-minute response. Then, you might all discuss settling the case, followed if necessary by private meetings of each party with the mediator. The mediator may travel back and forth between separate rooms where each party is located. The process may go on for hours, and it is frequently successful.

If a settlement is reached, the mediator will instruct you on how to have it translated into a Judgment.

Arbitration

Instead of mediation, many courts require arbitration before a case is set for trial. In judicial arbitration, each party presents witnesses and other evidence in what is usually a short version of what they would do at a trial. The parties can present evidence using experts' written reports and witnesses' statements, instead of incurring the expense of bringing them to court. You can also have witnesses appear at the hearing and present their testimony in person. The basic rules are in California Rules of Court 3.811–3.829.

After the hearing and within ten days, the arbitrator issues a written award, similar to a judgment. Each party has 30 days to accept or reject the decision and proceed to trial.

The Difference Between Arbitration and a Trial

In judicial arbitration, you present a short, informal version of a trial to the arbitrator. The arbitrator makes a ruling, much like a judge. But the difference between arbitration and a trial is that unless both parties agree to be bound by the arbitrator's decision, the ruling isn't final. Each side can accept or reject the arbitrator's opinion and ask for a court trial. If a side rejects the opinion, however, that side could be substantially penalized. (This penalty system is described in "The Arbitration Decision," below.) A high percentage of small and medium-sized cases are resolved by arbitration.

Since arbitration proceedings are less formal and rule-bound than a court trial, the level of stress felt by participants is normally much lower than what they experience in a trial. Your arbitration will normally be held in the lawyer-arbitrator's office or conference room, not in a courtroom. The formal rules of evidence enforced in most courts will be relaxed; you and the other side will simply hand much of the evidence to the arbitrator. The procedures are described in more detail in the rest of this chapter, but because of its informality, arbitration is usually a very good choice for a person without a lawyer.

Choosing an Arbitrator

When your case is referred to arbitration, you will receive a list of proposed arbitrators, containing the names of three or four lawyers, many of whom donate their time. You'll have the opportunity to strike one of the names (this person will no longer be considered). Your opponent will receive the same list and may also strike one name. Both of you will return your lists to the arbitration office.

You probably won't know any of the arbitrators on the list, which may make it hard to decide whom to strike. You may hear advice from lawyers or others to strike the name of any lawyer who defends insurance companies. But in my experience, a lawyer familiar with the other side's position can be sympathetic and make a fair decision, so I wouldn't proceed on this basis alone.

Getting Information About Potential Arbitrators

Unfortunately, you cannot call or interview potential arbitrators (in fact, doing so will result in that person being ineligible to hear your case). Many courts have arbitrators' resumes on file for you to look at. The file contains biographical information such as law school attended, awards received, and jobs held. You can also look up arbitrators in a lawyer directory called *Martindale-Hubbell*, found in most law libraries, which will give you the same sort of dry, biographical information.

Scheduling Your Arbitration

After the court administrator gets both forms, he or she will send you a notice naming the person who will hear your case. The administrator will check on the availability of eligible arbitrators and probably assign whomever can be reached first. Wait to be contacted by the arbitrator—don't initiate contact except to arrange for scheduling. Within 15 days after being selected, the arbitrator will contact you to set the date (usually 35–60 days after the date of appointment) and location of the hearing (probably the arbitrator's law office).

The arbitrator must notify the court administrator of the date and place of the hearing within 15 days of being appointed. Once the date is set, either side or the arbitrator can postpone it to accommodate a calendar conflict, but if the hearing hasn't taken place within 90 days of when the arbitrator was assigned, the arbitrator must return the case to the arbitration administrator for reassignment.

The person most likely to have a calendar conflict will be your opponent's lawyer, who may claim to be so busy with other cases that he or she can't get to this one for months. Litigation often involves date changes, and lawyers normally cooperate with one another. Judges want parties to work out scheduling conflicts, so be cooperative—the next conflict could be yours. But there's a limit—don't accommodate an attorney who wants to delay the hearing excessively, such as beyond 90 days. Let the arbitrator know you want it soon—as provided by law. If your opponent's lawyer and the arbitrator keep delaying, contact the arbitration administrator.

Preparing for the Arbitration Hearing

Preparing for the arbitration hearing involves deciding what evidence you will present. Be sure to read Chapter 13, which explains how to organize your material for an arbitration hearing or trial. Although you will prepare for the hearing in essentially the same way you'd prepare for a trial, the arbitration hearing itself is much less formal and much shorter.

As you'll read in Chapter 13, an important step will be preparing a chart of your evidence. In the left column of your chart, you will list all the facts in the Complaint that you (or your opponent, if you're the defendant) will have to prove during the hearing. In the right column, you'll list how you (or your opponent) will prove each fact. In a trial, you'd almost always use live witnesses. In an arbitration, however, you'll want to present all evidence—except the most crucial—in some way other than via live witnesses. This will save a lot of time and make the arbitrator happy.

Introducing Evidence Without Witnesses

The following evidence can be presented at a judicial arbitration as a substitute for live witnesses (California Rule of Court 3.823):

- expert witnesses' written reports (expert witnesses are discussed in "Using Written Declarations" in Chapter 13)
- medical records and bills (an example would be your doctor's report on your treatment and prognosis)
- for employees, evidence from an employer showing loss of income (such as pay stubs)
- for independent contractors, a list of income each month for six months or so before and after the incident involved in your suit (if you have an accountant, ask for such a list on the accountant's stationery, signed at the end)
- property damage repair bills or estimates, accompanied by a statement indicating whether the property was repaired and, if it was, whether it was repaired in full or in part; you must also attach a copy of the bill showing the items repaired and the amount paid
- other bills and invoices
- police reports; however, the arbitrator can't consider any opinion expressed in a police report about who was at fault for an accident
- purchase orders
- checks
- written contracts
- documents prepared and maintained in the ordinary course of business, which includes ledgers, books of account, profit and loss statements, and the like
- written statements of witnesses (declarations under penalty of perjury), and
- original transcripts of depositions.

If the evidence you want to present at your arbitration is not on this list, you will probably have to bring a live witness to testify.

Telling Your Opponent About Your Evidence

After you decide what physical evidence you will present, write a letter to the opposing side listing—and attaching copies of—all the evidence you will use at the hearing. You are not required to list the live witnesses whom you intend to present. Hand deliver the letter and copies of the attached items of evidence to the opposing side at least 20 days before the arbitration (25 days if you mail it instead). If you leave out any information or forget to attach a copy, you won't be able to use the evidence at the hearing, so be very thorough. If in doubt, overlist! If you list an item and then don't use it, you won't be penalized. The Sample Letter Listing Evidence shows how one litigant phrased her letter.

Sample Letter Listing Evidence

Gregory Dailey
Dailey and Weakly
2323 Mason Street
Santa Barbara, CA

July 5, 20xx

Re: Vincent vs. Higgins, Superior Court Limited Jurisdiction Case # 497233

Dear Mr. Dailey:

As required by California Rule of Court 3.823, I'm informing you of the documentary material (copies are attached) that I intend to offer into evidence at the arbitration hearing set for August 1, 20xx.

1. The following medical and hospital reports, records and bills:
   - bill from Washington Hospital dated January 8, 20xx;
   - report from Barbara Lazarus, M.D., dated February 2, 20xx; and
   - bill from Imaging of the World, Inc., for X-rays dated January 9, 20xx.
2. Declaration of Ken Rosen, my employer, dated June 17, 20xx, showing loss of income.
3. Property damage repair estimate dated March 22, 20xx, from Goodie's Garage, for damage to my car. Repairs have been made in part. See item 4 below.
4. Invoice from Goodie's Garage dated April 3, 20xx.
5. Police report from Officer O'Dell dated December 5, 20xx.
6. Declarations under penalty of perjury of Sadie Foster and Martha Conroy dated June 17, 20xx.

I also intend to offer into evidence defendant's Case Questionnaire dated July 2, 20xx, and his answers to interrogatories, also dated July 2, 20xx.

Yours very truly,

Sandra Vincent

Sandra Vincent

Your opponent should deliver to you (or mail to you) a similar letter, which you should receive at least 20 days before the hearing. If not, the opponent can't offer any evidence except live witnesses at the arbitration.

Discovery and Judicial Arbitration

One major advantage to judicial arbitration for a pro per is that discovery (formal methods used to gather evidence—see Chapter 10) must be completed at least 15 days before the arbitration hearing. Most pro pers do little or no discovery. The attorney on the other side, however, may try to wear you out with discovery, which may have begun before your case was referred to arbitration. You can use the cutoff date to save yourself at least from more discovery harassment. If your opponent schedules a deposition or attempts other discovery within the 15-day period, write him a letter stating that under California Rule of Court 3.822, you refuse to comply.

Objecting to Your Opponent's Proposed Evidence

You may want to object to items on your opponent's list if you don't believe it is reliable or if it appears to have been manufactured for the proceedings.

Unfortunately, objecting to the introduction of evidence won't keep this evidence out of the arbitration. In fact, you may end up with the same evidence coming in but via a more convincing channel—a live witness. As I'll explain below, you'll want to think carefully before trading a document for a witness.

How to Object

If you object to an expert witness's report or other documentary evidence, your remedy is to subpoena that witness or custodian of records to the hearing so that you may cross-examine him or her. As to a written statement being offered by a nonexpert, at least ten days before the hearing you should deliver to your opponent a written demand that the witness be produced at the hearing. If you make the demand and the witness does not appear at the hearing, the judge will not let the statement come in. The detailed rules about this subject are at California Rule of Court 3.823.

Get a subpoena from the court clerk and fill it out by listing the date and location of the arbitration and the name of the person whom you want to appear at the hearing. (See Chapter 13 for more information on how to fill out and serve the subpoena.)

Deciding Whether to Object to Proposed Evidence

You'll rarely want to force the other side into bringing a live witness to an arbitration hearing in place of documentary evidence or a declaration. If you demand that your opponent bring inconsequential witnesses, everyone else connected with the hearing is likely to think something along the lines of, "Here's a crazy pro per trying to make a federal case out of a fender bender."

However, one good reason to demand a live witness in place of documentary evidence is if the documentary evidence or written declaration is greatly exaggerated and you have no witness or evidence to show otherwise. For example, if your opponent's car was damaged slightly in the accident and she has submitted a bill showing repairs to the transmission, you may need to ask the mechanic if the transmission could have been damaged previously. But before relying on your opponent's witness, try hard to get your own evidence, especially a live witness. If your opponent's witness isn't at the hearing to refute your witness, you'll have the upper hand.

Of course, if your opponent's witness is wildly lying, consider having the witness come to the hearing just so the arbitrator can see it personally. Before sending a letter asking the witness to attend, try to talk to him or her yourself. If the witness seems believable or likely to impress the arbitrator, don't send your letter. But if you think some tough questions will expose the falsehoods, send the letter and require the witness to show up. Then, before you attend the hearing, have a mock hearing with your Sounding Board and make sure your tough questions are really tough.

Attending the Arbitration Hearing

As the arbitration hearing approaches, you may begin to feel nervous, which is perfectly understandable. The key to a successful arbitration (and to quieting your nerves) is to be prepared and spend some time trying to anticipate what your opponent might say. This is a perfect opportunity for your Sounding Board to play devil's advocate with you.

On the day of the arbitration hearing, be on time and dress appropriately. If you're a painter who has sued a homeowner for failing to pay, you are not expected to wear a suit and tie but, on the other hand, don't wear your work overalls.

The arbitrator will bring you, your opponent, your opponent's lawyer, and any witnesses into a room. Everyone usually sits around a table. If your opponent doesn't show up, the arbitrator will nevertheless proceed.

The arbitrator might have a tape recorder, but isn't required to tape the proceedings. No one else can record the hearing. The arbitrator usually starts things off by having all of the people who will testify swear to tell the truth. When it comes to your turn, raise your right hand. After the oath has been recited, answer clearly, "Yes, I do."

Next, the arbitrator will probably ask the plaintiff to explain the case. If you're the plaintiff, you should have rehearsed this. Start at the beginning and proceed chronologically. Talk in the first person. When you reach a place where a document or statement of a witness is relevant, hand it to the arbitrator. Your exhibits should be indexed and at your fingertips—nothing will undermine your self-confidence as much as hunting through a stack of papers for the third time in search of an elusive ambulance bill.

For an example of how to start your case, see the declarations in "Applying for a Judgment" in Chapter 9. Use it to outline your presentation. You might add a few details, if the incident involved was complicated, but don't get too specific. Your aim here is to get the basic scenario established.

After the plaintiff introduces the case, the arbitrator may ask some questions. The arbitrator may give the defendant a chance to ask the plaintiff questions or summarize his or her own case. If you (whether you are the plaintiff or defendant) have witnesses, be sure the arbitrator understands who they are and on what subject they will testify. To guide your witnesses through their testimony, the arbitrator may ask questions or tell you to do so.

> **Be Attuned to the Arbitrator's Clues**
>
> As a judge who heard lawyers and pro pers present cases every day for over 20 years, I saw many people ignore the clues I give about what I find important. This mistake often happens because the presentation has been over-rehearsed to the point of inflexibility. If you say something that results in the arbitrator perking up and saying, "Tell me more about that," follow that lead. Don't reply with, "I'll get back to that later; now I want to cover something else." The ultimate objective in the hearing is to convince the arbitrator to rule in your favor. Inflexibility will only work against you.

Arbitration hearings are informal and short—usually under two hours and often less. The absence of a courtroom and jury minimizes grandstanding. Normally few, if any, witnesses testify, since both sides bring documents and written witness statements (declarations). The arbitrator needs only the important facts, and few limited jurisdiction cases are complex. Also, the arbitrator has every reason to keep the proceeding short, since there's often no compensation involved.

If the arbitrator—or more likely your opponent's lawyer—mouths off about doing things more lawyer-like, point to Code of Civil Procedure § 1141.10. It provides that judicial arbitration hearings are to be simple, economical, and informal; and that the parties should have the maximum opportunity to participate directly in the resolution of their dispute. Don't be too heavy-handed, but protect yourself.

The Arbitration Decision

It's unlikely that the arbitrator will give you a decision at the end of the arbitration hearing. The arbitration rules provide ten days for the arbitrator to file a decision (called an "award") with the clerk and send each party a copy. You and your opponent then have 30 days (from the date the award was filed with the clerk or given in writing at the end of the hearing) to reject the decision and request a trial. If neither of you requests a trial, the award becomes a judgment of the court and your case is over. Of course, if you are awarded damages, you still have to collect.

Deciding Whether to Reject the Award and Go to Trial

If you lose, you may be tempted to reject the award and request a trial. Except in unusual cases, this would be a mistake. If you have a trial and do the same or worse than you did in the arbitration, you must pay any fee charged by the arbitrator. You must also pay your opponent's court costs, such as filing fees, fees paid to process servers, deposition costs, and—this is the big one—money paid to expert witnesses for their fees to prepare for and present testimony at the hearing. (Code of Civil Procedure § 1141.21(a).) These costs can amount to thousands of dollars, especially if your opponent calls several experts to testify at the trial.

While doing research for this book, I reviewed every case for a three-year period in one California county, in which one party rejected the arbitrator's award and went to trial. In over 80% of the cases, the party who requested the trial did the same or worse the second time. In effect, these people lost their battle and then, after spending more energy and money to fight a second time, shot themselves in the foot.

Demanding a Trial

It's a rare case in which you'll have a good reason for rejecting the arbitrator's award and going to trial. Now and then, however, arbitrators and judges make mistakes about who is telling the truth. Or, you may now have evidence that you couldn't present at the arbitration (in a trial, you aren't limited by what you presented at the hearing). Before assuming that your case falls into one of these categories, have a serious discussion with a lawyer coach.

If you decide to pursue a trial, you must file a Request for Trial De Novo After Judicial Arbitration form with the clerk. Remember—it must be filed within 30 days after the arbitrator filed the award with the clerk. Use Form ADR-102, Request for Trial De Novo After Judicial Arbitration, which is very simple to fill out.

FORM
The appendix contains a tear-out version of Form ADR-102, *Request for Trial De Novo After Judicial Arbitration*, and you can download one from the Judicial Council at www.courrtinfo.ca.gov. The form's first page is shown below.

Ask a friend to serve (by mail) the Request for a Trial De Novo on your opponent. File the Request and the Proof of Service by Mail with the court clerk, not the arbitration administrator.

After you file your Request, the clerk must put your case back on the list of cases awaiting trial. You're entitled to the same spot (or place in line) your case had before the arbitration. (Code of Civil Procedure § 1141.20.) Not all clerks follow this procedure. To protect yourself, ask to speak to the trial setting clerk when your file your Request. If the clerk asks you to submit a new Case Management Statement, do it. You don't have to do so under the law, but it's not worth fighting about.

Unless you somehow settle the case soon, you're headed for a trial. It's time to again ask yourself if you want a lawyer to take over. I'm not saying you should, but you should consider the option.

	ADR-102
ATTORNEY OR PARTY WITHOUT ATTORNEY *(Name, state bar number, and address)*: TELEPHONE NO.: FAX NO. *(Optional)*: E-MAIL ADDRESS *(Optional)*: ATTORNEY FOR *(Name)*:	FOR COURT USE ONLY

SUPERIOR COURT OF CALIFORNIA, COUNTY OF
STREET ADDRESS:
MAILING ADDRESS:
CITY AND ZIP CODE:
BRANCH NAME:

PLAINTIFF/PETITIONER:

DEFENDANT/RESPONDENT:

REQUEST FOR TRIAL DE NOVO AFTER JUDICIAL ARBITRATION	CASE NUMBER:

NOTE:
If you do not want the arbitrator's award to become the judgment in the case, you must file a request for a trial de novo within 30 days after the arbitration award is filed with the clerk. If you do not request a trial de novo by this deadline, the arbitrator's award will be final and it will be entered as the judgment in the case. The 30-day period cannot be extended (California Rules of Court, rule 3.826).

Copies of the request for a trial de novo must be served on all parties and the request and a proof of service must be filed with the clerk.

☐ Plaintiff ☐ Defendant ☐ Other *(specify)*:

(name):

requests trial de novo in this action, under Code of Civil Procedure, section 1141.20 and rule 3.826 of the California Rules of Court.

Date:

_____ _____
(TYPE OR PRINT NAME) (SIGNATURE OF PARTY OR ATTORNEY)

Page 1 of 2

Form Approved for Optional Use
Judicial Council of California
ADR-102 [Rev. January 1, 2007]

REQUEST FOR TRIAL DE NOVO AFTER JUDICIAL ARBITRATION
(Alternative Dispute Resolution)

Code of Civil Procedure, § 1141.20;
Cal. Rules of Court, Rule 3.826
www.courtinfo.ca.gov

CHAPTER 13

Preparing for a Trial or Arbitration

A Short Course in the Rules of Evidence	236
Dealing With Your Opponent's Objections	236
The Basic Rules	237
Live Witnesses or Written Declarations	239
Using Written Declarations	239
Declarations From Experts	239
Declarations From Nonexperts	242
Serving Your Declarations	242
Having Witnesses Attend a Trial or Arbitration Hearing	246
When to Use a Subpoena	246
Preparing a Subpoena for Appearance at Trial	246
Preparing a Subpoena for a Witness and Documents	248
Making a Chart of Your Evidence	252
Making a Trial Binder	253
Drafting Questions to Ask Your Witnesses	253
Attending a Settlement Conference	254
Cases That Settle	254
Cases That Don't Settle	255

In a Small Claims Court dispute, presenting your evidence is simple: You stand up and tell the judge what happened. Unfortunately, presenting evidence in a Superior Court case is quite a bit more complicated. The process is governed by hundreds of rules developed by lawyers, judges, and legislatures over the years. Although you don't need to know all the rules, you will have to learn some of them. This chapter will help you prepare for trial by explaining the basics of assembling and presenting your evidence.

A Short Course in the Rules of Evidence

To understand what kinds of evidence will be accepted in court or arbitration, you must have a general understanding of the rules of evidence. Understanding these rules will not only help you to put on your case, it will also help you to object if your opponent presents inappropriate evidence at the trial. If you don't object to inappropriate evidence, the judge will normally allow the evidence to be presented and won't make an objection for you.

The rules of evidence are the subject of an excruciating course in law school and are a major part of the bar exam. Still, many lawyers never really grasp them, and you cannot expect to master them after reading one chapter in a book. Below I give you the basic rules, which should suffice, especially if your trial is before a judge who is reasonably sensitive to the challenges facing self-represented people.

Dealing With Your Opponent's Objections

Your introduction to the rules of evidence will no doubt come when your opponent objects to a question you pose to a witness. If your opponent objects, the witness should stop talking to let the judge rule on the objection. If the judge says that the objection is "sustained," it means the question is bad, the objection correct, and the witness

---

The Rules of the Game

As you begin preparing for trial, keep these principles in mind:

The plaintiff must prove every important fact stated in the Complaint. Unless the plaintiff does this, the defendant can just sit back and do nothing—and if the unproven fact(s) are crucial to the case, the defendant will win.

The plaintiff must prove each important fact by "a preponderance of the evidence." A preponderance means that at least 51% of all the evidence supports the plaintiff's side. If the evidence is exactly even, neither side has established a preponderance and the plaintiff loses. This is what is meant by "the burden of proof"—the responsibility lies with the plaintiff.

The rules of evidence control how the plaintiff must prove the facts. The most basic rule—the hearsay rule—requires that only people with firsthand knowledge can testify about given events. Thus, the head electrician can't testify about what the other electricians said happened on the job. Each electrician who actually saw what happened must testify.

Don't assume that the judge (or arbitrator or jury) knows any important fact. For example, if your case involves an accident on an important freeway in your area, don't assume the judge knows the locations of the off-ramps. Be ready to bring a map to court. By the same token, don't assume the judge knows that plumbers in your area charge about $50 an hour for their time. The plumber will have to testify in person or by written declaration (if allowed). Of course, certain common facts (such as Monday follows Sunday) need no proof. But don't assume too much.

shouldn't answer. If the judge says the objection is "overruled," the question was fine, the objection invalid, and the witness should answer.

Some objectionable questions can be rephrased to not violate the rules of evidence. If you don't understand why your question was no good, politely ask the judge to explain the ruling. Although judges are supposed to act like a neutral baseball umpire calling the balls and strikes—and are not supposed to coach—most judges want cases resolved on the merits, not on technicalities. Many will provide limited help to self-represented litigants as they try to introduce relevant evidence and deal with opposing lawyers' objections.

If you offer evidence that violates a rule of evidence, you can expect your opponent to object. When preparing your case for the trial, don't rely on evidence that violates these rules. Just because a judge may help you around a technical problem doesn't mean you will be allowed to present evidence that is clearly inadmissible.

The Basic Rules

Here are the basic rules of evidence you'll need to understand. I've presented them in the words that your opponent is likely to use.

"Objection! Irrelevant!"

Evidence is irrelevant if it does not prove or disprove any disputed fact necessary to determine the case. There is one exception, however: Some evidence that is irrelevant to the outcome of the case but goes to the believability of a witness is allowed in. For example, if a witness to your automobile accident told you at the scene of the accident that he saw the whole thing and you had a green light, your opponent can probably introduce evidence that the witness was convicted of a felony several years ago or has a poor reputation for truth in the local community.

"Objection! Leading the Witness!"

A leading question is one that suggests the answer you want given. ("Isn't it true, Mr. Carlton, that you've never been to Mendocino County?") With a few exceptions, you may not ask leading questions of witnesses you call. You may, however, ask leading questions of your opponent's witnesses. A question that does not suggest a particular answer is not leading. ("Did you or did you not just return from Mendocino County?") Nor is a question that focuses on a particular incident. ("Turning to Tuesday, July 3, did you see anything unusual as you drove to work that day?") Acceptable nonleading questions include:
- "Did you feel nauseated the next day?"
- "What happened next?"
- "Was the car coming toward you on the right or the left?"
- "What did you tell Mr. Carlton when he said the computer wouldn't work?"

"Objection! The Witness Is Not Responding to the Question!"

A witness must answer the question asked, not a question he or she wishes you had asked. If an answer to a question you asked of an unfriendly witness is not responsive and you object, the judge should order the answer stricken—which means that everyone is supposed to forget the witness ever said it.

How to Object

"Objection, the question calls for an opinion."
"Objection, the question calls for hearsay."
"Objection, the question is unintelligible (or vague or ambiguous)."
"Objection, the question is argumentative."
"Objection, counsel is harassing the witness."

"Objection! The Question Calls for an Opinion!"

Unless the judge recognizes a witness as an expert, the witness cannot give an opinion when testifying. To qualify as an expert, the witness must convince the judge that special education or experience gives the witness the tools to draw conclusions about the facts. For example, a nonexpert cannot give an opinion regarding the point of impact in an accident (an accident reconstruction engineer might be able to do so) or the reasonable cost of a car repair (an experienced mechanic could probably do so). If you want to offer opinion testimony, first ask the witness what training or experience he or she has had in the area. Then say to the judge, for example, "I request permission to question this witness as an expert on body and fender repair."

There is one exception to this opinion rule: A nonexpert can give an opinion in areas of common experience, such as sobriety, age, and race.

"Objection! Hearsay!"

This is the most complicated rule of evidence. Yet, at its most basic level, it is quite simple: Only a firsthand witness can give testimony. Testimony that recounts what someone else said or saw, and that is offered for the truth of the statement's subject matter, is hearsay and, as a general rule, is not admissible.

For example, your testimony that Bob told you he saw the red car run into the green car is hearsay that a judge will disallow if the other side makes a timely objection. By contrast, Bob's testimony that he saw the red car run into the green car is obviously not hearsay and, therefore, will be admitted.

A statement that's offered not to prove the truth of its contents, but for some other relevant point, is not hearsay. For example, your testimony, "Bob told me he forgot to close the gate" is hearsay if you're trying to show who closed the gate or whether or not the gate was open. But if you want to show that Bob didn't have laryngitis (assuming that is a relevant issue in the case), then your testimony of what Bob said is admissible.

Justifications for the hearsay rule have been offered for years, but none is satisfactory. The common reason given today is that because the person who made the statement can't be cross-examined, the evidence isn't trustworthy. But since even prior hearsay statements by a witness present in the courtroom are not admissible, that's not the real reason. I guess no one really knows why we have the hearsay rule, which is why we have developed so many exceptions. Here are the ones you are likely to need:

- Photographs, contracts, and street signs brought into court are not considered hearsay because those objects speak for themselves.
- Business records, such as bills, letters, business records, and police reports, brought to court by the person who keeps the business's records, are an exception to the hearsay rule. There are a few shortcuts you can use to present business records at a trial or arbitration. See "Using Written Declarations," below (for a trial), and "Preparing for the Arbitration Hearing" in Chapter 12 (for an arbitration hearing).
- Statements a party previously made, which damage that party's own case, are considered an admission and may be offered in court as an exception to the hearsay rule. For example, if Lucy exclaimed, "I'm so sorry I hit you—I was changing radio stations" right after your accident with her and she now denies she ever said it, you can offer it as evidence.

Don't worry if you're unclear about all the hearsay exceptions. Few people understand them all. I have otherwise rational lawyer friends who can debate their peculiarities at parties for hours. You can rely on most judges to know the subject and to rule correctly. When your opponent presents some evidence that sounds like hearsay, say, "Objection, hearsay." If your opponent objects similarly to something your witness (or you) says, instead of trying to argue the point, it's often best to say "Your honor, I am not trained in the law; I submit the issue to you."

RESOURCE

Detailed help on how to present evidence, question your witnesses, and, where necessary, challenge your opponent's testimony and evidence, is available in *Represent Yourself in Court: How to Prepare & Try a Winning Case*, by Paul Bergman and Sarah J. Berman (Nolo).

Live Witnesses or Written Declarations

Written statements of witnesses—called declarations—are now admissible in arbitration hearings and limited jurisdiction trials as a substitute for the live testimony of a witness. (Examples are in "Using Written Declarations," below.) Until quite recently, witnesses always had to be present to give live testimony, so this is a big change.

But just because you can substitute a written statement for a live witness doesn't mean you necessarily should. You've got to weigh the advantages of the arbitrator seeing a live witness.

A witness whose testimony will be extremely supportive of your side—for example, a person who didn't know any of the parties (and thus has no motive to lie) and saw a traffic accident from a spot on the sidewalk—should testify in person if possible. This witness is likely to be much more persuasive in person than on paper. For a witness who will testify to routine facts—such as a billing clerk from your doctor's office who would testify that payment was received for a particular bill—save time, money, and hassle by using a declaration instead of personal testimony.

Using Written Declarations

To use written testimony at an arbitration hearing, you simply prepare a declaration under penalty of perjury, signed by the witness who would otherwise testify in person, and deliver it to your opponent(s) at least 20 days before the hearing. If your opponent wants to keep a statement (other than the report of an expert) out, he or she must deliver to you (at least ten days before the hearing) a written demand that you bring the statement's author to the hearing. If you want to have the testimony considered, you must then bring that person to the hearing.

The rules are quite different for dealing with written testimony at a trial (Code of Civil Procedure § 98). In that setting you can prepare a declaration under penalty of perjury of any witness (including an expert) and serve it on your opponent at least 30 days prior to trial together with a current address for the witness that is within 150 miles of the place of trial. You must also state that the witness will be available at that address for the service of process for "a reasonable period of time during the 20 days immediately prior to trial." The same procedure can be followed with regard to a portion of a deposition taken during the discovery phase of the case provided your opponent had an opportunity to participate in the deposition. If your opponent wants the witness to testify in person—presumably to unleash a withering cross-examination—he or she must serve a subpoena on the witness. The statement will be admissible as long as it does not violate the rules of evidence explained above.

If your opponent doesn't serve a subpoena, the declaration becomes evidence as if the witness was sitting on the witness stand. That means that if any part of the declaration is hearsay or otherwise not admissible under the rules of evidence, it's still inadmissible; it doesn't become admissible just because it's in the form of a declaration.

Declarations From Experts

There are special rules for expert witness declarations. If your expert witness uses a declaration to give an opinion, you will have to "qualify" the expert by presenting his or her credentials in the declaration's first paragraph. Explain the expert's special training, experience, and standing in the field in which the expert works. The judge will not

1	JUDY PINES
	166 Euclid Street
2	Monterey, CA 93001
	408-555-8989
3	Plaintiff In Pro Per

SUPERIOR COURT OF CALIFORNIA—LIMITED JURISDICTION

COUNTY OF MONTEREY

JUDY PINES,	)	Case No. 56-2323
Plaintiff,	)	
	)	DECLARATION OF LEE
vs.	)	ANDERSON, M.D.
	)	
DANIEL MCMURTRY and	)	
CARLOS RIVERA,	)	
Defendants.	)	

Lee Anderson declares:

I am a physician licensed by the State of California with a specialty in internal and sports medicine. I have maintained an active practice in this field in Monterey County since 1977. My resume describing my education and experience is attached to this declaration and marked Exhibit A.

I first had occasion to treat Judy Pines on July 3, 20xx, when she was brought to the Monterey Peninsula Hospital Emergency Room, where I was on duty. She appeared to have severely injured her left hand and was in a great deal of pain.

I gave her medication for her pain and had her hand X-rayed. The bones in her left index finger, middle finger, and ring finger were broken. I set the breaks, applied splints, gave her more pain medication, and sent her home with instructions for care.

I saw Ms. Pines four more times over the succeeding two months for treatment of her broken fingers. Four weeks after her first visit she had a reasonable amount of movement in her fingers. By eight weeks after the injury, I believe she had fully recovered.

My charges for my medical services were $1,055, which I believe to be reasonable and customary in this community.

I declare under penalty of perjury that the foregoing is true and correct.

Executed at Pacific Grove, California, on December 12, 20xx.

Lee Anderson
Lee Anderson, M.D.

consider the expert's opinion unless convinced that the declarant is, in fact, entitled to "expert" status.

A declaration from your doctor should include a description of your injuries, a description of the doctor's treatment, the amount of the bill, the reasonableness of the bill, and your prognosis. Write a draft and make sure the witness agrees to it. If so, type it up and have the witness sign it. There's a sample declaration of a medical expert below. Be sure to use legal pleading paper.

> **TIP**
> **If your opponent serves a subpoena on your expert, who is now forced to come to the trial, who pays the expert's fee?** The answer is unclear. If the sum and substance of the live testimony turns out to be little different than the written declaration, you can argue that nothing was gained by forcing the expert to come to court—and that your opponent should foot the bill for this unnecessary trip.

You can use the sample Declaration above as a guide when preparing declarations for other experts. For example, a declaration from an auto repairperson might read something like this:

"I am the owner of the Automotive Body Repair Shop, 8935 Fifth Street, Los Angeles, California. I have been in the business of body and fender work for 11 years and have attended numerous classes conducted by manufacturers in this field. I have repaired hundreds of cars damaged in accidents and believe that I am very knowledgeable about my work.

"The plaintiff had his 1990 Chevrolet towed to my shop on September 2, 20xx. It had extensive body damage on the right side of the car. The attached bill shows the work that was done to repair the damage under my supervision. All of the work appeared to me to be necessary to repair the damage to this car. The bill shows my charges for the repair of the automobile, which have been paid. I believe the charges are reasonable under the standards of what is normally charged in Los Angeles for similar work by competent persons."

Declarations From Nonexperts

Allowing testimony by written declaration from nonexperts is particularly helpful when you need to bring business or other noncontroversial records into court. In this situation, the live witness wouldn't add much; and using a written statement will speed up the trial. The Sample Declaration of Jill Bates is below.

You might also want to use a declaration in place of live testimony when you already have a live witness, at trial or arbitration, who will testify to similar facts. In other words, the declaration will corroborate the live witness. Especially if you know that your opponent is bringing a strong contrary witness to court, you'll want to have more than one source for your side of the story. The Sample Declaration of Paul Goldberg, below, illustrates this tactic.

Serving Your Declarations

Make at least one copy of each declaration. Keep the originals and have your friend (who by now is well known at the post office) send one copy of each to your opponent at least 35 days before the trial date. Enclose a letter like the Sample Letter Accompanying Declarations, below. Make sure your friend fills out a Proof of Service.

LLOYD DAVIS
1515 Marshall Street
San Francisco, CA 94129
Plaintiff In Pro Per

SUPERIOR COURT OF CALIFORNIA—LIMITED JURISDICTION

COUNTY OF SAN FRANCISCO

LLOYD DAVIS,) Case No. 4962214
    Plaintiff,)
) DECLARATION OF JILL BATES
vs.)
)
AARON GREENE)
    Defendant.)

    I reside at 1411 Willow Street, Walnut Creek, California. I am employed as a paralegal in San Francisco. I am 29 years old and am a graduate of St. Mary's University, Moraga.

    At approximately 5:10 p.m. July 30, 20xx I was standing at the corner of Tenth and Spear Streets, San Francisco. I had a clear view of the intersection. I saw a Red Pontiac Firebird approach from the east on Spear Street traveling far faster than the 25-mph speed limit and weaving in and out of traffic abruptly. Other cars were slowing quickly and pulling to the side to avoid being hit by the speeding Pontiac.

    I intended to cross Spear Street and as the light changed to allow me to cross, I hesitated to see if the Pontiac would stop. There was a green light for traffic on Tenth Street and a red light for traffic on Spear Street. The Pontiac ignored the red light and entered the intersection, crashing into a gray Lexus that, with the green light in its favor, had pulled slowly into the intersection. The crash sent the Lexus across the intersection and onto the northeast sidewalk near me.

    The driver of the Pontiac was a male white person of about 20 years of age with black hair and wearing a purple windbreaker.

Declaration of Jill Bates   Page 1

I declare under penalty of perjury the foregoing is true and correct.

Executed at Walnut Creek, California, September 4, 20xx.

Jill Bates
Jill Bates

LAWRENCE BOOTY
12 Kings Highway
Petaluma, CA 93001
707-555-8989
Plaintiff In Pro Per

SUPERIOR COURT OF CALIFORNIA

COUNTY OF SONOMA

LAWRENCE BOOTY,   ) Case No. 809-SC-1992
)
        Plaintiff,   )
) DECLARATION OF PAUL GOLDBERG
vs.   )
)
MYER KIM,   )
)
        Defendant.   )

Paul Goldberg declares:

I am the head of the records section at Civic Center Hospital in Santa Rosa. The patient records of the hospital are under my supervision and control.

Attached to this declaration are the records of the hospital's treatment of Lawrence Booty for the period between September 3, 20xx, and September 24, 20xx. The charges listed are the normal and customary charges for the listed services in this community.

Executed at Santa Rosa, California, on January 4, 20xx. I declare under penalty of perjury that the foregoing is true and correct.

Paul Goldberg
Paul Goldberg

Sample Letter Accompanying Declarations

> Martin Canseco, Esq.
> Henderson, LaRussa, and Canseco
> 1800 Forrest Road, Suite 1311
> Gilroy, CA
>
> March 9, 20xx
>
> Re: Pines vs. McMurtry and Rivera, Case # 56-2323
>
> Dear Mr. Canseco:
>
> I am the plaintiff in the above-referred case. The attached declaration of Lee Anderson, M.D., is served on you pursuant to Code of Civil Procedure § 98. Dr. Anderson's current address is 3400 Medical Row, Pacific Grove, California. Dr. Anderson will be available there for a reasonable period of time during the 20 days immediately prior to trial.
>
> Yours very truly,
>
> *Judy Pines*
>
> Judy Pines

Having Witnesses Attend a Trial or Arbitration Hearing

By now you may have decided that you want a witness to attend the trial or hearing, not to merely write a declaration. There are two ways to get the witness to the hearing or trial. You can simply ask or subpoena the witness.

A subpoena is a one-page form issued by the court but filled out by you. It requires a witness to attend a trial or arbitration. Subpoenas are also used to require a witness to attend a deposition. This section explains when to use a subpoena in either situation, how to also demand that the witness bring along documents or other physical evidence, and how to complete a subpoena.

When to Use a Subpoena

Any witness "friendly" to your case—that is, someone who will give testimony in your favor—should initially be asked to appear in court voluntarily. If the witness is a family member or close friend who you are sure will show up when asked, you need not do anything else. If, however, the person is less than reliable, someone whom you don't really know (a person who witnessed an accident, for example), or is a witness friendly to your opponent, you will also want to serve a subpoena.

Serving a subpoena has a few advantages. A forgetful witness is likely to remember the trial date if served with a subpoena. If the witness doesn't show up and you have proof of service, the judge or arbitrator is more likely to postpone ("continue") the trial or hearing rather than proceed without the person's testimony. And a subpoena can provide the necessary excuse for an employed witness to get some time off from work to testify.

Preparing a Subpoena for Appearance at Trial

You can get a subpoena from the court clerk at the counter in the main clerk's office. If you can convince the clerk that you are a party to a pending case, you will be entrusted with a signed subpoena. You are expected to fill in the name of the person who is ordered to come to court later. Obviously, handling the subpoena irresponsibly could bring you a load of trouble.

FORM

The appendix contains a tear-out version of Form SUBP-001, *Civil Subpoena for Personal Appearance at Trial or Hearing*, and you can download one from the Judicial Council website at www.courtinfo.ca.gov. A filled-out sample is below.

ATTORNEY OR PARTY WITHOUT ATTORNEY (Name, State Bar number, and address): James Garcia 82 Southwest Drive San Mateo, CA 94404 TELEPHONE NO.: 415-555-2044 FAX NO.: 415-555-2045 ATTORNEY FOR (Name): Plaintiff in pro per	FOR COURT USE ONLY

NAME OF COURT: SUPERIOR COURT, COUNTY OF SAN MATEO STREET ADDRESS: 800 North Humboldt Street MAILING ADDRESS: CITY AND ZIP CODE: San Mateo, CA 94401 BRANCH NAME:
PLAINTIFF/ PETITIONER: James Garcia, dba Flour Power DEFENDANT/ RESPONDENT: Anne Warren, individually and dba Anne's Pie Shop

CIVIL SUBPOENA For Personal Appearance at Trial or Hearing	CASE NUMBER: 555934

SUBP-001

THE PEOPLE OF THE STATE OF CALIFORNIA, TO *(name, address, and telephone number of witness, if known)*:

Fiona Richey

1. **YOU ARE ORDERED TO APPEAR AS A WITNESS** in this action at the date, time, and place shown in the box below UNLESS you make an agreement with the person named in item 2:

   a. Date: March 6, 20xx   Time: 9 a.m.   [X] Dept.: 17   [ ] Div.:   [ ] Room:
   b. Address: 800 North Humboldt St.
      San Mateo, CA 04401

2. **IF YOU HAVE ANY QUESTIONS ABOUT THE TIME OR DATE FOR YOU TO APPEAR, OR IF YOU WANT TO BE CERTAIN THAT YOUR PRESENCE IS REQUIRED, CONTACT THE FOLLOWING PERSON BEFORE THE DATE ON WHICH YOU ARE TO APPEAR:**
   a. Name of subpoenaing party or attorney:
      James Garcia
   b. Telephone number:
      415-555-2044

3. **Witness Fees:** You are entitled to witness fees and mileage actually traveled both ways, as provided by law, if you request them at the time of service. You may request them before your scheduled appearance from the person named in item 2.

DISOBEDIENCE OF THIS SUBPOENA MAY BE PUNISHED AS CONTEMPT BY THIS COURT. YOU WILL ALSO BE LIABLE FOR THE SUM OF FIVE HUNDRED DOLLARS AND ALL DAMAGES RESULTING FROM YOUR FAILURE TO OBEY.

Date issued:

_____   ▶ _____
(TYPE OR PRINT NAME)   (SIGNATURE OF PERSON ISSUING SUBPOENA)

DEPUTY SUPERIOR COURT CLERK
(TITLE)

Requests for Accommodations

Assistive listening systems, computer-assisted real-time captioning, or sign language interpreter services are available if you ask at least 5 days before the date on which you are to appear. Contact the clerk's office or go to *www.courtinfo.ca.gov/forms* for *Request for Accommodations by Persons With Disabilities and Order* (form MC-410). (Civil Code, § 54.8.)

(Proof of service on reverse)

Form Adopted for Mandatory Use
Judicial Council of California
SUBP-001 [Rev. January 1, 2007]

CIVIL SUBPOENA FOR PERSONAL APPEARANCE AT TRIAL OR HEARING

Code of Civil Procedure, §§ 1985, 1986, 1987
www.courtinfo.ca.gov

Filling out the subpoena is easy. Type in the witness's name, the address of the courthouse or arbitration hearing (be sure to include the room number or department), and the time the witness must appear. Put down the time the trial or hearing is scheduled to begin. If the trial or hearing will last more than one day, however, let your witness know that it won't be necessary to attend until the actual day he or she testifies. (Code of Civil Procedure § 1985.1.)

Preparing a Subpoena for a Witness and Documents

You may want a trial witness to bring documents to trial, but may be nervous about whether the witness will comply, especially if they're likely to forget or not a "friendly" witness. In this situation, you need use yet another form, one that allows you to require the witness appear and bring the items you've listed on the form along to trial (you can also opt to have the witness simply mail the documents to the court). Use Form SUBP-002, *Civil Subpoena (Duces Tecum)*. As with the regular Civil Subpoena, the clerk will sign and seal this subpoena in blank if you establish that you are a party to a pending case. (Code of Civil Procedure § 1985 (c).) Attorneys representing a party in the case are allowed to sign and issue one of these themselves without going to the clerk.

FORM
The appendix contains a tear-out version of Form SUBP-002, *Civil Subpoena (Duces Tecum)*, and you can download one from the Judicial Council website at www.courtinfo.ca.gov.

The form has three pages. The first is addressed to the witness whom you want to produce the records, explaining when and where to appear at your trial or hearing. If you are dealing with a large business, you may simply identify the witness by their title, such as "custodian of check records at Central Bank." The second page describes the papers you want the witness to produce. The person who personally serves these papers on the witness will complete the third page.

First page. Fill in the top portion of the form as you have done with all of the other documents in this case. Just above Item 1, fill in the name and descriptive data you have for the witness.

Item 1. Put the time you want the witness to appear and the address of the court.

Item 3. This portion of the form allows you to choose how you want the documents brought before the court. If the items are routine business records, you'll normally choose option b, which allows the witness to mail the records to court. Choose this option if the records—not the custodian—are what's important in your case. For example, if you're dealing with bank or medical records that speak for themselves, you won't need a records clerk (usually referred to in court as "the custodian of records") to take the witness stand. Choosing this method of delivery avoids the difficulty of trying to schedule the clerk into a hearing that may begin at an unpredictable time, and it's simple courtesy not to make someone wait for a long time in the hallway only to give rather perfunctory testimony.

If the items are not business records or if there is some reason you want the person with the items to come to court personally to present testimony about the records or other matters, check Box 3a.

Item 4. Insert your name and phone number. Now go on to page two, fill in the top box as usual, and check the second box ("the following declaration") below the caption box.

Item 1. Check your status as either a plaintiff or defendant.

Item 2. Identify exactly what you want in a manner that will be understood by the person receiving your subpoena. For example, "all cancelled checks processed by the subject bank between April 21, 20xx and December 10, 20xx on account 839902-88865 in the name of John Springfield," or "all medical records maintained

ATTORNEY OR PARTY WITHOUT ATTORNEY *(Name, State Bar number, and address):* Judy Pines 166 Euclid Street Monterey, CA 94001 TELEPHONE NO.: 408-555-8989 FAX NO.: ATTORNEY FOR *(Name):* In pro per	**SUBP-002** **FOR COURT USE ONLY**

NAME OF COURT: Superior Court of California, County of Monterey
STREET ADDRESS: 1200 Aguajito Road
MAILING ADDRESS:
CITY AND ZIP CODE: Monterey, CA 93942-4896
BRANCH NAME: Monterey Division

PLAINTIFF/PETITIONER: Judy Pines

DEFENDANT/RESPONDENT: Daniel McMurtry

CIVIL SUBPOENA (DUCES TECUM) for Personal Appearance and Production of Documents and Things at Trial or Hearing AND DECLARATION	CASE NUMBER: 56-2323

THE PEOPLE OF THE STATE OF CALIFORNIA, TO *(name, address, and telephone number of witness, if known):*

Lee Anderson, M.D., 49 Ocean St., Monterey, 408-231-9292

1. **YOU ARE ORDERED TO APPEAR AS A WITNESS** in this action at the date, time, and place shown in the box below UNLESS your appearance is excused as indicated in box 3b below or you make an agreement with the person named in item 4 below.

   a. Date: 2-14-20xx   Time: 10:45 a.m.   [X] Dept.: 13   [ ] Div.:   [ ] Room:
   b. Address: 1200 Aguajito Road, Monterey

2. **IF YOU HAVE BEEN SERVED WITH THIS SUBPOENA AS A CUSTODIAN OF CONSUMER OR EMPLOYEE RECORDS UNDER CODE OF CIVIL PROCEDURE SECTION 1985.3 OR 1985.6 AND A MOTION TO QUASH OR AN OBJECTION HAS BEEN SERVED ON YOU, A COURT ORDER OR AGREEMENT OF THE PARTIES, WITNESSES, *AND* CONSUMER OR EMPLOYEE AFFECTED MUST BE OBTAINED BEFORE YOU ARE REQUIRED TO PRODUCE CONSUMER OR EMPLOYEE RECORDS.**

3. **YOU ARE** *(item a or b must be checked):*

   a. [X] Ordered to appear in person and to produce the records described in the declaration on page two or the attached declaration or affidavit. The personal attendance of the custodian or other qualified witness and the production of the original records are required by this subpoena. The procedure authorized by Evidence Code sections 1560(b), 1561, and 1562 will not be deemed sufficient compliance with this subpoena.

   b. [ ] Not required to appear in person if you produce (i) the records described in the declaration on page two or the attached declaration or affidavit and (ii) a completed declaration of custodian of records in compliance with Evidence Code sections 1560, 1561, 1562, and 1271. (1) Place a copy of the records in an envelope (or other wrapper). Enclose the original declaration of the custodian with the records. Seal the envelope. (2) Attach a copy of this subpoena to the envelope or write on the envelope the case name and number; your name; and the date, time, and place from item 1 in the box above. (3) Place this first envelope in an outer envelope, seal it, and mail it to the clerk of the court at the address in item 1. (4) Mail a copy of your declaration to the attorney or party listed at the top of this form.

4. **IF YOU HAVE ANY QUESTIONS ABOUT THE TIME OR DATE YOU ARE TO APPEAR, OR IF YOU WANT TO BE CERTAIN THAT YOUR PRESENCE IS REQUIRED, CONTACT THE FOLLOWING PERSON BEFORE THE DATE ON WHICH YOU ARE TO APPEAR:**

   a. Name of subpoenaing party or attorney: Judy Pines   b. Telephone number: 408-555-8989

5. **Witness Fees:** You are entitled to witness fees and mileage actually traveled both ways, as provided by law, if you request them at the time of service. You may request them before your scheduled appearance from the person named in item 4.

DISOBEDIENCE OF THIS SUBPOENA MAY BE PUNISHED AS CONTEMPT BY THIS COURT. YOU WILL ALSO BE LIABLE FOR THE SUM OF FIVE HUNDRED DOLLARS AND ALL DAMAGES RESULTING FROM YOUR FAILURE TO OBEY.

Date issued: _____

_____   ▶ _____
(TYPE OR PRINT NAME)   (SIGNATURE OF PERSON ISSUING SUBPOENA)

(Declaration in support of subpoena on reverse)   (TITLE)

Page 1 of 3

Form Adopted for Mandatory Use
Judicial Council of California
SUBP-002 [Rev. July 1, 2009]

CIVIL SUBPOENA (DUCES TECUM) FOR PERSONAL APPEARANCE AND PRODUCTION OF DOCUMENTS AND THINGS AT TRIAL OR HEARING AND DECLARATION

Code of Civil Procedure,
§ 1985 et seq.
www.courtinfo.ca.gov

	SUBP-002
PLAINTIFF/PETITIONER: Judy Pines DEFENDANT/RESPONDENT: Daniel McMurtry	CASE NUMBER: 56-2323

The production of the documents or the other things sought by the subpoena on page one is supported by *(check one)*:
☐ the attached affidavit or declaration ☒ the following declaration:

DECLARATION IN SUPPORT OF CIVIL SUBPOENA (DUCES TECUM) FOR PERSONAL APPEARANCE AND PRODUCTION OF DOCUMENTS AND THINGS AT TRIAL OR HEARING
(Code Civ. Proc., §§ 1985, 1987.5)

1. I, the undersigned, declare I am the ☒ plaintiff ☐ defendant ☐ petitioner ☐ respondent ☐ attorney for *(specify)*: ☐ other *(specify)*:
in the above-entitled action.

2. The witness has possession or control of the following documents or other things and shall produce them at the time and place specified in the *Civil Subpoena for Personal Appearance and Production of Documents and Things at Trial* or *Hearing* on page one of this form *(specify the exact documents or other things to be produced)*:

    All records in your possession regarding medical treatment of plaintiff in the years 20xx, 20xx, and 20xx.

    ☐ Continued on Attachment 2.

3. Good cause exists for the production of the documents or other things described in paragraph 2 for the following reasons:

    They are necessary to show the extent of the injury and recovery time for plaintiff regarding the subject automobile accident.

    ☐ Continued on Attachment 3.

4. These documents or other things described in paragraph 2 are material to the issues involved in this case for the following reasons:

    Damages can not be determined without these records.

    ☐ Continued on Attachment 4.

I declare under penalty of perjury under the laws of the State of California that the foregoing is true and correct.
Date:

Judy Pines   *Judy Pines*
(TYPE OR PRINT NAME)   (SIGNATURE OF ☒ SUBPOENAING PARTY ☐ ATTORNEY FOR SUBPOENAING PARTY)

Request for Accommodations

Assistive listening systems, computer-assisted real-time captioning, or sign language interpreter services are available if you ask at least five days before the date on which you are to appear. Contact the clerk's office or go to www.courtinfo.ca.gov/forms for *Request for Accommodations by Persons With Disabilities and Response* (form MC-410). (Civil Code, § 54.8).

(Proof of service on page 3)

SUBP-002 [Rev. July 1, 2009] **CIVIL SUBPOENA (DUCES TECUM) FOR PERSONAL APPEARANCE AND PRODUCTION OF DOCUMENTS AND THINGS AT TRIAL OR HEARING AND DECLARATION**

| PLAINTIFF/PETITIONER: Judy Pines | CASE NUMBER: |
| DEFENDANT/RESPONDENT: Daniel McMurtry | 56-2323 |

SUBP-002

**PROOF OF SERVICE OF CIVIL SUBPOENA (DUCES TECUM)
FOR PERSONAL APPEARANCE AND PRODUCTION OF DOCUMENTS
AND THINGS AT TRIAL OR HEARING AND DECLARATION**

1. I served this *Civil Subpoena (Duces Tecum) for Personal Appearance and Production of Documents and Things at Trial or Hearing and Declaration* by personally delivering a copy to the person served as follows:
   a. Person served *(name)*:
   b. Address where served:

   c. Date of delivery:
   d. Time of delivery:
   e. Witness fees *(check one)*:
      (1) ☐ were offered or demanded and paid. Amount: . . . . . . $ _____
      (2) ☐ were not demanded or paid.
   f. Fee for service: . . . . $ _____

2. I received this subpoena for service on *(date)*:

3. Person serving:
   a. ☐ Not a registered California process server.
   b. ☐ California sheriff or marshal.
   c. ☐ Registered California process server.
   d. ☐ Employee or independent contractor of a registered California process server.
   e. ☐ Exempt from registration under Business and Professions Code section 22350(b).
   f. ☐ Registered professional photocopier.
   g. ☐ Exempt from registration under Business and Professions Code section 22451.
   h. Name, address, telephone number, and, if applicable, county of registration and number:

I declare under penalty of perjury under the laws of the State of California that the foregoing is true and correct.

Date:

▶ _____
(SIGNATURE)

(For California sheriff or marshal use only)
I certify that the foregoing is true and correct.

Date:

▶ _____
(SIGNATURE)

SUBP-002 [Rev. July 1, 2009]

**PROOF OF SERVICE OF CIVIL SUBPOENA (DUCES TECUM) FOR
PERSONAL APPEARANCE AND PRODUCTION OF DOCUMENTS
AND THINGS AT TRIAL OR HEARING AND DECLARATION**

by your office relating to the treatment of John Springfield for a broken ankle between March 4, 20xx and the present."

If you need more space to answer this question and the two following, use an attachment page.

Item 3. This question asks you to explain why you need to ask the witness to produce the items you are requesting. You can say something such as, "These records are not available from any other source."

Item 4. This question asks you to explain why the documents you're asking for are relevant or important to your case. Add something such as, "I am suing defendant for failure to pay for goods delivered to him and this account is his main business account. It will show exactly what he did pay me."

Sign at the bottom of the page as the "subpoenaing party." Page three simply calls for the facts of the personal service (you can't use mail service). See Chapter 7 for instructions on how to personally serve someone.

Making a Chart of Your Evidence

It will help you if you know in advance exactly what you will have to prove at the trial or hearing and what evidence you will present to prove each point. If you're the defendant, it's equally helpful to organize what you think will be coming at you. Whether you're the plaintiff or defendant, this type of preparation will make your trial experience less nerve-wracking.

Begin by making a two-column chart like the one below, "Sample Evidence Chart." Label the top of the left column "Facts," and look again at the Complaint. List each fact the plaintiff will have to prove. If you are the plaintiff (or a cross-complainant), label the top of the right column "Evidence," and list exactly what evidence you will use to prove the corresponding fact. Review "A Short Course in the Rules of Evidence," above, to be sure your evidence is admissible. If you are the defendant (or a cross-defendant), note in the left column the facts asserted in the Complaint (or Cross-Complaint) that you will challenge and, in the right column, what evidence you'll use to do so. If you raised affirmative defenses in your Answer, list them in the left column and the evidence you'll use to prove them in the right.

The Sample Evidence Chart, below, is for a hypothetical case in which you're suing your brother-in-law, Harold, for failing to repay money you loaned him.

Sample Evidence Chart

Separate Statement of Undisputed Material Facts in Support of Defendant Dawson's Motion for Summary Judgment

Facts in Complaint	Evidence
4/12/xx—loaned $10,000 to Harold	My testimony. Also Yvonne Reilly who lives in Long Beach can confirm she was in next room
Terms of loan—$250 per month with 9% interest	Note on back of envelope initialed by Harold
Harold paid for six months	Admitted in his answer
Harold made no more payments	My testimony; copies of his bank records subpoenaed from bank.
Harold owes me $11,978 plus costs	Declaration from Roger Hamilton, C.P.A.

Making a Trial Binder

About a month before the date of your trial or arbitration hearing, make a trial binder. This consists of a loose-leaf notebook containing all documents you need to bring to the trial or hearing. Make a tab for each major document filed with the court, each item of discovery, and each item of evidence. Your binder for your case against Harold (see the Sample Evidence Chart, above) might include tabs for the following:
- Complaint
- Answer
- plaintiff's Case Questionnaire
- defendant's Case Questionnaire
- interrogatories sent by plaintiff and defendant's answers
- interrogatories sent by defendant and plaintiff's answers
- copy of April 12, 20xx contract and amendments to the contract
- letters between the parties before the lawsuit was filed
- letters between parties after the lawsuit was filed
- outline of your opening statement (see Chapter 14)
- declaration of Roger Hamilton, C.P.A.
- matters to be covered in plaintiff's testimony
- questions to ask witness Yvonne Reilly
- questions to ask defendant on cross-examination, and
- closing argument.

Drafting Questions to Ask Your Witnesses

Many careful lawyers plan their direct examinations of their witnesses very carefully, often writing out the questions they intend to ask. You too may find it helpful to write out each question. You want to establish why your witness was present and what he or she saw. If possible, it's best to elicit the information so that it is told chronologically.

Designing questions to ask your witnesses is a challenging task. Fortunately, there are books in the law library that can help you. Take a look at either *Trials* or *Proof of Facts*, multivolume sets that contain suggested questions for typical types of civil lawsuits. They are written for use anywhere in the United States. Small law libraries won't have them, but larger ones and law schools will.

Although *Trials* and *Proof of Facts* are written for lawyers, they are relatively simple to use. Turn to either publication's General Index and look up your type of case. You'll see references to hundreds of articles. Many articles include a list of suggested questions. Many questions won't be relevant to your case. You can obviously discard those. For example, if speed was not an issue in your auto accident, don't include questions asking the witness to describe how fast a car was going at various sites. Adapt these questions to your case—don't be a slave to them.

Questioning a Traffic Accident Witness

Here are some questions you might ask a witness to a traffic accident. You'll want to take your witness through enough questions to tell the full story.
- Ms. Dillingham, do you customarily drive down Interstate 53 at about 2 a.m. in the morning?
- Where are you coming from and where are you going at that hour?
- Were you driving south down Interstate 53 at about 2 a.m. February 14 of last year? (Your opponent could object to this question as being leading, but most judges allow you to ask one or two leading questions to set the scene.)
- Was there anyone else in your car? Who?
- Did you see a brown Ford automobile driving on Interstate 53 at that time?
- What did you see the brown Ford do?
- Did you later see me at the scene of the accident?
- Did you notice anything unusual about me? What?

SKIP AHEAD
If your case is on its way to an arbitration hearing (not a trial), skip the rest of this chapter and read Chapter 12 if you haven't already done so.

Attending a Settlement Conference

Some courts hold a settlement conference before a trial. If your court does, you'll receive a notice from the clerk telling you when and where to appear for such a conference. Because over 80% of cases settle before trial, courts try to speed up the settlement process by forcing you to come to meet with a judge to talk turkey. The judge may be the judge scheduled to hear the trial, a different judge, or a volunteer lawyer who helps the court.

Settlement conferences are informal proceedings, normally held in a judge's office (which, for some strange historical reason, is called the judge's "chambers"). The settlement conference notice may state that you must file a Settlement Conference Statement before the conference itself. If the notice doesn't say what needs to be in the Statement, check your local rules. The Statement gives the judge a chance to get familiar with your case. Be sure to comply with any requirement of filing a Statement. If you don't, the judge may fine you.

Judges' settlement styles vary widely, but all will expect you to outline the strengths of your case and to handle some probing (and at times unfriendly) questions from the judge about your case's weaknesses. Have in mind your bottom line—the figure you'd accept in settlement—and a higher (or lower if you're the defendant) figure you plan to open with.

The judge may ask to speak to each party separately. Most judges keep what you say in these meetings confidential. That's a sign of a good settlement judge—someone who is trustworthy and whose advice people follow. Of course, because you don't come to court regularly, you'll have to operate on a certain amount of blind faith. After all, if you can't trust a judge, whom can you trust?

But not all judges keep things confidential, so ask what will stay in the room and what will be told to your opponent. And let the judge know what you want. For example, if you reveal your absolute bottom line amount to the judge, make it clear that you don't want your opponent told the amount unless the judge is confident your opponent will pay (or accept) that amount.

TIP
Don't be afraid to make a settlement offer out of fear that the amount you are willing to compromise for will be used against you at the trial. By law, settlement offers made while there is a genuine dispute on fault or amount of damages are not admissible during a trial.

During the settlement conference, the judge should evaluate the strengths and weaknesses of your case and give you some indication of what he or she thinks of your chance of success at the trial. The judge may also suggest a settlement figure—possibly far less than what you expected (or far more, if you're a defendant). Nevertheless, consider it seriously.

Cases That Settle

Some judges dislike doing settlement conferences and provide very little help in arriving at a resolution. Some judges zealously try to settle cases, almost without regard to their true value. Such a judge might think that in your inexperience you'll accept less than your case is worth (or will pay more than you should). If the judge's suggestion seems too low—and the judge doesn't give you a satisfactory explanation why—let the judge know you're not interested in settling for that amount.

If you reach a settlement, the judge will "put it on the record" so that the plaintiff can enforce it if the defendant later has a change of heart. The judge normally does this by bringing the clerk or court reporter into chambers and stating the terms of the settlement, such as, "Defendant will pay plaintiff $10,000 in ten monthly installments of $1,000. Payments are to made on the first day of each month beginning June 1, 20xx and ending on March 1, 20xx." If you want some time to think about the settlement, tell that to the judge and ask for a second conference in a few days. Then talk things over with your Sounding Board.

Cases That Don't Settle

Despite the settlement judge's best efforts—and the genuine efforts of one of the parties, too—some cases don't settle at this stage. If yours does not, the judge may ask you questions designed to make the next phase—trial or arbitration—go smoothly. The judge may ask you to make several decisions at the conference, such as:

- Are you willing to go to arbitration instead of a trial? (Answer yes.)
- If the other side demands a jury trial, will you accept fewer than 12 jurors? (Answer yes—six or eight will be fine.)
- Will you accept a pro tem (temporary) judge in place of a regular judge? (Yes.)

CHAPTER 14

Trial Before a Judge

Sizing Up the Judge	258
Commissioners	258
Judges Pro Tem	259
Regular Judges	259
Rules of Courtroom Etiquette	261
The Trial Begins	262
Plaintiff's Case	262
Presenting Witnesses	262
Presenting Documents or Objects	265
After Presenting the Evidence	265
Responding to the Defendant's Motions	265
Defendant's Case	266
Plaintiff's Rebuttal	266
Closing Arguments	267
Judgment	268

> **SKIP AHEAD**
>
> **Most limited civil cases that don't settle are tried before a judge with no jury—only a few limited jurisdiction cases are heard by a judge and jury together.** If yours is a jury trial, skip ahead to Chapter 15, "Trial Before a Jury." Then come back to this chapter to read material that is applicable to both judge trials and jury trials.

The day has arrived for your trial. You've prepared your evidence, your witnesses are ready to testify, and you want to get this matter over with. It's time to grab your trial binder and head for the courtroom.

Courthouses usually contain several courtrooms. To find where you need to go, look at the Notice of Trial you received from the court. It will direct you to appear in a certain courtroom—called a "department." This may be a court that sends cases to other courtrooms where the trials are conducted (the first judge is called either the "master calendar" judge or the "presiding" judge), or it may be the actual courtroom where your trial will be (the judge is called the "trial" judge).

When you find the courtroom, check the court schedule—called a "calendar"—on the bulletin board outside or inside your courtroom. If it's not there, ask the uniformed deputy in the courtroom or the clerk in the room where you filed your papers for help.

When you've confirmed you're in the right courtroom, wait until the court is in recess—when the judge is not on the bench—and approach the clerk sitting in the front of the courtroom. Show the clerk your Notice of Trial. He or she will make a note that you are present. This is called "checking in." If the judge doesn't take a recess and you don't get a chance to check in, don't get concerned. The judge or clerk will still announce (or "call") your case.

Courtrooms can be very busy. You may have to wait around for a while. You can use your waiting time to hold any last-minute settlement discussions with your opponent—even on the morning of trial, it's not too late to settle a case, which parties often do by conferring in the hallway. In fact, so many cases settle on the day of trial that on a given day, courts often schedule two or three times as many trials as there are judges available. If fewer cases than expected settle, however, the court will have to reschedule some of the cases.

Eventually, the judge will "call" your case. If you've reached a settlement, let the judge know. Otherwise, the judge is likely to ask you to estimate how long your trial will last. Explain that because you are self-represented, it is difficult for you to make such an estimate. Tell the judge how many witnesses you plan to call and state that you will do all you can to expedite the case.

If you are in the courtroom with the master calendar judge, he or she may ask you to step into chambers (the judge's office) to try and settle the case, assign the case to another judge, or tell you that there's no judge available. In the latter situation, you may be instructed to wait, come back in a few hours, or come back in a few days.

Sizing Up the Judge

Once you reach the courtroom with the trial judge, spend some time sizing the judge up. Take note whether the judge is patient, treats self-helpers with respect, or has any quirks. It's possible that the judge is actually an experienced lawyer hired by the court to handle certain cases. These lawyers are called "commissioners" if this is their regular job, or "judges pro tem" if they volunteer to serve as judges only occasionally. Commissioners have most of the powers of a regular judge.

No matter what kind of judge is scheduled to hear your case, you can remove that judge from your case if you don't want that particular judge to decide it. But exercise this right sparingly.

Commissioners

Commissioners are usually competent and will handle the case like a judge. If you're assigned a commissioner, you may be asked to sign an agreement stating that the commissioner is acceptable. Agree to accept a commissioner unless you know that the particular commissioner is unfair or incompetent. Refusing the commissioner often means a substantial delay in getting to trial. And the judge you wind up with may be no better.

Judges Pro Tem

If you're assigned a judge pro tem (temporary judge), you may be asked to sign an agreement stating that the lawyer who will hear your case as judge pro tem is acceptable. Whether to accept a judge pro tem is not as clear-cut as with a commissioner. While many judges pro tem are capable, experienced, and fair, some are none of these things. I have encountered several judges pro tem who seem to think that small or medium-sized cases are of little importance. Some are big-time trial lawyers who are not familiar with the legal rules that apply to your type of case.

If you know before your trial date that a particular judge pro tem will hear your case, go watch the pro tem handle other cases. If you don't do this bit of reconnoitering, you'll have to rely on your intuition in deciding whether to accept the pro tem. If you are in a hurry to resolve your case, you may want to accept the pro tem unless it is clear he or she is unfair or incompetent. If you don't accept the pro tem, it could be a few days, a few weeks, or possibly even months before you get assigned to a judge. And in some counties, where criminal cases consume all the regular judges, you'll only be assigned another pro tem, at which point you'll get another chance to say yes or no.

Regular Judges

You have the right to one removal ("challenge") of a regular trial judge assigned to your case. (Code of Civil Procedure § 170.6.) Once you've exercised this right, you cannot remove another regular judge assigned to replace the first one.

Deciding whether to remove a particular judge from hearing your case isn't easy, unless you have reliable information that the judge is awful. Otherwise, figuring out whom to challenge, who the new judge will be, and whether the new judge will be better or worse can be quite complex. It is usually not worth it unless you've determined that a particular judge is awful, or especially awful to pro pers.

The rules for challenging a judge differ depending on when the judge is assigned to your case.

Judge Assigned Before the Trial Date

In some counties, you will receive a notice from the court before the trial naming the trial judge or the department where the trial will be. If you get such a notice, call the court and find out the next time the judge in that department will hear a case. If you can, visit the court that day and watch the judge in action.

If you decide the judge is too tough on pro pers or otherwise unacceptable, you must file a Peremptory Challenge Motion at least five days before the trial. A sample Peremptory Challenge is below.

Once you've prepared your form, file it with the office of the Court Clerk (where you filed your Complaint or Answer) and deliver a copy to the clerk in the courtroom of the trial judge you are challenging, at least five days before the trial. If you follow this procedure carefully, your challenge will be granted automatically.

Judge Assigned the Day of Trial

In many counties, especially larger ones, you won't know the judge's identity until the day of your trial. If you have the chance to observe the judge and don't like what you see, you can make your challenge when your case is called. Just stand up and state that you wish to challenge the trial judge. The clerk will administer an oath, where you swear to tell the truth. After taking the oath, state "I believe Judge Angler is prejudiced against my

JUDY PINES
166 Euclid Street
Monterey, CA 93001
408-555-8989
Plaintiff In Pro Per

SUPERIOR COURT OF CALIFORNIA—IMITED JURISDICTION

COUNTY OF MONTEREY

JUDY PINES, 　　　　Plaintiff, vs. DANIEL MCMURTRY and CARLOS RIVERA, 　　　　Defendants.	Case No. 56-2323 PEREMPTORY CHALLENGE

Judy Pines declares:

I am the plaintiff to the within action. I believe that Judge Ernest Angler, before whom the trial in this case is pending, is prejudiced against my interest so that I cannot have a fair and impartial trial before him.

I declare under penalty of perjury that the foregoing is true and correct.

Executed on June 4, 20xx, at Carmel, California.

Judy Pines
Judy Pines

Plaintiff's Peremptory Challenge　　　　Page 1

interest so that I cannot have a fair and impartial trial before him."

Then sit down and wait for another assignment. You may have to wait several hours or even days before you get assigned to another judge.

Rules of Courtroom Etiquette

Going to court can be scary for anyone who has never been there before. As I've mentioned several times in this book, you'll probably benefit greatly by reading *Represent Yourself in Court*, by Paul Bergman and Sarah J. Berman (Nolo), a handy guide to all the ins and outs of handling your own trial. Also consider getting a copy of *The First Trial*, by Goldberg (Nutshell Series, West Publishing Co.). It's designed for new lawyers who have recently completed law school. Nevertheless, it has some helpful advice.

The following suggestions should also serve as helpful guidelines:

1. Call the judge "Your Honor" or, if you wish, the more global term "the Court." While there is nothing inherently wrong with calling the judge "Judge" or "Judge Ford," it's a bit jarring and usually not done.
2. Be on time. If an emergency occurs and you're going to be late or absent, call the courtroom directly, or the Court Clerk's office if you don't have the courtroom phone number. Once you're in court, be back on time after a recess or lunch break.
3. Be courteous to everyone, particularly the clerk, the court reporter, and the deputy sheriff. Don't make insulting, sarcastic, or angry remarks about your opponent.
4. Address your opponent, opponent's lawyer, and all witnesses as "Mr." or "Ms." and their last name. Never use their first name.
5. Don't sit on the courtroom railings or try to use the court's telephones. There should be a public phone in the hall. Never use your cell phone in the courtroom.
6. Don't be overly fussy about your attire. It's best to dress as you usually do. If yours is a business dispute, wear your normal business clothing. If you're a construction worker who wasn't paid for work you did, however, there's nothing wrong with wearing clean work clothes.
7. Stay behind the table where you are seated (called the "counsel table") except when handing something to the clerk or a witness, or when you need to point to an item on the exhibit board. Don't walk between the counsel table and where the judge sits unless the construction of the courtroom makes it necessary or the judge asks you to.
8. Stand when you are speaking. A possible exception is when you are making an objection or a statement of only a few words.
9. Address all objections, statements, and arguments to the judge, prefacing your remarks with "Your Honor" or "the Court," not to your opponent's lawyer or a witness.
10. Don't interrupt the judge. No matter how wrong you think he or she is, don't argue while the judge talks. If the other side objects to one of your questions, don't ask another one until the judge rules on the objection.
11. If the judge rules that an objection is "sustained," it means the objection is allowed and your statement or question is stricken. Continue to argue the matter at your own peril. If you ask to say a few more things about the matter, most judges won't let you.
12. Tell your witnesses that at no time prior to their testimony should they discuss their testimony with any other witnesses.
13. When you are asking questions or watching your opponent ask questions, don't nod your head or grimace. Act as though everything is going just as your expected it would.

The Trial Begins

The proceedings begin when the trial judge or clerk calls out the name of your case. When this happens, go to the long table in front of the judge, remain standing, and state your name. If the table doesn't have signs identifying the plaintiff's and defendant's sides, the plaintiff should stand on the side closer to the witness box.

What happens next depends on how the judge runs a courtroom. Here are the three most likely scenarios:

- The judge, ever hopeful of saving time by arranging a settlement, will take the parties (and any attorneys) into his or her office for a few minutes to find out what the case is all about and perhaps suggest a settlement.
- The judge will ask the plaintiff to make an opening statement—some brief remarks that outline how the plaintiff plans to proceed.
- The judge will ask the plaintiff to "call your first witness." A judge who does this wants you to know that he or she is busy and wants to get down to business.

Even if the judge holds a settlement conference or tells the plaintiff to call the first witness, each party has the right to make a brief opening statement outlining their case and how they plan to prove it. If the judge doesn't offer the chance and you want to make such a statement, you can ask to do so.

If you just had a settlement conference with the judge and then ask to make an opening statement, the judge may say no, feeling that it's a waste of time. Even if there was no conference, the judge (especially in a short trial) may prefer that you get right to the evidence, which, after all, really determines who wins and loses. At this early stage of the trial, it's often best to skip the opening statement to avoid making waves. Remember—this judge will determine the outcome of your case. If you appear difficult to deal with, the judge may subconsciously be prejudiced (despite the best intentions) against you.

If the judge allows opening statements, the plaintiff goes first. Give a short explanation of who your witnesses will be and what each is expected to say. End by stating that after all the evidence is presented, you believe His or Her Honor (the judge) will conclude you're entitled to an award of whatever amount you are seeking.

The defendant, too, should give a short explanation of his or her witnesses and their testimony and end with a similar statement that after the evidence is given, His or Her Honor will conclude that the plaintiff is entitled to nothing and the defendant is entitled to the costs of the lawsuit.

To help you prepare, put an outline of your opening statement in your trial binder. See the sample Plaintiff's Opening Statement, below, for an example of a plaintiff's opening statement in a contract case.

Plaintiff's Case

After any opening statement from the defendant (unless the judge ordered that the opening statements be skipped), the plaintiff begins the case. The defendant can give an opening statement next, but can also wait until the end of the plaintiff's entire case.

Presenting Witnesses

Before you call your first witness, state, "Your Honor, I move to have all witnesses excluded from the courtroom." The judge will grant your motion and announce that all persons who expect to be witnesses in the trial must leave the courtroom. This request will protect against a later witness changing his or her testimony to conform to an earlier witness.

Look around and see who stays. If anyone in the courtroom (with the exception of the defendant) is later called as a witness by your opponent, you can point out that that person should not be allowed to testify because he or she did not obey the judge's order to leave the courtroom.

Plaintiff's Opening Statement

"My name is Jean Harvey. I am representing myself in this case against Marvin Montgomery doing business as Mad Monty's Used Cars, located at 1121 Fresno Street in this city. I will have two witnesses in this case: Frank Cartwright and myself.

"I am a single person working as a secretary at the office of the Superintendent of Schools. I have owned several cars during my life, but have no particular knowledge of how cars operate or are repaired.

"On February 26, 20xx I went to Mr. Montgomery's business to shop for a used car. Mr. Montgomery waited on me and after discussing the type of car I was interested in, asked me how much I wanted to spend. I told him that $15,000 was the top price I could afford. After we looked at several cars, he took me to see a 1998 Volvo sedan and told me he thought it would be the best buy for me. He said he had known the prior owner of the car since the car was purchased new and that the car had had very good care. I asked if it had been in any accidents and he assured me it had not. The odometer showed that the car had a little over 60,000 miles and he told me that figure was accurate.

"On February 27, I purchased the car from Mr. Montgomery and paid him $14,350 cash. I drove it home and over the next two weeks drove it to work several days. All told, I drove it less than 150 miles.

"On March 10, 20xx the car wouldn't start at my home and I called Mr. Montgomery to ask him to take a look at it. He said it was my car now and he couldn't help me. I then contacted Mr. Cartwright, who has operated Frank's Dependable Garage near my home for over 15 years, and asked him to look at the car. Mr. Cartwright had the car towed to his garage. He will testify that at my request he checked records and found the car had well over 100,000 miles on it and had been in three serious accidents with several different owners. He said his inspection of the car indicated it had a bent frame, a defective transmission, and serious engine problems. He will describe the problems in more detail for the court.

"Mr. Cartwright will also tell the court that because he buys and sells used cars frequently, he is an expert on what used cars are worth and that in his opinion, the car I purchased was only worth about $2,500. At the conclusion of my case I will ask the court for a judgment against Mr. Montgomery for $11,850. Thank you."

Now you are ready to call your first witness. Simply state, "Plaintiff calls (name of your first) as a witness." Often your best first witness will be yourself, in which case say, "Plaintiff calls herself as a witness." The witness goes to the witness stand and is sworn to tell the truth by the clerk. Then you begin asking questions, which should be in your trial binder. Start out by asking the witness's name (unless the clerk already has done so) and home address or occupation if either is relevant to the case.

If you call yourself first, you get the opportunity to outline your case early and fill in details later with other witnesses. You may hesitate to call yourself because you may be unsure how to question yourself. The judge may let you testify in a narrative without questions and answers—just explain what happened more or less chronologically. But since doing this makes it difficult for your opponent (or his lawyer) to object to your testimony, some judges may insist that you ask yourself a question and then answer it. (Sorry, you can't use a nonlawyer friend to ask the questions.) See "Questioning Yourself," below, for an example of the verbal game you may have to play.

> **Questioning Yourself**
>
> Here's an example of how a plaintiff might pose questions to herself:
> YOU: Ms. Harvey, where do you live?
> YOU: 1121 Fresno Street in this city.
> YOU: Did you go to Mad Monty's car lot sometime earlier this year?
> YOU: Yes, on February 26, I went there to look at used cars and on February 27, I went there and bought a car.

Once your witness is on the stand, go through the questions you've prepared until you've heard the witness's whole story. When you are finished, say, "No further questions." The judge will turn to your opponent and say, "Cross-examine."

> **How to Elicit Testimony**
>
> When you're standing in front of the judge asking questions, you may be tempted to skip the questions and just tell the judge what the case is all about. Don't. Evidence (other than documents) must come to the judge by way of questions and answers. (See Chapter 13 for examples of questions to ask.) If you're surprised by a witness's answer to a question, don't argue or make a speech to the judge about how the witness is lying.
>
> Also, avoid the practice of burying your nose in your trial binder and never looking up to see how the judge or a witness reacts. You may miss a great opportunity if, for example, you don't see a witness blush or falter. If you're not looking, you also won't see the judge yawning and looking bored. It's often wise to alter your plans after noticing signs like these.

Now the defendant gets to cross-examine the witness, explained more fully below. The plaintiff's job is to listen carefully and object to improper questions. An objection should be made immediately—don't let the witness answer the question. You object by saying, "Objection, the question calls for an opinion [calls for hearsay, is leading, or whatever]." Then stop. The judge may ask you or your opponent for more information. Then the judge will rule. "Sustained" means you win and the question is stricken. "Overruled" means you lose and the witness must answer.

After the defendant finishes the cross-examination, the judge will ask the plaintiff if he or she has anything on "redirect." Redirect examination is simply an opportunity for the plaintiff to ask more questions of the witness. These questions must relate specifically to something that came up in the cross-examination. You can't bring up a new issue or clarify something the witness said during your first examination, unless the defendant asked about it in the cross-examination. If nothing important came up that you feel needs rebutting, simply say, "No questions."

> **EXAMPLE:** Mark, a plaintiff's witness, testifies that he saw an accident. On cross-examination by the defendant, he says he isn't 100% sure it was the way he just described, since it was getting dark. On redirect, Carl (the plaintiff) wants to convince the judge that Mark *was* sure or almost sure of what he saw. Carl elicits from Mark the details of where he was standing (close to the accident), his unobstructed view, and his clear memory of that day. Carl doesn't ask Mark why he said he wasn't absolutely sure on cross-examination. Carl has made his point.

If the plaintiff asks questions on redirect, the defendant can ask questions in response. In this case, these might try to establish that there are details about which Mark isn't sure. This back and forth rebuttal will go on until one party passes or the judge looses patience.

If you have any written declarations—statements from absent witnesses—to submit, it's time to do so after your live witnesses have testified. You can say something like, "Your Honor, in accordance with Section 98 of the Code of

Civil Procedure, on June 3, I served on Mr. Dane [the defendant or his lawyer] declarations of Dr. Rudolph Dimes and Ms. Patricia Gonzalez. I also served the notice required by that section. I ask that the declarations be admitted in evidence." Then hand the declaration to the clerk and a copy of it to your opponent. There should be no objection to this procedure, but strange as it may seem, some lawyers and judges may not be familiar with this practice, which can be used in a limited jurisdiction trial, but not in the rest of Superior Court. If you meet with skepticism from the judge, or from a lawyer representing the other side, just smile confidently and mention Code of Civil Procedure § 98.

Presenting Documents or Objects

To introduce documents (other than declarations) and other physical objects into evidence, you need a witness to identify the object, testify to its authenticity, and connect it up to the case. Here are the steps to take:

Step 1. Show the object—or give a copy of it—to your opponent. The best time to do this is before you call your first witness. Say to your opponent, "This is a copy of a letter I want to offer in evidence. I'm showing it to you now to save time later."

Step 2. When the witness who will identify the object reaches that portion of his or her testimony, hand the item to the clerk and say, "I'd like to have this document (or object) marked for identification—I have already furnished a copy of it to my opponent." The clerk will attach a letter or number ID tag. Open your trial binder to your sheet marked exhibits and record the number or letter that has been given. Then put down a brief description of the item. Later you can refer to the item simply by its exhibit number or letter.

Step 3. Hand the item to the witness and say, "Mr. Smyth, I am handing you Plaintiff's Exhibit 4. Can you tell me what that is?" The witness then replies, "Yes, it is a bill I gave you last March for the repair of your 2000 Toyota Camry" or "Yes, it is the letter I received from the defendant around Christmas last year." Then turn to the judge and say, "Your Honor, I offer Plaintiff's Exhibit 4 into evidence."

Your opponent can object to the introduction of this evidence by claiming it is irrelevant, hearsay, or otherwise inadmissible. The judge then rules that it is either admitted or not. If it's admitted, you can refer to it during the case and the judge can consider it in making the decision. If it is not admitted, you can't refer to it and the judge can't consider it.

After Presenting the Evidence

After the plaintiff's witnesses have testified and the plaintiff has introduced declarations and physical evidence, he or she should say, "I rest my case." This means that the plaintiff has no more witnesses at this time.

Responding to the Defendant's Motions

After the plaintiff rests, if the defendant believes the plaintiff has not proven a crucial element of the case, he or she can ask the judge, by way of a motion, for immediate judgment in the defendant's favor. These motions are granted infrequently, but can be dangerous for a self-represented plaintiff.

If the defendant makes such a motion (sometimes called a Motion for Non-Suit, described in Code of Civil Procedure § 631.8), control your desire to panic. Listen carefully to what the defendant claims you left out, and if the judge seems sympathetic to the defendant's request, ask for permission to reopen your case to supply the missing evidence—if you can. If the judge grants your request, your best bet often is to put yourself back on the witness stand and introduce what's missing.

If you don't feel you need to offer more evidence (or you have no more), open your binder to the chart of your evidence. Identify each aspect of your case that you needed to prove and explain to the judge how you've proven each. If the judge agrees, the defendant's motion will be denied. If the judge grants the defendant's motion, state that under Code of Civil Procedure § 632, you are entitled to a statement of the judge's reason for granting the motion and that you are requesting such a statement.

There are two reasons to ask for this statement. If the judge gives you an oral statement from the bench (instead of in writing later), you may have an opportunity to point out politely that the judge has disregarded important testimony that should have resulted in a different ruling. The other reason involves the possibility that you will file an appeal in the case. Without a statement from the judge, an appellate court won't know what persuaded the judge to rule against you. With such a statement, the appellate court has an opportunity to disagree with the judge's reasons and might reverse the decision.

Defendant's Case

After the plaintiff rests, it's the defendant's turn. The defendant may call witnesses, present written declarations, and introduce physical objects. If you're the defendant, you should read the previous section. What applies to plaintiffs applies equally to defendants. Here are a few other points to consider:

Opening statement. The defendant can make an opening statement right after the plaintiff makes his or her opening statement or after the plaintiff rests his or her case. Unless you have surprise evidence the plaintiff doesn't expect, make your opening statement right away. This way the judge will know your theory while listening to the plaintiff.

Presenting witnesses. You may be your most important and best witness. If so, take the witness stand to lead off your case. Remember that you must prove any affirmative defense you raised in your answer. (See Chapter 8.)

Motion for judgment when the plaintiff rests. If the plaintiff hasn't proven one of the elements of his or her case, you can ask for judgment when the plaintiff rests. Say, "Your Honor, defendant moves for judgment under Code of Civil Procedure Section 631.8." Then state why. For example, if you are being sued for damaging someone's car, you might say, "Plaintiff has not produced any evidence showing that I owned or was driving the car that struck her car." The judge will tell you whether you need to elaborate.

> ### Concerns About Cross-Examination
>
> Both the plaintiff and defendant are entitled to cross-examine any witness called by the other. Don't cross-examine a witness just for the sake of cross-examination. Have some attainable goal in mind. If you cross-examine a strong defense witness without achieving something, all you have done is let the witness repeat strong testimony given on direct examination.

RESOURCE
If your opponent is relying on an obvious lie to contest your case, you may want to read up on successful methods of cross-examination. Start with *Represent Yourself in Court*, by Paul Bergman & Sara Berman (Nolo). A more specific and advanced reference is *Effective Direct and Cross-Examination*, by Brockett and Keker (California Continuing Education of the Bar (CEB)). Also, *Trials*, a multivolume set published by American Jurisprudence, can be helpful. Each of these books should be available at your local law library.

Plaintiff's Rebuttal

After the defendant has called witnesses and introduced declarations and physical objects and rests, the plaintiff can call a new witness or recall a previous witness to rebut (answer) something that came up during the defendant's case. Don't do this just to have a witness repeat what was said before. Use rebuttal to raise an issue you would have brought up earlier had you known what the defendant's witnesses would say.

Closing Arguments

Each side is entitled to make a final speech to the judge, summarizing the important evidence. This is called a closing argument. Plaintiff goes first. Then the defendant gives a closing argument. After the defendant finishes, the plaintiff can rebut anything the defendant said.

Before the trial begins, prepare an outline of a closing argument and put it in your Trial Binder. Most judges take a short recess after all the witnesses have testified to give the parties a little time to prepare their closing arguments. During the recess, you can revise your closing argument based on evidence presented during the trial. If you were able to take verbatim notes of any important testimony given during the trial, try to work some of that language into your closing argument.

If the judge wants you to jump right into your closing argument without taking a break, you can ask for a short recess (ten minutes or so) to review your notes and revise the closing statement you had planned to make. But a recess is discretionary with the judge and if the judge refuses, you will have to press ahead and do the best you can.

Although you will probably want to summarize the evidence, in a trial that has lasted only a few hours the judge will probably have a pretty good recollection of what the important testimony was. Don't waste everyone's time going over the whole case as if the judge just walked into the room. A plaintiff might say something like this:

"Your Honor, you have heard the evidence and I am confident you understand why it has been necessary for me to bring this lawsuit and go through these unfamiliar legal procedures to get to this moment. If my inexperience and unfamiliarity with court procedures has caused problems, I apologize.

"Your Honor, of all the testimony given today, I thought the most important was that of Mr. Jara, the plumber who inspected the job after the defendant, Mr. Warren, had finished. Mr. Jara testified, and I think I got his exact words here, 'I would have been ashamed to have left a repair job in that sort of condition.' Mr. Jara said that elbow joints were improperly installed and were the cause of my damage.

"Your Honor, I am asking for damages in the sum of $12,459 plus my court costs in the amount of $136. My damages are composed of [break down the components]. If you have any questions, I will be happy to attempt to answer them. Thank you for the opportunity to put on this trial today."

If you're a self-represented defendant, keep in mind that the plaintiff has two chances to summarize his or her case while you have only one. You can't rebut the plaintiff's rebuttal. Thus, be complete when it is your turn. You would argue something as follows:

"Your Honor, you have heard the evidence and I am confident you understand why it has been necessary for me to defend this lawsuit and go through these unfamiliar legal procedures to get to this moment. If my inexperience and unfamiliarity with court procedures has caused problems, I apologize.

"Your Honor, the plaintiff called my shop and asked for an emergency repair. When we stopped her leak, as Mr. Warren testified, he called her at her office and told her what we had done. He said, 'There may be other problems further on down the pipe, but it would take me another hour or two to check it out.' She said she couldn't afford that work right now. What more could we do under the circumstances? I think we acted very responsibly. I ask for judgment for the defendant."

Then the plaintiff might offer the following rebuttal:

"Your Honor, I realize Mr. Warren claims to have called me and asked if I wanted more work done. But when pressed, Mr. Warren said he was not absolutely sure he had called me. He said he knew he didn't use the kitchen telephone, and he could not recall what phone he did use. As I testified, however, I do remember the details of this debacle very carefully. I am sure he did not call me. If he had called me, I would have authorized the work, given that I had over a thousand dollars in the bank and would not have left a leaking pipe in my basement. Thank you again."

The judge may ask questions during the closing arguments, especially if he has concerns with some part of the case. Although it can be stressful, treat it as the most important part of the trial and answer as directly and thoroughly as possible.

Judgment

The judgment, of course, is the ultimate moment you are waiting for. It may seem anticlimactic after preparing for, and conducting, a trial. And what's worse, you may have to wait for it. When the closing arguments have ended, the judge may do one of three things: announce the decision immediately, take a short recess (30 minutes or so) before announcing a decision, or "take the matter under submission." The latter means that the judge needs a few days to make a decision and you'll be informed by mail.

If you win—and are either told in court or sent the decision in the mail—the courtroom clerk may prepare a written form containing the actual judgment, or you may be expected to prepare it. Once you know you have won, contact the clerk's office and ask who prepares the judgment. If you're required to prepare it, use the judgment form in "Applying for a Judgment" in Chapter 9.

Usually, the day the judge signs the judgment (or the day after), the clerk (where you filed your papers) "enters the judgment." This means that the clerk notes the judgment in a record book—called the "register of actions" or the "judgment book"— kept in the clerk's office, and sends you a "Notice of Entry of Judgment." If you won, within ten days of when the clerk enters the judgment, you must file a form (called a "cost bill") stating your legal costs—filing fee, process server fees, deposition costs, statutory witness fees (not experts), and court reporter fees. The form is available from the clerk.

CHAPTER 15

Trial Before a Jury

If Your Opponent Requests a Jury Trial 270
Jury Selection 270
Challenging Jurors 272
Preparing Jury Instructions 273
The Trial 274
    Opening Statement 274
    Presenting Evidence and Making Objections 274
    Closing Argument 275
Jury Deliberations 275

have served as judge for several jury trials where one of the parties was self-represented. I didn't enjoy it and no one else did, either.

- **Not the jurors:** "I thought juries were used only for important cases. This case is pretty small, and nobody seems to know what they are doing. What am I doing here?"
- **Not the attorney for the other side:** "If I'm not careful, I will end up making the jury sympathetic for the pro per. I'm supposed to be a lawyer, but I feel more like a baby-sitter," and
- **Not the self-represented person:** "I knew it wouldn't be like television, but this is ridiculous and way more complicated than it needs to be. The judge keeps asking me to make decisions—I just wish he'd tell me what my choices were."

What all of this adds up to is one simple rule—avoid a jury trial if it is at all possible.

If Your Opponent Requests a Jury Trial

Unfortunately, you don't always have the choice of avoiding a jury trial. Your opponent might request one in a misguided effort to discourage you from proceeding with your lawsuit.

If your opponent requests a jury trial, you have three options:

- **Reconsider your decision not to use a lawyer.** Few lawyers relish taking over a case just to do the trial, but if you're persistent and willing to pay several hundred dollars an hour for their time, you'll find someone.
- **Make another effort to settle,** especially if you rejected a decent settlement offer in the past. However, bear in mind that some insurance companies have had success in the past by intimidating self-represented parties with the prospect of a jury trial. No matter how strong your case, they may not improve their offer until you're in the courtroom where the case will be tried and you have actually started to select a jury.
- **Proceed as planned.** This chapter will guide you through the procedure. I won't make you an expert in a few pages, but I can show you some methods for helping the jury to feel empathetic to a pro per, which may yield a good result.

In general, you should freely acknowledge to the judge and jury that conducting a jury trial is difficult and unfamiliar for you. In addition, many successful pro pers find the opportunity to let the jury know they didn't request a jury trial—their opponent did.

Finally, place as much of the responsibility as possible on the judge to take the actions necessary for you to get a fair trial. Most judges will understand that you did not create the need for a jury. As long as you don't pretend to possess a level of expertise you don't have, the judge is likely to give you a hand.

A jury trial is more formal than a trial before a judge. A judge can't help you through the rough spots as easily as the judge could if there were no jury. If the jury sees a judge advising you, the jury may conclude that the judge wants you to win and be influenced accordingly.

Jury Selection

If your opponent requests a jury trial, you're going to have to help select the actual jurors. When you are in the judge's office before the start of the trial (to discuss settlement and motions in limine—see below), the judge should explain how jury selection will proceed. If the judge doesn't tell you, ask. Until several years ago, most judges used juries of 12. But now, many judges ask the parties to agree to eight. You should agree. It will shorten the process. With 12-person juries, a minimum of nine must agree on a verdict. With eight jurors, six must agree.

Jury selection begins with the judge's clerk reading the names of a number of potential jurors, who leave the audience area and sit in the jury box. The judge makes some remarks and introduces the parties and any lawyers to the potential jurors. First impressions are important. When you are introduced, rise, smile and nod to the people in the jury box and then the people in the audience.

The object of jury selection is to choose people who can decide the case without being influenced by preexisting prejudice or sympathy. Your aim is to find 12 people (or eight, if so agreed) who appear not to dislike you and who sound as though they can be fair. You do this by asking questions and excusing ("challenging") potential jurors you don't like. Unfortunately, many lawyers believe it's their role to find jurors predisposed to their client's side. These lawyers sometimes question and challenge for hours. Don't get sucked into this. Jurors hate it and frequently get an early bad impression of a lawyer who overdoes it.

Questioning potential jurors begins with the judge. Then each side asks questions. The judge may restrict the amount of time or the number of questions, but you must be given the chance to ask questions that might reveal some prejudice from a potential juror. These are the methods the judge may use:

Traditional. The 12 (or eight) potential jurors are seated in the box. The judge questions each of them, one at a time. After the judge is done asking questions of all of them, the plaintiff questions potential Juror One and then the defendant questions potential Juror One. Then the plaintiff questions potential Juror Two and the defendant questions potential Juror Two. The process is repeated until all potential jurors are questioned.

Traditional with a twist. Same as above, but after the judge questions all potential jurors, the plaintiff does the same thing followed by the defendant who takes a turn.

Packs. Same as above, except that in addition to the potential jurors in the box, the judge seats six (called a "six-pack"), 12, or any other number of potential jurors in the front rows of the audience.

Motions in Limine

Before the trial actually starts, the judge will probably hold a conference to explore last-minute settlement possibilities and to plan the trial. While you're in the meeting, your opponent may orally make some "motions in limine." This archaic term translates roughly as motions at the threshold of the trial. Normally, these motions address problems either party anticipates will arise during the trial.

For example, if your opponent's lawyer was hired by an insurance company, the lawyer won't want you to state that fact in front of the jury and will make a motion asking the judge to order you not to do so. Don't bother opposing the motion. The judge will grant it—so be careful of what you say once the trial starts.

Your opponent's lawyer will probably also make a motion to prevent you from introducing evidence he or she feels is so prejudicial that the jury should not be allowed to see it. For example, your opponent may say, "Your Honor, the photo the plaintiff wants to introduce showing his injury at the scene of the accident is so bloody that it will inflame the jury. I ask that it be excluded."

You probably won't be able to anticipate the other side's motions and you surely won't know the law that applies. Here is where you apply a basic "trust the judge" approach. Tell the judge you believe you should be allowed to use all evidence that supports your case, that the photo (or other evidence) is important to show your injuries, but that you will rely on the judge to decide what is right in the situation.

When your opponent is finished making these motions in limine, be sure you understand all of the judge's rulings clearly. You don't want to introduce evidence or say something during the trial that the judge has excluded.

As seats open up in the jury box (when a party exercises a challenge), these potential jurors fill them.

When the questioning of the potential jurors begins, be prepared to track their relevant answers. Before the trial, divide a large sheet of paper into 12 (or eight) squares, each one representing a different jury seat. If the judge uses a six- or 12-pack, add more squares. (See diagram, below.)

As each potential juror takes a seat, write his or her name in the square corresponding to the seat he or she sits in. If the potential juror is later removed, cross out the name and write in the replacement. If he or she says something you don't like, note in the box that you might want to challenge the person. Or, if the person seems particularly fair or good for you, make an appropriate note.

Your case is likely to be fairly routine and the average jury panel will give you a fair hearing. In fact, accepting the first panel of 12 (or eight) that sits down can be a good strategy for a pro per. I've seen pro pers stand up, and rather than ask questions of each potential juror, simply say, "I would have been satisfied to have a trial before a judge alone, but my opponent requested a jury trial. I have only one question for the jury: Will anyone hold it against me because I can't talk and act like a lawyer?"

Challenging Jurors

There are two ways to eliminate potential jurors, using juror challenges. The first type is a challenge "for cause," in which you ask to excuse jurors because they've demonstrated that they cannot be fair or competent. Challenges for cause are for people who have a problem such as a limited grasp of English, prior knowledge of the case or the parties, or an admitted prejudice that will make it difficult for them to be fair. Sometimes the judge will excuse these people without your saying anything. Other times, you'll have to challenge the person yourself, specifying why you think the person should be excused. There is no limit to the number of challenges for cause that you and the court can exercise.

Peremptory challenges are different. You make them without having to give an explanation. You can challenge anyone you don't feel right about, but you are limited to six peremptory challenges in a 12-person jury. In an eight-person jury, the judge will probably cut your peremptory challenges to four.

EXAMPLE 1: A potential juror whose spouse was injured as a pedestrian in a crosswalk says in answer to a question that she thinks she can

Jury Panel Chart

Juror 6	Juror 5	Juror 4	Juror 3	Juror 2	Juror 1
Juror 12	Juror 11	Juror 10	Juror 9	Juror 8	Juror 7

be fair. But if you are a driver being sued for having struck a pedestrian in a crosswalk, you should challenge her when the time comes. As impartial as she might want to be, she probably resents the driver who hit her husband and she may unconsciously take it out on you.

EXAMPLE 2: A potential juror answers a question posed by the judge by saying his uncle is a plumber. You can say, "Juror Three, Mr. Edgars—you said that your uncle is a plumber. As you know, I am suing a plumber. How close are you to this uncle?" If he says he is fairly close, ask, "Will that cause you at all to be prejudiced against me?" Listen carefully to the answer. If you have any question about his ability to be fair and impartial, challenge him at the appropriate time.

After the judge and parties are done asking questions, the judge will probably ask if you have any challenges for cause. Most of these will have been taken care of by the judge. But if the judge missed one, say, "I challenge Juror number X for cause." You can make an unlimited number of challenges for cause, but you must explain your reason. For example, if a potential juror admits to not being sure she can be fair, say, "The juror has a state of mind which is likely to lead her to be prejudiced against me."

Once challenges for cause are done with, the judge will ask if you have any peremptory challenges. If you do, simply say, "Plaintiff (or defendant) thanks and excuses Juror number X." If you don't wish to challenge anyone, say, "Plaintiff (or defendant) passes." Your opponent will also have an opportunity to challenge, and if he or she passes too, the challenging of these jurors is over. If your opponent exercises a challenge, you get another chance to challenge a juror if you wish.

If a potential juror is challenged, a person from the audience (or the six-pack) is called as a replacement. These replacements are questioned and challenged in the same manner as described above. If the trial will take more than one day, the judge may decide to pick one or two alternate jurors in case a regular juror becomes ill. The alternates are questioned and challenged similarly. You have unlimited challenges for cause and one peremptory challenge for each alternate seat to be filled.

Jury selection ends when 12 (or eight) jurors and any alternates are seated and both sides have either passed or exercised all their peremptory challenges. Once jurors and alternates are selected, the clerk administers an oath in which they swear to do their job.

Preparing Jury Instructions

When a trial is over but before the jurors retire to the jury room to reach a decision ("deliberate"), the judge reads them some instructions on the law to guide them in their work. These are called "jury instructions." They:
- explain the law that applies in the case
- direct the jurors to apply that law to the facts of the case they just heard
- explain general legal principles, and
- outline the deliberation process.

The judge's presentation of the jury instructions usually takes about 15 minutes. The jury often takes the instructions very seriously. Jurors usually believe in the judicial system and in following rules. I have seen more than a few cases in which the jurors come into court profoundly disturbed by the verdict they are about to render, but convinced they must do it "because that is the law the judge read us and we have sworn to uphold the law." Other jurors struggle to avoid applying instructions they feel are unfair.

The judge does not manufacture the instructions out of thin air. At the beginning of the trial, the judge will usually ask each party to submit a written set of instructions that party wants the judge to read. The parties get the instructions primarily from a book called *California Forms of Jury Instruction*, published by Mathew Bender and Company. The book is in all law libraries.

How can you come up with useful jury instructions? There are two ways:

- **Hire a lawyer to prepare jury instructions for you.** Hire a lawyer to learn something about your case and then choose instructions from the book mentioned above and other sources to develop a set of instructions. This will take at least two to three hours. If you intend to find a lawyer who will do this, make the arrangements several weeks before your trial date so the lawyer has the time to do the work before the trial.
- **Rely on the judge to construct even-handed jury instructions without contributions from you.** If you follow this plan, when you meet before the trial begins, tell the judge that you haven't hired a lawyer because the amount involved does not justify the expense; and that you'd hoped for a trial by the judge alone, but the other side requested a jury trial. Explain that you realize you are expected to produce instructions, but that it is beyond your abilities. End by saying that you will accept whatever instructions the judge deems appropriate—but recognize the instructions could come from your opponent.

The Trial

The basic outline of a jury trial is the same as a trial before a judge. Each side makes an opening statement, presents evidence, introduces documents, cross-examines the other side's witnesses, and makes a closing argument. If you haven't already done so, read Chapter 14. This section supplements that material.

Opening Statement

Your opening statement in a jury trial is more important than in a judge trial. It is the jury's first real opportunity to hear from you, and you should make the most of it. The jurors will be inclined to identify with you, not the lawyer representing your opponent. By being friendly and frank when telling them what the case is about and why they are being asked to resolve your dispute, you can build a rapport. Some self-represented parties use this as an opportunity to "apologize in advance" for the fact that they don't have the skills of a lawyer and that they will undoubtedly make mistakes while representing themselves. Some make mention of the fact that they were willing to have the judge decide the case, but that the defendant wanted a jury.

In your opening statement, you'll want to outline your case. You should state what you think the testimony will be and what you expect the jury to do after they have heard the evidence, but you cannot argue the case or attempt to persuade the jury. If you start arguing, your opponent is likely to object and the judge may admonish you.

If you are the plaintiff, conclude your opening statement by saying something like, "After you have heard all of the evidence, I will ask you to return a verdict for me in the amount of $17,800." If you are a defendant, conclude with, "After you have heard from all of the witnesses, I will ask that you return a verdict finding for me and awarding the plaintiff nothing."

Presenting Evidence and Making Objections

The chief difference between a jury trial and trial before a judge is that in a jury trial you need to be especially careful to object to improper questions before a witness blurts out something the jury should not hear. While you can expect a judge to ignore an improper statement made by a witness, you can't expect a jury to do so. If a witness gives an answer before you object, the fact that you eventually win your objection may be irrelevant.

If you hear a question that calls for hearsay or other inadmissible evidence, don't be shy. Loudly state, "Objection." The witness should stop talking.

If not, interrupt the witness and ask the judge to tell him or her to stop talking until the judge rules on the objection.

The judge may rule on your objection without your having to specify why you are objecting. But don't count on it. Some judges will ask you what your objection is. If your judge does, explain it as best you can, for example, "The question calls for an answer that is hearsay" or "The question is leading."

Closing Argument

In your closing argument, you have wide latitude to persuade the jury you are right, as long as your argument is based upon evidence presented during the trial. You can't refer to what someone "probably would have said had he been here" or talk about "facts" you believe to be true unless there was supporting testimony during the trial.

If you're uncertain about whether you can say something in your closing argument, during a recess before the closing arguments begin, ask the clerk to set up a meeting with both sides and the judge.

Regardless of whether they have mentioned this in their opening statement, many pro pers find it helpful to begin their closing argument by explaining to the jury that they have done their best under the circumstances, but that they feel like a fish out of water doing battle against a highly trained lawyer on the other side. If you follow such a statement with a cogent recapitulation of the evidence, it may be quite effective with the jury, especially if your opponent's lawyer has been stuffy.

Jury Deliberations

After the closing arguments, the judge will read the jury instructions. (Some judges read the instructions before the closing arguments.) Then the judge's clerk swears the deputy to keep the jury private and to bring the jurors back when they have reached a verdict. Stand as the jury leaves the courtroom. Do not attempt to communicate with the jurors or do anything—other than smile confidently—as they walk out.

You are expected to stay close by while the jury deliberates. The jurors may want to come back into the court and ask a question of the judge or have some of the evidence read by the court reporter. If you need to leave the courtroom for more than a few minutes, tell the judge's clerk where you will be.

When the jury reaches a decision (verdict), the jurors are brought back to the courtroom. The head juror (foreperson) hands a written verdict to the marshal, who hands it to the judge. The judge makes sure it is in proper form, and then hands it to the clerk who reads it aloud. The judge then asks if anyone wants the individual jurors polled. Don't bother. Jurors never change their vote. If either side says yes, the clerk asks each juror if he or she agrees with the verdict. The winner needs three-quarters (nine of 12 or six of eight).

The judge will probably thank the jurors and make a speech about how important their service has been, then announce that court is recessed and, unless he or she has directed you otherwise, you are free to talk to the jurors. They can refuse to talk to you, however, so don't badger them if they want to be left alone.

CHAPTER 16

After the Trial

Requesting a New Trial 278
Appealing the Judgment 279

The trial is over. You survived. If you followed the directions in this book, you may even have received compliments from the clerk about how "professional" you were. But what if, despite all of that, you lost—the judge or jury ruled in favor of your opponent? You may think it's over. That's not necessarily true. If you believe that the judge or jury made a serious mistake either before or during the trial, you can make a motion for a new trial or file an appeal. If you won the case, of course your opponent has the right to ask for a new trial or to appeal.

Appealing or requesting a new trial are complicated, time-consuming procedures and beyond the ability of all but the most determined pro per. They require legal research, legal writing, and the preparation of a formal brief. This chapter only describes the two procedures briefly. If you want to pursue either one, you'll need to hire a lawyer right away or, for the next several months, make a career out of fighting your case.

Requesting a New Trial

You request a new trial by filing a Motion for New Trial with the trial judge. In it, you ask the judge to throw out everything that happened at the trial and to start over. The judge may grant the motion if you show that any of the following materially affected your rights and the outcome of the case (Code of Civil Procedure § 657):

- An irregularity in the proceedings of the court, jury, or your opponent, or an order of the court, prevented you from having a fair trial.
- Misconduct by the jury, such as talking to a party during the trial, unauthorized viewing of the scene of the accident or incident, or doing any other independent research during the trial seriously affected the jury's ability to decide the case on the evidence presented.
- An accident or surprise happened at the trial (such as a fire alarm interrupting the trial, resulting in your key witness leaving without testifying), which ordinary prudence could not have guarded against.
- Newly found evidence that could not have been discovered and produced during the trial would likely have changed the outcome.
- The jury awarded excessive or inadequate damages.
- There was insufficient evidence to justify the decision—after a jury trial, this allows the judge to overrule the jury if the judge believes the verdict was clearly wrong, or
- The judge made an error when applying the law.

CAUTION
You must file a Motion for New Trial within 15 days of when the court or your opponent mails you a paper called a Notice of Entry of Judgment. Begin counting the day after the Notice was mailed. If no one sends you a Notice of Entry, you have 180 days after entry took place.

As hopeful as it may sound, a Motion for New Trial is granted infrequently. A judge who heard the case without a jury seldom grants one because, in essence, the judge would be admitting to having made a major mistake during the trial. After a jury trial, the judge usually will grant a Motion for a New Trial only if the jury was way off base in its decision.

If your opponent files a Motion for a New Trial and any supporting declarations, carefully read the papers filed in support of the Motion. Your opponent has ten days after filing the Motion to support it with a legal brief (called points and authorities) and declarations. Your response and any declarations you may want to file must be filed within ten days after you are served with supporting papers. (Code of Civil Procedure § 659a.) If your opponent's papers are so full of legalese that they are incoherent, consider hiring a lawyer for the limited job of defending your victory. If your opponent has simply written a diatribe about the unfairness of the result, you can probably file your own response.

RESOURCE

An excellent source for drafting a response to a Motion for a New Trial is *California Points and Authorities*, Volume 15, § 155.60 (Matthew Bender).

Whether you file your own response or hire a lawyer to do so, the response must be filed within the time described above. The court will set a hearing date. If the judge doesn't rule on the motion within 60 days after it was filed, it is deemed denied.

Appealing the Judgment

Frequently, when the media covers a big trial, the loser (or the loser's lawyer) promises to appeal to a higher court and is "confident that the decision will be overturned." This is conventional lawyer talk. In truth, few cases are appealed and even fewer are reversed. This is because an appellate court can reverse a decision only if the trial judge made a serious mistake in applying the law. A factual finding by a jury—or by a judge—normally cannot be reversed. Most Superior Court judges have handled hundreds of vehicle accident and contract cases and make very few errors.

If your case was held before a pro tem judge (a volunteer lawyer) and not a regular judge, however, you may have a better chance of winning an appeal. Although pro tems may be fine lawyers, they haven't attended the many training programs offered to California judges and are somewhat more likely to make a serious legal error that could result in a reversal.

To appeal a limited jurisdiction case decision, you must file a paper called a Notice of Appeal in the clerk's office within 30 days of when you are sent the Notice of Entry of Judgment. You must also pay a filing fee. If you are not sent a Notice, you must file your Notice of Appeal within 90 days after the judgment is actually entered (noted in the official court books by the court clerk).

After your Notice is filed, the case will be transferred to the Superior Court's Appellate Division for review. If you are not happy with the decision of the Appellate Division, there is no practical way for you to appeal to a higher court.

Within ten days of filing your notice of appeal, you must file several other documents with the court identifying certain papers you must file as identified in California Rules of Court 8.830 and the following.

When reviewing the case, the Appellate Court reads only the court reporter's transcript of what happened at the trial. The Appellate Court does not see or judge the credibility of the witnesses. In essence, the Appellate Court must accept the judge or jury's belief of one witness and disbelief of another.

RESOURCE

If you want to represent yourself in the appeal, as the appellant (you lost below) or the appellee (you won below), you'll have your work cut out for you, but you can get some help from reading Chapter 10 in *California Civil Appellate Practice*, 3d ed., (Continuing Education of the Bar).

CHAPTER 17

Finding a Good Lawyer

Your Choices 282
    Referrals From Friends 283
    County and State Bar Referrals 283
    Referrals From Other Good Lawyers 283

Checking Out the Lawyer 284

There are several reasons you may want to find a good lawyer to assist you in bringing or defending the lawsuit that brought you to this book:

- you may have decided that this whole process is just more than you have the time or patience to get started with and you want to have a lawyer represent you
- you have done some of the preliminary work in suing or defending yourself, but your opponent has become so difficult that you now want to turn the whole thing over to a lawyer to handle things from now on, or
- you have decided you are going to continue to represent yourself in this lawsuit, but you want to have a lawyer coach and consult with you from time to time as the case continues.

As I pointed out in the second chapter of this book, forming a coaching relationship with a lawyer can be a very wise step if you are going to represent yourself in court. The lawyer can help you choose the correct step to take at many of the points that arise during litigation, such as:

- Whom should you name as defendants?
- How much should you sue for or agree to settle for?
- In which county or branch courts are you most likely to find judges and clerks who are friendly or unfriendly to self-represented persons?
- If you reach a settlement, what should your settlement agreement say?
- How many causes of action should you include in your Complaint or Cross-Complaint?
- Should you take a deposition?
- How do you defend against a Motion for Summary Judgment?
- If you are going to trial, should you be represented by a lawyer?

To follow this coaching/counseling path, you choose an attorney and discuss your case, at an agreed hourly rate whenever you feel you need some advice. If you need to file or respond to a particular legal paper not covered in this book, the lawyer will draw it up for you to present to the court.

What I've described is not a traditional type of lawyer-client relationship, and many lawyers are very hesitant to get involved in anything that isn't traditional. But there are an increasing number of lawyers who will agree to do this kind of work for you. These lawyers will probably want you to sign an agreement that says they are not becoming your lawyer for all purposes of the case, and that their liability is limited to giving you advice on the facts you present to them. Whether you want a full-service lawyer or a lawyer coach, the problem is finding the right lawyer.

Your Choices

I've probably read most every book published in the U.S. in the last ten years discussing how to choose a lawyer. I've certainly tried to. And I've concluded that there is no surefire way to find a good attorney.

That's not to say there aren't good lawyers in California—there are many. Unfortunately, however, there are a substantial number who do an inadequate job even on a simple case. And using the selection methods recommended by, for example, a bar association could easily land you in the office of someone who will do a poor job. So before explaining how to find a lawyer, let's first eliminate the types of lawyers you are *not* looking for:

- **The Showman.** This is the expensive, flamboyant lawyer who gets his or her name in the newspaper a lot. This lawyer will probably charge you a bundle (upwards of $250 an hour) and pass your case on to an inexperienced employee fresh out of law school.
- **The Bigwig.** This is the associate or partner at a giant law firm that represents big businesses. These lawyers often charge $300–$400 an hour and few know much about simple cases or keeping costs down.

- **The Don't-Bother-Me Professional.** This is the lawyer who won't tell you how he or she plans to handle your case and wants to make all decisions alone. These lawyers are annoyed—and intimidated—by clients who know anything about the law. What they want is a passive client who doesn't ask a lot of questions and pays the bill on time each month.

What you do want is a dedicated, smart, and skilled small-office lawyer who regularly handles small and medium-sized cases. If you are looking for a coach, the lawyer should understand that you prefer to handle your case as a pro per whenever possible, and be willing to charge you a reasonable rate to consult as difficulties arise. If the case turns so complex that you change your mind about going pro per, the lawyer should be willing to take it over.

Referrals From Friends

Some people recommend that you ask friends and relatives for names of lawyers they've used and liked. The problem with this approach, however, is that your friends and relatives don't necessarily know if they got the best possible result at a reasonable price. They know if the lawyer treated them decently and returned their phone calls, which is important—but only a part of the picture! Maybe the case was such a winner that even the most incompetent lawyer couldn't have lost it. Maybe the result obtained was only a fraction of what the case was worth. And maybe not even Clarence Darrow himself could have won their case.

County and State Bar Referrals

Other people recommend using a lawyer referral program run by a county bar association or commercial network. I don't. These programs usually take the names of any lawyer who has passed the bar examination and agrees to follow certain (minimal) rules. However, the State Bar does have some helpful advice and a list of some referral sources at www.courtinfo.ca.gov. Click the Self Help icon in the upper left corner and then click the Free and Low-Cost Legal Help heading.

Similarly, I'd suggest steering clear of the lawyers that advertise on television. They claim to be "reasonably priced," but my experience is that they charge about the same as other lawyers. There also tends to be a lot of turnover in their lawyer staff.

Referrals From Other Good Lawyers

Another approach is to contact any good lawyer whom you or anyone you know has access to, even if that lawyer specializes in a field of law different from the area where you need help. For example, you might ask a divorce lawyer for the name of a personal injury lawyer. This isn't a bad approach—lawyers often know competent attorneys in other fields—but it can also be dangerous. Instead of referring you to the best lawyer for your case, the lawyer may give you the name of a law school friend or brother-in-law who just opened his own law office. In short, if you follow this route, you'll want to check to be sure the recommended lawyer really is competent.

RESOURCE

Nolo's Lawyer Directory. Although many online directories don't differ much from county bar or commercial referral services, Nolo offers a directory that provides a detailed profile for each attorney with information to help you select the right lawyer for you. The profiles describe the lawyer's experience, education, and fees, and also tell you something about the lawyer's general approach to practicing law. (For example, each lawyer states whether he or she is willing to review documents or coach clients who are doing their own legal work.) Nolo has confirmed that every listed attorney has a valid license and is in good standing with their bar association. Check out www.nolo.com to get interesting information about lawyers who advertise there—information that you probably won't find elsewhere.

Checking Out the Lawyer

Once you get the names of some lawyers, your most important job is to talk to them in person. Call and ask for a brief interview. You may have to pay a small fee for the lawyer's time, but many don't charge for an initial consultation. Be ready to explain your case and exactly what services you want from the lawyer. Note how the lawyer responds to your pro per efforts.

Remember, having read this book, you know far more about the legal process than the average person. Does the lawyer seem comfortable with that? Does the lawyer give you clear, concise answers to your questions—or does the lawyer want to maintain an aura of mystery about the legal system? Pay attention to your own intuition.

Once, when I was practicing law, a scientist called me and said he had selected five possible lawyers to handle his case. He wanted to meet with me for 30 minutes to ask me some questions and decide whether or not to hire me. I was intrigued and asked him to come in. During the 30 minutes, he asked good questions about how I worked on a case, how I felt about settlements (as opposed to taking every case to trial), my billing practices, and the like. I was impressed with his involvement in his case. It was the only time in my 15 years of practice that anyone did this.

Once you choose a lawyer, be sure to get a written fee agreement outlining exactly what the lawyer promises to do and what you're expected to pay. If appropriate, include something stating the maximum fee you are willing to pay unless you agree in writing otherwise.

APPENDIX

Tear-Out Forms

A

Request for Dismissal

Blank Pleading Paper

Attachment to Judicial Council Form

Complaint—Personal Injury, Property Damage, Wrongful Death

Cause of Action—Motor Vehicle

Cause of Action—Premises Liability

Cause of Action—General Negligence

Cause of Action—Intentional Tort

Exemplary Damages Attachment

Complaint—Contract

Cause of Action—Breach of Contract

Cause of Action—Breach of Warranty (Merchantability)

Cause of Action—Breach of Warranty (Fitness)

Civil Case Cover Sheet

Civil Case Cover Sheet Addendum and Statement of Location

Case Questionnaire—For Limited Civil Cases (Under $25,000)

Request to Waive of Court Fees

Summons

Notice and Acknowledgement of Receipt—Civil

Proof of Service by First-Class Mail—Civil

Application and Order for Appointment of Guardian ad Litem—Civil

Proof of Service of Summons

Answer—Personal Injury, Property Damage, Wrongful Death

Answer—Contract

General Denial

Cross-Complaint—Personal Injury, Property Damage, Wrongful Death

Request for Entry of Default

Judgment

Declaration

Attached Declaration

Form Interrogatories—Limited Civil Cases (Economic Litigation)

Requests for Admission

Amendment to Complaint (Fictitious/Incorrect Name)

Case Management Statement

Request for Statement of Witnesses and Evidence

Civil Subpoena for Personal Appearance at Trial or Hearing

Request for Trial De Novo After Judicial Arbitration

Civil Subpoena (Duces Tecum)

CIV-110

ATTORNEY OR PARTY WITHOUT ATTORNEY (Name, State Bar number, and address):	FOR COURT USE ONLY
TELEPHONE NO.: FAX NO. (Optional): E-MAIL ADDRESS (Optional): ATTORNEY FOR (Name):	

SUPERIOR COURT OF CALIFORNIA, COUNTY OF
STREET ADDRESS:
MAILING ADDRESS:
CITY AND ZIP CODE:
BRANCH NAME:

PLAINTIFF/PETITIONER:

DEFENDANT/RESPONDENT:

REQUEST FOR DISMISSAL ☐ **Personal Injury, Property Damage, or Wrongful Death** ☐ Motor Vehicle ☐ Other ☐ **Family Law** ☐ **Eminent Domain** ☐ **Other** (specify):	CASE NUMBER:

— A conformed copy will not be returned by the clerk unless a method of return is provided with the document. —

1. TO THE CLERK: Please **dismiss** this action as follows:
   a. (1) ☐ With prejudice   (2) ☐ Without prejudice

   b. (1) ☐ Complaint   (2) ☐ Petition
      (3) ☐ Cross-complaint filed by (name):   on (date):
      (4) ☐ Cross-complaint filed by (name):   on (date):
      (5) ☐ Entire action of all parties and all causes of action
      (6) ☐ Other (specify):*

2. (Complete in all cases except family law cases.)
   ☐ Court fees and costs were waived for a party in this case. (This information may be obtained from the clerk. If this box is checked, the declaration on the back of this form must be completed).

Date:

_____   ▶ _____
(TYPE OR PRINT NAME OF ☐ ATTORNEY ☐ PARTY WITHOUT ATTORNEY)   (SIGNATURE)

*If dismissal requested is of specified parties only of specified causes of action only, or of specified cross-complaints only, so state and identify the parties, causes of action, or cross-complaints to be dismissed.

Attorney or party without attorney for:
☐ Plaintiff/Petitioner   ☐ Defendant/Respondent
☐ Cross-Complainant

3. **TO THE CLERK:** Consent to the above dismissal is hereby given.**
   Date:

_____   ▶ _____
(TYPE OR PRINT NAME OF ☐ ATTORNEY ☐ PARTY WITHOUT ATTORNEY)   (SIGNATURE)

** If a cross-complaint – or Response (Family Law) seeking affirmative relief – is on file, the attorney for cross-complainant (respondent) must sign this consent if required by Code of Civil Procedure section 581 (i) or (j).

Attorney or party without attorney for:
☐ Plaintiff/Petitioner   ☐ Defendant/Respondent
☐ Cross-Complainant

(To be completed by clerk)
4. ☐ Dismissal entered as requested on (date):
5. ☐ Dismissal entered on (date):   as to only (name):
6. ☐ Dismissal **not entered** as requested for the following reasons (specify):

7. a. ☐ Attorney or party without attorney notified on (date):
   b. ☐ Attorney or party without attorney not notified. Filing party failed to provide
       ☐ a copy to be conformed   ☐ means to return conformed copy

Date: Clerk, by _____, Deputy

Form Adopted for Mandatory Use
Judicial Council of California
CIV-110 [Rev. July 1, 2009]

REQUEST FOR DISMISSAL

Code of Civil Procedure, § 581 et seq.;
Gov. Code, § 68637(c); Cal. Rules of Court, rule 3.1390
www.courtinfo.ca.gov

		CIV-110
PLAINTIFF/PETITIONER: DEFENDANT/RESPONDENT:	CASE NUMBER:	

Declaration Concerning Waived Court Fees

The court has a statutory lien for waived fees and costs on any recovery of $10,000 or more in value by settlement, compromise, arbitration award, mediation settlement, or other recovery. The court's lien must be paid before the court will dismiss the case.

1. The court waived fees and costs in this action for *(name):*
2. The person in item 1 *(check one):*
   a. ☐ is not recovering anything of value by this action.
   b. ☐ is recovering less than $10,000 in value by this action.
   c. ☐ is recovering $10,000 or more in value by this action. *(If item 2c is checked, item 3 must be completed.)*
3. ☐ All court fees and costs that were waived in this action have been paid to the court *(check one):* ☐ Yes ☐ No

I declare under penalty of perjury under the laws of the State of California that the information above is true and correct.

Date: _____

_____   ▶ _____
(TYPE OR PRINT NAME OF ☐ ATTORNEY ☐ PARTY MAKING DECLARATION)   (SIGNATURE)

CIV-110 [Rev. July 1, 2009] — **REQUEST FOR DISMISSAL**

SHORT TITLE:	CASE NUMBER:

ATTACHMENT *(Number):* _____

(This Attachment may be used with any Judicial Council form.)

(If the item that this Attachment concerns is made under penalty of perjury, all statements in this Attachment are made under penalty of perjury.)

Page _____ of _____

(Add pages as required)

Form Approved for Optional Use
Judicial Council of California
MC-025 [Rev. July 1, 2009]

ATTACHMENT
to Judicial Council Form

www.courtinfo.ca.gov

MC-025

PLD-PI-001

ATTORNEY OR PARTY WITHOUT ATTORNEY (Name, State Bar number, and address):	FOR COURT USE ONLY
TELEPHONE NO: FAX NO. (Optional):	
E-MAIL ADDRESS (Optional):	
ATTORNEY FOR (Name):	

SUPERIOR COURT OF CALIFORNIA, COUNTY OF
 STREET ADDRESS:
 MAILING ADDRESS:
 CITY AND ZIP CODE:
 BRANCH NAME:

PLAINTIFF:

DEFENDANT:

☐ DOES 1 TO _____

COMPLAINT—Personal Injury, Property Damage, Wrongful Death
 ☐ **AMENDED** *(Number):*
Type *(check all that apply):*
☐ **MOTOR VEHICLE** ☐ **OTHER** *(specify):*
 ☐ **Property Damage** ☐ **Wrongful Death**
 ☐ **Personal Injury** ☐ **Other Damages** *(specify):*

Jurisdiction *(check all that apply):*	CASE NUMBER:
☐ **ACTION IS A LIMITED CIVIL CASE**	
Amount demanded ☐ does not exceed $10,000	
☐ exceeds $10,000, but does not exceed $25,000	
☐ **ACTION IS AN UNLIMITED CIVIL CASE (exceeds $25,000)**	
☐ **ACTION IS RECLASSIFIED by this amended complaint**	
☐ from limited to unlimited	
☐ from unlimited to limited	

1. **Plaintiff** *(name or names):*

 alleges causes of action against **defendant** *(name or names):*

2. This pleading, including attachments and exhibits, consists of the following number of pages:

3. Each plaintiff named above is a competent adult
 a. ☐ **except** plaintiff *(name):*
 (1) ☐ a corporation qualified to do business in California
 (2) ☐ an unincorporated entity *(describe):*
 (3) ☐ a public entity *(describe):*
 (4) ☐ a minor ☐ an adult
 (a) ☐ for whom a guardian or conservator of the estate or a guardian ad litem has been appointed
 (b) ☐ other *(specify):*
 (5) ☐ other *(specify):*
 b. ☐ **except** plaintiff *(name):*
 (1) ☐ a corporation qualified to do business in California
 (2) ☐ an unincorporated entity *(describe):*
 (3) ☐ a public entity *(describe):*
 (4) ☐ a minor ☐ an adult
 (a) ☐ for whom a guardian or conservator of the estate or a guardian ad litem has been appointed
 (b) ☐ other *(specify):*
 (5) ☐ other *(specify):*

☐ Information about additional plaintiffs who are not competent adults is shown in Attachment 3.

Form Approved for Optional Use
Judicial Council of California
PLD-PI-001 [Rev. January 1, 2007]

COMPLAINT—Personal Injury, Property Damage, Wrongful Death

Code of Civil Procedure, § 425.12
www.courtinfo.ca.gov

SHORT TITLE:	CASE NUMBER:

PLD-PI-001

4. ☐ Plaintiff (name):
   is doing business under the fictitious name (specify):

   and has complied with the fictitious business name laws.

5. Each defendant named above is a natural person
   a. ☐ **except** defendant (name):
      (1) ☐ a business organization, form unknown
      (2) ☐ a corporation
      (3) ☐ an unincorporated entity (describe):

      (4) ☐ a public entity (describe):

      (5) ☐ other (specify):

   c. ☐ **except** defendant (name):
      (1) ☐ a business organization, form unknown
      (2) ☐ a corporation
      (3) ☐ an unincorporated entity (describe):

      (4) ☐ a public entity (describe):

      (5) ☐ other (specify):

   b. ☐ **except** defendant (name):
      (1) ☐ a business organization, form unknown
      (2) ☐ a corporation
      (3) ☐ an unincorporated entity (describe):

      (4) ☐ a public entity (describe):

      (5) ☐ other (specify):

   d. ☐ **except** defendant (name):
      (1) ☐ a business organization, form unknown
      (2) ☐ a corporation
      (3) ☐ an unincorporated entity (describe):

      (4) ☐ a public entity (describe):

      (5) ☐ other (specify):

   ☐ Information about additional defendants who are not natural persons is contained in Attachment 5.

6. The true names of defendants sued as Does are unknown to plaintiff.
   a. ☐ Doe defendants (specify Doe numbers): _____ were the agents or employees of other named defendants and acted within the scope of that agency or employment.
   b. ☐ Doe defendants (specify Doe numbers): _____ are persons whose capacities are unknown to plaintiff.

7. ☐ Defendants who are joined under Code of Civil Procedure section 382 are (names):

8. This court is the proper court because
   a. ☐ at least one defendant now resides in its jurisdictional area.
   b. ☐ the principal place of business of a defendant corporation or unincorporated association is in its jurisdictional area.
   c. ☐ injury to person or damage to personal property occurred in its jurisdictional area.
   d. ☐ other (specify):

9. ☐ Plaintiff is required to comply with a claims statute, **and**
   a. ☐ has complied with applicable claims statutes, **or**
   b. ☐ is excused from complying because (specify):

COMPLAINT—Personal Injury, Property Damage, Wrongful Death

SHORT TITLE:	CASE NUMBER:

10. The following causes of action are attached and the statements above apply to each *(each complaint must have one or more causes of action attached)*:
    a. ☐ Motor Vehicle
    b. ☐ General Negligence
    c. ☐ Intentional Tort
    d. ☐ Products Liability
    e. ☐ Premises Liability
    f. ☐ Other *(specify):*

11. Plaintiff has suffered
    a. ☐ wage loss
    b. ☐ loss of use of property
    c. ☐ hospital and medical expenses
    d. ☐ general damage
    e. ☐ property damage
    f. ☐ loss of earning capacity
    g. ☐ other damage *(specify):*

12. ☐ The damages claimed for wrongful death and the relationships of plaintiff to the deceased are
    a. ☐ listed in Attachment 12.
    b. ☐ as follows:

13. The relief sought in this complaint is within the jurisdiction of this court.

14. **Plaintiff prays** for judgment for costs of suit; for such relief as is fair, just, and equitable; and for
    a. (1) ☐ compensatory damages
       (2) ☐ punitive damages
    The amount of damages is *(in cases for personal injury or wrongful death, you must check (1)):*
    (1) ☐ according to proof
    (2) ☐ in the amount of: $

15. ☐ The paragraphs of this complaint alleged on information and belief are as follows *(specify paragraph numbers):*

Date:

_____   ▶   _____
(TYPE OR PRINT NAME)   (SIGNATURE OF PLAINTIFF OR ATTORNEY)

PLD-PI-001 [Rev. January 1, 2007]

COMPLAINT—Personal Injury, Property Damage, Wrongful Death

SHORT TITLE:	CASE NUMBER:

PLD-PI-001(1)

CAUSE OF ACTION—Motor Vehicle

_____ (number)

ATTACHMENT TO ☐ Complaint ☐ Cross - Complaint

(Use a separate cause of action form for each cause of action.)

Plaintiff *(name):*

MV- 1. Plaintiff alleges the acts of defendants were negligent; the acts were the legal (proximate) cause of injuries and damages to plaintiff; the acts occurred
on *(date):*
at *(place):*

MV- 2. DEFENDANTS
a. ☐ The defendants who operated a motor vehicle are *(names):*

☐ Does _____ to _____

b. ☐ The defendants who employed the persons who operated a motor vehicle in the course of their employment are *(names):*

☐ Does _____ to _____

c. ☐ The defendants who owned the motor vehicle which was operated with their permission are *(names):*

☐ Does _____ to _____

d. ☐ The defendants who entrusted the motor vehicle are *(names):*

☐ Does _____ to _____

e. ☐ The defendants who were the agents and employees of the other defendants and acted within the scope of the agency were *(names):*

☐ Does _____ to _____

f. ☐ The defendants who are liable to plaintiffs for other reasons and the reasons for the liability are
☐ listed in Attachment MV-2f ☐ as follows:

☐ Does _____ to _____

Page _____

Page 1 of 1

Form Approved for Optional Use
Judicial Council of California
PLD-PI-001(1) [Rev. January 1, 2007]

CAUSE OF ACTION—Motor Vehicle

Code of Civil Procedure 425.12
www.courtinfo.ca.gov

SHORT TITLE:	CASE NUMBER:

PLD-PI-001(4)

_____ **CAUSE OF ACTION—Premises Liability**   Page _____
(number)

ATTACHMENT TO   ☐ Complaint   ☐ Cross - Complaint
(Use a separate cause of action form for each cause of action.)

Prem.L-1. Plaintiff *(name):*
   alleges the acts of defendants were the legal (proximate) cause of damages to plaintiff.
   On *(date):* _____ plaintiff was injured on the following premises in the following
   fashion *(description of premises and circumstances of injury):*

Prem.L-2.   ☐ **Count One—Negligence** The defendants who negligently owned, maintained, managed and operated the described premises were *(names):*

   ☐ Does _____ to _____

Prem.L-3.   ☐ **Count Two—Willful Failure to Warn** [Civil Code section 846] The defendant owners who willfully or maliciously failed to guard or warn against a dangerous condition, use, structure, or activity were *(names):*

   ☐ Does _____ to _____
   Plaintiff, a recreational user, was   ☐ an invited guest   ☐ a paying guest.

Prem.L-4.   ☐ **Count Three—Dangerous Condition of Public Property** The defendants who owned public property on which a dangerous condition existed were *(names):*

   ☐ Does _____ to _____
   a. ☐ The defendant public entity had ☐ actual ☐ constructive notice of the existence of the dangerous condition in sufficient time prior to the injury to have corrected it.
   b. ☐ The condition was created by employees of the defendant public entity.

Prem.L-5. a. ☐ **Allegations about Other Defendants** The defendants who were the agents and employees of the other defendants and acted within the scope of the agency were *(names):*

   ☐ Does _____ to _____
   b. ☐ The defendants who are liable to plaintiffs for other reasons and the reasons for their liability are
      ☐ described in attachment Prem.L-5.b   ☐ as follows *(names):*

Page 1 of 1

Form Approved for Optional Use
Judicial Council of California
PLD-PI-001(4) [Rev. January 1, 2007]

CAUSE OF ACTION—Premises Liability

Code of Civil Procedure, § 425.12
www.courtinfo.ca.gov

SHORT TITLE:	CASE NUMBER:

PLD-PI-001(2)

CAUSE OF ACTION—General Negligence   Page _____

_____ (number)

ATTACHMENT TO ☐ Complaint ☐ Cross - Complaint

(Use a separate cause of action form for each cause of action.)

GN-1. Plaintiff *(name)*:

   alleges that defendant *(name)*:

   ☐ Does _____ to _____

   was the legal (proximate) cause of damages to plaintiff. By the following acts or omissions to act, defendant negligently caused the damage to plaintiff
   on *(date)*:
   at *(place)*:

   (description of reasons for liability):

Form Approved for Optional Use
Judicial Council of California
PLD-PI-001(2) [Rev. January 1, 2007]

CAUSE OF ACTION—General Negligence

Page 1 of 1
Code of Civil Procedure 425.12
www.courtinfo.ca.gov

SHORT TITLE:	CASE NUMBER

PLD-PI-001(3)

_____ **CAUSE OF ACTION—Intentional Tort**   Page _____
(number)

ATTACHMENT TO   ☐ Complaint   ☐ Cross - Complaint

(Use a separate cause of action form for each cause of action.)

IT-1. Plaintiff *(name)*:

   alleges that defendant *(name)*:

   ☐ Does _____ to _____

was the legal (proximate) cause of damages to plaintiff. By the following acts or omissions to act, defendant intentionally caused the damage to plaintiff
on *(date)*:
at *(place)*:

(description of reasons for liability):

Form Approved for Optional Use
Judicial Council of California
PLD-PI-001(3) [Rev. January 1, 2007]

CAUSE OF ACTION–Intentional Tort

Code of Civil Procedure, § 425.12
www.courtinfo.ca.gov

SHORT TITLE:	CASE NUMBER:

PLD-PI-001(6)

Exemplary Damages Attachment

Page: _____

ATTACHMENT TO ☐ Complaint ☐ Cross - Complaint

EX-1. As additional damages against defendant *(name)*:

Plaintiff alleges defendant was guilty of
☐ malice
☐ fraud
☐ oppression

as defined in Civil Code section 3294, and plaintiff should recover, in addition to actual damages, damages to make an example of and to punish defendant.

EX-2. The facts supporting plaintiff's claim are as follows:

EX-3. The amount of exemplary damages sought is
 a. ☐ not shown, pursuant to Code of Civil Procedure section 425.10.
 b. ☐ $

Form Approved for Optional Use
Judicial Council of California
PLD-PI-001(6) [Rev. January 1, 2007]

Exemplary Damages Attachment

Code of Civil Procedure, § 425.12
www.courtinfo.ca.gov

PLD-C-001

ATTORNEY OR PARTY WITHOUT ATTORNEY *(Name, State Bar number, and address)*:	*FOR COURT USE ONLY*
TELEPHONE NO: FAX NO. *(Optional)*:	
E-MAIL ADDRESS *(Optional)*:	
ATTORNEY FOR *(Name)*:	

SUPERIOR COURT OF CALIFORNIA, COUNTY OF
STREET ADDRESS:
MAILING ADDRESS:
CITY AND ZIP CODE:
BRANCH NAME:

PLAINTIFF:

DEFENDANT:

☐ DOES 1 TO _____

CONTRACT
☐ **COMPLAINT**   ☐ **AMENDED COMPLAINT** *(Number)*:
☐ **CROSS-COMPLAINT**   ☐ **AMENDED CROSS-COMPLAINT** *(Number)*:

Jurisdiction *(check all that apply)*:
☐ **ACTION IS A LIMITED CIVIL CASE**
    Amount demanded   ☐ does not exceed $10,000
                                     ☐ exceeds $10,000 but does not exceed $25,000
☐ **ACTION IS AN UNLIMITED CIVIL CASE** (exceeds $25,000)
☐ **ACTION IS RECLASSIFIED** by this amended complaint or cross-complaint
    ☐ from limited to unlimited
    ☐ from unlimited to limited

CASE NUMBER:

1. **Plaintiff*** *(name or names)*:

   alleges causes of action against **defendant*** *(name or names)*:

2. This pleading, including attachments and exhibits, consists of the following number of pages:
3. a. Each plaintiff named above is a competent adult
   ☐ **except** plaintiff *(name)*:
      (1) ☐ a corporation qualified to do business in California
      (2) ☐ an unincorporated entity *(describe)*:
      (3) ☐ other *(specify)*:

   b. ☐ Plaintiff *(name)*:
      a. ☐ has complied with the fictitious business name laws and is doing business under the fictitious name *(specify)*:
      b. ☐ has complied with all licensing requirements as a licensed *(specify)*:
   c. ☐ Information about additional plaintiffs who are not competent adults is shown in Attachment 3c.
4. a. Each defendant named above is a natural person
   ☐ **except** defendant *(name)*:   ☐ **except** defendant *(name)*:
      (1) ☐ a business organization, form unknown   (1) ☐ a business organization, form unknown
      (2) ☐ a corporation   (2) ☐ a corporation
      (3) ☐ an unincorporated entity *(describe)*:   (3) ☐ an unincorporated entity *(describe)*:

      (4) ☐ a public entity *(describe)*:   (4) ☐ a public entity *(describe)*:

      (5) ☐ other *(specify)*:   (5) ☐ other *(specify)*:

* If this form is used as a cross-complaint, plaintiff means cross-complainant and defendant means cross-defendant.

COMPLAINT—Contract

Form Approved for Optional Use
Judicial Council of California
PLD-C-001 [Rev. January 1, 2007]

Code of Civil Procedure, § 425.12

SHORT TITLE:	CASE NUMBER:

PLD-C-001

4. *(Continued)*
   b. The true names of defendants sued as Does are unknown to plaintiff.
      (1) ☐ Doe defendants *(specify Doe numbers):* _____ were the agents or employees of the named defendants and acted within the scope of that agency or employment.
      (2) ☐ Doe defendants *(specify Doe numbers):* _____ are persons whose capacities are unknown to plaintiff.
   c. ☐ Information about additional defendants who are not natural persons is contained in Attachment 4c.
   d. ☐ Defendants who are joined under Code of Civil Procedure section 382 are *(names):*

5. ☐ Plaintiff is required to comply with a claims statute, **and**
   a. ☐ has complied with applicable claims statutes, *or*
   b. ☐ is excused from complying because *(specify):*

6. ☐ This action is subject to ☐ Civil Code section 1812.10 ☐ Civil Code section 2984.4.

7. This court is the proper court because
   a. ☐ a defendant entered into the contract here.
   b. ☐ a defendant lived here when the contract was entered into.
   c. ☐ a defendant lives here now.
   d. ☐ the contract was to be performed here.
   e. ☐ a defendant is a corporation or unincorporated association and its principal place of business is here.
   f. ☐ real property that is the subject of this action is located here.
   g. ☐ other *(specify):*

8. The following causes of action are attached and the statements above apply to each *(each complaint must have one or more causes of action attached):*
   ☐ Breach of Contract
   ☐ Common Counts
   ☐ Other *(specify):*

9. ☐ Other allegations:

10. **Plaintiff prays** for judgment for costs of suit; for such relief as is fair, just, and equitable; and for
    a. ☐ damages of: $
    b. ☐ interest on the damages
       (1) ☐ according to proof
       (2) ☐ at the rate of *(specify):* ____ percent per year from *(date):*
    c. ☐ attorney's fees
       (1) ☐ of: $
       (2) ☐ according to proof.
    d. ☐ other *(specify):*

11. ☐ The paragraphs of this pleading alleged on information and belief are as follows *(specify paragraph numbers):*

Date:

_____   ▶ _____
(TYPE OR PRINT NAME)   (SIGNATURE OF PLAINTIFF OR ATTORNEY)

(If you wish to verify this pleading, affix a verification.)

COMPLAINT—Contract

SHORT TITLE:	CASE NUMBER:

PLD-C-001(1)

CAUSE OF ACTION—Breach of Contract

_____
(number)

ATTACHMENT TO ☐ Complaint ☐ Cross - Complaint

(Use a separate cause of action form for each cause of action.)

BC-1. Plaintiff *(name):*

alleges that on or about *(date):*
a ☐ written ☐ oral ☐ other *(specify):*
agreement was made between *(name parties to agreement):*

☐ A copy of the agreement is attached as Exhibit A, or
☐ The essential terms of the agreement ☐ are stated in Attachment BC-1 ☐ are as follows *(specify):*

BC-2. On or about *(dates):*
defendant breached the agreement by ☐ the acts specified in Attachment BC-2 ☐ the following acts *(specify):*

BC-3. Plaintiff has performed all obligations to defendant except those obligations plaintiff was prevented or excused from performing.

BC-4. Plaintiff suffered damages legally (proximately) caused by defendant's breach of the agreement
☐ as stated in Attachment BC-4 ☐ as follows *(specify):*

BC-5. ☐ Plaintiff is entitled to attorney fees by an agreement or a statute
☐ of $
☐ according to proof.

BC-6. ☐ Other:

Page _____

Page 1 of 1

Form Approved for Optional Use
Judicial Council of California
PLD-C-001(1) [Rev. January 1, 2007]

CAUSE OF ACTION—Breach of Contract

Code of Civil Procedure, § 425.12
www.courtinfo.ca.gov

SHORT TITLE:	CASE NUMBER:

_____
(number)

CAUSE OF ACTION—Breach of Warranty (Merchantability)

Page _____

ATTACHMENT TO ☐ Complaint   ☐ Cross-Complaint

BWM-1. Plaintiff (*name*):

   alleges that on or about (*date*):

   defendant(s) (*seller*):

   sold plaintiff (*quantity and description of goods*):

   at retail and plaintiff brought such goods from defendant(s) for a price of (*amount*): $_____.

   ☐ A true copy of a memorandum or contract regarding this sale is attached to this Cause of Action as Exhibit BWM-1.

BWM-2. ☐ On or about (*date*):

   defendant(s) (*manufacturer*):

   manufactured such goods for the purpose of their eventual sale to retail buyers.

BWM-3. ☐ On or about (*date*):

   defendant(s) (*distributor*):

   acquired such goods from defendant(s) manufacturer and distributed them to defendant(s) seller for eventual retail sale to consumers.

BWM-4. ☐ In the process, defendants (*name*):

   appended to such goods a written warranty which is attached to this Cause of Action as Exhibit BWM-4.

BWM-5. Such retail sale to plaintiff was accompanied separately and individually by the implied warranty that such goods were merchantable by defendant(s) (*name*):

SHORT TITLE:	CASE NUMBER:

_____
(number)

CAUSE OF ACTION—Breach of Warranty (Merchantability)

Page _____

BWM-6. Defendant(s) breached their respective warranties implied in the sale in that (*describe*):

As a result of the breach by defendant(s), plaintiff did not receive merchantable goods as impliedly warranted by defendant(s).

BWM-7. Plaintiff discovered such breach of warranty on or about (date):

    a. ☐ On or about (date):

        plaintiff notified defendant(s) (*name*):

    b. ☐ By letter, a true copy of which is attached to this Cause of Action as Exhibit BWM-7.

    c. ☐ Other (*describe*):

BWM-8. As a legal result of such breach of the warranty of merchantability by defendant(s), plaintiff has been damaged in the amount $_____ .

SHORT TITLE:	CASE NUMBER:

_____
(number)

CAUSE OF ACTION—Breach of Warranty (Fitness)

Page _____

ATTACHMENT TO ☐ Complaint   ☐ Cross-Complaint

BWF-1. Plaintiff (*name*):

   alleges that on or about (*date*):

   plaintiff required (*quantity and description of goods*):

   for the particular purpose of (*describe*):

   To select and furnish suitable goods for such purpose, plaintiff relied on the skill and judgment of defendant(s) (*name*):

BWF-2. ☐ On or about (*date*):

   defendant(s) sold to plaintiff (*quantity and description of goods*):

   and plaintiff bought such goods from defendant(s), in such reliance, for amount of (*price paid*): $_____

   ☐ A true copy of the memorandum or contract of the sale is attached to this Cause of Action as Exhibit BWF-2.

BWF-3. At the time of the retail sale of such goods, defendant(s) had reason to know the particular purpose for which the goods were required because plaintiff expressly communicated such purposes to defendant(s). Defendant(s) further knew plaintiff was relying on the skill and judgment of defendant(s) to select and furnish suitable goods; thus there was an implied warranty that goods were fit for such purpose.

SHORT TITLE:	CASE NUMBER:

_____
(number)

CAUSE OF ACTION—Breach of Warranty (Fitness)

Page _____

BWF-4. Defendant(s) breached such warranty in that plaintiff did not receive suitable goods and such goods were not fit for the particular purpose for which they were required in that (*describe failure*):

BWF-5. Plaintiff discovered such breach of warranty on or about (date):

    a. ☐ On or about (*date*):

        plaintiff notified defendant(s) (*name*):

    b. ☐ By letter, a true copy of which is attached to this Cause of Action as Exhibit BWM-7.

    c. ☐ Other (*describe*):

BWF-6. As a result of such breach of the warranty of fitness by defendant(s), plaintiff has been damaged in the amount $_____ .

		CM-010

ATTORNEY OR PARTY WITHOUT ATTORNEY *(Name, State Bar number, and address)*:
 	
 TELEPHONE NO.:   FAX NO.:
 ATTORNEY FOR *(Name)*:
 SUPERIOR COURT OF CALIFORNIA, COUNTY OF
    STREET ADDRESS:
    MAILING ADDRESS:
    CITY AND ZIP CODE:
    BRANCH NAME:
 CASE NAME:
		FOR COURT USE ONLY

CIVIL CASE COVER SHEET	**Complex Case Designation**	CASE NUMBER:
☐ Unlimited ☐ Limited (Amount (Amount demanded demanded is exceeds $25,000) $25,000 or less)	☐ Counter ☐ Joinder Filed with first appearance by defendant (Cal. Rules of Court, rule 3.402)	JUDGE: DEPT:

Items 1–6 below must be completed (see instructions on page 2).

1. Check **one** box below for the case type that best describes this case:

   Auto Tort
   - ☐ Auto (22)
   - ☐ Uninsured motorist (46)

   Other PI/PD/WD (Personal Injury/Property Damage/Wrongful Death) Tort
   - ☐ Asbestos (04)
   - ☐ Product liability (24)
   - ☐ Medical malpractice (45)
   - ☐ Other PI/PD/WD (23)

   Non-PI/PD/WD (Other) Tort
   - ☐ Business tort/unfair business practice (07)
   - ☐ Civil rights (08)
   - ☐ Defamation (13)
   - ☐ Fraud (16)
   - ☐ Intellectual property (19)
   - ☐ Professional negligence (25)
   - ☐ Other non-PI/PD/WD tort (35)

   Employment
   - ☐ Wrongful termination (36)
   - ☐ Other employment (15)

   Contract
   - ☐ Breach of contract/warranty (06)
   - ☐ Rule 3.740 collections (09)
   - ☐ Other collections (09)
   - ☐ Insurance coverage (18)
   - ☐ Other contract (37)

   Real Property
   - ☐ Eminent domain/Inverse condemnation (14)
   - ☐ Wrongful eviction (33)
   - ☐ Other real property (26)

   Unlawful Detainer
   - ☐ Commercial (31)
   - ☐ Residential (32)
   - ☐ Drugs (38)

   Judicial Review
   - ☐ Asset forfeiture (05)
   - ☐ Petition re: arbitration award (11)
   - ☐ Writ of mandate (02)
   - ☐ Other judicial review (39)

   Provisionally Complex Civil Litigation (Cal. Rules of Court, rules 3.400–3.403)
   - ☐ Antitrust/Trade regulation (03)
   - ☐ Construction defect (10)
   - ☐ Mass tort (40)
   - ☐ Securities litigation (28)
   - ☐ Environmental/Toxic tort (30)
   - ☐ Insurance coverage claims arising from the above listed provisionally complex case types (41)

   Enforcement of Judgment
   - ☐ Enforcement of judgment (20)

   Miscellaneous Civil Complaint
   - ☐ RICO (27)
   - ☐ Other complaint *(not specified above)* (42)

   Miscellaneous Civil Petition
   - ☐ Partnership and corporate governance (21)
   - ☐ Other petition *(not specified above)* (43)

2. This case ☐ is ☐ is not complex under rule 3.400 of the California Rules of Court. If the case is complex, mark the factors requiring exceptional judicial management:
   - a. ☐ Large number of separately represented parties
   - b. ☐ Extensive motion practice raising difficult or novel issues that will be time-consuming to resolve
   - c. ☐ Substantial amount of documentary evidence
   - d. ☐ Large number of witnesses
   - e. ☐ Coordination with related actions pending in one or more courts in other counties, states, or countries, or in a federal court
   - f. ☐ Substantial postjudgment judicial supervision

3. Remedies sought *(check all that apply)*: a. ☐ monetary   b. ☐ nonmonetary; declaratory or injunctive relief   c. ☐ punitive
4. Number of causes of action *(specify)*:
5. This case ☐ is ☐ is not a class action suit.
6. If there are any known related cases, file and serve a notice of related case. *(You may use form CM-015.)*

Date:

_____   ▶   _____
(TYPE OR PRINT NAME)   (SIGNATURE OF PARTY OR ATTORNEY FOR PARTY)

NOTICE
- Plaintiff must file this cover sheet with the first paper filed in the action or proceeding (except small claims cases or cases filed under the Probate Code, Family Code, or Welfare and Institutions Code). (Cal. Rules of Court, rule 3.220.) Failure to file may result in sanctions.
- File this cover sheet in addition to any cover sheet required by local court rule.
- If this case is complex under rule 3.400 et seq. of the California Rules of Court, you must serve a copy of this cover sheet on **all** other parties to the action or proceeding.
- Unless this is a collections case under rule 3.740 or a complex case, this cover sheet will be used for statistical purposes only.

CM-010

INSTRUCTIONS ON HOW TO COMPLETE THE COVER SHEET

To Plaintiffs and Others Filing First Papers. If you are filing a first paper (for example, a complaint) in a civil case, you **must** complete and file, along with your first paper, the *Civil Case Cover Sheet* contained on page 1. This information will be used to compile statistics about the types and numbers of cases filed. You must complete items 1 through 6 on the sheet. In item 1, you must check **one** box for the case type that best describes the case. If the case fits both a general and a more specific type of case listed in item 1, check the more specific one. If the case has multiple causes of action, check the box that best indicates the **primary** cause of action. To assist you in completing the sheet, examples of the cases that belong under each case type in item 1 are provided below. A cover sheet must be filed only with your initial paper. Failure to file a cover sheet with the first paper filed in a civil case may subject a party, its counsel, or both to sanctions under rules 2.30 and 3.220 of the California Rules of Court.

To Parties in Rule 3.740 Collections Cases. A "collections case" under rule 3.740 is defined as an action for recovery of money owed in a sum stated to be certain that is not more than $25,000, exclusive of interest and attorney's fees, arising from a transaction in which property, services, or money was acquired on credit. A collections case does not include an action seeking the following: (1) tort damages, (2) punitive damages, (3) recovery of real property, (4) recovery of personal property, or (5) a prejudgment writ of attachment. The identification of a case as a rule 3.740 collections case on this form means that it will be exempt from the general time-for-service requirements and case management rules, unless a defendant files a responsive pleading. A rule 3.740 collections case will be subject to the requirements for service and obtaining a judgment in rule 3.740.

To Parties in Complex Cases. In complex cases only, parties must also use the *Civil Case Cover Sheet* to designate whether the case is complex. If a plaintiff believes the case is complex under rule 3.400 of the California Rules of Court, this must be indicated by completing the appropriate boxes in items 1 and 2. If a plaintiff designates a case as complex, the cover sheet must be served with the complaint on all parties to the action. A defendant may file and serve no later than the time of its first appearance a joinder in the plaintiff's designation, a counter-designation that the case is not complex, or, if the plaintiff has made no designation, a designation that the case is complex.

CASE TYPES AND EXAMPLES

Auto Tort
    Auto (22)–Personal Injury/Property
        Damage/Wrongful Death
    Uninsured Motorist (46) *(if the*
        case involves an uninsured
        motorist claim subject to
        arbitration, check this item
        instead of Auto)

Other PI/PD/WD (Personal Injury/ Property Damage/Wrongful Death) Tort
    Asbestos (04)
        Asbestos Property Damage
        Asbestos Personal Injury/
            Wrongful Death
    Product Liability *(not asbestos or*
        toxic/environmental) (24)
    Medical Malpractice (45)
        Medical Malpractice–
            Physicians & Surgeons
        Other Professional Health Care
            Malpractice
    Other PI/PD/WD (23)
        Premises Liability (e.g., slip
            and fall)
        Intentional Bodily Injury/PD/WD
            (e.g., assault, vandalism)
        Intentional Infliction of
            Emotional Distress
        Negligent Infliction of
            Emotional Distress
        Other PI/PD/WD

Non-PI/PD/WD (Other) Tort
    Business Tort/Unfair Business
        Practice (07)
    Civil Rights (e.g., discrimination,
        false arrest) *(not civil*
        harassment) (08)
    Defamation (e.g., slander, libel)
        (13)
    Fraud (16)
    Intellectual Property (19)
    Professional Negligence (25)
        Legal Malpractice
        Other Professional Malpractice
            (not medical or legal)
    Other Non-PI/PD/WD Tort (35)

Employment
    Wrongful Termination (36)
    Other Employment (15)

Contract
    Breach of Contract/Warranty (06)
        Breach of Rental/Lease
            Contract *(not unlawful detainer*
            or wrongful eviction)
        Contract/Warranty Breach–Seller
            Plaintiff *(not fraud or negligence)*
        Negligent Breach of Contract/
            Warranty
        Other Breach of Contract/Warranty
    Collections (e.g., money owed, open
        book accounts) (09)
        Collection Case–Seller Plaintiff
        Other Promissory Note/Collections
            Case
    Insurance Coverage *(not provisionally*
        complex) (18)
        Auto Subrogation
        Other Coverage
    Other Contract (37)
        Contractual Fraud
        Other Contract Dispute

Real Property
    Eminent Domain/Inverse
        Condemnation (14)
    Wrongful Eviction (33)
    Other Real Property (e.g., quiet title) (26)
        Writ of Possession of Real Property
        Mortgage Foreclosure
        Quiet Title
        Other Real Property *(not eminent*
            domain, landlord/tenant, or
            foreclosure)

Unlawful Detainer
    Commercial (31)
    Residential (32)
    Drugs (38) *(if the case involves illegal*
        drugs, check this item; otherwise,
        report as Commercial or Residential)

Judicial Review
    Asset Forfeiture (05)
    Petition Re: Arbitration Award (11)
    Writ of Mandate (02)
        Writ–Administrative Mandamus
        Writ–Mandamus on Limited Court
            Case Matter
        Writ–Other Limited Court Case
            Review
    Other Judicial Review (39)
        Review of Health Officer Order
        Notice of Appeal–Labor
            Commissioner Appeals

Provisionally Complex Civil Litigation (Cal. Rules of Court Rules 3.400–3.403)
    Antitrust/Trade Regulation (03)
    Construction Defect (10)
    Claims Involving Mass Tort (40)
    Securities Litigation (28)
    Environmental/Toxic Tort (30)
    Insurance Coverage Claims
        (arising from provisionally complex
        case type listed above) (41)

Enforcement of Judgment
    Enforcement of Judgment (20)
        Abstract of Judgment (Out of
            County)
        Confession of Judgment *(non-*
            domestic relations)
        Sister State Judgment
        Administrative Agency Award
            (not unpaid taxes)
        Petition/Certification of Entry of
            Judgment on Unpaid Taxes
        Other Enforcement of Judgment
            Case

Miscellaneous Civil Complaint
    RICO (27)
    Other Complaint *(not specified*
        above) (42)
        Declaratory Relief Only
        Injunctive Relief Only *(non-*
            harassment)
        Mechanics Lien
        Other Commercial Complaint
            Case *(non-tort/non-complex)*
        Other Civil Complaint
            (non-tort/non-complex)

Miscellaneous Civil Petition
    Partnership and Corporate
        Governance (21)
    Other Petition *(not specified*
        above) (43)
        Civil Harassment
        Workplace Violence
        Elder/Dependent Adult
            Abuse
        Election Contest
        Petition for Name Change
        Petition for Relief From Late
            Claim
        Other Civil Petition

CIVIL CASE COVER SHEET

SHORT TITLE:	CASE NUMBER

CIVIL CASE COVER SHEET ADDENDUM AND STATEMENT OF LOCATION
(CERTIFICATE OF GROUNDS FOR ASSIGNMENT TO COURTHOUSE LOCATION)

This form is required pursuant to LASC Local Rule 2.0 in all new civil case filings in the Los Angeles Superior Court.

Item I. Check the types of hearing and fill in the estimated length of hearing expected for this case:

JURY TRIAL? ☐ YES   CLASS ACTION? ☐YES   LIMITED CASE? ☐YES   TIME ESTIMATED FOR TRIAL _____ ☐ HOURS/ ☐ DAYS

Item II. Select the correct district and courthouse location (4 steps – If you checked "Limited Case", skip to Item III, Pg. 4):

Step 1: After first completing the Civil Case Cover Sheet Form, find the main civil case cover sheet heading for your case in the left margin below, and, to the right in Column **A**, the Civil Case Cover Sheet case type you selected.

Step 2: Check **one** Superior Court type of action in Column **B** below which best describes the nature of this case.

Step 3: In Column **C**, circle the reason for the court location choice that applies to the type of action you have checked. For any exception to the court location, see Los Angeles Superior Court Local Rule 2.0.

Applicable Reasons for Choosing Courthouse Location (see Column C below)

1. Class Actions must be filed in the County Courthouse, Central District.
2. May be filed in Central (Other county, or no Bodily Injury/Property Damage).
3. Location where cause of action arose.
4. Location where bodily injury, death or damage occurred.
5. Location where performance required or defendant resides.
6. Location of property or permanently garaged vehicle.
7. Location where petitioner resides.
8. Location wherein defendant/respondent functions wholly.
9. Location where one or more of the parties reside.
10. Location of Labor Commissioner Office.

Step 4: Fill in the information requested on page 4 in Item III; complete Item IV. Sign the declaration.

	A Civil Case Cover Sheet Category No.	B Type of Action (Check only one)	C Applicable Reasons - See Step 3 Above
Auto Tort	Auto (22)	☐ A7100 Motor Vehicle - Personal Injury/Property Damage/Wrongful Death	1., 2., 4.
	Uninsured Motorist (46)	☐ A7110 Personal Injury/Property Damage/Wrongful Death – Uninsured Motorist	1., 2., 4.
Damage/Wrongful Death Tort	Asbestos (04)	☐ A6070 Asbestos Property Damage ☐ A7221 Asbestos - Personal Injury/Wrongful Death	2. 2.
	Product Liability (24)	☐ A7260 Product Liability (not asbestos or toxic/environmental)	1., 2., 3., 4., 8.
	Medical Malpractice (45)	☐ A7210 Medical Malpractice - Physicians & Surgeons ☐ A7240 Other Professional Health Care Malpractice	1., 2., 4. 1., 2., 4.
	Other Personal Injury Property Damage Wrongful Death (23)	☐ A7250 Premises Liability (e.g., slip and fall) ☐ A7230 Intentional Bodily Injury/Property Damage/Wrongful Death (e.g., assault, vandalism, etc.) ☐ A7270 Intentional Infliction of Emotional Distress ☐ A7220 Other Personal Injury/Property Damage/Wrongful Death	1., 2., 4. 1., 2., 4. 1., 2., 3. 1., 2., 4.
Damage/Wrongful Death Tort	Business Tort (07)	☐ A6029 Other Commercial/Business Tort (not fraud/breach of contract)	1., 2., 3.
	Civil Rights (08)	☐ A6005 Civil Rights/Discrimination	1., 2., 3.
	Defamation (13)	☐ A6010 Defamation (slander/libel)	1., 2., 3.
	Fraud (16)	☐ A6013 Fraud (no contract)	1., 2., 3.

LACIV 109 (Rev. 01/07)
LASC Approved 03-04

**CIVIL CASE COVER SHEET ADDENDUM
AND STATEMENT OF LOCATION**

LASC, rule 2.0

SHORT TITLE:	CASE NUMBER

A Civil Case Cover Sheet Category No.	B Type of Action (Check only one)	C Applicable Reasons -See Step 3 Above
Non-Personal Injury/Property Damage/Wrongful Death Tort (Cont'd.)		
Professional Negligence (25)	☐ A6017 Legal Malpractice ☐ A6050 Other Professional Malpractice (not medical or legal)	1., 2., 3. 1., 2., 3.
Other (35)	☐ A6025 Other Non-Personal Injury/Property Damage tort	2.,3.
Employment		
Wrongful Termination (36)	☐ A6037 Wrongful Termination	1., 2., 3.
Other Employment (15)	☐ A6024 Other Employment Complaint Case ☐ A6109 Labor Commissioner Appeals	1., 2., 3. 10.
Contract		
Breach of Contract/ Warranty (06) (not insurance)	☐ A6004 Breach of Rental/Lease Contract (not Unlawful Detainer or wrongful eviction) ☐ A6008 Contract/Warranty Breach -Seller Plaintiff (no fraud/negligence) ☐ A6019 Negligent Breach of Contract/Warranty (no fraud) ☐ A6028 Other Breach of Contract/Warranty (not fraud or negligence)	2., 5. 2., 5. 1., 2., 5. 1., 2., 5.
Collections (09)	☐ A6002 Collections Case-Seller Plaintiff ☐ A6012 Other Promissory Note/Collections Case	2., 5., 6. 2., 5.
Insurance Coverage (18)	☐ A6015 Insurance Coverage (not complex)	1., 2., 5., 8.
Other Contract (37)	☐ A6009 Contractual Fraud ☐ A6031 Tortious Interference ☐ A6027 Other Contract Dispute(not breach/insurance/fraud/negligence)	1., 2., 3., 5. 1., 2., 3., 5. 1., 2., 3., 8.
Real Property		
Eminent Domain/Inverse Condemnation (14)	☐ A7300 Eminent Domain/Condemnation Number of parcels_____	2.
Wrongful Eviction (33)	☐ A6023 Wrongful Eviction Case	2., 6.
Other Real Property (26)	☐ A6018 Mortgage Foreclosure ☐ A6032 Quiet Title ☐ A6060 Other Real Property (not eminent domain, landlord/tenant, foreclosure)	2., 6. 2., 6. 2., 6.
Unlawful Detainer		
Unlawful Detainer-Commercial (31)	☐ A6021 Unlawful Detainer-Commercial (not drugs or wrongful eviction)	2., 6.
Unlawful Detainer-Residential (32)	☐ A6020 Unlawful Detainer-Residential (not drugs or wrongful eviction)	2., 6.
Unlawful Detainer-Drugs (38)	☐ A6022 Unlawful Detainer-Drugs	2., 6.
Judicial Review		
Asset Forfeiture (05)	☐ A6108 Asset Forfeiture Case	2., 6.
Petition re Arbitration (11)	☐ A6115 Petition to Compel/Confirm/Vacate Arbitration	2., 5.

SHORT TITLE:	CASE NUMBER

	A Civil Case Cover Sheet Category No.	B Type of Action (Check only one)	C Applicable Reasons - See Step 3 Above
Judicial Review (Cont'd.)	Writ of Mandate (02)	☐ A6151 Writ - Administrative Mandamus ☐ A6152 Writ - Mandamus on Limited Court Case Matter ☐ A6153 Writ - Other Limited Court Case Review	2., 8. 2. 2.
	Other Judicial Review (39)	☐ A6150 Other Writ /Judicial Review	2., 8.
Provisionally Complex Litigation	Antitrust/Trade Regulation (03)	☐ A6003 Antitrust/Trade Regulation	1., 2., 8.
	Construction Defect (10)	☐ A6007 Construction defect	1., 2., 3.
	Claims Involving Mass Tort (40)	☐ A6006 Claims Involving Mass Tort	1., 2., 8.
	Securities Litigation (28)	☐ A6035 Securities Litigation Case	1., 2., 8.
	Toxic Tort Environmental (30)	☐ A6036 Toxic Tort/Environmental	1., 2., 3., 8.
	Insurance Coverage Claims from Complex Case (41)	☐ A6014 Insurance Coverage/Subrogation (complex case only)	1., 2., 5., 8.
Enforcement of Judgment	Enforcement of Judgment (20)	☐ A6141 Sister State Judgment ☐ A6160 Abstract of Judgment ☐ A6107 Confession of Judgment (non-domestic relations) ☐ A6140 Administrative Agency Award (not unpaid taxes) ☐ A6114 Petition/Certificate for Entry of Judgment on Unpaid Tax ☐ A6112 Other Enforcement of Judgment Case	2., 9. 2., 6. 2., 9. 2., 8. 2., 8. 2., 8., 9.
Miscellaneous Civil Complaints	RICO (27)	☐ A6033 Racketeering (RICO) Case	1., 2., 8.
	Other Complaints (Not Specified Above) (42)	☐ A6030 Declaratory Relief Only ☐ A6040 Injunctive Relief Only (not domestic/harassment) ☐ A6011 Other Commercial Complaint Case (non-tort/non-complex) ☐ A6000 Other Civil Complaint (non-tort/non-complex)	1., 2., 8. 2., 8. 1., 2., 8. 1., 2., 8.
Miscellaneous Civil Petitions	Partnership Corporation Governance(21)	☐ A6113 Partnership and Corporate Governance Case	2., 8.
	Other Petitions (Not Specified Above) (43)	☐ A6121 Civil Harassment ☐ A6123 Workplace Harassment ☐ A6124 Elder/Dependent Adult Abuse Case ☐ A6190 Election Contest ☐ A6110 Petition for Change of Name ☐ A6170 Petition for Relief from Late Claim Law ☐ A6100 Other Civil Petition	2., 3., 9. 2., 3., 9. 2., 3., 9. 2. 2., 7. 2., 3., 4., 8. 2., 9.

SHORT TITLE:	CASE NUMBER

Item III. Statement of Location: Enter the address of the accident, party's residence or place of business, performance, or other circumstance indicated in Item II., Step 3 on Page 1, as the proper reason for filing in the court location you selected.

REASON: CHECK THE NUMBER UNDER COLUMN C WHICH APPLIES IN THIS CASE ☐1. ☐2. ☐3. ☐4. ☐5. ☐6. ☐7. ☐8. ☐9. ☐10.	ADDRESS:
CITY: STATE: ZIP CODE:	

Item IV. *Declaration of Assignment*: I declare under penalty of perjury under the laws of the State of California that the foregoing is true and correct and that the above-entitled matter is properly filed for assignment to the _____ courthouse in the _____ District of the Los Angeles Superior Court (Code Civ. Proc., § 392 et seq., and LASC Local Rule 2.0, subds. (b), (c) and (d)).

Dated: _____

_____
(SIGNATURE OF ATTORNEY/FILING PARTY)

PLEASE HAVE THE FOLLOWING ITEMS COMPLETED AND READY TO BE FILED IN ORDER TO PROPERLY COMMENCE YOUR NEW COURT CASE:

1. Original Complaint or Petition.
2. If filing a Complaint, a completed Summons form for issuance by the Clerk.
3. Civil Case Cover Sheet form CM-010.
4. Complete Addendum to Civil Case Cover Sheet form LACIV 109 (Rev. 01/07), LASC Approved 03-04.
5. Payment in full of the filing fee, unless fees have been waived.
6. Signed order appointing the Guardian ad Litem, JC form FL-935, if the plaintiff or petitioner is a minor under 18 years of age, or if required by Court.
7. Additional copies of documents to be conformed by the Clerk. Copies of the cover sheet and this addendum must be served along with the summons and complaint, or other initiating pleading in the case.

LACIV 109 (Rev. 01/07)   **CIVIL CASE COVER SHEET ADDENDUM**   LASC, rule 2.0
LASC Approved 03-04   **AND STATEMENT OF LOCATION**

DO NOT FILE WITH THE COURT
THIS IS NOT AN ANSWER OR RESPONSE TO THE COMPLAINT

DISC-010

SUPERIOR COURT OF CALIFORNIA, COUNTY OF	
PLAINTIFF (Name):	CASE NUMBER
DEFENDANT (Name):	

CASE QUESTIONNAIRE—FOR LIMITED CIVIL CASES
(Under $25,000)

REQUESTING PARTY (Name):

RESPONDING PARTY (Name):

—INSTRUCTIONS—

A. The purpose of the case questionnaire is to help the parties settle their differences without spending a lot of money. This is accomplished by exchanging information about the case early in the lawsuit. The exchange of case questionnaires may be started only by a plaintiff (or cross-complainant) in a limited civil case. The case questionnaire is optional, and if plaintiff (or cross-complainant) exercises the option, only this form may be used.

B. **Instructions for plaintiffs (and cross-complainants)**

1. Under Code of Civil Procedure section 93, a plaintiff (or cross-complainant) may serve a completed case questionnaire and a blank questionnaire with a complaint (or cross-complaint).

2. This is the only way you can require defendants (or cross-defendants) to serve you with a completed case questionnaire.

C. **Instructions for defendants (and cross-defendants)**

1. If you have been served with a completed case questionnaire by a plaintiff (or cross-complainant), then you must fill in the blank case questionnaire. Your completed case questionnaire must be served on that same plaintiff (or cross-complainant) with your answer to the complaint (or cross-complaint).

2. **THIS IS NOT AN ANSWER OR RESPONSE TO THE COMPLAINT.**

D. **Instructions for all parties**

1. **ALL QUESTIONS REFER TO THE INCIDENT OR AGREEMENT IN THIS LAWSUIT ONLY.**

2. Answer each question. If a question is not applicable, answer "NA."

3. Your answers are not limited to your personal knowledge, but you are required to furnish information available to you or to anyone acting on your behalf, whether you are a plaintiff, defendant, cross-complainant, or cross-defendant.

4. Type or legibly print your answer below each question. If you cannot completely answer a question in the space provided on the case questionnaire, check the "attachment" box and put the number of the question and the complete answer on an attached sheet of paper or form MC-025. You should *not* put part of an answer on the case questionnaire and part on the attachment. You may put more than one answer on each attached page.

5. When you have completed the case questionnaire, sign the verification and serve the original.

6. You may compel compliance with these requirements under Code of Civil Procedure section 93.

7. **DO NOT FILE THIS CASE QUESTIONNAIRE WITH THE COURT.**

DO NOT FILE WITH THE COURT　　　　　　　　　　　　　　DISC-010

PLAINTIFF (Name):	CASE NUMBER:
DEFENDANT (Name):	

—QUESTIONS—

1. **FOR ALL CASES**

   a. State your name and street address.

   b. State your current business name and street address, the type of business entity, and your title.

   c. Describe in detail your claims or defenses and the facts on which they are based, giving relevant dates.

   ☐ See attachment for answer number 1c.

   d. State the name, street address, and telephone number of each person who has knowledge of facts relating to this lawsuit, and specify his or her area of knowledge.

   ☐ See attachment for answer number 1d.

   e. Describe each document or photograph that relates to the issues or facts. You are encouraged to attach a copy of each. For each that you have described but not attached, state the name, street address, and telephone number of each person who has it.

   ☐ See attachment for answer number 1e.

CASE QUESTIONNAIRE—FOR LIMITED CIVIL CASES
(Under $25,000)

DO NOT FILE WITH THE COURT

DISC-010

PLAINTIFF (Name):	CASE NUMBER:
DEFENDANT (Name):	

1. f. Describe each item of physical evidence that relates to the issues and facts; give its location; and state the name, street address, and telephone number of each person who has it.
   ☐ See attachment for answer number 1f.

   g. State the name and street address of each insurance company and the number of each policy that may cover you in whole or part for the damages claimed.
   ☐ See attachment for answer number 1g.

2. FOR PERSONAL INJURY OR PROPERTY DAMAGE CASES
   a. Describe each injury or illness that you received and your present complaints about each.
   ☐ See attachment for answer number 2a.

   b. State the name, street address, and telephone number of each physician, dentist, or other health care provider who treated or examined you; the type of treatment; the dates of treatment; and the charges by each to date.
   ☐ See attachment for answer number 2b.

   c. Itemize the medical expenses you anticipate in the future.
   ☐ See attachment for answer number 2c.

   d. Itemize your loss of income to date, give the name and street address of each source, and show how the loss is computed.
   ☐ See attachment for answer number 2d.

**CASE QUESTIONNAIRE—FOR LIMITED CIVIL CASES
(Under $25,000)**

DO NOT FILE WITH THE COURT　　　　　　　　　　DISC-010

PLAINTIFF *(Name):*	CASE NUMBER:
DEFENDANT *(Name):*	

2. e. Itemize the loss of income you anticipate in the future, give the name and street address of each source, and show how the loss is computed.
    ☐ See attachment for answer number 2e.

   f. Itemize your property damage, and state the amount or attach an itemized bill or estimate.
    ☐ See attachment for answer number 2f.

   9. Describe each other item of damage or cost that you claim, and state the amount.
    ☐ See attachment for answer number 2g.

3. FOR CASES BASED ON AGREEMENTS
    a. In addition to your answer to 1e, state all the terms and give the date of any part of the agreement that is not in writing.
    ☐ See attachment for answer number 3a.

    b. Describe each item of damage or cost you claim, state the amount, and show how it is computed.
    ☐ See attachment for answer number 3b.

VERIFICATION

I declare under penalty of perjury under the laws of the State of California that the foregoing is true and correct.

Date:

_____ ▶ _____
(TYPE OR PRINT NAME)   (SIGNATURE)

DISC-010 [Rev. January 1, 2007]

**CASE QUESTIONNAIRE—FOR LIMITED CIVIL CASES
(Under $25,000)**

FW-001 Request to Waive Court Fees

CONFIDENTIAL

If you are getting public benefits, are a low-income person, or do not have enough income to pay for household's basic needs and your court fees, you may use this form to ask the court to waive all or part of your court fees. The court may order you to answer questions about your finances. If the court waives the fees, you may still have to pay later if:
- You cannot give the court proof of your eligibility,
- Your financial situation improves during this case, or
- You settle your civil case for **$10,000** or more. The trial court that waives your fees will have a lien on any such settlement in the amount of the waived fees and costs. The court may also charge you any collection costs.

Clerk stamps date here when form is filed.

Fill in court name and street address:

Fill in case number and name:

Case Number:

Case Name:

(1) **Your Information** *(person asking the court to waive the fees):*
Name: _____
Street or mailing address: _____
City: _____ State: _____ Zip: _____
Phone number: _____

(2) **Your Job,** if you have one *(job title):* _____
Name of employer: _____
Employer's address: _____

(3) **Your lawyer,** if you have one *(name, firm or affiliation, address, phone number, and State Bar number):*
_____

a. The lawyer has agreed to advance all or a portion of your fees or costs *(check one):* Yes ☐ No ☐
b. *(If yes, your lawyer must sign here)* Lawyer's signature: _____
If your lawyer is not providing legal-aid type services based on your low income, you may have to go to a hearing to explain why you are asking the court to waive the fees.

(4) **What court's fees or costs are you asking to be waived?**
☐ Superior Court (See *Information Sheet on Waiver of Superior Court Fees and Costs* (form FW-001-INFO).)
☐ Supreme Court, Court of Appeal, or Appellate Division of Superior Court (See *Information Sheet on Waiver of Appellate Court Fees and Costs* (form APP-015/FW-015-INFO).)

(5) **Why are you asking the court to waive your court fees?**
a. ☐ I receive *(check all that apply):* ☐ Medi-Cal ☐ Food Stamps ☐ SSI ☐ SSP ☐ County Relief/General Assistance ☐ IHSS (In-Home Supportive Services) ☐ CalWORKS or Tribal TANF (Tribal Temporary Assistance for Needy Families) ☐ CAPI (Cash Assistance Program for Aged, Blind and Disabled)
b. ☐ My gross monthly household income (before deductions for taxes) is less than the amount listed below. *(If you check 5b you must fill out 7, 8 and 9 on page 2 of this form.)*

Family Size	Family Income	Family Size	Family Income	Family Size	Family Income	
1	$1,128.13	3	$1,907.30	5	$2,686.46	*If more than 6 people at home, add $389.59 for each extra person.*
2	$1,517.71	4	$2,296.88	6	$3,076.05	

c. ☐ I do not have enough income to pay for my household's basic needs *and* the court fees. I ask the court to *(check one):* ☐ waive all court fees ☐ waive some of the court fees ☐ let me make payments over time *(Explain):* _____ *(If you check 5c, you must fill out page 2.)*

(6) ☐ Check here if you asked the court to waive your court fees for this case in the last six months. *(If your previous request is reasonably available, please attach it to this form and check here:* ☐ *)*

I declare under penalty of perjury under the laws of the State of California that the information I have provided on this form and all attachments is true and correct.

Date: _____

Print your name here ▶ *Sign here*

Request to Waive Court Fees

Case Number:	

Your name: _____

*If you checked 5a on page 1, do not fill out below. If you checked 5b, fill out questions 7, 8, and 9 only. If you checked 5c, you **must** fill out this entire page. If you need more space, attach form MC-025 or attach a sheet of paper and write Financial Information and your name and case number at the top.*

⑦ ☐ Check here if your income changes a lot from month to month. Fill out below based on your average income for the past 12 months.

⑧ **Your Monthly Income**
  a. Gross monthly income *(before deductions):* $ _____
     List each payroll deduction and amount below:
     (1) _____ $ _____
     (2) _____ $ _____
     (3) _____ $ _____
     (4) _____ $ _____
  b. Total deductions *(add 8a (1)-(4) above):* $ _____
  c. Total monthly take-home pay *(8a minus 8b):* $ _____
  d. List the source and amount of *any* other income you get each month, including: spousal/child support, retirement, social security, disability, unemployment, military basic allowance for quarters (BAQ), veterans payments, dividends, interest, trust income, annuities, net business or rental income, reimbursement for job-related expenses, gambling or lottery winnings, etc.
     (1) _____ $ _____
     (2) _____ $ _____
     (3) _____ $ _____
     (4) _____ $ _____
  e. **Your total monthly income is** *(8c plus 8d):* $ _____

⑨ **Household Income**
  a. List all other persons living in your home and their income; include only your spouse and all individuals who depend in whole or in part on you for support, or on whom you depend in whole or in part for support.

	Name	Age	Relationship	Gross Monthly Income
(1)				$
(2)				$
(3)				$
(4)				$

  b. **Total monthly income of persons above:** $ _____

  Total monthly income *and* household income *(8e plus 9b):* $ _____

To list any other facts you want the court to know, such as unusual medical expenses, family emergencies, etc., attach form MC-025. Or attach a sheet of paper, and write Financial Information and your name and case number at the top. Check here if you attach another page. ☐

Important! **If your financial situation or ability to pay court fees improves, you must notify the court within five days on form FW-010.**

⑩ **Your Money and Property**
  a. Cash -------------------------------- $ _____
  b. All financial accounts *(List bank name and amount):*
     (1) _____ $ _____
     (2) _____ $ _____
     (3) _____ $ _____
     (4) _____ $ _____
  c. Cars, boats, and other vehicles

Make / Year	Fair Market Value	How Much You Still Owe
(1)	$	$
(2)	$	$
(3)	$	$

  d. Real estate

Address	Fair Market Value	How Much You Still Owe
(1)	$	$
(2)	$	$
(3)	$	$

  e. Other personal property (jewelry, furniture, furs, stocks, bonds, etc.):

Describe	Fair Market Value	How Much You Still Owe
(1)	$	$
(2)	$	$
(3)	$	$

⑪ **Your Monthly Expenses**
  (Do not include payroll deductions you already listed in 8b.)
  a. Rent or house payment & maintenance $ _____
  b. Food and household supplies $ _____
  c. Utilities and telephone $ _____
  d. Clothing $ _____
  e. Laundry and cleaning $ _____
  f. Medical and dental expenses $ _____
  g. Insurance (life, health, accident, etc.) $ _____
  h. School, child care $ _____
  i. Child, spousal support (another marriage) $ _____
  j. Transportation, gas, auto repair and insurance $ _____
  k. Installment payments (list each below):
     Paid to:
     (1) _____ $ _____
     (2) _____ $ _____
     (3) _____ $ _____
  l. Wages/earnings withheld by court order $ _____
  m. Any other monthly expenses *(list each below).* $
     Paid to: How Much?
     (1) _____ $ _____
     (2) _____ $ _____
     (3) _____ $ _____

  Total monthly expenses *(add 11a – 11m above):* $ _____

Request to Waive Court Fees

SUMMONS
(CITACION JUDICIAL)

SUM-100

FOR COURT USE ONLY
(SOLO PARA USO DE LA CORTE)

NOTICE TO DEFENDANT:
(AVISO AL DEMANDADO):

YOU ARE BEING SUED BY PLAINTIFF:
(LO ESTÁ DEMANDANDO EL DEMANDANTE):

NOTICE! You have been sued. The court may decide against you without your being heard unless you respond within 30 days. Read the information below.

You have 30 CALENDAR DAYS after this summons and legal papers are served on you to file a written response at this court and have a copy served on the plaintiff. A letter or phone call will not protect you. Your written response must be in proper legal form if you want the court to hear your case. There may be a court form that you can use for your response. You can find these court forms and more information at the California Courts Online Self-Help Center (*www.courtinfo.ca.gov/selfhelp*), your county law library, or the courthouse nearest you. If you cannot pay the filing fee, ask the court clerk for a fee waiver form. If you do not file your response on time, you may lose the case by default, and your wages, money, and property may be taken without further warning from the court.

There are other legal requirements. You may want to call an attorney right away. If you do not know an attorney, you may want to call an attorney referral service. If you cannot afford an attorney, you may be eligible for free legal services from a nonprofit legal services program. You can locate these nonprofit groups at the California Legal Services Web site (*www.lawhelpcalifornia.org*), the California Courts Online Self-Help Center (*www.courtinfo.ca.gov/selfhelp*), or by contacting your local court or county bar association. **NOTE:** The court has a statutory lien for waived fees and costs on any settlement or arbitration award of $10,000 or more in a civil case. The court's lien must be paid before the court will dismiss the case.

¡AVISO! Lo han demandado. Si no responde dentro de 30 días, la corte puede decidir en su contra sin escuchar su versión. Lea la información a continuación.

Tiene 30 DÍAS DE CALENDARIO después de que le entreguen esta citación y papeles legales para presentar una respuesta por escrito en esta corte y hacer que se entregue una copia al demandante. Una carta o una llamada telefónica no lo protegen. Su respuesta por escrito tiene que estar en formato legal correcto si desea que procesen su caso en la corte. Es posible que haya un formulario que usted pueda usar para su respuesta. Puede encontrar estos formularios de la corte y más información en el Centro de Ayuda de las Cortes de California (www.sucorte.ca.gov), en la biblioteca de leyes de su condado o en la corte que le quede más cerca. Si no puede pagar la cuota de presentación, pida al secretario de la corte que le dé un formulario de exención de pago de cuotas. Si no presenta su respuesta a tiempo, puede perder el caso por incumplimiento y la corte le podrá quitar su sueldo, dinero y bienes sin más advertencia.

Hay otros requisitos legales. Es recomendable que llame a un abogado inmediatamente. Si no conoce a un abogado, puede llamar a un servicio de remisión a abogados. Si no puede pagar a un abogado, es posible que cumpla con los requisitos para obtener servicios legales gratuitos de un programa de servicios legales sin fines de lucro. Puede encontrar estos grupos sin fines de lucro en el sitio web de California Legal Services, (www.lawhelpcalifornia.org), en el Centro de Ayuda de las Cortes de California, (www.sucorte.ca.gov) o poniéndose en contacto con la corte o el colegio de abogados locales. AVISO: Por ley, la corte tiene derecho a reclamar las cuotas y los costos exentos por imponer un gravamen sobre cualquier recuperación de $10,000 ó más de valor recibida mediante un acuerdo o una concesión de arbitraje en un caso de derecho civil. Tiene que pagar el gravamen de la corte antes de que la corte pueda desechar el caso.

The name and address of the court is:
(El nombre y dirección de la corte es):

CASE NUMBER:
(Número del Caso):

The name, address, and telephone number of plaintiff's attorney, or plaintiff without an attorney, is:
(El nombre, la dirección y el número de teléfono del abogado del demandante, o del demandante que no tiene abogado, es):

DATE: Clerk, by   , Deputy
(Fecha)   *(Secretario)*   *(Adjunto)*

(For proof of service of this summons, use Proof of Service of Summons *(form POS-010).)*
(Para prueba de entrega de esta citatión use el formulario Proof of Service of Summons, *(POS-010)).*

[SEAL]

NOTICE TO THE PERSON SERVED: You are served
1. ☐ as an individual defendant.
2. ☐ as the person sued under the fictitious name of *(specify):*
3. ☐ on behalf of *(specify):*

     under: ☐ CCP 416.10 (corporation)   ☐ CCP 416.60 (minor)
             ☐ CCP 416.20 (defunct corporation)   ☐ CCP 416.70 (conservatee)
             ☐ CCP 416.40 (association or partnership) ☐ CCP 416.90 (authorized person)
             ☐ other *(specify):*

4. ☐ by personal delivery on *(date):*

Form Adopted for Mandatory Use
Judicial Council of California
SUM-100 [Rev. July 1, 2009]

SUMMONS

Code of Civil Procedure §§ 412.20, 465
www.courtinfo.ca.gov

POS-015

ATTORNEY OR PARTY WITHOUT ATTORNEY *(Name, State Bar number, and address)*:	FOR COURT USE ONLY
TELEPHONE NO.: FAX NO. *(Optional)*: E-MAIL ADDRESS *(Optional)*: ATTORNEY FOR *(Name)*:	

SUPERIOR COURT OF CALIFORNIA, COUNTY OF
    STREET ADDRESS:
    MAILING ADDRESS:
    CITY AND ZIP CODE:
    BRANCH NAME:

PLAINTIFF/PETITIONER:

DEFENDANT/RESPONDENT:

NOTICE AND ACKNOWLEDGMENT OF RECEIPT—CIVIL	CASE NUMBER:

TO *(insert name of party being served)*: _____

NOTICE

The summons and other documents identified below are being served pursuant to section 415.30 of the California Code of Civil Procedure. Your failure to complete this form and return it within 20 days from the date of mailing shown below may subject you (or the party on whose behalf you are being served) to liability for the payment of any expenses incurred in serving a summons on you in any other manner permitted by law.

If you are being served on behalf of a corporation, an unincorporated association (including a partnership), or other entity, this form must be signed by you in the name of such entity or by a person authorized to receive service of process on behalf of such entity. In all other cases, this form must be signed by you personally or by a person authorized by you to acknowledge receipt of summons. If you return this form to the sender, service of a summons is deemed complete on the day you sign the acknowledgment of receipt below.

Date of mailing:

_____   ▶   _____
           (TYPE OR PRINT NAME)   (SIGNATURE OF SENDER—MUST NOT BE A PARTY IN THIS CASE)

ACKNOWLEDGMENT OF RECEIPT

This acknowledges receipt of *(to be completed by sender before mailing)*:
1. ☐ A copy of the summons and of the complaint.
2. ☐ Other *(specify)*:

(To be completed by recipient):

Date this form is signed:

_____   ▶   _____
(TYPE OR PRINT YOUR NAME AND NAME OF ENTITY, IF ANY,   (SIGNATURE OF PERSON ACKNOWLEDGING RECEIPT, WITH TITLE IF
ON WHOSE BEHALF THIS FORM IS SIGNED)   ACKNOWLEDGMENT IS MADE ON BEHALF OF ANOTHER PERSON OR ENTITY)

Form Adopted for Mandatory Use
Judicial Council of California
POS-015 [Rev. January 1, 2005]

NOTICE AND ACKNOWLEDGMENT OF RECEIPT — CIVIL

Code of Civil Procedure,
§§ 415.30, 417.10
www.courtinfo.ca.gov

POS-030

ATTORNEY OR PARTY WITHOUT ATTORNEY *(Name, State Bar number, and address)*:	FOR COURT USE ONLY
TELEPHONE NO.:	
E-MAIL ADDRESS *(Optional)*: FAX NO. *(Optional)*:	
ATTORNEY FOR *(Name)*:	

SUPERIOR COURT OF CALIFORNIA, COUNTY OF
STREET ADDRESS:
MAILING ADDRESS:
CITY AND ZIP CODE:
BRANCH NAME:

PETITIONER/PLAINTIFF:

RESPONDENT/DEFENDANT:

PROOF OF SERVICE BY FIRST-CLASS MAIL—CIVIL	CASE NUMBER:

(Do not use this Proof of Service to show service of a Summons and Complaint.)

1. I am over 18 years of age and **not a party to this action.** I am a resident of or employed in the county where the mailing took place.

2. My residence or business address is:

3. On *(date)*:   I mailed from *(city and state)*:
   the following **documents** *(specify)*:

   ☐ The documents are listed in the *Attachment to Proof of Service by First-Class Mail—Civil (Documents Served)* (form POS-030(D)).

4. I served the documents by enclosing them in an envelope and *(check one)*:
   a. ☐ **depositing** the sealed envelope with the United States Postal Service with the postage fully prepaid.
   b. ☐ **placing** the envelope for collection and mailing following our ordinary business practices. I am readily familiar with this business's practice for collecting and processing correspondence for mailing. On the same day that correspondence is placed for collection and mailing, it is deposited in the ordinary course of business with the United States Postal Service in a sealed envelope with postage fully prepaid.

5. The envelope was addressed and mailed as follows:
   a. **Name** of person served:
   b. **Address** of person served:

   ☐ The name and address of each person to whom I mailed the documents is listed in the *Attachment to Proof of Service by First-Class Mail—Civil (Persons Served)* (POS-030(P)).

I declare under penalty of perjury under the laws of the State of California that the foregoing is true and correct.

Date:

_____   ▶   _____
(TYPE OR PRINT NAME OF PERSON COMPLETING THIS FORM)   (SIGNATURE OF PERSON COMPLETING THIS FORM)

Form Approved for Optional Use
Judicial Council of California
POS-030 [New January 1, 2005]

PROOF OF SERVICE BY FIRST-CLASS MAIL—CIVIL
(Proof of Service)

Code of Civil Procedure, §§ 1013, 1013a
www.courtinfo.ca.gov

INFORMATION SHEET FOR PROOF OF SERVICE BY FIRST-CLASS MAIL—CIVIL

(This information sheet is not part of the Proof of Service and does not need to be copied, served, or filed.)

NOTE: This form should **not** be used for proof of service of a summons and complaint. For that purpose, use *Proof of Service of Summons* (form POS-010).

Use these instructions to complete the *Proof of Service by First-Class Mail—Civil* (form POS-030).

A person over 18 years of age must serve the documents. There are two main ways to serve documents: (1) by personal delivery and (2) by mail. Certain documents must be personally served. You must determine whether personal service is required for a document. Use the *Proof of Personal Service–Civil* (form POS-020) if the documents were personally served.

The person who served the documents by mail must complete a proof of service form for the documents served. **You cannot serve documents if you are a party to the action.**

INSTRUCTIONS FOR THE PERSON WHO SERVED THE DOCUMENTS

The proof of service should be printed or typed. If you have Internet access, a fillable version of the Proof of Service form is available at *www.courtinfo.ca.gov/forms*.

Complete the top section of the proof of service form as follows:

First box, left side: In this box print the name, address, and telephone number of the person *for* whom you served the documents.

Second box, left side: Print the name of the county in which the legal action is filed and the court's address in this box. The address for the court should be the same as on the documents that you served.

Third box, left side: Print the names of the Petitioner/Plaintiff and Respondent/Defendant in this box. Use the same names as are on the documents that you served.

First box, top of form, right side: Leave this box blank for the court's use.

Second box, right side: Print the case number in this box. The case number should be the same as the case number on the documents that you served.

Complete items 1–5 as follows:

1. You are stating that you are over the age of 18 and that you are not a party to this action. You are also stating that you either live in or are employed in the county where the mailing took place.

2. Print your home or business address.

3. Provide the date and place of the mailing and list the name of each document that you mailed. If you need more space to list the documents, check the box in item 3, complete the *Attachment to Proof of Service by First-Class Mail—Civil (Documents Served)* (form POS-030(D)), and attach it to form POS-030.

4. For item 4:

    Check box a if you personally put the documents in the regular U.S. mail.
    Check box b if you put the documents in the mail at your place of business.

5. Provide the name and address of each person to whom you mailed the documents. If you mailed the documents to more than one person, check the box in item 5, complete the *Attachment to Proof of Service by First-Class Mail—Civil (Persons Served)* (form POS-030(P)), and attach it to form POS-030.

At the bottom, fill in the date on which you signed the form, print your name, and sign the form. By signing, you are stating under penalty of perjury that all the information you have provided on form POS-030 is true and correct.

POS-030 [New January 1, 2005]

PROOF OF SERVICE BY FIRST CLASS MAIL—CIVIL
(Proof of Service)

CIV-010

ATTORNEY (Name, State Bar number, and address):	FOR COURT USE ONLY
TELEPHONE NO.: FAX NO. (Optional): E-MAIL ADDRESS (Optional): ATTORNEY FOR (Name):	

SUPERIOR COURT OF CALIFORNIA, COUNTY OF
STREET ADDRESS:
MAILING ADDRESS:
CITY AND ZIP CODE:
BRANCH NAME:

PLAINTIFF/PETITIONER:

DEFENDANT/RESPONDENT:

APPLICATION AND ORDER FOR APPOINTMENT OF GUARDIAN AD LITEM—CIVIL ☐ EX PARTE	CASE NUMBER:

NOTE: This form is for use in civil proceedings in which a party is a minor, an incapacitated person, or a person for whom a conservator has been appointed. A party who seeks the appointment of a guardian ad litem in a family law or juvenile proceeding should use form FL-935. A party who seeks the appointment of a guardian ad litem in a probate proceeding should use form DE-350/GC-100. An individual cannot act as a guardian ad litem unless he or she is represented by an attorney or is an attorney.

1. Applicant *(name):* is
   a. ☐ the parent of *(name):*
   b. ☐ the guardian of *(name):*
   c. ☐ the conservator of *(name):*
   d. ☐ a party to the suit.
   e. ☐ the minor to be represented *(if the minor is 14 years of age or older).*
   f. ☐ another interested person *(specify capacity):*

2. This application seeks the appointment of the following person as guardian ad litem *(state name, address, and telephone number):*

3. The guardian ad litem is to represent the interests of the following person *(state name, address, and telephone number):*

4. The person to be represented is:
   a. ☐ a minor *(date of birth):*
   b. ☐ an incompetent person.
   c. ☐ a person for whom a conservator has been appointed.

5. The court should appoint a guardian ad litem because:
   a. ☐ the person named in item 3 has a cause or causes of action on which suit should be brought *(describe):*

☐ Continued on Attachment 5a.

Form Adopted for Mandatory Use
Judicial Council of California
CIV-010 [Rev. January 1, 2008]

APPLICATION AND ORDER FOR APPOINTMENT OF GUARDIAN AD LITEM—CIVIL

Code of Civil Procedure, § 372 et seq.

	CIV-010
PLAINTIFF/PETITIONER: DEFENDANT/RESPONDENT:	CASE NUMBER:

5. b. ☐ more than 10 days have elapsed since the summons in the above-entitled matter was served on the person named in item 3, and no application for the appointment of a guardian ad litem has been made by the person identified in item 3 or any other person.

   c. ☐ the person named in item 3 has no guardian or conservator of his or her estate.

   d. ☐ the appointment of a guardian ad litem is necessary for the following reasons *(specify)*:

   ☐ Continued on Attachment 5d.

6. The proposed guardian ad litem's relationship to the person he or she will be representing is:
   a. ☐ related *(state relationship)*:
   b. ☐ not related *(specify capacity)*:

7. The proposed guardian ad litem is fully competent and qualified to understand and protect the rights of the person he or she will represent and has no interests adverse to the interests of that person. *(If there are any issues of competency or qualification or any possible adverse interests, describe and explain why the proposed guardian should nevertheless be appointed)*:

   ☐ Continued on Attachment 7.

_____ ▶ _____
(TYPE OR PRINT NAME)   (SIGNATURE OF ATTORNEY)

I declare under penalty of perjury under the laws of the State of California that the foregoing is true and correct.
Date:

_____ ▶ _____
(TYPE OR PRINT NAME)   (SIGNATURE OF APPLICANT)

CONSENT TO ACT AS GUARDIAN AD LITEM

I consent to the appointment as guardian ad litem under the above petition.
Date:

_____ ▶ _____
(TYPE OR PRINT NAME)   (SIGNATURE OF PROPOSED GUARDIAN AD LITEM)

ORDER ☐ EX PARTE

THE COURT FINDS that it is reasonable and necessary to appoint a guardian ad litem for the person named in item 3 of the application, as requested.

THE COURT ORDERS that *(name)*:
is hereby appointed as the guardian ad litem for *(name)*:
for the reasons set forth in item 5 of the application.
Date:

JUDICIAL OFFICER
☐ SIGNATURE FOLLOWS LAST ATTACHMENT

APPLICATION AND ORDER FOR APPOINTMENT OF GUARDIAN AD LITEM—CIVIL

POS-010

ATTORNEY OR PARTY WITHOUT ATTORNEY *(Name, State Bar number, and address)*:	FOR COURT USE ONLY
TELEPHONE NO.: FAX NO. *(Optional):* E-MAIL ADDRESS *(Optional):* ATTORNEY FOR *(Name):*	

SUPERIOR COURT OF CALIFORNIA, COUNTY OF
STREET ADDRESS:
MAILING ADDRESS:
CITY AND ZIP CODE:
BRANCH NAME:

PLAINTIFF/PETITIONER:

DEFENDANT/RESPONDENT:

PROOF OF SERVICE OF SUMMONS	CASE NUMBER:
	Ref. No. or File No.:

(Separate proof of service is required for each party served.)

1. At the time of service I was at least 18 years of age and not a party to this action.
2. I served copies of:
   a. ☐ summons
   b. ☐ complaint
   c. ☐ Alternative Dispute Resolution (ADR) package
   d. ☐ Civil Case Cover Sheet *(served in complex cases only)*
   e. ☐ cross-complaint
   f. ☐ other *(specify documents):*

3. a. Party served *(specify name of party as shown on documents served):*

   b. ☐ Person (other than the party in item 3a) served on behalf of an entity or as an authorized agent (and not a person under item 5b on whom substituted service was made) *(specify name and relationship to the party named in item 3a):*

4. Address where the party was served:

5. I served the party *(check proper box)*
   a. ☐ **by personal service.** I personally delivered the documents listed in item 2 to the party or person authorized to receive service of process for the party (1) on *(date):*   (2) at *(time):*
   b. ☐ **by substituted service.** On *(date):*   at *(time):*   I left the documents listed in item 2 with or in the presence of *(name and title or relationship to person indicated in item 3):*

   (1) ☐ **(business)** a person at least 18 years of age apparently in charge at the office or usual place of business of the person to be served. I informed him or her of the general nature of the papers.

   (2) ☐ **(home)** a competent member of the household (at least 18 years of age) at the dwelling house or usual place of abode of the party. I informed him or her of the general nature of the papers.

   (3) ☐ **(physical address unknown)** a person at least 18 years of age apparently in charge at the usual mailing address of the person to be served, other than a United States Postal Service post office box. I informed him or her of the general nature of the papers.

   (4) ☐ I thereafter mailed (by first-class, postage prepaid) copies of the documents to the person to be served at the place where the copies were left (Code Civ. Proc., § 415.20). I mailed the documents on *(date):*   from *(city):*   **or** ☐ a declaration of mailing is attached.

   (5) ☐ I attach a **declaration of diligence** stating actions taken first to attempt personal service.

Page 1 of 2

Form Adopted for Mandatory Use
Judicial Council of California
POS-010 [Rev. January 1, 2007]

PROOF OF SERVICE OF SUMMONS

Code of Civil Procedure, § 417.10

PLAINTIFF/PETITIONER:	CASE NUMBER:
DEFENDANT/RESPONDENT:	

5. c. ☐ **by mail and acknowledgment of receipt of service.** I mailed the documents listed in item 2 to the party, to the address shown in item 4, by first-class mail, postage prepaid,

    (1) on *(date):*   (2) from *(city):*

    (3) ☐ with two copies of the *Notice and Acknowledgment of Receipt* and a postage-paid return envelope addressed to me. *(Attach completed* Notice and Acknowledgement of Receipt.*)* (Code Civ. Proc., § 415.30.)

    (4) ☐ to an address outside California with return receipt requested. (Code Civ. Proc., § 415.40.)

  d. ☐ **by other means** *(specify means of service and authorizing code section):*

    ☐ Additional page describing service is attached.

6. The "Notice to the Person Served" (on the summons) was completed as follows:
   a. ☐ as an individual defendant.
   b. ☐ as the person sued under the fictitious name of *(specify):*
   c. ☐ as occupant.
   d. ☐ On behalf of *(specify):*
      under the following Code of Civil Procedure section:

      ☐ 416.10 (corporation)   ☐ 415.95 (business organization, form unknown)
      ☐ 416.20 (defunct corporation)   ☐ 416.60 (minor)
      ☐ 416.30 (joint stock company/association)   ☐ 416.70 (ward or conservatee)
      ☐ 416.40 (association or partnership)   ☐ 416.90 (authorized person)
      ☐ 416.50 (public entity)   ☐ 415.46 (occupant)
                                           ☐ other:

7. **Person who served papers**
   a. Name:
   b. Address:
   c. Telephone number:
   d. **The fee** for service was: $
   e. I am:
      (1) ☐ not a registered California process server.
      (2) ☐ exempt from registration under Business and Professions Code section 22350(b).
      (3) ☐ a registered California process server:
         (i) ☐ owner   ☐ employee   ☐ independent contractor.
         (ii) Registration No.:
         (iii) County:

8. ☐ **I declare** under penalty of perjury under the laws of the State of California that the foregoing is true and correct.

   or

9. ☐ **I am a California sheriff or marshal and** I certify that the foregoing is true and correct.

Date:

_____   ▶   _____
(NAME OF PERSON WHO SERVED PAPERS/SHERIFF OR MARSHAL)   (SIGNATURE)

POS-010 [Rev. January 1, 2007]   **PROOF OF SERVICE OF SUMMONS**

PLD-PI-003

ATTORNEY OR PARTY WITHOUT ATTORNEY (NAME AND ADDRESS):	TELEPHONE NO.:	FOR COURT USE ONLY
ATTORNEY FOR (NAME):		
Insert name of court, judicial district or branch court, if any, and post office and street address:		
PLAINTIFF:		
DEFENDANT:		

ANSWER—Personal Injury, Property Damage, Wrongful Death
☐ **COMPLAINT OF** (name):
☐ **CROSS-COMPLAINT OF** (name):

CASE NUMBER:

1. This pleading, including attachments and exhibits, consists of the following number of pages: _____

DEFENDANT OR CROSS-DEFENDANT (name):

2. ☐ Generally **denies** each allegation of the unverified complaint or cross-complaint.

3. a. ☐ DENIES each allegation of the following numbered paragraphs:

   b. ☐ ADMITS each allegation of the following numbered paragraphs:

   c. ☐ DENIES, ON INFORMATION AND BELIEF, each allegation of the following numbered paragraphs:

   d. ☐ DENIES, BECAUSE OF LACK OF SUFFICIENT INFORMATION OR BELIEF TO ANSWER, each allegation of the following numbered paragraphs:

   e. ☐ ADMITS the following allegations and generally denies all other allegations:

Form Approved for Optional Use
Judicial Council of California
PLD-PI-003 [Rev. January 1, 2007]

ANSWER—Personal Injury, Property Damage, Wrongful Death

Code of Civil Procedure, § 425.12
www.courtinfo.ca.gov

SHORT TITLE:	CASE NUMBER:

PLD-PI-003

ANSWER—Personal Injury, Property Damage, Wrongful Death

    f. ☐ DENIES the following allegations and admits all other allegations:

    g. ☐ Other *(specify)*:

AFFIRMATIVELY ALLEGES AS A DEFENSE

4. ☐ The comparative fault of plaintiff or cross-complainant *(name)*:
   as follows:

5. ☐ The expiration of the Statute of Limitations as follows:

6. ☐ Other *(specify)*:

7. DEFENDANT OR CROSS - DEFENDANT PRAYS
   For costs of suit and that plaintiff or cross-complainant take nothing.
   ☐ Other *(specify)*:

_____   _____
(Type or print name)   (Signature of party or attorney)

PLD-C-010

ATTORNEY OR PARTY WITHOUT ATTORNEY (NAME AND ADDRESS): TELEPHONE:	FOR COURT USE ONLY:
ATTORNEY FOR (NAME):	

Insert name of court, judicial district or branch court, if any, and post office and street address:

PLAINTIFF:

DEFENDANT:

ANSWER—Contract
☐ TO COMPLAINT OF (name):
☐ TO CROSS-COMPLAINT (name):

CASE NUMBER:

1. This pleading, including attachments and exhibits, consists of the following number of pages: _____
2. DEFENDANT (name):
   answers the complaint or cross-complaint as follows:
3. Check ONLY ONE of the next two boxes:
   a. ☐ Defendant generally denies each statement of the complaint or cross-complaint. *(Do not check this box if the verified complaint or cross-complaint demands more than $1,000.)*
   b. ☐ Defendant admits that all of the statements of the complaint or cross-complaint are true EXCEPT:
      (1) Defendant claims the following statements are false *(use paragraph numbers or explain):*

      ☐ Continued on Attachment 3.b.(1).
      (2) Defendant has no information or belief that the following statements are true, so defendant denies them *(use paragraph numbers or explain):*

      ☐ Continued on Attachment 3.b.(2).

If this form is used to answer a cross-complaint, plaintiff means cross-complainant and defendant means cross-defendant.

Form Approved for Optional Use
Judicial Council of California
PLD-C-010 [Rev. January 1, 2007]

ANSWER—Contract

Code of Civil Procedure, § 425.12
www.courtinfo.ca.gov

SHORT TITLE:	CASE NUMBER:

PLD-C-010

ANSWER—Contract

4. ☐ AFFIRMATIVE DEFENSES Defendant alleges the following additional reasons that plaintiff is not entitled to recover anything:

☐ Continued on Attachment 4.

5. ☐ Other

6. DEFENDANT PRAYS
   a. that plaintiff take nothing.
   b. ☐ for costs of suit.
   c. ☐ other *(specify):*

.... _____
(Type or print name)   (Signature of party or attorney)

ANSWER—Contract

PLD-050

ATTORNEY OR PARTY WITHOUT ATTORNEY (Name, State Bar number, and address):	TELEPHONE NO.	FOR COURT USE ONLY
ATTORNEY FOR (Name):		

NAME OF COURT:
STREET ADDRESS:
MAILING ADDRESS:
CITY AND ZIP CODE:
BRANCH NAME:

PLAINTIFF:

DEFENDANT:

GENERAL DENIAL	CASE NUMBER:

You MUST use this form for your general denial if the amount asked for in the complaint or the value of the property involved is $1000 or less.

You MAY use this form if:
1. The complaint is not verified, OR
2. The complaint is verified, and the action is subject to the economic litigation procedures of the municipal and justice courts, EXCEPT

You MAY NOT use this form if the complaint is verified and involves a claim for more than $1000 that has been assigned to a third party for collection.

(See Code of Civil Procedure sections 90-100, 431.30, and 431.40).

---

1. DEFENDANT (name):
   generally denies each and every allegation of plaintiff's complaint.

2. ☐ DEFENDANT states the following FACTS as separate affirmative defenses to plaintiff's complaint *(attach additional pages if necessary)*:

Date:

....
(TYPE OR PRINT NAME)   ▶   (SIGNATURE OF DEFENDANT OR ATTORNEY)

If you have a claim for damages or other relief against the plaintiff, the law may require you to state your claim in a special pleading called a cross-complaint or you may lose your claim. (See Code of Civil Procedure sections 426.10–426.40.)

The original of this General Denial must be filed with the clerk of this court with proof that a copy was served on each plaintiff's attorney and on each plaintiff not represented by an attorney. *(See the other side for a proof of service.)*

Form Adopted for Mandatory Use
Judicial Council of California
PLD-050 [Rev. January 1, 2007]

GENERAL DENIAL

Code Civ. Procedure, §§ 431.30, 431.40
www.courtinfo.ca.gov

	PLD-050
PLAINTIFF (name):	CASE NUMBER:
DEFENDANT (name):	

PROOF OF SERVICE
☐ Personal Service   ☐ Mail

> A General Denial may be served by anyone at least 18 years of age EXCEPT you or any other party to this legal action. Service is made in one of the following ways:
> (1) Personally delivering a copy to the attorney for the other party or, if no attorney, to the other party.
>   **OR**
> (2) Mailing a copy, postage prepaid, to the last known address of the attorney for the other party or, if no attorney, to the other party.
> Be sure whoever serves the General Denial fills out and signs a proof of service. File the proof of service with the court as soon as the General Denial is served.

1. At the time of service I was at least 18 years of age and **not a party to this legal action.**

2. I served a copy of the General Denial as follows (check either a or b):

   a. ☐ **Personal service.** I personally delivered the General Denial as follows:
      (1) Name of person served:
      (2) Address where served:

      (3) Date served:
      (4) Time served:

   b. ☐ **Mail.** I deposited the General Denial in the United States mail, in a sealed envelope with postage fully prepaid. The envelope was addressed and mailed as follows:
      (1) Name of person served:
      (2) Address:

      (3) Date of mailing:
      (4) Place of mailing (city and state):
      (5) I am a resident of or employed in the county where the General Denial was mailed.

   c. My residence or business address is (specify):

   d. My phone number is (specify):

I declare under penalty of perjury under the laws of the State of California that the foregoing is true and correct.

Date:

....
(TYPE OR PRINT NAME OF PERSON WHO SERVED THE GENERAL DENIAL)

▶ _____
(SIGNATURE OF PERSON WHO SERVED THE GENERAL DENIAL)

GENERAL DENIAL
(Proof of Service)

PLD-PI-002

ATTORNEY OR PARTY WITHOUT ATTORNEY *(Name, state bar number, and address)*:	FOR COURT USE ONLY
TELEPHONE NO: FAX NO. *(Optional)*:	
E-MAIL ADDRESS *(Optional)*:	
ATTORNEY FOR *(Name)*:	

NAME OF COURT:
STREET ADDRESS:
MAILING ADDRESS:
CITY AND ZIP CODE:
BRANCH NAME:

SHORT TITLE:

CROSS-COMPLAINANT:

CROSS-DEFENDANT:

☐ DOES 1 TO _____

CROSS-COMPLAINT—Personal Injury, Property Damage, Wrongful Death
    ☐ **AMENDED** *(Number)*:
Causes of Action *(check all that apply)*:
☐ Apportionment of Fault   ☐ Declaratory Relief
☐ Indemnification   ☐ Other *(specify)*:

Jurisdiction *(check all that apply)*:
☐ **ACTION IS A LIMITED CIVIL CASE ($25,000 or less)**
☐ **ACTION IS AN UNLIMITED CIVIL CASE (exceeds $25,000)**
    It ☐ is ☐ is not reclassified as unlimited by this cross-complaint

CASE NUMBER:

1. CROSS-COMPLAINANT *(name)*:

    alleges causes of action against CROSS-DEFENDANT *(name)*:

2. This pleading, including exhibits and attachments, consists of the following number of pages: _____

3. Each cross-complainant named above is a competent adult
    a. ☐ **except** cross-complainant *(name)*:
        (1) ☐ a corporation qualified to do business in California
        (2) ☐ an unincorporated entity *(describe)*:
        (3) ☐ a public entity *(desciribe)*:
        (4) ☐ a minor ☐ an adult
            (a) ☐ for whom a guardian or conservator of the estate or a guardian ad litern has been appointed
            (b) ☐ other *(specify)*:
        (5) ☐ other *(specify)*:

☐ Information about additional cross-complainants who are not competent adults is contained in Cross-Complaint—Attachment 3.

Form Approved for Optional Use
Judicial Council of California
PLD-PI-002 [Rev. January 1, 2007]

**CROSS-COMPLAINT—Personal Injury,
Property Damage, Wrongful Death**

Code of Civil Procedure, § 425.12

SHORT TITLE:	CASE NUMBER:

PLD-PI-002

4. Each cross-defendant named above is a natural person
    a. ☐ **except** cross-defendant *(name)*:
        (1) ☐ a business organization, form unknown
        (2) ☐ a corporation
        (3) ☐ an unincorporated entity *(describe)*:
        (4) ☐ a public entity *(describe)*:
        (5) ☐ other *(specify)*:
    b. ☐ **except** cross-defendant *(name)*:
        (1) ☐ a business organization, form unknown
        (2) ☐ a corporation
        (3) ☐ an unincorporated entity *(describe)*:
        (4) ☐ a public entity *(describe)*:
        (5) ☐ other *(specify)*:

☐ Information about additional cross-defendants who are not natural persons is contained in Cross-Complaint—Attachment 4.

5. The true names and capacities of cross-defendants sued as Does are unknown to cross-complainant.

6. ☐ Cross-complainant is required to comply with a claims statute, **and**
    a. ☐ has complied with applicable claims statutes, **or**
    b. ☐ is excused from complying because *(specify)*:

7. ☐ _____ **Cause of Action—Indemnification**
    (NUMBER)
    a. Cross-defendants were the agents, employees, co-venturers, partners, or in some manner agents or principals, or both, for each other and were acting within the course and scope of their agency or employment.
    b. The principal action alleges, among other things, conduct entitling plaintiff to compensatory damages against me. I contend that I am not liable for events and occurrences described in plaintiff's complaint.
    c. If I am found in some manner responsible to plaintiff or to anyone else as a result of the incidents and occurrences described in plaintiff's complaint, my liability would be based solely upon a derivative form of liability not resulting from my conduct, but only from an obligation imposed upon me by law; therefore, I would be entitled to complete indemnity from each cross-defendant.

8. ☐ _____ **Cause of Action—Apportionment of Fault**
    (NUMBER)
    a. Each cross-defendant was responsible, in whole or in part, for the injuries, if any, suffered by plaintiff.
    b. If I am judged liable to plaintiff, each cross-defendant should be required: (1) to pay a share of plaintiffs judgment which is in proportion to the comparative negligence of that cross-defendant in causing plaintiff's damages; and (2) to reimburse me for any payments I make to plaintiff in excess of my proportional share of all cross-defendants' negligence.

CROSS-COMPLAINT—Personal Injury, Property Damage, Wrongful Death

SHORT TITLE:	CASE NUMBER:

PLD-PI-002

9. ☐ _____ **Cause of Action—Declaratory Relief**
   (NUMBER)

   An actual controversy exists between the parties concerning their respective rights and duties because cross-complainant contends and cross-defendant disputes ☐ as specified in Cross-Complaint—Attachment 9
   ☐ as follows:

10. ☐ _____ **Cause of Action—*(specify)*:**
    (NUMBER)

11. ☐ The following additional causes of action are attached and the statements below apply to each *(in each of the attachments, "plaintiff" means "cross-complainant" and "defendant" means "cross-defendant")*:
    a. ☐ Motor Vehicle
    b. ☐ General Negligence
    c. ☐ Intentional Tort
    d. ☐ Products Liability
    e. ☐ Premises Liability
    f. ☐ Other *(specify)*:

12. **CROSS-COMPLAINANT PRAYS** for judgment for costs of suit; for such relief as is fair, just, and equitable; and for
    a. ☐ total and complete indemnity for any judgments rendered against me.
    b. ☐ judgment in a proportionate share from each cross-defendant.
    c. ☐ a judicial determination that cross-defendants were the legal cause of any injuries and damages sustained by plaintiff and that cross-defendants indemnify me, either completely or partially, for any sums of money which may be recovered against me by plaintiff.
    d. ☐ compensatory damages
        (1) ☐ (unlimited civil cases) according to proof.
        (2) ☐ (limited civil cases) in the amount of: $
    e. ☐ other *(specify)*:

13. ☐ The paragraphs of this cross-complaint alleged on information and belief are as follows *(specify paragraph numbers)*:

Date:

_____   ▶   _____
(TYPE OR PRINT NAME)   (SIGNATURE OF CROSS-COMPLAINANT OR ATTORNEY)

PLD-PI-002 [Rev. January 1, 2007] **CROSS-COMPLAINT—Personal Injury, Property Damage, Wrongful Death**

CIV-100

ATTORNEY OR PARTY WITHOUT ATTORNEY *(Name, State Bar number, and address)*:	FOR COURT USE ONLY
TELEPHONE NO.: FAX NO. *(Optional)*: E-MAIL ADDRESS *(Optional)*: ATTORNEY FOR *(Name)*:	

SUPERIOR COURT OF CALIFORNIA, COUNTY OF
STREET ADDRESS:
MAILING ADDRESS:
CITY AND ZIP CODE:
BRANCH NAME:

PLAINTIFF/PETITIONER:

DEFENDANT/RESPONDENT:

REQUEST FOR (Application)	☐ Entry of Default ☐ Clerk's Judgment ☐ Court Judgment	CASE NUMBER:

1. **TO THE CLERK:** On the complaint or cross-complaint filed
   a. on *(date)*:
   b. by *(name)*:
   c. ☐ Enter default of defendant *(names)*:

   d. ☐ I request a court judgment under Code of Civil Procedure sections 585(b), 585(c), 989, etc., against defendant *(names)*:

   (Testimony required. Apply to the clerk for a hearing date, unless the court will enter a judgment on an affidavit under Code Civ. Proc., § 585(d).)
   e. ☐ Enter clerk's judgment
      (1) ☐ for restitution of the premises only and issue a writ of execution on the judgment. Code of Civil Procedure section 1174(c) does not apply. (Code Civ. Proc., § 1169.)
         ☐ Include in the judgment all tenants, subtenants, named claimants, and other occupants of the premises. The *Prejudgment Claim of Right to Possession* was served in compliance with Code of Civil Procedure section 415.46.
      (2) ☐ under Code of Civil Procedure section 585(a). *(Complete the declaration under Code Civ. Proc., § 585.5 on the reverse (item 5).)*
      (3) ☐ for default previously entered on *(date)*:

2. **Judgment to be entered.**

	Amount	Credits acknowledged	Balance
a. Demand of complaint	$	$	$
b. Statement of damages *			
(1) Special	$	$	$
(2) General	$	$	$
c. Interest	$	$	$
d. Costs *(see reverse)*	$	$	$
e. Attorney fees	$	$	$
f. **TOTALS**	$	$	$

   g. **Daily damages** were demanded in complaint at the rate of: $ per day beginning *(date)*:
   (* Personal injury or wrongful death actions; Code Civ. Proc., § 425.11.)

3. ☐ *(Check if filed in an unlawful detainer case)* **Legal document assistant or unlawful detainer assistant** information is on the reverse *(complete item 4).*

Date:

_____ ▶ _____
(TYPE OR PRINT NAME)   (SIGNATURE OF PLAINTIFF OR ATTORNEY FOR PLAINTIFF)

FOR COURT USE ONLY
(1) ☐ Default entered as requested on *(date)*:
(2) ☐ Default NOT entered as requested *(state reason)*:

Clerk, by _____, Deputy

Form Adopted for Mandatory Use
Judicial Council of California
CIV-100 [Rev. January 1, 2007]

REQUEST FOR ENTRY OF DEFAULT
(Application to Enter Default)

Code of Civil Procedure,
§§ 585–587, 1169
www.courtinfo.ca.gov

PLAINTIFF/PETITIONER:	CASE NUMBER:
DEFENDANT/RESPONDENT:	

CIV-100

4. **Legal document assistant or unlawful detainer assistant (Bus. & Prof. Code, § 6400 et seq.).** A legal document assistant or unlawful detainer assistant ☐ did ☐ did **not** for compensation give advice or assistance with this form. *(If declarant has received **any** help or advice for pay from a legal document assistant or unlawful detainer assistant, state):*

   a. Assistant's name:
   b. Street address, city, and zip code:
   c. Telephone no.:
   d. County of registration:
   e. Registration no.:
   f. Expires on *(date):*

5. ☐ **Declaration under Code of Civil Procedure Section 585.5** *(required for entry of default under Code Civ. Proc., § 585(a)).* This action
   a. ☐ is ☐ is not on a contract or installment sale for goods or services subject to Civ. Code, § 1801 et seq. (Unruh Act).
   b. ☐ is ☐ is not on a conditional sales contract subject to Civ. Code, § 2981 et seq. (Rees-Levering Motor Vehicle Sales and Finance Act).
   c. ☐ is ☐ is not on an obligation for goods, services, loans, or extensions of credit subject to Code Civ. Proc., § 395(b).

6. **Declaration of mailing (Code Civ. Proc., § 587).** A copy of this *Request for Entry of Default* was
   a. ☐ **not mailed** to the following defendants, whose addresses are **unknown** to plaintiff or plaintiff's attorney *(names):*
   b. ☐ **mailed** first-class, postage prepaid, in a sealed envelope addressed to each defendant's attorney of record or, if none, to each defendant's last known address as follows:
      (1) Mailed on *(date):*
      (2) To *(specify names and addresses shown on the envelopes):*

I declare under penalty of perjury under the laws of the State of California that the foregoing items 4, 5, and 6 are true and correct.
Date:

▶

_____ _____
(TYPE OR PRINT NAME) (SIGNATURE OF DECLARANT)

7. **Memorandum of costs** *(required if money judgment requested).* Costs and disbursements are as follows (Code Civ. Proc., § 1033.5):
   a. Clerk's filing fees . . . . $
   b. Process server's fees . . . . $
   c. Other *(specify):* . . . . $
   d. . . . . $
   e. **TOTAL** . . . . $ _____
   f. ☐ Costs and disbursements are waived.
   g. I am the attorney, agent, or party who claims these costs. To the best of my knowledge and belief this memorandum of costs is correct and these costs were necessarily incurred in this case.

I declare under penalty of perjury under the laws of the State of California that the foregoing is true and correct.
Date:

▶

_____ _____
(TYPE OR PRINT NAME) (SIGNATURE OF DECLARANT)

8. ☐ **Declaration of nonmilitary status** *(required for a judgment).* No defendant named in item 1c of the application is in the military service so as to be entitled to the benefits of the Servicemembers Civil Relief Act (50 U.S.C. App. § 501 et seq.).

I declare under penalty of perjury under the laws of the State of California that the foregoing is true and correct.
Date:

▶

_____ _____
(TYPE OR PRINT NAME) (SIGNATURE OF DECLARANT)

REQUEST FOR ENTRY OF DEFAULT
(Application to Enter Default)

JUD-100

ATTORNEY OR PARTY WITHOUT ATTORNEY *(Name, state bar number, and address):*	FOR COURT USE ONLY
TELEPHONE NO.: FAX NO. *(Optional):* E-MAIL ADDRESS *(Optional):* ATTORNEY FOR *(Name):*	

SUPERIOR COURT OF CALIFORNIA, COUNTY OF
STREET ADDRESS:
MAILING ADDRESS:
CITY AND ZIP CODE:
BRANCH NAME:

PLAINTIFF:

DEFENDANT:

JUDGMENT ☐ By Clerk ☐ By Default ☐ After Court Trial ☐ By Court ☐ On Stipulation ☐ Defendant Did Not Appear at Trial	CASE NUMBER:

JUDGMENT

1. ☐ **BY DEFAULT**
    a. Defendant was properly served with a copy of the summons and complaint.
    b. Defendant failed to answer the complaint or appear and defend the action within the time allowed by law.
    c. Defendant's default was entered by the clerk upon plaintiff's application.
    d. ☐ **Clerk's Judgment** (Code Civ. Proc., § 585(a)). Defendant was sued only on a contract or judgment of a court of this state for the recovery of money.
    e. ☐ **Court Judgment** (Code Civ. Proc., § 585(b)). The court considered
        (1) ☐ plaintiff's testimony and other evidence.
        (2) ☐ plaintiff's written declaration (Code Civ. Proc., § 585(d)).

2. ☐ **ON STIPULATION**
    a. Plaintiff and defendant agreed (stipulated) that a judgment be entered in this case. The court approved the stipulated judgment and
    b. ☐ the signed written stipulation was filed in the case.
    c. ☐ the stipulation was stated in open court   ☐ the stipulation was stated on the record.

3. ☐ **AFTER COURT TRIAL.** The jury was waived. The court considered the evidence.
    a. The case was tried on *(date and time):*
       before *(name of judicial officer):*
    b. Appearances by:
       ☐ Plaintiff *(name each):*   ☐ Plaintiff's attorney *(name each):*
       (1)   (1)
       (2)   (2)
       ☐ Continued on Attachment 3b.

       ☐ Defendant *(name each):*   ☐ Defendant's attorney *(name each):*
       (1)   (1)
       (2)   (2)
       ☐ Continued on Attachment 3b.

    c. ☐ Defendant did not appear at trial. Defendant was properly served with notice of trial.

    d. ☐ A statement of decision (Code Civ. Proc., § 632) ☐ was not ☐ was requested.

Form Approved for Optional Use
Judicial Council of California
JUD-100 [New January 1, 2002]

JUDGMENT

Code of Civil Procedure, §§ 585, 664.6

PLAINTIFF:	CASE NUMBER:
DEFENDANT:	

JUDGMENT IS ENTERED AS FOLLOWS BY: ☐ THE COURT ☐ THE CLERK

4. ☐ **Stipulated Judgment.** Judgment is entered according to the stipulation of the parties.

5. **Parties.** Judgment is
   a. ☐ for plaintiff (name each):

   and against defendant (names):

   ☐ Continued on Attachment 5a.

   b. ☐ for defendant (name each):

   c. ☐ for cross-complainant (name each):

   and against cross-defendant (name each):

   ☐ Continued on Attachment 5c.

   d. ☐ for cross-defendant (name each):

6. **Amount.**
   a. ☐ Defendant named in item 5a above must pay plaintiff on the complaint:

(1) ☐ Damages	$
(2) ☐ Prejudgment interest at the annual rate of %	$
(3) ☐ Attorney fees	$
(4) ☐ Costs	$
(5) ☐ Other (specify):	$
(6) **TOTAL**	$

   c. ☐ Cross-defendant named in item 5c above must pay cross-complainant on the cross-complaint:

(1) ☐ Damages	$
(2) ☐ Prejudgment interest at the annual rate of %	$
(3) ☐ Attorney fees	$
(4) ☐ Costs	$
(5) ☐ Other (specify):	$
(6) **TOTAL**	$

   b. ☐ Plaintiff to receive nothing from defendant named in item 5b.
      ☐ Defendant named in item 5b to recover costs $
         ☐ and attorney fees $

   d. ☐ Cross-complainant to receive nothing from cross-defendant named in item 5d.
      ☐ Cross-defendant named in item 5d to recover costs $
         ☐ and attorney fees $

7. ☐ Other (specify):

Date: _____ ☐ _____
                              JUDICIAL OFFICER

Date: _____ ☐ Clerk, by _____ , Deputy

(SEAL)

CLERK'S CERTIFICATE (Optional)

I certify that this is a true copy of the original judgment on file in the court.

Date:

Clerk, by _____ , Deputy

JUD-100 [New January 1, 2002] **JUDGMENT**

ATTORNEY OR PARTY WITHOUT ATTORNEY *(Name, State Bar number, and address):*	FOR COURT USE ONLY
TELEPHONE NO.: FAX NO. *(Optional):* E-MAIL ADDRESS *(Optional):* ATTORNEY FOR *(Name):*	
SUPERIOR COURT OF CALIFORNIA, COUNTY OF STREET ADDRESS: MAILING ADDRESS: CITY AND ZIP CODE: BRANCH NAME:	
PLAINTIFF/PETITIONER: DEFENDANT/RESPONDENT:	
DECLARATION	CASE NUMBER:

MC-030

I declare under penalty of perjury under the laws of the State of California that the foregoing is true and correct.

Date:

_____   _____
(TYPE OR PRINT NAME)   (SIGNATURE OF DECLARANT)

☐ Attorney for   ☐ Plaintiff   ☐ Petitioner   ☐ Defendant
☐ Respondent   ☐ Other *(Specify):*

Form Approved for Optional Use
 Judicial Council of California
 MC-030 [Rev. January 1, 2006]

DECLARATION

	MC-031
PLAINTIFF/PETITIONER: DEFENDANT/RESPONDENT:	CASE NUMBER:

DECLARATION

(This form must be attached to another form or court paper before it can be filed in court.)

I declare under penalty of perjury under the laws of the State of California that the foregoing is true and correct.

Date:

_____
(TYPE OR PRINT NAME)

_____
(SIGNATURE OF DECLARANT)

☐ Attorney for ☐ Plaintiff ☐ Petitioner ☐ Defendant
☐ Respondent ☐ Other *(Specify):*

Form Approved for Optional Use
Judicial Council of California
MC-031 [Rev. July 1, 2005]

ATTACHED DECLARATION

DISC-004

ATTORNEY OR PARTY WITHOUT ATTORNEY (Name, State Bar number, and address):
TELEPHONE NO.:
FAX NO. (Optional):
E-MAIL ADDRESS (Optional):
ATTORNEY FOR (Name):

SUPERIOR COURT OF CALIFORNIA, COUNTY OF

SHORT TITLE:

FORM INTERROGATORIES—LIMITED CIVIL CASES (Economic Litigation)
Asking Party:
Answering Party:
Set No.:

CASE NUMBER:

Sec. 1. Instructions to All Parties

(a) Interrogatories are written questions prepared by a party to an action that are sent to any other party in the action to be answered under oath. The interrogatories below are form interrogatories approved for use in economic litigation.

(b) For time limitations, requirements for service on other parties, and other details, see Code of Civil Procedure sections 2030.010–2030.410 and the cases construing those sections.

(c) These form interrogatories do not change existing law relating to interrogatories, nor do they affect an answering party's right to assert any privilege or make any objection.

Sec. 2. Instructions to the Asking Party

(a) These interrogatories are designed for optional use by parties under economic litigation in limited civil cases. See Code of Civil Procedure sections 90 through 100. However, these interrogatories also may be used in unlimited civil cases.

(b) There are restrictions on discovery for most limited civil cases. These restrictions limit the number of interrogatories that may be asked. For details, read Code of Civil Procedure section 94.

(c) Some of these interrogatories are similar to questions in the *Case Questionnaire for Limited Civil Cases* (form DISC-010) and may be omitted if the information sought has already been provided in a completed *Case Questionnaire*.

(d) Check the box next to each interrogatory that you want the answering party to answer. Use care in choosing those interrogatories that apply to the case and are within the restrictions discussed above.

(e) You may insert your own definition of **INCIDENT** in Section 4, but only where the action arises from a course of conduct or a series of events occurring over a period of time.

(f) The interrogatories in section 116.0, Defendant's Contentions - Personal Injury, should not be used until defendant has had a reasonable opportunity to conduct an investigation or discovery of plaintiff's injuries and damages.

(g) Additional interrogatories may be attached, subject to the restrictions discussed above.

Sec. 3. Instructions to the Answering Party

(a) Subject to the restrictions discussed above, you must answer or provide another appropriate response to each interrogatory that has been checked below.

(b) As a general rule, within 30 days after you are served with these interrogatories, you must serve your responses on the asking party and serve copies of your responses on all other parties who have appeared. See Code of Civil Procedure sections 2030.260–2030.270 for details.

(c) Each answer must be as complete and straight-forward as the information reasonably available to you permits. If an interrogatory cannot be answered completely, answer it to the extent possible.

(d) If you do not have enough personal knowledge to fully answer an interrogatory, say so, but make a reasonable and good faith effort to get the information by asking other persons or organizations, unless the information is equally available to the asking party.

(e) Whenever an interrogatory may be answered by referring to a document, the document may be attached as an exhibit to the response and referred to in the response. If the document has more than one page, refer to the page and section where the answer to the interrogatory can be found.

(f) Whenever an address and telephone number for the same person are requested in more than one interrogatory, you are required to furnish them in answering only the first interrogatory asking for that information.

(g) Your answers to these interrogatories must be verified, dated, and signed. You may wish to use the following form at *the end of your answers:*

I declare under penalty of perjury under the laws of the State of California that the foregoing answers are true and correct.

_____   _____
(DATE)   (SIGNATURE)

Sec. 4. Definitions

Words in **BOLDFACE CAPITALS** in these interrogatories are defined as follows:
(Check one of the following):

(a) ☐ (1) **INCIDENT** includes the circumstances and events surrounding the alleged accident, injury, or other occurrence or breach of contract giving rise to this action or proceeding.

Form Approved for Optional Use Judicial Council of California
DISC-004 [Rev. January 1, 2007]

FORM INTERROGATORIES – LIMITED CIVIL CASES
(Economic Litigation)

Code of Civil Procedure, §§ 94, 2030.010-2030.410, 2033.710

☐ **(2) INCIDENT** means *(insert your definition here or on a separate, attached sheet labeled "Sec. 4(a) (2)")*:

(b) **YOU OR ANYONE ACTING ON YOUR BEHALF** includes you, your agents, your employees, your insurance companies, their agents, their employees, your attorneys, your accountants, your investigators, and anyone else acting on your behalf.

(c) **PERSON** includes a natural person, firm, association, organization, partnership, business, trust, corporation, or public entity.

(d) **DOCUMENT** means a writing, as defined in Evidence Code section 250, and includes the original or a copy of handwriting, typewriting, printing, photostating, photographing, electronically stored information, and every other means of recording upon any tangible thing and form of communicating or representation, including letters, words, pictures, sounds, or symbols, or combinations of them.

(e) **HEALTH CARE PROVIDER** includes any **PERSON** referred to in Code of Civil Procedure section 667.7(e)(3).

(f) **ADDRESS** means the street address, including the city, state, and zip code.

Sec. 5. Interrogatories

The following interrogatories have been approved by the Judicial Council under Code of Civil Procedure section 2033.710:

CONTENTS
101.0 Identity of Persons Answering These Interrogatories
102.0 General Background Information - Individual
103.0 General Background Information - Business Entity
104.0 Insurance
105.0 *[Reserved]*
106.0 Physical, Mental, or Emotional Injuries
107.0 Property Damage
108.0 Loss of Income or Earning Capacity
109.0 Other Damages
110.0 Medical History
111.0 Other Claims and Previous Claims
112.0 Investigation - General
113.0 *[Reserved]*
114.0 Statutory or Regulatory Violations
115.0 Claims and Defenses
116.0 Defendant's Contentions - Personal Injury
117.0 *[Reserved]*
120.0 How the Incident Occurred - Motor Vehicle
125.0 *[Reserved]*
130.0 *[Reserved]*
135.0 *[Reserved]*
150.0 Contract
160.0 *[Reserved]*
170.0 *[Reserved]*

101.0 Identity of Persons Answering These Interrogatories

☐ 101.1 State the name, **ADDRESS**, telephone number, and relationship to you of each **PERSON** who prepared or assisted in the preparation of the responses to these interrogatories. (Do not identify anyone who simply typed or reproduced the responses.)

102.0 General Background Information - Individual

☐ 102.1 State your name, any other names by which you have been known, and your **ADDRESS.**

☐ 102.2 State the date and place of your birth.

☐ 102.3 State, as of the time of the **INCIDENT**, your driver's license number, the state of issuance, the expiration date, and any restrictions.

☐ 102.4 State each residence **ADDRESS** for the last five years and the dates you lived at each **ADDRESS.**

☐ 102.5 State the name, **ADDRESS**, and telephone number of each employer you have had over the past five years and the dates you worked for each.

☐ 102.6 Describe your work for each employer you have had over the past five years.

☐ 102.7 State the name and **ADDRESS** of each academic or vocational school you have attended, beginning with high school, and the dates you attended each.

☐ 102.8 If you have ever been convicted of a felony, state, for each, the offense, the date and place of conviction, and the court and case number.

☐ 102.9 State the name, **ADDRESS,** and telephone number of any **PERSON** for whom you were acting as an agent or employee at the time of the **INCIDENT.**

☐ 102.10 Describe any physical, emotional, or mental disability or condition that you had that may have contributed to the occurrence of the **INCIDENT.**

☐ 102.11 Describe the nature and quantity of any alcoholic beverage, marijuana, or other drug or medication of any kind that you used within *24* hours before the **INCIDENT.**

103.0 General Background Information - Business Entity

☐ 103.1 State your current business name and **ADDRESS,** type of business entity, and your title.

104.0 Insurance

☐ 104.1 State the name and **ADDRESS** of each insurance company and the policy number and policy limits of each policy that may cover you, in whole or in part, for the damages related to the **INCIDENT.**

105.0 *[Reserved]*

106.0 Physical, Mental, or Emotional Injuries

☐ 106.1 Describe each injury or illness related to the **INCIDENT.**

☐ 106.2 Describe your present complaints about each injury or illness related to the **INCIDENT.**

☐ 106.3 State the name, **ADDRESS**, and telephone number of each **HEALTH CARE PROVIDER** who treated or examined you for each injury or illness related to the **INCIDENT** and the dates of treatment or examination.

FORM INTERROGATORIES–LIMITED CIVIL CASES
(Economic Litigation)

DISC-004

☐ 106.4 State the type of treatment or examination given to you by each **HEALTH CARE PROVIDER** for each injury or illness related to the **INCIDENT**.

☐ 106.5 State the charges made by each **HEALTH CARE PROVIDER** for each injury or illness related to the **INCIDENT**.

☐ 106.6 State the nature and cost of each health care service related to the **INCIDENT** not previously listed (for example, medication, ambulance, nursing, prosthetics).

☐ 106.7 State the nature and cost of the health care services you anticipate in the future as a result of the **INCIDENT**.

☐ 106.8 State the name and **ADDRESS** of each **HEALTH CARE PROVIDER** who has advised you that you may need future health care services as a result of the **INCIDENT**.

107.0 Property Damage

☐ 107.1 Itemize your property damage and, for each item, state the amount or attach an itemized bill or estimate.

108.0 Loss of Income or Earning Capacity

☐ 108.1 State the name and **ADDRESS** of each employer or other source of the earnings or income you have lost as a result of the **INCIDENT**.

☐ 108.2 Show how you compute the earnings or income you have lost, from each employer or other source, as a result of the **INCIDENT**.

☐ 108.3 State the name and **ADDRESS** of each employer or other source of the earnings or income you expect to lose in the future as a result of the **INCIDENT**.

☐ 108.4 Show how you compute the earnings or income you expect to lose in the future, from each employer or other source, as the result of the **INCIDENT**.

109.0 Other Damages

☐ 109.1 Describe each other item of damage or cost that you attribute to the **INCIDENT**, stating the dates of occurrence and the amount.

110.0 Medical History

☐ 110.1 Describe and give the date of each complaint or injury, whether occurring *before or after* **INCIDENT**, that involved the same part of your body claimed to have been injured in the **INCIDENT**.

☐ 110.2 State the name, **ADDRESS**, and telephone number of each **HEALTH CARE PROVIDER** who examined or treated you for each injury or complaint, whether occurring *before or after* the **INCIDENT**, that involved the same part of your body claimed to have been injured in the **INCIDENT** and the dates of examination or treatment.

111.0 Other Claims and Previous Claims

☐ 111.1 Identify each personal injury claim that **YOU OR ANYONE ACTING ON YOUR BEHALF** have made within the past ten years and the dates.

☐ 111.2 State the case name, court, and case number of each personal injury action or claim filed by **YOU OR ANYONE ACTING ON YOUR BEHALF** within the past ten years.

112.0 Investigation - General

☐ 112.1 State the name, **ADDRESS**, and telephone number of each individual who has knowledge of facts relating to the **INCIDENT**, and specify his or her area of knowledge.

☐ 112.2 State the name, **ADDRESS**, and telephone number of each individual who gave a written or recorded statement relating to the **INCIDENT** and the date of the statement.

☐ 112.3 State the name, **ADDRESS**, and telephone number of each **PERSON** who has the original or a copy of a written or recorded statement relating to the **INCIDENT**.

☐ 112.4 Identify each document or photograph that describes or depicts any place, object, or individual concerning the **INCIDENT** or plaintiff's injuries, or attach a copy. (if you do not attach a copy, state the name, **ADDRESS**, and telephone number of each **PERSON** who had the original document or photograph or a copy.)

☐ 112.5 Identify each other item of physical evidence that shows how the **INCIDENT** occurred or the nature or extent of plaintiff's injuries, and state the location of each item, and the name, **ADDRESS**, and telephone number of each **PERSON** who has it.

113.0 *[Reserved]*

114.0 Statutory or Regulatory Violations

☐ 114.1 If you contend that any **PERSON** involved in the **INCIDENT** violated any statute, ordinance, or regulation and that the violation was a cause of the **INCIDENT**, identify each **PERSON** and the statute, ordinance, or regulation.

115.0 Claims and Defenses

☐ 115.1 State in detail the facts upon which you base your claims that the **PERSON** asking this interrogatory is responsible for your damages.

☐ 115.2 State in detail the facts upon which you base your contention that you are not responsible, in whole or in part, for plaintiff's damages.

☐ 115.3 State the name, **ADDRESS**, and the telephone number of each **PERSON**, other than the **PERSON** asking this interrogatory, who is responsible, in whole or in part, for damages claimed in this action.

116.0 Defendant's Contentions - Personal Injury

[See Instruction 2(f)]

☐ 116.1 If you contend that any **PERSON,** other than you or plaintiff, contributed to the occurrence of the **INCIDENT** or the injuries or damages claimed by plaintiff, state the name, **ADDRESS,** and telephone number of each individual who has knowledge of the facts upon which you base your contention.

☐ 116.2 If you contend that plaintiff was not injured in the **INCIDENT,** state the name, **ADDRESS,** and telephone number of each individual who has knowledge of the facts upon which you base your contention.

☐ 116.3 If you contend that the injuries or the extent of the injuries claimed by plaintiff were not caused by the **INCIDENT,** state the name, **ADDRESS,** and telephone number of each individual who has knowledge of the facts upon which you base your contention.

☐ 116.4 If you contend that any of the services furnished by any **HEALTH CARE PROVIDER** were not related to the **INCIDENT,** state the name, **ADDRESS,** and telephone number of each individual who has knowledge of the facts upon which you base your contention.

☐ 116.5 If you contend that any of the costs of services furnished by any **HEALTH CARE PROVIDER** were unreasonable, identify each service that you dispute, the cost, and the **HEALTH CARE PROVIDER.**

☐ 116.6 If you contend that any part of the loss of earnings or income claimed by plaintiff was unreasonable, identify each part of the loss that you dispute and each source of the income or earnings.

☐ 116.7 If you contend that any of the property damage claimed by plaintiff was not caused by the **INCIDENT,** identify each item of property damage that you dispute.

☐ 116.8 If you contend that any of the costs of repairing the property damage claimed by plaintiff were unreasonable, identify each cost item that you dispute.

☐ 116.9 If you contend that, within the last ten years, plaintiff made a claim for personal injuries that are related to the injuries claimed in the **INCIDENT,** identify each related injury and the date.

☐ 116.10 If you contend that, within the past ten years, plaintiff made a claim for personal injuries that are related to the injuries claimed in the **INCIDENT,** state the name, court, and case number of each action filed.

117.0 *[Reserved]*

120.0 How the Incident Occurred - Motor Vehicle

☐ 120.1 State how the **INCIDENT** occurred.

☐ 120.2 For each vehicle involved in the **INCIDENT,** state the year, make, model, and license number.

☐ 120.3 For each vehicle involved in the **INCIDENT,** state the name, **ADDRESS,** and telephone number of the driver.

☐ 120.4 For each vehicle involved in the **INCIDENT,** state the name, **ADDRESS,** and telephone number of each occupant other than the driver.

☐ 120.5 For each vehicle involved in the **INCIDENT,** state the name, **ADDRESS,** and telephone number of each registered owner.

☐ 120.6 For each vehicle involved in the **INCIDENT,** state the name, **ADDRESS,** and telephone number of each lessee.

☐ 120.7 For each vehicle involved in the **INCIDENT,** state the name, **ADDRESS,** and telephone number of each owner other than the registered owner or lien holder.

☐ 120.8 For each vehicle involved in the **INCIDENT,** state the name of each owner who gave permission or consent to the driver to operate the vehicle.

150.0 Contract

☐ 150.1 Identify all **DOCUMENTS** that are part of the agreement and for each state the name, **ADDRESS, and** telephone number of the **PERSON** who has each **DOCUMENT.**

☐ 150.2 State each part of the agreement not in writing, the name, **ADDRESS,** and telephone number of each **PERSON** agreeing to that provision, and the date that part of the agreement was made.

☐ 150.3 Identify all **DOCUMENTS** that evidence each part of the agreement not in writing, and for each state the name, **ADDRESS,** and telephone number of the **PERSON** who has each **DOCUMENT.**

☐ 150.4 Identify all **DOCUMENTS** that are part of each modification to the agreement, and for each state the name **ADDRESS,** and telephone number of the **PERSON** who has each **DOCUMENT.**

☐ 150.5 State each modification not in writing, the date, and the name, **ADDRESS,** and telephone number of the **PERSON** agreeing to the modification, and the date the modification was made.

☐ 150.6 Identify all **DOCUMENTS** that evidence each modification of the agreement not in writing and for each state the name, **ADDRESS,** and telephone number of the **PERSON** who has each **DOCUMENT.**

☐ 150.7 Describe and give the date of every act or omission that you claim is a breach of the agreement.

☐ 150.8 Identify each agreement excused and state why performance was excused.

☐ 150.9 Identify each agreement terminated by mutual agreement and state why it was terminated, including dates.

☐ 150.10 Identify each unenforceable agreement and state the facts upon which your answer is based.

☐ 150.11 Identify each ambiguous agreement and state the facts upon which your answer is based.

	DISC-020
ATTORNEY OR PARTY WITHOUT ATTORNEY *(Name, State Bar number, and address):* TELEPHONE NO.:　　　　　　　FAX NO. *(Optional):* E-MAIL ADDRESS *(Optional):* ATTORNEY FOR *(Name):*	FOR COURT USE ONLY

SUPERIOR COURT OF CALIFORNIA, COUNTY OF
STREET ADDRESS:
MAILING ADDRESS:
CITY AND ZIP CODE:
BRANCH NAME:

SHORT TITLE:

REQUESTS FOR ADMISSION ☐ Truth of Facts　　☐ Genuineness of Documents Requesting Party: Answering Party: Set No.:	CASE NUMBER:

INSTRUCTIONS

Requests for admission are written requests by a party to an action requiring that any other party to the action either admit or deny, under oath, the truth of certain facts or the genuineness of certain documents. For information on timing, the number of admissions a party may request from any other party, service of requests and responses, restrictions on the style, format, and scope of requests for admission and responses to requests, and other details, see Code of Civil Procedure sections 94–95, 1013, and 2033.010–2033.420 and the case law relating to those sections.

An answering party should consider carefully whether to admit or deny the truth of facts or the genuineness of documents. With limited exceptions, an answering party will not be allowed to change an answer to a request for admission. There may be penalties if an answering party fails to admit the truth of any fact or the genuineness of any document when requested to do so and the requesting party later proves that the fact is true or that the document is genuine. These penalties may include, among other things, payment of the requesting party's attorney's fees incurred in making that proof.

Unless there is an agreement or a court order providing otherwise, the answering party must respond in writing to requests for admission within 30 days after they are served, or within 5 days after service in an unlawful detainer action. There may be significant penalties if an answering party fails to provide a timely written response to each request for admission. These penalties may include, among other things, an order that the facts in issue are deemed true or that the documents in issue are deemed genuine for purposes of the case.

Answers to *Requests for Admission* must be given under oath. The answering party should use the following language at the end of the responses:

I declare under penalty of perjury under the laws of the State of California that the foregoing answers are true and correct.

_____　　_____
　　　　　　(DATE)　　　　　　　　　　　　　　　　　(SIGNATURE)

These instructions are only a summary and are not intended to provide complete information about requests for admission. This *Requests for Admission* form does not change existing law relating to requests for admissions, nor does it affect an answering party's right to assert any privilege or to make any objection.

REQUESTS FOR ADMISSION

You are requested to admit within 30 days after service, or within 5 days after service in an unlawful detainer action, of this *Requests for Admission* that:

1. ☐　Each of the following facts is true *(if more than one, number each fact consecutively):*

　　☐ Continued on Attachment 1

2. ☐　The original of each of the following documents, copies of which are attached, is genuine *(if more than one, number each document consecutively):*

　　☐ Continued on Attachment 2

▶

_____　　　　　　　　　　_____
　　(TYPE OR PRINT NAME)　　　　　　　　　　　　(SIGNATURE OF PARTY OR ATTORNEY)

Form Approved for Optional Use
Judicial Council of California
DISC-020 [Rev. January 1, 2008]

REQUESTS FOR ADMISSION

Code of Civil Procedure,
§§ 94–95, 2033.010–2033.420, 2033.710

NAME, ADDRESS, AND TELEPHONE NUMBER OF ATTORNEY OR PARTY WITHOUT ATTORNEY:	STATE BAR NUMBER	Reserved for Clerk's File Stamp
ATTORNEY FOR (Name):		

SUPERIOR COURT OF CALIFORNIA, COUNTY OF LOS ANGELES

COURTHOUSE ADDRESS:

PLAINTIFF:

DEFENDANT:

AMENDMENT TO COMPLAINT (Fictitious /Incorrect Name)	CASE NUMBER:

☐ **FICTITIOUS NAME** *(No order required)*

Upon the filing of the complaint, the plaintiff, being ignorant of the true name of the defendant and having designated the defendant in the complaint by the fictitious name of:

FICTITIOUS NAME

and having discovered the true name of the defendant to be:

TRUE NAME

amends the complaint by substituting the true name for the fictitious name wherever it appears in the complaint.

DATE	TYPE OR PRINT NAME	SIGNATURE OF ATTORNEY

☐ **INCORRECT NAME** *(Order required)*

The plaintiff, having designated a defendant in the complaint by the incorrect name of:

INCORRECT NAME

and having discovered the true name of the defendant to be:

TRUE NAME

amends the complaint by substituting the true name for the incorrect name wherever it appears in the complaint.

DATE	TYPE OR PRINT NAME	SIGNATURE OF ATTORNEY

ORDER

THE COURT ORDERS the amendment approved and filed.

_____   _____
Dated   Judicial Officer

LACIV 105 (Rev. 01/07)
LASC Approved 03-04

AMENDMENT TO COMPLAINT
(Fictitious / Incorrect Name)

Code Civ. Proc., §§ 471.5,
472, 473, 474

CM-110

ATTORNEY OR PARTY WITHOUT ATTORNEY *(Name, State Bar number, and address)*:	FOR COURT USE ONLY
TELEPHONE NO.: FAX NO. *(Optional)*: E-MAIL ADDRESS *(Optional)*: ATTORNEY FOR *(Name)*:	
SUPERIOR COURT OF CALIFORNIA, COUNTY OF STREET ADDRESS: MAILING ADDRESS: CITY AND ZIP CODE: BRANCH NAME:	
PLAINTIFF/PETITIONER: DEFENDANT/RESPONDENT:	
CASE MANAGEMENT STATEMENT *(Check one):* ☐ **UNLIMITED CASE** ☐ **LIMITED CASE** (Amount demanded exceeds $25,000) (Amount demanded is $25,000 or less)	CASE NUMBER:

A **CASE MANAGEMENT CONFERENCE** is scheduled as follows:

Date: Time: Dept.:   Div.:   Room:

Address of court *(if different from the address above)*:

☐ Notice of Intent to Appear by Telephone, by *(name)*:

INSTRUCTIONS: All applicable boxes must be checked, and the specified information must be provided.

1. **Party or parties** *(answer one)*:
   a. ☐ This statement is submitted by party *(name)*:
   b. ☐ This statement is submitted **jointly** by parties *(names)*:

2. **Complaint and cross-complaint** *(to be answered by plaintiffs and cross-complainants only)*
   a. The complaint was filed on *(date)*:
   b. ☐ The cross-complaint, if any, was filed on *(date)*:

3. **Service** *(to be answered by plaintiffs and cross-complainants only)*
   a. ☐ All parties named in the complaint and cross-complaint have been served, or have appeared, or have been dismissed.
   b. ☐ The following parties named in the complaint or cross-complaint
      (1) ☐ have not been served *(specify names and explain why not)*:
      (2) ☐ have been served but have not appeared and have not been dismissed *(specify names)*:
      (3) ☐ have had a default entered against them *(specify names)*:
   c. ☐ The following additional parties may be added *(specify names, nature of involvement in case, and the date by which they may be served)*:

4. **Description of case**
   a. Type of case in ☐ complaint   ☐ cross-complaint   *(Describe, including causes of action)*:

Form Adopted for Mandatory Use
 Judicial Council of California
 CM-110 [Rev. January 1, 2009]

CASE MANAGEMENT STATEMENT

Page 1 of 4
 Cal. Rules of Court, <br> rules 3.720–3.730 <br> www.courtinfo.ca.gov

PLAINTIFF/PETITIONER:	CASE NUMBER:
DEFENDANT/RESPONDENT:	

4. b. Provide a brief statement of the case, including any damages. *(If personal injury damages are sought, specify the injury and damages claimed, including medical expenses to date [indicate source and amount], estimated future medical expenses, lost earnings to date, and estimated future lost earnings. If equitable relief is sought, describe the nature of the relief.)*

☐ *(If more space is needed, check this box and attach a page designated as Attachment 4b.)*

5. **Jury or nonjury trial**
   The party or parties request ☐ a jury trial ☐ a nonjury trial. *(If more than one party, provide the name of each party requesting a jury trial):*

6. **Trial date**
   a. ☐ The trial has been set for *(date):*
   b. ☐ No trial date has been set. This case will be ready for trial within 12 months of the date of the filing of the complaint *(if not, explain):*
   c. Dates on which parties or attorneys will not be available for trial *(specify dates and explain reasons for unavailability):*

7. **Estimated length of trial**
   The party or parties estimate that the trial will take *(check one):*
   a. ☐ days *(specify number):*
   b. ☐ hours (short causes) *(specify):*

8. **Trial representation** *(to be answered for each party)*
   The party or parties will be represented at trial ☐ by the attorney or party listed in the caption ☐ by the following:
   a. Attorney:
   b. Firm:
   c. Address:
   d. Telephone number:
   e. Fax number:
   f. E-mail address:
   g. Party represented:
   ☐ Additional representation is described in Attachment 8.

9. **Preference**
   ☐ This case is entitled to preference *(specify code section):*

10. **Alternative Dispute Resolution (ADR)**
    a. Counsel ☐ has ☐ has not provided the ADR information package identified in rule 3.221 to the client and has reviewed ADR options with the client.
    b. ☐ All parties have agreed to a form of ADR. ADR will be completed by *(date):*
    c. ☐ The case has gone to an ADR process *(indicate status):*

CASE MANAGEMENT STATEMENT

CM-110

PLAINTIFF/PETITIONER:	CASE NUMBER:
DEFENDANT/RESPONDENT:	

10. d. The party or parties are willing to participate in *(check all that apply)*:
    (1) ☐ Mediation
    (2) ☐ Nonbinding judicial arbitration under Code of Civil Procedure section 1141.12 (discovery to close 15 days before arbitration under Cal. Rules of Court, rule 3.822)
    (3) ☐ Nonbinding judicial arbitration under Code of Civil Procedure section 1141.12 (discovery to remain open until 30 days before trial; order required under Cal. Rules of Court, rule 3.822)
    (4) ☐ Binding judicial arbitration
    (5) ☐ Binding private arbitration
    (6) ☐ Neutral case evaluation
    (7) ☐ Other *(specify):*

   e. ☐ This matter is subject to mandatory judicial arbitration because the amount in controversy does not exceed the statutory limit.
   f. ☐ Plaintiff elects to refer this case to judicial arbitration and agrees to limit recovery to the amount specified in Code of Civil Procedure section 1141.11.
   g. ☐ This case is exempt from judicial arbitration under rule 3.811 of the California Rules of Court *(specify exemption):*

11. Settlement conference
☐ The party or parties are willing to participate in an early settlement conference *(specify when):*

12. Insurance
   a. ☐ Insurance carrier, if any, for party filing this statement *(name):*
   b. Reservation of rights: ☐ Yes ☐ No
   c. ☐ Coverage issues will significantly affect resolution of this case *(explain):*

13. Jurisdiction
Indicate any matters that may affect the court's jurisdiction or processing of this case, and describe the status.
☐ Bankruptcy ☐ Other *(specify):*
Status:

14. Related cases, consolidation, and coordination
   a. ☐ There are companion, underlying, or related cases.
      (1) Name of case:
      (2) Name of court:
      (3) Case number:
      (4) Status:
      ☐ Additional cases are described in Attachment 14a.
   b. ☐ A motion to ☐ consolidate ☐ coordinate will be filed by *(name party):*

15. Bifurcation
☐ The party or parties intend to file a motion for an order bifurcating, severing, or coordinating the following issues or causes of action *(specify moving party, type of motion, and reasons):*

16. Other motions
☐ The party or parties expect to file the following motions before trial *(specify moving party, type of motion, and issues):*

CM-110 [Rev. January 1, 2009] **CASE MANAGEMENT STATEMENT**

PLAINTIFF/PETITIONER:	CASE NUMBER:
DEFENDANT/RESPONDENT:	

17. **Discovery**
    a. ☐ The party or parties have completed all discovery.
    b. ☐ The following discovery will be completed by the date specified *(describe all anticipated discovery)*:

    Party   Description   Date

    c. ☐ The following discovery issues are anticipated *(specify)*:

18. **Economic litigation**
    a. ☐ This is a limited civil case (i.e., the amount demanded is $25,000 or less) and the economic litigation procedures in Code of Civil Procedure sections 90 through 98 will apply to this case.
    b. ☐ This is a limited civil case and a motion to withdraw the case from the economic litigation procedures or for additional discovery will be filed *(if checked, explain specifically why economic litigation procedures relating to discovery or trial should not apply to this case)*:

19. **Other issues**
    ☐ The party or parties request that the following additional matters be considered or determined at the case management conference *(specify)*:

20. **Meet and confer**
    a. ☐ The party or parties have met and conferred with all parties on all subjects required by rule 3.724 of the California Rules of Court *(if not, explain)*:

    b. After meeting and conferring as required by rule 3.724 of the California Rules of Court, the parties agree on the following *(specify)*:

21. Total number of pages attached *(if any)*: _____

I am completely familiar with this case and will be fully prepared to discuss the status of discovery and ADR, as well as other issues raised by this statement, and will possess the authority to enter into stipulations on these issues at the time of the case management conference, including the written authority of the party where required.

Date:

_____   ▶ _____
(TYPE OR PRINT NAME)   (SIGNATURE OF PARTY OR ATTORNEY)

_____   ▶ _____
(TYPE OR PRINT NAME)   (SIGNATURE OF PARTY OR ATTORNEY)

☐ Additional signatures are attached.

CASE MANAGEMENT STATEMENT

DO NOT FILE WITH THE COURT DISC-015

ATTORNEY OR PARTY WITHOUT ATTORNEY (Name and Address):	
TELEPHONE NO.:	FAX NO. (Optional):
E-MAIL ADDRESS (Optional):	
ATTORNEY FOR (Name):	

SUPERIOR COURT OF CALIFORNIA, COUNTY OF
STREET ADDRESS:
MAILING ADDRESS:
CITY AND ZIP CODE:
BRANCH NAME:

PLAINTIFF:

DEFENDANT:

REQUEST FOR STATEMENT OF WITNESSES AND EVIDENCE—FOR LIMITED CIVIL CASES (UNDER $25,000)	CASE NUMBER:
Requesting Party (name):	
Responding Party (name):	

Under Code of Civil Procedure section 96, you are requested to serve on the undersigned, within 20 days, a statement of:

1. The names and street addresses of witnesses you intend to call at trial (except for any individual who is a party to this action).

2. A description of each document that you intend to offer at trial. Attach a copy of each document available to you.

3. A description of each photograph and other physical evidence you intend to offer at trial.

Witnesses and evidence that will be used only for impeachment need not be included.

You Will Not Be Permitted To Call Any Witness Or Introduce Any Evidence Not Included In Your Statement in Response To This Request, Except As Otherwise Provided By Law.

Date:

_____   ▶   _____
(TYPE OR PRINT NAME)   (SIGNATURE OF PARTY OR ATTORNEY)

Form Adopted for Mandatory Use
Judicial Council of California
DISC-015 [Rev. January 1, 2007]

REQUEST FOR STATEMENT OF WITNESSES AND EVIDENCE—FOR LIMITED CIVIL CASES (UNDER $25,000)

Code of Civil Procedure, §§ 96, 97

SUBP-001

ATTORNEY OR PARTY WITHOUT ATTORNEY *(Name, State Bar number, and address):*	FOR COURT USE ONLY
TELEPHONE NO.: FAX NO.: ATTORNEY FOR *(Name):*	
NAME OF COURT: STREET ADDRESS: MAILING ADDRESS: CITY AND ZIP CODE: BRANCH NAME:	
PLAINTIFF/ PETITIONER: DEFENDANT/ RESPONDENT:	
CIVIL SUBPOENA For Personal Appearance at Trial or Hearing	CASE NUMBER:

THE PEOPLE OF THE STATE OF CALIFORNIA, TO *(name, address, and telephone number of witness, if known):*

1. **YOU ARE ORDERED TO APPEAR AS A WITNESS** in this action at the date, time, and place shown in the box below UNLESS you make an agreement with the person named in item 2:

   a. Date: Time: ☐ Dept.:   ☐ Div.:   ☐ Room:

   b. Address:

2. **IF YOU HAVE ANY QUESTIONS ABOUT THE TIME OR DATE FOR YOU TO APPEAR, OR IF YOU WANT TO BE CERTAIN THAT YOUR PRESENCE IS REQUIRED, CONTACT THE FOLLOWING PERSON BEFORE THE DATE ON WHICH YOU ARE TO APPEAR:**

   a. Name of subpoenaing party or attorney: b. Telephone number:

3. **Witness Fees:** You are entitled to witness fees and mileage actually traveled both ways, as provided by law, if you request them at the time of service. You may request them before your scheduled appearance from the person named in item 2.

DISOBEDIENCE OF THIS SUBPOENA MAY BE PUNISHED AS CONTEMPT BY THIS COURT. YOU WILL ALSO BE LIABLE FOR THE SUM OF FIVE HUNDRED DOLLARS AND ALL DAMAGES RESULTING FROM YOUR FAILURE TO OBEY.

Date issued:

_____   ▶ _____
(TYPE OR PRINT NAME)   (SIGNATURE OF PERSON ISSUING SUBPOENA)

_____
(TITLE)

Requests for Accommodations

Assistive listening systems, computer-assisted real-time captioning, or sign language interpreter services are available if you ask at least 5 days before the date on which you are to appear. Contact the clerk's office or go to www.courtinfo.ca.gov/forms for *Request for Accommodations by Persons With Disabilities and Order* (form MC-410). (Civil Code, § 54.8.)

(Proof of service on reverse)

Form Adopted for Mandatory Use
Judicial Council of California
SUBP-001 [Rev. January 1, 2007]

CIVIL SUBPOENA FOR PERSONAL APPEARANCE AT TRIAL OR HEARING

Code of Civil Procedure, §§ 1985, 1986, 1987
www.courtinfo.ca.gov

PLAINTIFF/PETITIONER: DEFENDANT/RESPONDENT:	CASE NUMBER:

SUBP-001

PROOF OF SERVICE OF CIVIL SUBPOENA
FOR PERSONAL APPEARANCE AT TRIAL OR HEARING

1. I served this *Civil Subpoena for Personal Appearance at Trial or Hearing* by personally delivering a copy to the person served as follows:

   a. Person served *(name)*:

   b. Address where served:

   c. Date of delivery:

   d. Time of delivery:

   e. Witness fees *(check one)*:
      (1) ☐ were offered or demanded and paid. Amount: . . . . . . $ _____
      (2) ☐ were not demanded or paid.

   f. Fee for service: . . . . $ _____

2. I received this subpoena for service on *(date)*:

3. Person serving:
   a. ☐ Not a registered California process server.
   b. ☐ California sheriff or marshal.
   c. ☐ Registered California process server.
   d. ☐ Employee or independent contractor of a registered California process server.
   e. ☐ Exempt from registration under Business and Professions Code section 22350(b).
   f. ☐ Registered professional photocopier.
   g. ☐ Exempt from registration under Business and Professions Code section 22451.
   h. Name, address, telephone number, and, if applicable, county of registration and number:

I declare under penalty of perjury under the laws of the State of California that the foregoing is true and correct.

Date:

▶ _____
(SIGNATURE)

(For California sheriff or marshal use only)
I certify that the foregoing is true and correct.

Date:

▶ _____
(SIGNATURE)

SUBP-001 [Rev. January 1, 2007]

**PROOF OF SERVICE OF
CIVIL SUBPOENA FOR
PERSONAL APPEARANCE AT TRIAL OR HEARING**

ADR-102

ATTORNEY OR PARTY WITHOUT ATTORNEY *(Name, state bar number, and address)*:	FOR COURT USE ONLY
TELEPHONE NO.: FAX NO. *(Optional)*:	
E-MAIL ADDRESS *(Optional)*:	
ATTORNEY FOR *(Name)*:	

SUPERIOR COURT OF CALIFORNIA, COUNTY OF
STREET ADDRESS:
MAILING ADDRESS:
CITY AND ZIP CODE:
BRANCH NAME:

PLAINTIFF/PETITIONER:

DEFENDANT/RESPONDENT:

REQUEST FOR TRIAL DE NOVO AFTER JUDICIAL ARBITRATION	CASE NUMBER:

NOTE:
If you do not want the arbitrator's award to become the judgment in the case, you must file a request for a trial de novo within 30 days after the arbitration award is filed with the clerk. If you do not request a trial de novo by this deadline, the arbitrator's award will be final and it will be entered as the judgment in the case. The 30-day period cannot be extended (California Rules of Court, rule 3.826).

Copies of the request for a trial de novo must be served on all parties and the request and a proof of service must be filed with the clerk.

☐ Plaintiff   ☐ Defendant   ☐ Other *(specify)*:

(name):

requests trial de novo in this action, under Code of Civil Procedure, section 1141.20 and rule 3.826 of the California Rules of Court.

Date:

_____
(TYPE OR PRINT NAME)

_____
(SIGNATURE OF PARTY OR ATTORNEY)

Form Approved for Optional Use
Judicial Council of California
ADR-102 [Rev. January 1, 2007]

REQUEST FOR TRIAL DE NOVO AFTER JUDICIAL ARBITRATION
(Alternative Dispute Resolution)

Code of Civil Procedure, § 1141.20;
Cal. Rules of Court, Rule 3.826
www.courtinfo.ca.gov

ADR-102

SHORT TITLE:	CASE NUMBER:

PROOF OF SERVICE

☐ Mail   ☐ Personal Service

1. At the time of service I was at least 18 years of age and **not a party to this legal action.**

2. My residence or business address is *(specify):*

3. I mailed or personally delivered a copy of the *Request for Trial De Novo After Judicial Arbitration* as follows *(complete either a or b):*

   a. ☐ **Mail.** I am a resident of or employed in the county where the mailing occurred.
      (1) I enclosed a copy in an envelope and
         (a) ☐ **deposited** the sealed envelope with the United States Postal Service, with the postage fully prepaid.
         (b) ☐ **placed** the envelope for collection and mailing on the date and at the place shown in items below, following our ordinary business practices. I am readily familiar with this business's practice for collecting and processing correspondence for mailing. On the same day that correspondence is placed for collection and mailing, it is deposited in the ordinary course of business with the United States Postal Service, in a sealed envelope with postage fully prepaid.
      (2) The envelope was addressed and mailed as follows:
         (a) Name of person served:
         (b) Address on envelope:

         (c) Date of mailing:
         (d) Place of mailing *(city and state):*

   b. ☐ **Personal delivery.** I personally delivered a copy as follows:
      (1) Name of person served:
      (2) Address where delivered:

      (3) Date delivered:
      (4) Time delivered:

I declare under penalty of perjury under the laws of the State of California that the foregoing is true and correct.

Date:

_____   _____
(TYPE OR PRINT NAME)   (SIGNATURE OF DECLARANT)

REQUEST FOR TRIAL DE NOVO AFTER JUDICIAL ARBITRATION
(Alternative Dispute Resolution)

	SUBP-002
ATTORNEY OR PARTY WITHOUT ATTORNEY *(Name, State Bar number, and address):*	FOR COURT USE ONLY
TELEPHONE NO.: FAX NO.:	
ATTORNEY FOR *(Name)*:	
NAME OF COURT:	
STREET ADDRESS:	
MAILING ADDRESS:	
CITY AND ZIP CODE:	
BRANCH NAME:	
PLAINTIFF/ PETITIONER:	
DEFENDANT/ RESPONDENT:	
CIVIL SUBPOENA (DUCES TECUM) for Personal Appearance and Production of Documents and Things at Trial or Hearing AND DECLARATION	CASE NUMBER:

THE PEOPLE OF THE STATE OF CALIFORNIA, TO *(name, address, and telephone number of witness, if known)*:

1. **YOU ARE ORDERED TO APPEAR AS A WITNESS** in this action at the date, time, and place shown in the box below UNLESS your appearance is excused as indicated in box 3b below or you make an agreement with the person named in item 4 below.
   a. Date: Time: ☐ Dept.:   ☐ Div.:   ☐ Room:
   b. Address:

2. **IF YOU HAVE BEEN SERVED WITH THIS SUBPOENA AS A CUSTODIAN OF CONSUMER OR EMPLOYEE RECORDS UNDER CODE OF CIVIL PROCEDURE SECTION 1985.3 OR 1985.6 AND A MOTION TO QUASH OR AN OBJECTION HAS BEEN SERVED ON YOU, A COURT ORDER OR AGREEMENT OF THE PARTIES, WITNESSES, *AND* CONSUMER OR EMPLOYEE AFFECTED MUST BE OBTAINED BEFORE YOU ARE REQUIRED TO PRODUCE CONSUMER OR EMPLOYEE RECORDS.**

3. **YOU ARE** *(item a or b must be checked)*:
   a. ☐ Ordered to appear in person and to produce the records described in the declaration on page two or the attached declaration or affidavit. The personal attendance of the custodian or other qualified witness and the production of the original records are required by this subpoena. The procedure authorized by Evidence Code sections 1560(b), 1561, and 1562 will not be deemed sufficient compliance with this subpoena.
   b. ☐ Not required to appear in person if you produce (i) the records described in the declaration on page two or the attached declaration or affidavit and (ii) a completed declaration of custodian of records in compliance with Evidence Code sections 1560, 1561, 1562, and 1271. (1) Place a copy of the records in an envelope (or other wrapper). Enclose the original declaration of the custodian with the records. Seal the envelope. (2) Attach a copy of this subpoena to the envelope or write on the envelope the case name and number; your name; and the date, time, and place from item 1 in the box above. (3) Place this first envelope in an outer envelope, seal it, and mail it to the clerk of the court at the address in item 1. (4) Mail a copy of your declaration to the attorney or party listed at the top of this form.

4. **IF YOU HAVE ANY QUESTIONS ABOUT THE TIME OR DATE YOU ARE TO APPEAR, OR IF YOU WANT TO BE CERTAIN THAT YOUR PRESENCE IS REQUIRED, CONTACT THE FOLLOWING PERSON BEFORE THE DATE ON WHICH YOU ARE TO APPEAR:**
   a. Name of subpoenaing party or attorney: b. Telephone number:

5. **Witness Fees:** You are entitled to witness fees and mileage actually traveled both ways, as provided by law, if you request them at the time of service. You may request them before your scheduled appearance from the person named in item 4.

DISOBEDIENCE OF THIS SUBPOENA MAY BE PUNISHED AS CONTEMPT BY THIS COURT. YOU WILL ALSO BE LIABLE FOR THE SUM OF FIVE HUNDRED DOLLARS AND ALL DAMAGES RESULTING FROM YOUR FAILURE TO OBEY.

Date issued:

_____ ▶ _____
(TYPE OR PRINT NAME)   (SIGNATURE OF PERSON ISSUING SUBPOENA)

(Declaration in support of subpoena on reverse)   (TITLE)

Form Adopted for Mandatory Use
Judicial Council of California
SUBP-002 [Rev. July 1, 2009]

CIVIL SUBPOENA (DUCES TECUM) FOR PERSONAL APPEARANCE AND PRODUCTION OF DOCUMENTS AND THINGS AT TRIAL OR HEARING AND DECLARATION

Code of Civil Procedure,
§ 1985 et seq.
www.courtinfo.ca.gov

	SUBP-002
PLAINTIFF/PETITIONER:	CASE NUMBER:
DEFENDANT/RESPONDENT:	

The production of the documents or the other things sought by the subpoena on page one is supported by *(check one)*:
☐ the attached affidavit or declaration ☐ the following declaration:

DECLARATION IN SUPPORT OF CIVIL SUBPOENA (DUCES TECUM) FOR PERSONAL APPEARANCE AND PRODUCTION OF DOCUMENTS AND THINGS AT TRIAL OR HEARING
(Code Civ. Proc., §§ 1985, 1987.5)

1. I, the undersigned, declare I am the ☐ plaintiff ☐ defendant ☐ petitioner ☐ respondent
   ☐ attorney for *(specify)*: ☐ other *(specify)*:
   in the above-entitled action.

2. The witness has possession or control of the following documents or other things and shall produce them at the time and place specified in the *Civil Subpoena for Personal Appearance and Production of Documents and Things at Trial or Hearing* on page one of this form *(specify the exact documents or other things to be produced)*:

   ☐ Continued on Attachment 2.

3. Good cause exists for the production of the documents or other things described in paragraph 2 for the following reasons:

   ☐ Continued on Attachment 3.

4. These documents or other things described in paragraph 2 are material to the issues involved in this case for the following reasons:

   ☐ Continued on Attachment 4.

I declare under penalty of perjury under the laws of the State of California that the foregoing is true and correct.

Date:

....
(TYPE OR PRINT NAME)

▶ _____
(SIGNATURE OF ☐ SUBPOENAING PARTY ☐ ATTORNEY FOR SUBPOENAING PARTY)

Request for Accommodations

Assistive listening systems, computer-assisted real-time captioning, or sign language interpreter services are available if you ask at least five days before the date on which you are to appear. Contact the clerk's office or go to www.courtinfo.ca.gov/forms for *Request for Accommodations by Persons With Disabilities and Response* (form MC-410). (Civil Code, § 54.8.)

(Proof of service on page 3)

CIVIL SUBPOENA (DUCES TECUM) FOR PERSONAL APPEARANCE AND PRODUCTION OF DOCUMENTS AND THINGS AT TRIAL OR HEARING AND DECLARATION

PLAINTIFF/PETITIONER:	CASE NUMBER:
DEFENDANT/RESPONDENT:	

PROOF OF SERVICE OF CIVIL SUBPOENA (DUCES TECUM) FOR PERSONAL APPEARANCE AND PRODUCTION OF DOCUMENTS AND THINGS AT TRIAL OR HEARING AND DECLARATION

1. I served this *Civil Subpoena (Duces Tecum) for Personal Appearance and Production of Documents and Things at Trial or Hearing and Declaration* by personally delivering a copy to the person served as follows:
   a. Person served *(name)*:
   b. Address where served:

   c. Date of delivery:

   d. Time of delivery:

   e. Witness fees *(check one)*:
      (1) ☐ were offered or demanded and paid. Amount: ...... $
      (2) ☐ were not demanded or paid.

   f. Fee for service: .... $

2. I received this subpoena for service on *(date)*:

3. Person serving:
   a. ☐ Not a registered California process server.
   b. ☐ California sheriff or marshal.
   c. ☐ Registered California process server.
   d. ☐ Employee or independent contractor of a registered California process server.
   e. ☐ Exempt from registration under Business and Professions Code section 22350(b).
   f. ☐ Registered professional photocopier.
   g. ☐ Exempt from registration under Business and Professions Code section 22451.
   h. Name, address, telephone number, and, if applicable, county of registration and number:

I declare under penalty of perjury under the laws of the State of California that the foregoing is true and correct.

Date:

▶ _____
(SIGNATURE)

(For California sheriff or marshal use only)
I certify that the foregoing is true and correct.

Date:

▶ _____
(SIGNATURE)

PROOF OF SERVICE OF CIVIL SUBPOENA (DUCES TECUM) FOR PERSONAL APPEARANCE AND PRODUCTION OF DOCUMENTS AND THINGS AT TRIAL OR HEARING AND DECLARATION

Index

A

Abuse of process, 87
Accident cases, 53
    Cause of Action—General Negligence (PLD-PI-001(2)), 79, 85–87
    Cause of Action—Motor Vehicle (Form PLD-PI-001(1)), 79–82
    Cause of Action—Premises Liability (Form PLD-PI-001(4)), 79, 82–84
    See also Slip-and-fall cases; Vehicle accidents
Accident insurance. See Automobile insurance
Accident reconstruction experts, 28
Administrator, 59–61
Admissibility of evidence, 24–25
ADR. See Alternative dispute resolution
Advisor. See Sounding board
Affirmative defense, 151, 154, 155, 158–159
Alternative dispute resolution (ADR), 9, 37, 122
    See also Arbitration; Mediation
Amended complaint, 203–204, 219
Amendment to Complaint (Fictitious/Incorrect Name), 204
Annotated code books, 19
Answer
    alternate responses, 144, 147–148
    in breach of contract cases, 155–159
    defined, 17, 26
    in limited jurisdiction cases, 159–160
    in tort cases, 150–155
    in unlimited jurisdiction case, 138
Answer—Contract (Form PLD-C-010), 155–159
Answer—General Denial (Form PLD-050), 159, 160
Answer—Personal Injury, Property Damage, Wrongful Death (Form PLD-PI-003), 150–155
Appeals, 13, 278

Appellate Court, 279
Application and Order for Appointment of Guardian *Ad Litem*—Civil (Form CIV-010), 130
Application for Waiver of Court Fees and Costs (FW-001), 113–117, 120
Arbitration, 227–233
    award, 232–233
    different from trial, 227–228
    discovery and, 230
    hearing, 228–232, 246
    mandatory arbitration clause in contracts, 9, 39
    rejecting award, 232–233
    scheduling, 228
    voluntary, 39
Arbitration hearing, 228–232, 246
Arbitrators, 39, 228
Assault, 73
Associations
    as defendants, 57
    fictitious business name, 50, 57
    owners' liability for debts, 52
    serving legal papers to, 129
    unincorporated, 5, 52, 57, 129
Assumption of risk, 154
Attachments
    Attachment to Judicial Council Form, 117
    Exemplary Damages Attachment, 79, 89–91
    See also Cause of Action attachments
Attachment to Judicial Council Form (Form MC-025), 117
Attorneys. See Lawyers
Automobile insurance, 7, 140–141
    coverage in DUI, 32
    reimbursement clause in, 32
    winning lawsuit against a minor, 62
Award (arbitration), 232

B

Back taxes, 11
Back wages, 11
Bankruptcy, of defendant, 29, 61, 154
Battery, 73, 87
Binding agreements. *See* Contracts
Bodily injury cases, statute of limitations, 22, 23
Breach of contract cases, 5, 7–9
    Answer—Contract (Form PLD-C-010), 155–159
    Cause of Action attachments, 96–107
    Cause of Action—Breach of Contract (PLD-C-001(1)), 96–100
    Cause of Action—Breach of Implied Warranty (Fitness), 104–107
    Cause of Action—Breach of Implied Warranty (Merchantability), 100–104
    Complaint, 70–72, 92–96, 107–108
    Complaint—Contract (PLD-C-001), 92–96
    Cross-Complaint, 162–163
    damage amount in, 33–34
    defendants in, 53–56
    examples of, 7, 8
    express warranty, 55–56, 104
    implied warranty of fitness, 55, 104–107
    implied warranty of merchantability, 55, 56, 100–104
    installment payments, 22–23
    minor as defendant in, 62
    purchase contracts, 55
    sample settlement agreement, 43
    sample settlement letter, 40–42
    selecting jurisdiction, 65
    service contracts, 54–55
    statute of limitations, 22–23, 158
    third party beneficiary, 51
    warranty issues, 55–56
Breach of Contract Cause of Action form, 96–100
Breach of contract Complaint
    Cause of Action attachments, 96–107
    Cause of Action—Breach of Contract (PLD-C-001(1)), 96–100
    Cause of Action—Breach of Implied Warranty (Fitness), 104–107
    Cause of Action—Breach of Implied Warranty (Merchantability), 100–104
    Complaint—Contract (PLD-C-001), 92–96
    instructions for filling out, 70–72, 92–96, 107–108
Businesses
    collecting judgments against, 29
    as defendants, 52, 56–58, 64
    fictitious business names, 50, 57, 92
    owners' liability for debts, 52
    as plaintiffs, 50
    serving of legal papers to, 129

C

Calendar (court), 258
California court rules, 19
California court system, 4
California Department of Consumer Affairs, 10
California Forms of Pleading and Practice, 108
California Judicial Council, 15, 100
California Labor Commissioner, 11
California statutes, 18–19
California Superior Court. *See* Superior Court
California Victims Compensation and Government Claims Board, 59
Caption
    Civil Case Cover Sheet, 110–111
    Complaint forms, 71–72
Car accidents. *See* Automobile insurance; Vehicle accidents
Case law, 19
Case Management Conference, 122, 224
Case Management Statement (CM-110), 122, 223–227
Case number, 72, 122
Case Questionnaire
    for Cross-Complaint, 163–164
    failure to respond to, 199–203
    photocopying, 120
    preparing, 112–113
Case Questionnaire—For Limited Civil Cases (Form DISC-010), 112–113, 126, 127
Cases, legal research, 19
Cause of Action, 218

Cause of Action attachments
    breach of contract Complaint, 96–107
    defendant review of, 137–138, 149–150
    responses to, 149–150
    tort cases, 79–89
Cause of Action—Breach of Contract (PLD-C-001(1)), 96–100
Cause of Action—Breach of Implied Warranty (Fitness), 104–107
Cause of Action—Breach of Implied Warranty (Merchantability), 100–104
Cause of Action—General Negligence (PLD-PI-001(2)), 79, 85–87
Cause of Action—Intentional Tort (PLD-PI-001(3)), 79, 87–89
Cause of Action—Motor Vehicle (Form PLD-PI-001(1)), 79–82
Cause of Action—Premises Liability (Form PLD-PI-001(4)), 79, 82–84
Challenging a judge, 258, 260
Challenging jurors, 272–273
Change of venue, 147, 148
Chapter 7 bankruptcy, 29
Chapter 13 bankruptcy, 29
Charitable ventures, owners' liability for debts, 52
Chart of evidence, 252
"Checking in," trial, 258
Chiropractor, treatment by, 27
Civil Case Cover Sheet (Form CM-010), 110–112
Civil Case Cover Sheet Addendum and Statement of Location, 111
Civil Code, 18
Civil rights and civil liberties cases, 6
Civil Subpoena (Duces Tecum) (Form SUBP-002), 186, 191, 248–252
Civil Subpoena for Personal Appearance at Trial or Hearing (Form SUBP-001), 246, 247
Clerks of the Superior Court, 15–17, 180
Closing arguments, 267–268, 275
Code of Civil Procedure, 18
Codes, legal research, 18–19
Collection (of judgments), 29–30, 48
Commissioners, 258, 258–259
Comparative negligence, 33

Compensatory damages, 79
Complaint, 70–117
    amending, 73, 203–204, 219
    breach of contract cases, 70–72, 92–96, 107–108
    Caption, 71–72
    defined, 17, 26
    filing, 120–123
    instructions for filling out, 19–20, 70–72, 92–96, 107–108, 109–110
    legal defects in, 148
    order of documents, 121
    photocopying, 120
    prayer, 77, 96, 138, 219
    review by defendant, 136–138
    selecting correct form, 71
    selecting county, 75
    selecting court, 75
    serving on defendant, 128–130, 134
    tort cases, 73–92
    verified complaints, 148
Complaint—Contract (PLD-C-001), 92–96
Complaint—Personal Injury, Property Damage, Wrongful Death, 73–79
Construction defects cases, statute of limitations, 23
Contingency fee contracts, 8, 14
Contracts
    arbitration requirements, 9, 39
    defined, 7
    illegal, 9–10
    oral or implied vs. written, 7, 23
    signed by minor, 62, 159
    Statute of Frauds, 8
    unwritten/unsigned, 8
    where entered into, 65
    See also Breach of contract cases
Conversion, 87
Copies. *See* Photocopying
Coplaintiffs, 50–51, 75, 96
Corporations
    collecting judgments against, 29
    as defendants, 57
    owners' liability for debts, 52

"piercing the corporate veil," 57
as plaintiff, 50
serving legal papers to, 129
Cost bill, 268
Counsel table, 261
County
choosing wrong county, 67–68, 147
Cover Sheets for, 111
filing in inconvenient county, 148
selecting county to sue in, 65
County government, as defendant, 58–59
Court
consequences of picking wrong county or branch, 67–68, 147–148
selecting court to sue in, 65–68, 111, 147–148
Self-Help Center, 121
See also Courtroom; Jurisdiction
Court cases (decisions). *See* Cases
Court clerk, 15–17
rejection of forms by, 121
Court costs. *See* Filing fees
Court judgment. *See* Judgment
Courtroom
counsel table, 261
court rules, 19
etiquette in, 261, 262
finding, 258
order of events in, 258
Cover sheet, 110–112, 120, 121
Creditor's Claim Form, 59
Criminal cases, 10
Cross-complainant, 161, 168
Cross-Complaint, 138, 160–164
in breach of contract cases, 162–163
Case Questionnaire for, 163–164
filing and serving, 164
preparing, 160–161
in tort cases, 160–163
Cross-Complaint—Personal Injury, Property Damage, Wrongful Death (Form PLD-PI-002), 161
Cross-defendant, 161, 163, 168
Cross-examining witnesses, 264, 266
Custodian, 25

D

Damages
in breach of contract cases, 33–34
compensatory damages, 79
determining amount of, 30–34, 36–37
emotional damage, 31, 87
exemplary (punitive) damages, 7, 73, 77, 79, 89–91
indicating on Complaint form, 77, 79
for medical bills, 30
noneconomic damages, 51
for pain and suffering, 31, 32, 51
settling out of court, 36–37
in tort cases, 30–33
See also Judgment
Declaration (Form MC-030), 175–180, 183
Declarations
as evidence, 239, 239–244
from experts, 239–242
from nonexperts, 242
Opposition to Motion for Summary Judgment, 214–216
service of, 242, 246
use at hearing, 239
use at trial, 239
Defamation action, 61, 62, 87
Default
applying for judgment, 174
court hearings on, 180–181
Request for Entry of Default (Form CIV-100), 169–173
self-representation after, 143
taking the defendant's default, 168–181
Default clerks, 180
Default judgment
about, 15, 122, 131, 134, 136
limited jurisdiction case, 17
setting aside, 181–183
Defective product cases, 34, 56
Defendants, 136–165
Answer, 17, 26, 144, 150–155, 155–159
assumption of risk defense, 154
bankruptcy and, 29, 61, 154
in breach of contract cases, 54–55

businesses as, 52, 56–58, 64
California jurisdiction of, 63–64
Causes of Action reviewed by, 137–138, 149–150
closing arguments, 267, 275
collecting judgments against, 29–30
in Complaint form Caption, 72
Complaint review by, 136–138
Cross-Complaint by, 138, 160–164
cross-examining witnesses, 264, 266
default by, 168–181
defenses, 154–155, 158
determining settlement amount, 37
Doe defendants, 63, 75, 91, 94, 107, 109, 130, 137, 180, 203–204
elusive defendants, 130
entrustment defendants, 53
estates as, 59, 61
government agency/entities as, 23, 58–59
initial actions for, 26
insurance policies reviewed by, 138–141
media outlets as, 61–62
mediation, 9, 37–38, 142
meeting with opponent, 222–223
minors as, 62–63
more time to respond to Complaint, 143–144, 145, 146
Motion for Judgment, 266
opening statement, 266, 274
out-of-state, 12
presenting case at trial, 266
presenting witnesses, 266
responding to Complaint, 144, 147–148
selecting, 51–68
self-defense claim, 154
self-representation, 5, 13–17, 142–143
serving with legal papers, 122, 126–134
settling out of court, 18, 36–48, 141–142
Summons review by, 136
unknown, 63
in vehicle accidents, 53
workers' compensation remedy as defense, 154–155
Defenses, 154–155, 158

Demand for Bill of Particulars, 219–220
Demurrer, 26, 73, 218–219
    General Demurrer, 144, 148, 218
    special demurrer, 148
Department of Consumer Affairs, 10
Deposition, 191–193
    attending, 194
    cost of, 5
    defined, 18, 42, 186
    limits on taking depositions, 187–188
    Notice of Deposition, 192, 193
    objecting to deposition questions, 194–195
    preparing for, 192
    rules for, 187
    scheduling, 193
Discovery, 186–204
    arbitration and, 230
    defined, 17
    depositions, 42, 186, 187, 188, 191–193, 191–195
    of Doe defendants, 203–204
    doing one's own discovery, 188–189
    failure to respond to, 199–203
    interrogatories, 18, 186, 187, 195–196
    limits on number of discovery requests, 188
    Motion to Compel, 200–203
    requests for admission, 186, 187, 197–198
    requests for physical examination, 186, 198–199
    requests for production of documents, 186, 188–191, 197
    responding to, 193–195
    rules and limits, 187
    subpoena duces tecum, 186, 191, 248–252
    time limits for, 187–188
    types of, 186
    witness list, 186, 199
    written interrogatories, 189
Discovery rules, 187
Discrimination cases, 6
Dismissal of lawsuit, 46–48, 164
Doe defendants, 63
    Amendment to Complaint (Fictitious/Incorrect Name), 203–204

Complaint, 75, 91, 94, 107, 109, 137
  discovery, 203–204
  dismissing, 180
  serving legal papers to, 130
Driving under the influence (DUI), 32

E

E-commerce, lawsuits resulting from, 64
Elements (of lawsuits), 26
Emancipated minor, 62
Emotional damage, 31, 87
Employer, as defendant, 54
Employer/employee lawsuits, 54
Entrustment, 53, 80
Estate, as defendants, 59, 61
Evidence
  admissibility of, 24–25
  at arbitration hearing, 229–231
  chart of evidence, 252
  evaluating, 23–26
  hearsay evidence, 238
  initial steps, 26
  medical evaluation, 27
  objecting to, 237–238, 274–275
  opinion evidence, 24–25
  pain diary, 28
  photographs as, 25, 27
  physical objects, 27
  police reports, 28
  presenting at trial, 265, 274–275
  recorded statements of witnesses, 27, 28
  recordkeeping, 26–28
  rules of evidence, 236–239
  videotaped statements of witnesses, 27, 28
  written statements as, 25, 239–245, 239–246, 265
  See also Discovery; Witnesses
Evidence chart, 252
Evidence Code, 18
Excusable neglect, 182
Executor, 59, 61
Exemplary damages (punitive damages), 7, 73, 77, 79, 89–91
Exemplary Damages Attachment (PLD-PI-001(6)), 79, 89–91

Exemptions (judgments), 29
Expert witnesses, 24–25, 199
Express warranty, 55, 56, 104
Extortion, 42

F

Failure to provide a service, 33–34
False imprisonment, 87
Fault
  in accident, 33
  settlement offer and, 37
Fax filing, 123
Federal government, as defendant, 58
Fees
  court costs waiver, 227
  deposition cost, 5
  filing fees, 5, 59, 113–117, 120, 123, 164
  lawyers' fees, 13, 14
  process server's fee, 5
  See also Filing fees
Fictitious business name, 50, 57, 92
Fictitious Names Index, 57
Filing fees
  Answer, 164
  Complaint and Summons, 5, 59, 120, 123
  waiver of, 113–117, 120, 122
Filing forms, 120–123
  case number, 72, 122
  Complaint, 120–123
  Cross-Complaint, 164
  local rules, 109
  by mail or fax, 122–123
  order of documents, 121
  in person, 121–122
  rejection of forms by clerk, 121
  Request for Trial De Novo After Judicial Arbitration, 233
  selecting where to file, 65–67
  Summons, 120, 122
  in wrong branch, 68, 147–148
  in wrong county, 68, 147
  in wrong state, 144, 147
Firearms, minors and, 63
Form Interrogatories—Limited Civil Cases (Form DISC-004), 189

Forms
    attachments to, 117
    downloading, 20
    filing. *See* Filing forms
    handwritten, 20, 70
    instructions for filling out, 19–20
    photocopying, 120
    pleading paper, 71, 137, 150
    selecting, 71, 109
    tips on preparing, 70
    typewritten, 70
    See also specific forms
Fraud as affirmative defense, 158
Fraud cases, 7, 87
Future income, loss of, 30, 77
Future waiver clause, 44–45

G

Gambling, 9
General damage, 77
General Demurrer, 144, 148, 218
General Denial form, 159, 160
General partnerships, 52, 57
General release, 44
Government agency/entity
    as defendant, 77
        serving legal papers to, 129
        suing, 23, 58–59
Government employees, as defendants, 58
Guardian *ad litem,* 63, 130
Guns, minors and, 63

H

Handwritten forms, 20, 70
Health insurance, 31
Hearings
    on default, 180–181
    trial binder, 253, 265, 267
    written declaration used at, 239
Hearsay evidence, 238
Homeowner's insurance, 7, 138–141

I

Illegal contracts, 9–10
Illegal interest rate, 9
Impartial witnesses, 25
Impeachment of witnesses, 28
Implied contracts, 7
Implied warranty, 55–56
    of fitness, 55, 104–107
    of merchantability, 55, 56, 100–104
Income, lost. *See* Lost wages and benefits
Independent contractors, as defendants, 54
Information Sheet on Waiver of Court Fees and Costs, 116
Injury cases. *See* Personal injury cases
In pro per (*in pro se*), 5
Installment loans, unpaid, 33
Installment payments, 23
Instructing the jury, 273–274, 275
Insurance
    dealing with insurance company, 140–141
    defendant's review of, 138–141
    denial of coverage, 140
    lien claim, 31
    pain and suffering, damage amount, 31, 32
    reimbursement clause in, 31
    settling out of court and, 42–43
    See also Automobile insurance; Health insurance; Homeowner's insurance
Intentional torts, 87
Interest rate, illegal, 9
Internet disputes, lawsuits resulting from, 64
Internet research. *See* Online resources
Interrogatories
    defined, 18, 186
    objecting to, 195
    responding to, 195–196
    rules for, 187
    written interrogatories, 189
Interviewing witnesses, 27
Invasion of privacy, 87
Issues of fact, 206–207
Issues of law, 206, 207

J

Joint ventures, owners' liability for debts, 52
"Judge pro tem," 258, 259, 279
Judges
    addressing, 261
    assignment of before trial date, 259
    assignment of on day of trial, 259, 261
    challenging, 258, 260
    types of, 258–259
Judgment
    amount of, 30
    appeals, 13, 278
    applying for, 174
    bankruptcy and, 29–30
    collecting, 29–30, 48
    default judgment, 15, 17, 122, 131, 134, 136, 181–183
    entering, 48, 268
    exemptions, 29
    Motion for Judgment, 266
    Notice of Entry of Judgment, 268, 279
    Small Claims judgment, 13
    trial proceedings, 268
    See also Damages
Judgment (Form JUD-100), 174
Judgment book, 268
Judicial arbitration, 227–233
    See also Arbitration
Jurisdiction, 5, 63–64
    Internet disputes, 64
    personal jurisdiction, 5
    See also Court
Jurors
    challenging, 272–273
    instructing, 273–274, 275
    misconduct by, 278
    questioning of, 270–272
    selecting, 270–272
    "six-pack," 273
Jury selection, 270–272
Jury trial, 18, 270–279
    appealing the judgment, 279
    jury deliberations, 275
    jury selection, 270–272

L

Large businesses, collecting judgments against, 29
Law library, 108
Lawsuits
    before filing, 50
    dismissal, 46–48, 164
    elements of, 26
    to "get even," 22
    participants in, 5
    self-representation, 4–5, 13–17
    Small Claims Court, 12–13
    statutes of limitations, 22–23, 26
    taking the defendant's default, 168–181
    types of, 10
    See also Damages; Default; Defendants; Judgment; Plaintiffs; Settling out of court; Trial
Lawyer referral program, 283
Lawyers, 282–284
    checking out, 284
    coaching relationship with, 282
    compliance with law, 209
    contingency fee contracts with, 8, 14
    fees, 13, 14
    negligence by, 182
    referral program, 283
    review of settlement agreement, 45
Leading the witness, 237
Leases, 8
Legal coach. *See* Sounding Board
Legal guardians
    liability for minor's actions, 62–63
    serving of legal papers to minor, 130
Legal research, 18, 108–110
    California statutes, 18–19
    choosing forms, 109
    law library, 108
    local rules, 109
Lemon law, 56, 100
Letters
    accompanying Notice and Acknowledgement Service, 128
    confirming productive meet and confer, 223
    confirming time extension, 144

demanding compliance with discovery request or Case Questionnaire, 199
listing evidence for arbitration hearing, 230–231
objecting to request for production of documents, 197
protesting denial of coverage, 140–141
requesting change of venue, 147
"reservation of rights" letter, 141
with service of Declaration, 246
settlement demand letter, 40–41
uncooperative opponent, 222
Letters (estate), 61
Liability, minor as defendant, 62–63
Libel/slander, 6–7, 61–62, 87–89
Licenses, 9–10
Lien claim, 31
Limited jurisdiction, 77
Limited jurisdiction cases, 4, 17–18, 66, 159, 160
Limited liability companies (LLCs), 50
fictitious name certificate, 57
owners' liability for debts, 52
serving legal papers to, 129
Limited liability partnerships (LLPs), serving legal papers to, 129
Limited partnerships
as defendants, 57
owners' liability for debts, 52
LLCs. *See* Limited liability companies
LLPs. *See* Limited liability partnerships
Loans, unpaid, 33
Local court rules, 19
Local government agency/entity, suing, 23
Local rules, filing forms, 109
Los Angeles County, 66, 67, 111, 120, 203
Loss of earning capacity, 30, 77
Lost wages and benefits, 30

M
Mail
filing forms by, 122–123
service of legal papers by, 126–128, 134
Mail Notice and Acknowledgement of Receipt form, 128

Malicious prosecution, 87
Malpractice cases, 6, 108
Mandatory arbitration clause, 39
Manufacturer, breach of warranty, 55–56
"Master calendar" judge, 258
Media outlets, as defendants, 61–62
Mediation, 9, 37–38, 142, 227
Mediators, 38, 227
Medical bills
damages for, 30
insurance payment for, 31
Medical evaluation, as evidence, 27
Merchantability, 55, 56, 100–104
Minors
contracts signed by, 62, 159
as defendants, 62–63
emancipated, 62
firearms and, 63
graffiti and, 63
guardian *ad litem,* 63
serving of legal papers to, 130
shoplifting by, 63
unemancipated, 62, 82
Mistake of fact affirmative defense, 159
Motion for Change of Venue, 147, 148
Motion for Judgment, 266
Motion for Judgment on the Pleadings, 218
Motion for New Trial, 278
Motion for Non-Suit, 265
Motion for Summary Adjudication of Issues, 217–218
Motion for Summary Judgment (MSJ)
about, 43, 165, 197, 206–217
defeating, 207
defending against, 217
defined, 43, 206
opposition to, 209–213
requesting sanctions, 217
time restrictions for, 207–208
Motion in limine, 271
Motions, 18
Motion to Compel, 200–203
Motion to Enter Judgment Per C.C.P., 47
Motion to Quash Service, 148, 219

Motion to Set Aside, 182–183, 183
Motion to Strike, 148, 219
Motor vehicle accidents. *See* Automobile insurance; Vehicle accidents
MSJ. *See* Motion for Summary Judgment
Municipal courts, 4

N

Negative pregnant, 151, 159
Negligence cases
    Cause of Action—General Negligence (PLD-PI-001(2)), 79, 85–87
    comparative negligence, 33
Negligent performance of duties. *See* Professional malpractice
Newspaper, libel and/or slander, 61–62
New trial, requesting, 278–279
Noneconomic damages, 51
Nonexpert testimony, 25
Nonprofit corporations, as defendants, 57–58
Notice and Acknowledgement of Receipt—Civil (POS-015), 127
Notice and Acknowledgement of Service, 126
Notice of Appeal, 279
Notice of Deposition, 192, 193
Notice of Entry of Judgment, 268, 278, 279
Notice of Trial, 258

O

Objections
    to deposition questions, 194–195
    to evidence and questions, 236–238, 274–275
    hearsay evidence, 238
    to interrogatories, 195
    leading the witness, 237
    letter objecting to request for production of documents, 197
    to opponent's proposed evidence at arbitration hearing, 231
    question calls for opinion, 238
    relevance, 237
    at trial, 236–238
Online resources
    Complaint forms, 71
    corporate and LLC information, 58
    court decisions, 19
    court rules, 19
    downloading court forms, 20
    law library, 108
    mediators, 38
    Superior Court, 19
Online shopping, lawsuits resulting from, 64
Opening statements
    defendants, 266
    at jury trial, 274
    plaintiffs, 263
Opinion evidence, 24–25
Opposition to Motion for Summary Judgment, 209–213
Oral contracts, 8, 22, 23
Order Granting Defendant's Motion for Extension of Time, 145, 146
Order on Application for Waiver of Court Fees and Costs, 117, 120
Out-of-state defendants, 12

P

Pain and suffering
    damage amount and, 31, 32, 51
    DUI cases, 32
    general damage, 77
Pain diary, 28
Paralegals, 70
Parents
    liability for minor's actions, 62–63
    serving of legal papers to minor, 130
Partners, as defendants, 57
Partnerships
    as defendants, 5, 57
    fictitious business name, 50, 57
    owners' liability for debts, 52
    as plaintiff, 50
    serving legal papers to, 129
Penalty of perjury, 197
Peremptory Challenge Motion, 259, 260
Personal injury cases, 14
    Answer—Personal Injury, Property Damage, Wrongful Death (Form PLD-PI-003), 150–155

Cause of Action—Intentional Tort (PLD-PI-001(3)), 79, 87–89
Complaint form, 73
Cross-Complaint, 160–163
written interrogatories, 189
Personal jurisdiction, 5
Personal property, 30
See also Property damage cases
Photocopying, 120, 134, 164
Photographs, as evidence, 25, 27
Physical examination, requests for, 186, 198–199
Physical objects. *See* Evidence
"Piercing the corporate veil," 57
Plaintiffs
assumption of risk, 154
attorney fees and, 13, 14
closing arguments, 267–268, 275
in Complaint form Caption, 72
coplaintiffs, 50–51, 75, 96
determining settlement amount, 36–37
mediation, 9, 37–38, 142
meeting with opponent, 222–223
mistakes in filing, 144, 147–148
opening statements, 263, 274
Peremptory Challenge Motion, 259, 260
presenting case at trial, 262–266
presenting evidence, 265
presenting witnesses, 262–264
rebuttal by, 266–267, 267–268
referring to, 71
responding to defendant's motions, 265–266
selection, 50–51
self-representation, 4–5, 13–17, 142–143
Separate Statement of Undisputed Material Facts, 208, 212–213
service of legal papers by, 122, 126–134
Pleading paper, 71, 137, 150
Pocket part, 18
Points and authorities, 278
Police reports, 28
Prayer (Complaint), 77, 96, 138, 219
Premises liability Cause of Action, 79, 82–84
"Presiding" judge, 259
Pretrial settlement conference, 254

Privacy, invasion of, 87
Probate, 61
Process server, 128, 129
Process server's fee, 5
Product liability cases, 7, 79, 89
Products
breach of warranty, 56
implied warranty of merchantability, 55, 56, 100–104
Lemon law, 56, 100
online shopping disputes, 64
Professional malpractice cases, 6, 108
Proof of Claim form, 61
Proof of service, legal papers, 130–134
Proof of Service by First-Class Mail—Civil (Form POS-030), 134
Proof of Service of Civil Subpoena (Duces Tecum), 251
Proof of Service of Summons (Form POS-010), 130–134
Property damage cases
Answer—Personal Injury, Property Damage, Wrongful Death (Form PLD-PI-003), 150–155
Cause of Action—Intentional Tort (PLD-PI-001(3)), 79, 87–89
Complaint form, 73
Cross-Complaint, 160–163
damage amount in, 30
statute of limitations, 23
written interrogatories, 189
Pro tem judge, 258, 259, 279
Punitive damages. *See* Exemplary damages
Purchase contracts, 55

Q

Questions
calling yourself as witness, 264
eliciting testimony, 264
leading the witness, 237
objections to, 237–238
to potential jurors, 270–272
relevance, 237

R

Radio stations, libel and/or slander, 61–62
Real estate contracts, 8
Real property, 30
　See also Property damage cases
Rebuttal, 266–267, 267–268
Recordkeeping
　chart of evidence, 252
　evidence, 26–28
　trial binder, 253, 265, 267
Redirect examination, 264
Rees-Levering Motor Vehicle Sales and Finance Act, 94
Register of actions, 268
Regular judges, 259
Reimbursement clause, in insurance policies, 31
Release, 43, 44, 45
Relevance, 237
Renter's insurance, 138–140
Request for admission, 186, 187, 197–198
Request for Admissions (Form DISC-020), 191
Request for Dismissal (Form CIV-110), 45–47
Request for Entry of Default (Form CIV-100), 169–173
Request for Extension of Time to Plead, 145–146
Request for Trial De Novo After Judicial Arbitration (Form ADR-102), 233–234
Requests for physical examination, 186, 198–199
Requests for production of documents, 186, 189–191, 197
Request to Enter Default, 148
"Reservation of rights" letter, 141
Response to Demand for Bill of Particulars, 219–220
Retailer, breach of warranty, 55–56
Retraction, libel/slander, 62
Riverside County, selecting courthouse, 66
Roster of Public Agencies, 58–59
Rules of evidence, 236–239

S

Sanctions, 200, 217
San Francisco County, 66
Santa Clara County, 66
S corporations, owners' liability for debts, 52
Section 1542 waiver, 44
Self-defense claim, 154
Self-representation, 5, 13–17, 142
　after default, 134
　with no defense, 143
Separate Statement of Undisputed Material Facts, 208, 212–213
Service contracts, 54
Service of legal papers, 122, 126–134
　Cross-Complaint, 164
　Declarations, 242, 245, 246
　discovery documents, 186
　improper service by plaintiff, 148
　by mail, 126–128, 134
　Motion to Quash Service, 148, 219
　process server, 128, 129
　proof of service, 130–134
　Request for Trial De Novo After Judicial Arbitration, 233
　requesting more time, 129
　serving elusive defendants, 130
　serving minors, 130
　serving on businesses, 129
Setting aside default, 182–183
Settlement agreement
　mandatory arbitration agreements, 39
　review by lawyer, 45
　turning into court judgment, 48
　written, 43–45, 48–50
Settlement amount, determining, 36–37
Settlement conference, 254
Settlement demand letters, 40–41
Settling out of court, 18, 36–48, 141–142
　advantages of, 36
　after lawsuit is filed, 42–43
　before lawsuit is filed, 39–42
　damage amount determination, 36–37
　dismissal of lawsuit, 45–47
　mediation and arbitration, 9, 37–39, 227–233
　negotiation tips, 40
　pretrial settlement conference, 254
　release, 43, 44, 45, 47
　written settlement agreement, 43–45

written settlement agreement turned into judgment, 48
Sexual harassment cases, 6
Shoplifting, by minors, 63
"Six-pack," 273
Slander/libel, 6–7, 61–62, 87–89
Slip-and-fall cases, defendants in, 53
Small businesses, collecting judgments against, 29
Small Claims Court, 12–13
Sole proprietorship
    as defendant, 5, 57
    fictitious business name, 50, 57
    owners' liability for debts, 52
    as plaintiff, 50
Song-Beverly Consumer Warranty Act, 56, 100
Sounding Board, 15, 17, 24, 26, 194
Special demurrer, 148
Spouses, as coplaintiffs, 50, 51
State agency/entity, suing, 23
State court rules, 18–19
Statute of Frauds, 8, 158
Statutes, 18–19
Statutes of limitations, 22–23, 26, 158
Stipulation for Entry of Judgment, 48
Subpoena duces tecum, 186, 191, 248–252
Subpoenas
    for appearance at trial, 246–248
    for witness and documents, 246–248
    for witnesses, 246–248
Summary judgment, Motion for Summary Judgment, 43, 165, 197, 206–217
Summons
    defined, 17
    filing, 120, 122
    for new cross-defendant, 163
    photocopying, 120
    preparing, 110, 126
    review by defendant, 26, 136
    serving on defendant, 128–130, 134
Summons (Form SUM-100), 110
Superior Court
    about, 4, 19, 68
    arbitration program, 227
    clerks, 15–17, 180
    selecting, county, 68
    selecting court branch, 65–68, 111, 147–148
    selecting jurisdiction, 68
    Self-Help Center, 122
    Unlimited Division of, 138

T

Taking the matter under submission, 18, 267
Taping, of witness testimony, 27–28
Television stations, libel and/or slander, 61–62
Temporary judge, 259
Tenants, as coplaintiffs, 51
Tentative ruling system, 217
Testimony
    eliciting testimony by questioning, 264
    nonexpert, 25
    See also Witnesses
Theft, 88–89
Third party beneficiary, 51
Threats, 42
Time extension, 143–144, 145, 146
Tort cases, 30–33
    Answer in, 150–155
    battery, 87
    Complaint forms, 73–92
    conversion, 87
    Cross-Complaint in, 160–163
    damage amount in, 30–33
    defined, 5
    elements of, 6
    intentional torts, 87
    minor as defendant in, 62–63
    sample settlement agreement, 44
    sample settlement letter, 41
    selecting courthouse in Los Angeles County, 66
    selecting jurisdiction, 65
    theft, 87
    types of, 6–7
    written interrogatories, 189
Traffic accidents. *See* Automobile insurance; Vehicle accidents
Trespass, 87
Trial, 18
    appealing the judgment, 278, 279

before a judge, 258–268
"checking in," 258
closing arguments, 267–268, 275
decision to go to trial, 233
defendant's case, 266
demanding, 233–234
different from arbitration, 227–228
judges, 258–259
judgment, 267
jury deliberations, 275
jury trial, 18, 270–279
Notice of Trial, 258
opening statements, 263, 266, 274
order of events, 263–268, 274–275
plaintiff's case, 262–266
plaintiff's rebuttal, 266–267, 267–268
preparing for, 236, 253–254
presenting evidence, 265, 274
pretrial settlement conference, 254
requesting new trial, 278–279
subpoenas for witnesses, 246–248
trial binder, 253, 265, 267
trial date, 222
verdict, 275
written declarations used at, 239
written testimony, 239–245, 239–246
See also Evidence; Judgment; Witnesses
Trial binder, 253, 265, 267
Trial date, 222
TV stations, libel and/or slander, 61–62
Typewritten forms, 70

U

Unemancipated minor, 62, 82
Unincorporated associations, 5
   as defendants, 57
   owners' liability for debts, 52
   serving legal papers to, 129
Uninsured drivers, 32
Unknown defendants, 63
Unlicensed services, 9–10
Unlimited jurisdiction cases, 4, 138
Unpaid loans, 33

Unwritten/unsigned contracts, 8
Usury, 9

V

Vehicle accidents
   accident reconstruction experts, 28
   automobile insurance, 7, 140–141
   Cause of Action—Motor Vehicle (Form PLD-PI-001(1)), 79–82
   Complaint form, 73
   defendants in, 53, 62
   drunk or uninsured drivers, 32
   evidence, 28
   minors as defendants, 62
   questioning witnesses of, 253
Vehicle Code, 18
Ventura County, 122
Venue, change of, 147, 148
Verdict, 275
Verification, 96
Verified complaints, 148
Victims Compensation and Government Claims Board, 59
Videotaping, of witness testimony, 27–28

W

Wages, lost. *See* Lost wages and benefits
Waiver of court costs, 227
Waiver of filing fee, 113–117, 122
Warranty
   express warranty, 55, 56, 104
   implied warranty, 55–56
   implied warranty of fitness, 55, 104–107
   implied warranty of merchantability, 55, 56, 100–104
   written warranty, 55
Warranty, breach of, 55–56
   See also Breach of contract cases
Websites, online shopping disputes, 64
Witnesses
   calling yourself as witness, 264
   cross-examining, 264, 266
   drafting questions for, 253

eliciting testimony, 264
excluding from courtroom, 262
expert witnesses, 24–25, 199
guidelines for, 24–25, 239
impartial, 25
impeaching, 28
interviewing, 27–28
objecting to questions for, 236–238
persuasiveness of, 239
plaintiff's case, 262–264
recorded statements of, 28
redirect examination, 264
subpoenas for, 246–248
written declaration, 239
See also Evidence
Witness list, discovery, 186, 199
Workers' compensation, 154–155
Written contracts, 8, 22, 23
Written estimates, for damage, 27
Written interrogatories, 189
Written statements, as evidence, 25, 239–245, 239–246, 265
Written warranty, 55
Wrongful death, 73, 150–155, 161

NOLO® Keep Up to Date

1 Go to **Nolo.com/newsletters/index.html** to sign up for free newsletters and discounts on Nolo products.

- **Nolo Briefs.** Our monthly email newsletter with great deals and free information.
- **BizBriefs.** Tips and discounts on Nolo products for business owners and managers.
- **Landlord's Quarterly.** Deals and free tips just for landlords and property managers, too.
- **Nolo's Special Offer.** A monthly newsletter with the biggest Nolo discounts around.

2 Don't forget to check for updates at **Nolo.com**. Under "Products," find this book and click "Legal Updates."

Let Us Hear From You

3 Comments on this book? We want to hear 'em. Email us at feedback@nolo.com.

SLWY4

NOLO and USA TODAY

Cutting-Edge Content, Unparalleled Expertise

The Busy Family's Guide to Money
by Sandra Block, Kathy Chu & John Waggoner • $19.99

The Work From Home Handbook
Flex Your Time, Improve Your Life
by Diana Fitzpatrick & Stephen Fishman • $19.99

Retire Happy
What You Can Do NOW to Guarantee a Great Retirement
by Richard Stim & Ralph Warner • $19.99

The Essential Guide for First-Time Homeowners
Maximize Your Investment & Enjoy Your New Home
by Ilona Bray & Alayna Schroeder • $19.99

Easy Ways to Lower Your Taxes
Simple Strategies Every Taxpayer Should Know
by Sandra Block & Stephen Fishman • $19.99

First-Time Landlord
Your Guide to Renting Out a Single-Family Home
by Attorney Janet Portman, Marcia Stewart & Michael Molinski • $19.99

Stopping Identity Theft
10 Easy Steps to Security
by Scott Mitic, CEO, TrustedID, Inc. • $19.99

The Mom's Guide to Wills & Estate Planning
by Attorney Liza Hanks • $21.99

Running a Side Business
How to Create a Second Income
by Attorneys Richard Stim & Lisa Guerin • $21.99

Nannies and Au Pairs
Hiring In-Home Child Care
by Ilona Bray, J.D. • $19.99

The Judge Who Hated Red Nail Polish
& Other Crazy But True Stories of Law and Lawyers
by Ilona Bray, Richard Stim & the Editors of Nolo • $19.99

Prices subject to change.

ORDER ANYTIME AT WWW.NOLO.COM OR CALL 800-728-3555

NOLO® Bestsellers

The Small Business Start-Up Kit
SMBU • $29.99

How to Write a Business Plan
SBS • $34.99

The Executor's Guide
EXEC • $39.99

The Criminal Law Handbook
KYR • $39.99

Make Your Own Living Trust
LITR • $39.99

Patent It Yourself
PAT • $49.99

ORDER ANYTIME AT WWW.NOLO.COM OR CALL 800-728-3555

NOLO® Bestsellers

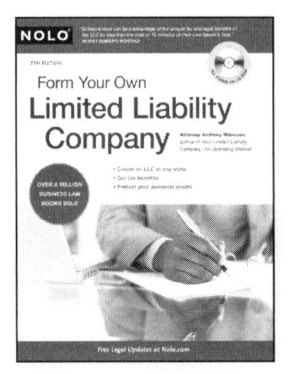

Form Your Own Limited Liability Company
LIAB • $44.99

Plan Your Estate
NEST • $44.99

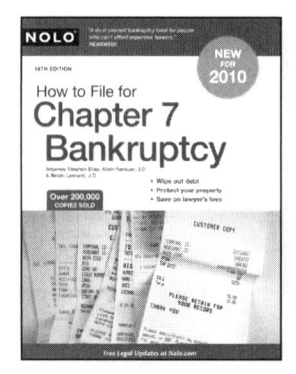

How to File for Chapter 7 Bankruptcy
HFB • $39.99

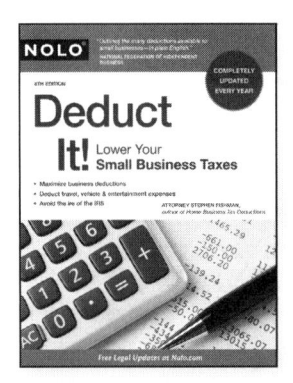

Deduct It! Lower Your Small Business Taxes
DEDU • $34.99

Retire Happy
US-RICH • $19.99

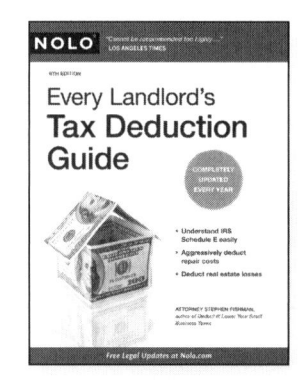

Every Landlord's Tax Deduction Guide
DELL • $39.99

ORDER ANYTIME AT **WWW.NOLO.COM** OR CALL 800-728-3555

NOLO® Online Legal Forms

Nolo offers a large library of legal solutions and forms, created by Nolo's in-house legal staff. These reliable documents can be prepared in minutes.

Create a Document

- **Incorporation.** Incorporate your business in any state.
- **LLC Formations.** Gain asset protection and pass-through tax status in any state.
- **Wills.** Nolo has helped people make over 2 million wills. Is it time to make or revise yours?
- **Living Trust (avoid probate).** Plan now to save your family the cost, delays, and hassle of probate.
- **Trademark.** Protect the name of your business or product.
- **Provisional Patent.** Preserve your rights under patent law and claim "patent pending" status.

Download a Legal Form

Nolo.com has hundreds of top quality legal forms available for download—bills of sale, promissory notes, nondisclosure agreements, LLC operating agreements, corporate minutes, commercial lease and sublease, motor vehicle bill of sale, consignment agreements and many, many more.

Review Your Documents

Many lawyers in Nolo's consumer-friendly lawyer directory will review Nolo documents for a very reasonable fee. Check their detailed profiles at **www.nolo.com/lawyers/index.html**.

Nolo's Bestselling Books

Everybody's Guide to Small Claims Court in California
$29.99

Nolo's Plain-English Law Dictionary
$29.99

Fight Your Ticket & Win in California
$29.99

Nolo's Guide to California Law
Know Your Rights, Survive the System
$39.99

Every Nolo title is available in print and for download at Nolo.com.

NOLO® Lawyer Directory

Find a Quality Attorney

- *Qualified lawyers*
- *In-depth profiles*
- *A pledge of respectful service*

When you want help with a serious legal problem, you don't want just any lawyer—you want an expert in the field who can give you and your family up-to-the-minute advice. You need a lawyer who has the experience and knowledge to answer your questions about personal injury, wills, family law, child custody, drafting a patent application or any other specialized legal area you are concerned with.

Nolo's Lawyer Directory is unique because it provides an extensive profile of every lawyer. You'll learn about not only each lawyer's education, professional history, legal specialties, credentials and fees, but also about their philosophy of practicing law and how they like to work with clients.

All lawyers listed in Nolo's directory are in good standing with their state bar association. Many will review Nolo documents, such as a will or living trust, for a fixed fee. They all pledge to work diligently and respectfully with clients—communicating regularly, providing a written agreement about how legal matters will be handled, sending clear and detailed bills and more.

www.nolo.com

The photos above are illustrative only. Any resemblance to an actual attorney is purely coincidental.